LEON BATTISTA ALBERTI

LEON BATTISTA ALBERTI

Franco Borsi

LEON BATTISTA ALBERTI

Harper & Row, Publishers
New York, Hagerstown, San Francisco, London

Design Diego Birelli
Art Director of Electa Editrice

Translated by Rudolf G. Carpanini

September 1977

First published in Italy under the title "Leon Battista Alberti"
© Copyright 1975 Milano-Industrie Grafiche Editoriali S.p.A.

LEON BATTISTA ALBERTI. English translation
Copyright © 1977 by Electa Editrice.

Printed in Italy.

For information address Harper & Row, Publishers Inc.,
10 East 53rd Street, New York, N.Y. 10022.

Published simultaneously in Canada by Fitzhenry & Whiteside Limited, Toronto.

FIRST U.S. EDITION

ISBN: 0-06-010411-2

LIBRARY OF CONGRESS CATALOG CARD NUMBER: 75-23870

CONTENTS

CHAPTER ONE
The Themes of Alberti's Life

Nobility, dialectical argument, erudition, and didacticism distinguish all Alberti's works and, indeed, the entire culture of his day. Yet the presence of these qualities does not prevent us from wondering whether Alberti, in spite of his monumentality and his renown as a complete man of the Renaissance, was not a deeply divided man, one whose subtle anguish and pessimism were the consequence of his realisation that a breach had opened between contemporary culture and society. At times he explored this division deliberately, taking refuge from harsh reality in the pleasures and *commoditas* of letters. At others he sought to overcome it in practical action and concrete commitment. His own particular interpretation of the architect's profession, an unusual one for his day (indeed, for any day), may be explained by this practical interest in civic affairs, in the dialogue between artist and patron, in the debate over ancient and modern, and in the relationship between symbol and reality. But Alberti's architecture cannot be understood, not even as meta-architecture, unless seen in relationship to the inner dialectic of the Albertian *animus*. For the more Alberti speaks of harmony and tranquillity, the further he may have been from such ideals, divided by "the anxiety of study", the complexity of his aims, and the multiplicity of his interests. His very gifts were a danger to him, for, as Landino says: "I recall the style of Battista Alberti, who, like a chameleon, always takes the form of what he writes about."[1] His many interests, the ambiguities inherent in his serenity and anguish, paganism and Christianity, theory and practice, 'virtue' and 'fortune', all suggest a rather different portrait than that drawn in the *Anonymous Life* (the work was most probably written by Alberti himself).

This tells us that "so great was his genius that he may be said to have been master of all the arts", and that "he enjoyed literature so much that it sometimes gave him the same pleasure as the buds of sweetly smelling flowers, and then neither hunger nor sleep could make him leave his books. But so late did he stay up sometimes that his books assumed the aspect of piles of scorpions, so that he could see nothing, let alone his books."[2] We shall now take a look at some of the main themes of Alberti's life, though our brief account does not claim to be an exhaustive treatment of their many-sidedness, if only to see how they are connected with his architecture. For only in this way can we understand his psychological make-up and the motives that guided him as an architect, such as they appear in a personality that was as aggressive on the intellectual level as it was prudent and elusive on the practical.

EXILE

It is known that Leon Battista was born in Genoa, on approximately 18 February 1403 (according to the Florentine calendar, 1404 according to our own). He was the illegitimate son of Lorenzo Alberti, a member of a very rich family that had been banished from Florence and sent into perilous exile with a price on its head: "from 1500 to 3000 florins together with important privileges to whosoever should deliver up dead or alive an Alberti declared rebel (1400)."[3] The theme of exile recurs with sad insistence in *I Libri della Famiglia*. In thinking back on his adolescence, when he learnt to put up with "the onslaughts of human adversity", Leon Battista makes his father say in one of the dialogues: "I leave you in exile and fatherless, without a country or a home. Let it be an incentive to you, my sons, in your tender years, if not in everything, at least in helping you to overcome the bitterness of hard necessity, and you will deserve to triumph over yourselves in old age, if you have learnt at all times in life to fear little the malice of fortune and to conquer its adversities."[4] The exile resulted in many deaths. During the years 1428–49, forty-six members of the family died in various Italian cities or abroad; only thirteen afterwards returning to their native Florence.[5] In exile: "Nothing is more difficult than life. And blessed were those who survived so many hardships to end their youthful years under their father's roofs in our own country! Happy were those who did not feel our misery, who did not have to wander in foreign lands without dignity or authority, far from parents, friends, and dear ones, scorned, looked down upon, rejected and hated by those to whom we paid homage and showed courtesy! Oh what unhappiness was ours to find comfort and solace from our adversities in foreign lands, to find pity and compassion amongst the strangers we encountered in our misfortunes, and to be denied for so long all show of mercy by our own fellow-citizens."[6] Exile bred a longing for his family's homes, both those in the city, which were fortresses providing refuge in difficult times, and those in the country, "our" places, "where the air is crystal clear, the countryside cheerful and beautiful wherever the eye roams, fog rare, the winds moderate, the water good, and everything healthy and pure. But we shall not mention those that are more like palaces or castles for great lords than villas. We shall not recall the magnificence of the Albertis, in this present moment, but forget rather those fine, excessively decorated buildings, which many, seeing their new occupants, now pass with a sigh."[7] Such as these must have been in Alberti's mind when he wrote that private houses, both in the town and in the country, should be

1. C. Landino, *Comento sopra la "Comedia"*, cf. R. Cardini, "La critica del Landino", Florence 1973, p. 130.
2. Anon., *Leonis Baptistae de Albertis Vita*, in "Rerum Italicarum Scriptores XXV", Milan 1723, 38, pp. 295–304.

3. G. Mancini, *Vita di Leon Battista Alberti*, Rome 1967, p. 8.
4. *I Libri della Famiglia*, Book I, in L.B. Alberti, *Opere Volgari*, Bari 1960, p. 26.
5. G. Mancini, op. cit., p. 16.
6. *I Libri della Famiglia*, Book I, in L.B. Alberti, op. cit., pp. 38–39.
7. *I Libri della Famiglia*, Book III, in L.B. Alberti, op. cit., p. 195.

built in proportion to the importance and social prestige of their occupants. It was better "for the rich to go without certain decorations in their private houses than to be accused, in some way, of extravagance by the more discreet and frugal."[8] And again: "in the decoration of private houses, therefore, one must have a very strict sense of proportion, even though a certain freedom may be allowed in most cases."[9]

But when he speaks of the town, not a single personal reference, not one memory, not a trace of nostalgia is to be found. The subject is dealt with universally; the schematic division of the variety of human nature and places is his main concern. To do this he had to make a special effort to sublimate his nostalgia. The result provides us with further proof that his state of mind was that of a man in perpetual exile: "Moderate your opinion and judgement, and you will temper the affections and impulses of the soul. Once love is tempered, the arbitrary will dies. Once the arbitrary will is extinguished, you will not desire. Not desiring, you will not grieve whether you have, or do not have, that which you do not esteem. People say, 'love your country and love your kin, doing them all the good they desire'. But they also say that the whole world is a man's country, and that the wise man makes his home wherever he happens to be. In doing this he does not escape from his country, but adopts another, and thus finds great good wherever he does not choose to find ill; in this way he will escape being a burden to himself."[10]

ALBERTI'S FAMILY

On 28 May 1421, when Leon Battista was sixteen years old, his father died at Padua. In his will Lorenzo left a sum of money to his illegitimate sons, Carlo and Battista. But on the death of Battista's uncle, Ricciardo, his cousins managed to delay the settlement of the will for years on the pretext of the complexity of the commercial affairs involved. "Fatherless, without influence, an outlaw in his own country, deprived not only of the whole of his father's fortune by his closest relatives, but banished from the latter's intimacy and companionship, he was so desperate as to have to beg from strangers."[11] Battista himself writes: "After the death of my father, Lorenzo Alberti, while I was studying canon law in Bologna and striving to succeed in my studies so as to be all the dearer to my family and a credit to it, some of my relatives became inhumanly jealous of my rising reputation, which I had almost established."[12] An orphan and a bastard, wronged and shunned by his relatives, Alberti, even when still a young boy felt the need to praise his family: "No man has ever rightly consi-

dered himself to have been unjustly or unkindly treated by us; no member of the Alberti family has ever broken faith or offended due honesty in matters of business. And as far as I can see, this honesty will always be observed by the Albertis, all the more so as I see our men are not greedy for profits, not unjust in their dealings with people, nor lazy in business."[13]

Of his family's wealth he says: "I say that one may glorify the house of Alberti, which for more than two hundred years now has never been so poor as not to be considered very rich by the other families of Florence. Our older men cannot remember, nor is there any trace in our family's letters of a time when the house of Alberti produced anything less than very great, famous, good, truthful, honest merchants. Nor will you find in our country such great wealth to have endured so long and so blamelessly as ours. Indeed, it seems that our family was the only one in our country whose wealth was not inherited by its grandchildren. Within a few days it all vanished into thin air, as the common people say, leaving some of the family in poverty, misery, and shame."[14] Exile made "real husbandry" difficult, since "we could never cramp our spirit or way of life with fixed rules."[15] The honesty of the Albertis was known the world over: "As in everything else our family was extremely honest in matters of money, having traded for a long time in the west and other parts of the world with honesty and integrity, ...so that no one has ever accused us of dishonesty in matters of trade."[16] Paying taxes was a point of honour: "Of the thirty-two denari our country spent in that period, more than one came from our family. A large sum, but not so great as our desire and readiness to serve our country, or our affection for it."[17] And again: "Messer Cipriano Alberti used to say that the command of others was bought from fortune with blood and gold. ... And according to Messer Benedetto Alberti, the richest state was not that with the greatest number of debtors or the greatest taxable wealth, but was loved by its moderately wealthy citizens, and to which all its richest citizens were most loyal and just."[18] After praising his family's virtues, Alberti proceeds to build a commercial myth around it: "Thus great profits are to be made in trading on a large scale, and I doubt whether luck has very much to do with the kind of trade carried on by the Albertis, such as when they used to bring by land, from the most distant parts of Flanders as far as Florence, wool enough for all the weavers of Florence and for those of a great part of Tuscany as well. ... We shall not mention all the other goods our men brought to Florence from the farthest provinces at great expense, over mountains and very steep, dif-

8. L.B. Alberti, *L'Architettura*, Book IX, chap. I, Milan 1966, p. 780.
9. L.B. Alberti, op. cit., Book IX, chap. I, p. 784.
10. *Profugiorum ab aerumna*, in L.B. Alberti, *Opere volgari*, Bari 1966, vol. II, p. 124.
11. G. Mancini, op. cit., pp. 51–52.
12. G. Mancini, op. cit., p. 54.

13. *I Libri della Famiglia*, Book, II, in L.B. Alberti, op. cit., Vol. I, pp. 143–144.
14. *I Libri della Famiglia*, Book II, in L.B. Alberti, op. cit., p. 143.
15. *I Libri della Famiglia*, Book, in L.B. Alberti, op. cit., p. 17.
16. *I Libri della Famiglia*, Vol. I, Book II, p. 142.
17. *I Libri della Famiglia*, ibid.
18. *I Libri della Famiglia*, ibid.

ficult passes. Did all that wool fall from the lap of fortune by chance? How many dangers were run, how many rivers crossed, how many difficulties overcome before their goods were brought safely home! Thieves, tyrants, wars, negligence, dishonest middlemen and the like were never lacking wherever my family went. And I think this is what happens in all great enterprises in trade and commerce worthy of so noble and honest a family. Thus, all merchants should be as our ancestors were, as we are now, and as no doubt we shall always be in the future."[19]

Nor does he neglect the cultural or humanistic vocation of his family, which "in letters was always most excellent", since "a young man without letters, though a gentleman, will always be considered a rustic."[20] He goes on to mention Benedetto, who "in natural philosophy and mathematics was reputed, as indeed he was, very learned"; Niccolò, who dedicated himself to "Holy Scripture"; Antonio, who "desired to enjoy the genius and art of all the great writers, who has been magnificently active in his very honest, idle pleasures, has already written a *History of Illustrious Men*, besides his amorous contentions, and is, as you know, a very famous astrologer"; Ricciardo, who was versed in "humanistic studies and the poets"; and Lorenzo, who was "superior to all in mathematics and music." Leon Battista stresses the connection between his vocation and his family descent, pointing out that the adversities of fortune had led him to develop virtues unlike those required for practical matters. In his attempt to establish a single vocation for himself and his family, Alberti tries to cancel the image of a *déraciné* and to overcome his position as an alienated solitary forced to work for a living. At the same time, he emphasises his social extraction in dynastic terms. His situation was the very modern one of a nobleman fallen on hard times and obliged to work.

BUREAUCRACY AND FREEDOM

"I have lived subject to others." Thus Alberti begins to explain how, after taking a degree in law at Bologna, he was compelled to seek employment in the service of Cardinal Aleman, the papal legate in Bologna, and later, with Cardinal Albergati, whom he accompanied on a long journey across the Alps. Finally, he became an "apostolic abbreviator" in the Papal chancery, under Biagio Molin, Eugenius IV's right-hand man. This required a special dispensation from the canonical laws that excluded illegitimate children from receiving holy orders and ecclesiastical benefices, and the conferring upon Battista of the priorate of S. Martino a Gangalandi near Lastra a Signa in the diocese of Florence.[21]

19. *I Libri della Famiglia*, Book II, p. 147.
20. *I Libri della Famiglia*, Book, I, p. 68.
21. G. Mancini, op. cit., p. 89.

If one considers that there were 101 Papal abbreviators, and that Eugenius IV nominated the 102nd in 1431, one may say that while Alberti's post had the advantage of security, it was not a particularly elevated one. However, in spite of the envy that surrounded him, his knowledge of literature and elegance of style soon distinguished him, especially as he matured and his fame as an architect grew.

His position as a member of the Papal civil service was probably the main reason for his obtaining commissions as an architect, since it is reasonable to suppose that in order to obtain his good offices in the settlement of certain affairs of the Curia, his superiors encouraged his architectural ambitions by giving him the opportunity to exercise his talent, almost certainly on a gratuitous basis. For when we find him at the court of the Malatestas or the Gonzagas, or in the house of the Rucellai, his position is never very clear, nor does he ever have any specific duties. At the same time, his appearance inevitably coincides with the need on the part of his potential clients to settle some question with the apostolic chancery. That Battista's good offices were obtained by playing upon his passion for architecture is confirmed in the *Ten Books*, where he advises architects not to give their services to all who seek them, but only to those who have particular confidence in them: "For why should I set about explaining the excellence and utility of my ideas when the only recompense I get is the confidence of the incompetent?"[22] A passage in the *Famiglia* confirms that this kind of employment helped Alberti to overcome the impatience he felt with his position as a bureaucrat: "I have always preferred every other kind of life to that of what we may call the civil servant. And who could possibly like that? A most troublesome life, full of suspicion, fatigue and every kind of servitude. What difference can you see between these men who work away at State affairs and slaves? One rushes about here and there, bowing before this man, competing with that, insulting another. One is suspected by many and envied by all. One has countless enemies but no loyal friendships, any number of promises and offers even though one is surrounded by pretence, vanity, and lies. And what you need most you cannot find—a single loyal, trustworthy person. And so everything you strive and hope for is suddenly swept away, to your damage, sorrow, and not a little to your undoing too. And if, after countless applications, you succeed in obtaining some favour, what have you achieved? There you are, seated in office, and what advantages do you have besides being able to steal and command with greater freedom? You will hear complaints, endless accusations, great uproars, and you will be surrounded by greedy, quarrelsome, wicked men, filling your ears with suspicion, your heart with greed, and your mind with fear and worry. Is it worthwhile leaving your own affairs in order to deal with the stupidity of others?"[23] This vivid description of the career of a bureaucrat then becomes in turn a yearning for freedom, that freedom which is man's true wealth, whether it be exercised for good or evil, and in which the body becomes an instrument of harmony: "Nature abhors the state wherein the soul loses control of the body. Above all, it leads man to love freedom, to love to live to himself, and to belong to himself."[24] It is clear that for Alberti, the bored bureaucrat, culture was the choice of freedom.

THE PRACTICE OF ARCHITECTURE

Alberti's post as an official of the Curia may have made it difficult for him to supervise his own works. His disinterest in the actual realisation of his designs may have been a consequence of the *forma mentis* he acquired in the cautious, reserved circles of the Curia. Or it may have been the result of a natural preference for the purely theoretical aspect of his art. The fact is that Alberti always withdrew into the background when the moment came to carry out a project, even though he had put everything into its design. He himself explains this attitude in what is clearly an autobiographical passage in the ninth book of the *De re aedificatoria*: "Therefore, a prudent man should take care to maintain his reputation, and it is sufficient to give honest advice and accurate designs to those who seek your services. If, afterwards, you decide to supervise and complete the work yourself, you will inevitably be held responsible for all the faults and mistakes made by others in their ignorance or negligence. So the work must be entrusted to skilful, prudent, thorough workmen, who will see that everything necessary is carried out with precision, care, and diligence."[25] The whole of Alberti's professional ethics is dominated by this preoccupation with the architect's dignity, which, if it is to be safeguarded, requires total commitment on the part of the architect. For he must "examine the nature of the task before him, the responsibility he intends to assume, what kind of reputation he wishes to have, how much work is involved, how much glory, profit, favour and fame he will acquire among posterity, if he carries out the work as he should; or, on the contrary, if he carries it out inexpertly, unadvisedly, or rashly, to how much disgrace and indignation he exposes himself, and what a clear, manifest, and enduring testimony of his own folly he leaves behind him."[26]

22. L.B. Alberti, *L'Architettura*, cit., Book IX, chap. XI, p. 862.

23. *I Libri della Famiglia*, Book III, pp. 179–180.
24. *I Libri della Famiglia*, Book III, pp. 168–169.
25. L.B. Alberti, *L'Architettura*, Book IX, chap. XI, pp. 862–864.
26. L.B. Alberti, *L'Architettura*, Book, IX chap. XI, pp. 852–854.

There are two things the architect must do if he is to be rewarded for his commitment. One is cultural and regards only himself; the other concerns his relationship with his client. As for the first: "The architect should follow the example of those who study letters. For in this field no one will think he has done enough until he has read and studied all the authors; and not just the best ones, but all those who have written anything at all on the subject. In the same way, the architect will go wherever there happen to be works that are universally admired and esteemed, and he will examine them all with the greatest care. He will make drawings of them, measure their proportions, and make models of them so as to have them near at hand. And he will study them, and understand the ordering, placing, nature and proportions of all the single parts".[27] Here, the relationship between literature and architecture, between philological enquiry and physical proportion has become the expression of a profound conviction. Thus, the treatise is also a diary, and it provides us with the best instrument for understanding Alberti—Alberti himself. Opposed to Vitruvius's vague universalism, Alberti found that architecture was rooted in the two disciplines of which he had had direct experience, painting and mathematics, which were as indispensable "as the knowledge of metric feet and syllables is to the poet, and I doubt whether a slight acquaintance with these matters is enough."[28] In the *De Pictura* Alberti asks: "Can anyone doubt that painting is the mistress of the arts, or at least something more than just the mere ornament of everything else? If I am not mistaken, the architect also took his architraves, bases, capitals, columns, façades and all similar things from the painter, and the rules and the art of the painter guide all artisans, sculptors, and workshops. Nor perhaps will you find any art of a noble kind which is not related to painting, so that whatever beauty you see may be said to be born of painting."[29]

As for the qualities to be looked for in a patron, Alberti advises the architect: "do everything possible to obtain commissions only from the most important people, who are generous and true lovers of the arts. For your work loses its value when done for persons of low social rank. Can't you see the advantages to be had in the furthering of your reputation if you have the support of the most influential people to whom you offer your services? For my part—besides the fact that when we listen to the opinions and advice of the great, we are nearly always, for some unknown reason, considered to be wiser than we really are—I believe that the architect must always be plentifully and readily supplied with everything he needs for the completion of his work."[30] Though this passage is steeped in class consciousness and courtly servility, Alberti redeems himself by his concern with the education not only of the architect but also of the patron. In the very prologue to the *Ten Books* he insists that "the safety, authority, and decorum of the State depend to a great extent on the work of the architect. Thanks to him we can spend our leisure time in a pleasant, tranquil, healthy way, and our hours of work in the profitable increase of our substance: in brief, with dignity and security. Considering, therefore, the extraordinary grace and beauty of his works, how indispensable and useful they are, and the benefits that posterity derives from them, it cannot be denied that the architect deserves to be honoured and esteemed as being amongst the greatest benefactors of mankind."[31] There are frequent references to the patron's responsibility in the treatise: "I do not think one should enter upon the construction of any building without considering carefully the labour and expense involved: apart from other disadvantages, it would be harmful to your reputation. For if it is true that a well-designed work furthers the reputations of all who dedicate their intelligence, study, and labour to it, it is also true that if any particular happens to reflect a lack of judgement on the part of its author, or of skill on that of the man who carries out the design, then the reputations of all suffer considerably from it."[32] Indeed, Alberti was far more concerned with the 'construction' of the patron than with the constructions themselves, and whenever he had to deal with clients, whether it was Malatesta, Rucellai, Nicholas V, Ludovico Gonzaga, or Federico da Montefeltro (with whom he had more indirect dealings), he never allowed his work to be shaped by their decisions. On the contrary, it was always he who exercised decisive influence in the end. But Alberti's first concern was not so much the design as the whole project; this took precedence over both the patron's wishes and the architect's plans. Alberti nearly always acted progressively. The explanation of this lies in his culture and in the quiet strength of his powers of persuasion. In fact, he often succeeded in converting clients from the conventional ideas of their day to a more authentic awareness of their own needs, whether these were motivated by love of prestige and culture, or inspired by a desire for something historic, capable of resisting the erosion of time, and worthy of taking its place among the *monumenta*. In every case, Alberti presented the princes of his day with a concept of architecture as a means of overcoming the dualism and antithesis of 'virtue' and 'fortune'. For when a building was the expression of highly civilised values, it was an embodiment

27. L.B. Alberti, *L'Architettura*, Book IX, chap. X, pp. 854–856.
28. L.B. Alberti, *L'Architettura*, Book IX, chap. X, p. 860.
29. *De pictura*, Book II, in L.B. Alberti, *Opere volgari*, Vol. III, Bari 1973, p. 46.
30. L.B. Alberti, *L'Architettura*, Book IX, chap XI, p. 864.
31. L.B. Alberti, *L'Architettura*, Preface, pp. 12–14.
32. L.B. Alberti, *L'Architettura*, Book II, chap. I, p. 94.

of virtue; and insofar as its walls were proof against change and destruction, it was an investment against fortune.

LATIN AND THE VERNACULAR

In the *Anonymous Life* it is said that the three books of the *Famiglia* were written in ninety days in Rome, but that they were "so rough and unpolished that one could not say they were written in the Florentine tongue. For as a result of his family's long exile, Alberti had been educated in foreign countries and did not know his native tongue. Unfamiliar with it, it was difficult for him to write it elegantly and concisely."[33] In the third book, Alberti discussed his choice of the vernacular: "I admit that the ancient Latin tongue is very rich and ornate, but I cannot see why our own modern Tuscan should be so disliked that even the finest works that adopt it are frowned upon."[34] The *certame coronario* Alberti promoted in Florence in 1441 was the clearest manifestation of his interest in the language question. He adopted a thoroughly modern attitude, rejecting the snobbery of the learned in favour of the advantages to be gained from the wider diffusion of knowledge, and urging writers to improve and develop the vernacular. The same ideas were later taken up by Lorenzo the Magnificent: "Nothing is less worthy because it is more common. Indeed, it has been shown that all good is the greater for being communicable and universal, as is the nature of what we call the Highest Good. For it would not be the highest if it were not infinite, nor can anything be called infinite unless it be common to all things. Nor does it seem that our mother tongue is any less dignified for being common to all Italy."[35]

In the introduction to his *Grammatica della lingua toscana* (which Grayson maintains was written at the same time as the letter to Matteo de' Pasti about the works at Rimini) Alberti writes: "I believe that those who maintain that the Latin language was not common to all the Latin peoples but used only by a few learned scholars, such as we see today, will realise their mistake after reading this book of ours, in which I have examined the usages of our language by means of very brief notes."[36] This was a step forward compared with the justification he was to elaborate in dedicating *Theogenius* (1440?) to the refined Lionello d'Este: "I thought I would write in such a way as to be understood by those fellow citizens of mine who had no great knowledge of letters... but they say I have offended literary decorum by not writing about so refined a subject in Latin."[37]

Alberti's clear position on the use of the vernacular[38] seems to have changed from one of justification on practical grounds to one of real conviction as to the partly unexplored, expressive wealth of his native tongue. The fact that Alberti used both Latin and the vernacular creates a problem. Of the treatises on art, only the *De pictura* and the *Elementa picturae* were written in both languages. It would seem that the first work was probably written first in Latin (though the question is still an open one), while there is no doubt that the vernacular version of the second preceded the Latin.[39] One can understand why the *Ludi Matematici* exists only in the vernacular since it was something of a popular *divertissement*. The *De re aedificatoria*, on the other hand, which appeared only in Latin, was addressed more to patrons than to architects and had elevated cultural aims.

Apart from circumstances one might describe as pre-editorial, significant though they may be, Alberti's architecture might also be explained in terms of Latin and the vernacular: the former clearly parallels the antique texts and monuments we find quoted in his works, while the latter corresponds to the later medieval tradition which Alberti inherited through Florentine town planning and the Roman-Romanesque element in Florence's architectural tradition. 'Vernacular' may also be used to describe the style he developed in progressing from the study of antique models to the unexplored expressive wealth of his mythological 'Etruscan' style. Certainly, his sense of history was a vital factor, both in the rejection of his contemporaries' "silly, extravagant novelties" and in the "deep sorrow" he felt at the sight of the gradual decay of works of antiquity. It is precisely when talking of the latter, at the beginning of the sixth book, that he writes in a moment of dejection: "I have examined all the buildings of antiquity that might be in the least important to see if anything was to be learnt from them. I have been tireless in seeking out, examining, measuring, and drawing everything possible, so as to master all that man's labour and intelligence offers in these monuments. Thus, I have found relief from the fatigue of writing in satisfying my passion for knowledge."[40] But Alberti was driven to undertake such a task not only by his thirst for documentary evidence and precise data, but by the fact that so many ancient texts had been lost, and by the inadequacy and incomprehensibility of Vitruvius, the only ancient author who had survived.

An even closer parallel may be drawn between his architecture and his position on the language question. For though he rejected the literary novelty and populism of a Burchiello, he defended the independence of the Latin tradition (which he more correctly called Italic) and the interrelationship of Latin and the vernacular,

33. A. Bonucci, *Vita di Leon Battista Alberti*, anon., pp. XCV-XCVII.

34. *I Libri della Famiglia*, Preface to Book III, in L.B. Alberti, *Opere volgari*, Bari 1960, Vol. I, p. 155.

35. Lorenzo de' Medici, *Opere*, Bari 1973, Vol. I, p. 18.

36. L.B. Alberti, *Opere volgari*, Vol. III, Bari 1973, p. 177.

37. L.B. Alberti, *Opere volgari*, II, *Teogenio*, pp. 55–6.

38. A. Tateo, *La Letteratura volgare in Toscana*, in "Il Quattrocento", Bari 1973, p. 177.

39. L.B. Alberti, *Opere volgari*, Vol. III, Bari 1973, pp. 304 ff. 345.

40. L.B. Alberti, *L'Architettura*, Book VI, chap. I, p. 442.

or, in other words, of ancient and modern in architecture. This was accompanied by his confidence in himself and in his times, his admiration of Brunelleschi, and his attempt to historicise the experience of his generation: "It was certainly less difficult for the ancients to attain to that knowledge of the supreme arts which we ourselves now find so very difficult, since they had models to learn from and imitate. But our reputation will be all the greater, if without teachers and without examples to follow, we achieve in the arts and sciences things as yet unseen and unheard of."[41] The dignifying of the vernacular through the *studia humanitatis* and the ennobling of architecture through the study of classical models were merely different aspects of a single endeavour. The result would be the same in the field of ethics too, for, as he maintains in the *Profugiorum ab aerumna*, the study of letters enables one to judge human things "not in accordance with erroneous opinion, but according to the truth and certitude of reason."[42]

The artist's imagination acts as a kind of sedative: "And sometimes it has happened that not only have I grown calm in my restlessness of spirit, but I have thought of things most rare and memorable. Sometimes I have designed and built finely proportioned buildings in my mind, arranging their orders and numerous columns with various capitals and unusual bases, and decorating them with cornices and panels. And I have occupied myself with constructions of this kind until overcome by sleep."[43] The nights of the fifteenth century were populated with images: Paolo di Dono lay awake at night thinking of "sweet perspective"; Leon Battista imagined buildings and mathematical demonstrations; and Leonardo was to praise "the straying of the imagination over the superficial features of forms when you lie in bed in the dark."

POLITICS AND ARCHITECTURE

For Alberti, the point of contact between the world of the present and that of the past was the town, which was both an urban and a social structure. The ambiguity with which he uses the word is deliberate and only underlines the fact that both structures were strictly connected in his mind. The variety of buildings has its origins in the variety of human nature, and the attempt to classify these buildings presupposes a clarification of the differences that exist among men. Ancient authorities such as Plutarch, Caesar, Aristotle, Plato, and all the other writers mentioned in the fourth book of the *De re aedificatoria*, provided Alberti with the basis for what is clearly an oligarchical concept: "You will select a small number of individuals from the rest of

41. *De pictura*, Preface, in L.B. Alberti, *Opere volgari*, cit., Vol. III.
42. *Profugiorum ab aerumna*, in L.B. Alberti, *Opere volgari*, cit., vol. III, Book I.
43. *Profugiorum ab aerumna*, in L.B. Alberti, *Opere volgari*, Vol. II, Book III.

the community, some distinguished for their learning, wisdom, and ability, others for their experience and practical knowledge, and others for their wealth and abundance of property. There is no doubt that these should be given the most important offices in the State."[44] These in turn, when they prefer meditation to action, will delegate the executive power to others who will then constitute the military and bureaucratic backbone of the State: "On entering into office, these will carry out their duties with flexibility and seriousness at home, with tenacity and patience abroad. They will be judges and generals, and they will dedicate both themselves and others to their country's cause. Finally, since they will realise that it is useless to try and carry out any enterprise unless one has the means, they will occupy a position immediately below the first mentioned persons, who have riches, whether in movable or immovable goods. All the other citizens ought to obey and collaborate with these."[45] The various kinds of building correspond to three social categories: "There is one kind of building fit for the whole community, another for the most important citizens, and another for the people. Some of the buildings set aside for the first citizens will be reserved for those who decide public policy, others for those who carry out decisions already taken, and still others for those whose business it is to accumulate wealth."[46] The city embodies the needs of all: "Everyone needs the city and the many public services that are a part of it." But there are symbolic needs as well as practical ones; above all, there is the problem of time. Here we touch upon the basic principle of Alberti's political thought: the love and respect for what endures—a feeling that finds its dogmatic expression in the following rule from the *De jure*: "permanentia non permanentibus anteponantur." According to Walter Pater, Plato, the philosopher of the immutable, tried "to establish the indefectibly immutable" in the *Republic*. In this Alberti was his disciple. But the difference between the two was that the Greek philosopher tried to achieve his purpose by means of a system of wise laws, whereas the Florentine humanist and architect, haunted by the memory of Rome, demanded that a material construction be the visible manifestation of the triumph of man over time."[47] Alberti resolved the various dichotomies between function and symbol, engineering and rhetoric, contemporary political reality and the historical past in the course of his experiences in Florence and Rome. His Florence was the Florence of Salutati, Bruni, and Cosimo the Elder, while Rome was the city of ruins that provoked his indignant denunciation not only of the damage caused by time, but of that caused by man; the same Rome that cher-

ished the myth of the *renovatio imperii*. Garin observes: "in point of fact [Alberti] makes a distinction between the new principalities and kingdoms and the free republics. The new principalities must seek refuge in the mountains and defend themselves with fear and suspicion, while the free populations may inhabit the comfortable cities in the plain. But apart from this, Alberti's town is built to stress class differences, and to accommodate a precise political structure within its walls and buildings. Thus the architect becomes the regulator and co-ordinator of all the town's activities according to a free restatement of the Aristotelian concept. Alberti presents architecture as the art of arts, the queen and sum of all the others. Town planning is not just connected with politics, it is part and parcel of political activity, almost its highest expression."[48] But Alberti never drew up a design of his ideal city, just as he never expressed his idea of the perfect republic. He preferred to concentrate on the genesis and purpose of both on the basis of a constant dialectic between virtue and rational purpose: "Therefore, it is our firm belief, as I think it is yours too, for you are all wise and prudent men, that in public affairs and human intercourse reason is to be esteemed more highly than fortune, prudence more than any kind of chance."[49] Tenenti has observed that in this concept of virtue there is "a fair dose of detached tolerance and scornful reserve, with a strong tendency to exalt the self-sufficiency of the family and the individual. We have already mentioned how his anti-Florentine politics were really a form of protest against the state."[50] His disgust with his own position as a political bureaucrat which, as we have seen, is often movingly and scornfully expressed, is accompanied by a pre-Guicciardinian concept of human nature: "The minds and hearts of men are different and various: some men are wrathful; some more easily moved to pity; some are sharp and suspicious; some credulous and pure; some are haughty, stubborn, and bitter; some human, malleable, obsequious; some are gay, open, and hearty; some shy, solitary and austere; some like to be praised, and suffer when they are criticised; some are stubborn and will heed nothing but the law; some are harsh in command, cruel in their arrogance, weak in danger, and so forth; it would be a waste of words to describe them all."[51] From this arises the necessary art of government: "It is the proper office of the father to command, and of the son to obey. Brothers ought to advise, the husband rules over his wife, the tutor over his pupils, the elder brother over his younger ones; and the friend feels he has a right to guide in some way. The architect commands his workmen, the helmsman the other sailors at sea, the doctor

44. L.B. Alberti, *L'Architettura*, cit., Book IV, chap. I, p. 268.
45. L.B. Alberti, op. cit., ibid., p. 270.
46. L.B. Alberti, op. cit., ibid.
47. D.H. Michel, *La Penseé de L.B. Alberti*, Paris 1930, pp. 275–277.

48. E. Garin, *Scienza e vita civile nel Rinascimento italiano*, Bari 1965, p. 49.
49. *I Libri della Famiglia*, Preface, in L.B. Alberti, op. cit., p. 9.
50. A. Tenenti, *Leon Battista Alberti*, Rome-Milan 1966, p. 63.
51. *De Iciarchia*, in L.B. Alberti, *Opere volgari*, Book III, p. 279.

his patient, the general his soldiers, and the magistrate the citizens."[52] But government must be firm, for when it is based on mere exhortation it is a pious illusion.[53]

This leads Alberti to the need to conceive the perfect prince and to the recognition that "when we see persons who excel in intelligence and who stand out above everyone else in a crowd, so that they are, in their different ways, extraordinary and therefore rare, nature moves us to call them divine, and we admire and honour them as gods."[54] The satire of *Momus* breaks out into a spirited criticism of Jove's simplicity and of the victory of malice over virtue. It then presents us with a picture of the ideal prince: "[He] must not behave in such a way that he does nothing, nor must he do everything himself, but what he does, he must do neither by himself nor together with everyone else. He must see that no one is too rich, and that there are not too many poor people without any opportunities at all. Let him reward the good, even against their own wishes, and punish the wicked only against his own inclinations. Let him judge people by giving more importance to facts that are known to a few than to those that are known by all. Let him abstain from reform unless he is driven to them by the need to save the decorum of the State. Let him be magnificent in public and thrifty in private life. He will procure tranquillity for his dear ones, and glory and popularity for himself, more through the arts of peace than by waging war. Let him listen patiently to petitions and tolerate with moderation the complaints of his humblest subjects, if he wants the common people to tolerate his pomp."[55] This last piece of advice must have been little heeded, except by Lionello d'Este and Federico da Montefeltro. Perhaps the satire, under the cover of its cautious and inscrutable allusions, was aimed at the Curia. In any case, the ideal prince remained an improbable ideal for Alberti, whose thought may easily be related to the anti-Republican controversy that had cost his family so much, and which had been the cause of his life's anguish.

What Alberti's political thought really boils down to is a distrust of human nature and political life, and this distrust expresses itself in a flight from all that had given birth to it, including the town. Tenenti has made the acute observation that "there were family reasons for his hostile attitude to the town, and he adopted quite different attitudes at times; the rest of Alberti's work shows how highly he valued the urban world. Moreover, his turning to the countryside reflects a profound, widespread tendency, which was not only characteristic of the Humanists but of a large part of the Italian élite."[56] The theme of the villa as a place where one

can "live to oneself" and escape from the alienation caused by political strife and the wickedness of man is taken up again in the third book of the *Famiglia*, where Alberti writes of the need to be economically self-sufficient and of the joys of nature: "You can also enjoy fresh, pure, free days of the happiest kind in a villa, for you are surrounded by the loveliest of views: leafy hillocks, verdant plains, and clear springs and streams skipping and diving amongst grassy tufts."[57] The same theme is dealt with in his *Villa*, where he repeats his theory of government, or "the industry of command"[58] as he calls it.

It reappears in the *De re aedificatoria*, coupled with that of the enjoyment of nature: "I do not think it necessary for the gentleman's house to stand in a particularly fertile part of his estate, but in one that is notable in other respects; in other words, where he has all the advantages and pleasures of good air, sun, and fine views. It should be connected with his farm by easily transitable roads and should have decorous avenues for the reception of guests. It should be visible to all, and enjoy the view perhaps of some town, fortress, the sea, a vast plain, the tops of some familiar hills or mountains, or beautiful gardens, and should offer plentiful opportunities for fishing and hunting."[59] He then speaks of the enjoyment of nature and 'works and days' in connection with the pleasure of reading one's favourite authors, but expresses nothing more on the political level than a snobbish theory of middle-class independence or autarchy.

At the time the *Ten Books* were written — in the middle of the 15th century — Alberti's thought might have looked like the escapism of an intellectual minority or frustrated faction. But when the treatise appeared in the vernacular a century later, his concept of a return to feudalism found fertile ground in the new form of tyranny established by Cosimo, tempered though this was by an ideal of service to the State. Thus the treatise, with its directions for farmhouses, villas, and thrifty housekeeping, became the standard work of reference for the territorial organisation that was to condition the economy, customs and the very look of Tuscan architecture for centuries. Guicciardini himself was to seek refuge in the villa after losing his freedom in the game of power politics.

If one looks at the historical context in which Alberti lived and worked, one realises how futile it is to expect him to have created an architectural vision out of a desire for progress or social and political equality. His awareness of the relationship between politics and architecture was limited to establishing the exact relationship between two class structures. The only saving note

52. *De Iciarchia*, ibid.
53. *De Iciarchia*, Vol. II, Book I, p. 194.
54. L.B. Alberti, *Momus*, ed. by G. Martini, Preface, Bologna 1942, p. 191.
55. *Momo o del Principe*, cit., p. 296.
56. A. Tenenti, op. cit., p. 64.

57. *I Libri della Famiglia*, Book III, in L.B. Alberti, op. cit., p. 200.
58. C. Grayson, *Villa, un opuscolo sconosciuto* in "Rinascimento", Florence, 1953, IV, p. 51.
59. L.B. Alberti, *L'Architettura*, cit., Book V, chap. XVII, p. 414.

in this schematic body of thought is the idea that culture helps one to educate princes and patrons and to understand human nature, so that one may guide it rationally. It also helps one to understand one's own alienation, and to overcome it in the effort to attain to "spiritual tranquillity". The disillusioned realism that takes political commitment as its object of satire in *Momus* is not an anticipation of Machiavelli's vision of the autonomy of politics. What it expresses is man's independence of politics. And this he achieves through the independence of art.

ALBERTI'S WILL

"Taciturnity, solitariness, and melancholy" are the almost Leopardian qualities attributed to Alberti by his anonymous biographer: "But he was also of an open affable disposition, and even when discussing serious matters with his relatives, he would address them respectfully, but cheerfully and gaily."[60] In the first book of the *Famiglia* Battista has his father Lorenzo say: "Yet the pleasure I feel at being here conversing with you and my friends, this delight at seeing my own things, turns to grief at the thought I must leave all."[61] But Alberti's noblest thoughts on the subject of death are to be found in the *Theogenius*: "Perhaps, just as we come into this life with so much sadness and bitterness, and then feel its full sweetness when the moment comes to leave it, so it is with the swan, which is said to die singing. All the needs of nature are full of delight, as eating, drinking, resting, sleeping and so forth, so that when our appetites and movements are at rest we are not unlike those becalmed in death. Thus, we may persuade ourselves that death too, may have some delight. But we must not think that death brings no sorrow at all. When we die, we lose our feelings; nor can one grieve who does not feel. So death does not bring sorrow, but cancels it."[62] The beauty of the passage does not prevent us from questioning the particular nature of Alberti's *pietas*, or even his faith. He affirms that religion is the prime source of morality: "Whosoever does not fear God, whosoever has lost the faith, may be reputed wicked in all things."[63] Moreover, according to his idea of harmony in the family, good wives are the gift of God, and it is the duty of all newly-weds to entreat God for the right use of the goods they share. Thus, though he reaffirms the basic principles of the Christian religion, the content of his faith is unusual nonetheless. In spite of Mancini's efforts to show he was a practising Catholic and that he may even have been ordained, given his clerical status, Tenenti has correctly observed: "In the whole of his work there is not the slightest reference to dogma; not

even to the Virgin or to Christ himself. One may even say that he ignores the whole religious patrimony of the Christian faith, and that his is not so much religion as religiosity."[64] There is no doubt that Alberti fully recognised the function of religion in the maintenance of social order and of the inner order of the individual conscience, but he may have felt that the same effect could be obtained by following the religion of the ancients or pagan mythology.

This explains the importance of the temple in his city, for its function was to inspire philosophical wisdom. It also explains the austerity of his forms, his rejection of pietism (even in painting) and superstition, and his preference for the clarity and abstract language of architecture, or, at the very most, sculpture. Finally, there is his appeal to early Christianity: "In the early years of our religion our ancestors, who were righteous men, used to meet together at supper, not to fill themselves with food, but to learn greater meekness in such intimacy, and so return home with their souls full of good counsel and hungry for virtue. Then, after those present had tasted rather than eaten the food that had been prepared most frugally, some theological text was read or sermon given, and all burnt with the desire to do good to others and cultivate virtue. ... Later, when the emperors allowed them to practise these customs publicly, they did not change them very much, though the food grew less as their numbers increased. The sermons preached by the most eloquent bishops of those days may still be read in many of the writings of the fathers. In those days there was only one altar around which the faithful used to gather, and only one sacrifice a day was celebrated."[65]

The detachment Alberti shows towards his age, which may be explained by his preference for a culture based wholly on the values of antiquity, is also reflected in his judgement of the ecclesiastical world, of which he was both an official and an impartial observer for the whole of his life. His bitter denunciation of the corrupt religious practices of his day makes him a precursor of certain laical tendencies that were to develop later: "Then our own times followed, which ought to be disapproved of by every serious man. Let this be said without offence to our bishops, who, on the pretext of maintaining their dignity, can hardly suffer to show themselves to the people once a year, on New Year's Day, though they have filled all the churches with altars to the point that ... but it is useless going on any further."[66] The same argument is put forward in the *Famiglia* and in the *Pontiphex*, but the tone is not so much that of a detached aesthete

---

60. A. Bonucci, *Vita di Leon Battista Alberti*, anon., p. CV.
61. *I Libri della Famiglia*, Book I, p. 15.
62. *Theogenius*, Book II, p. 102.
63. *I Libri della Famiglia*, Book I, p. 59.

64. A. Tenenti, op. cit., p. 68.
65. L.B. Alberti, *L'Architettura*, Book, chap. XIII, pp. 626–628.
66. L.B. Alberti, *L'Architettura*, ibid.

as that of an indignant moralist: "Nor do I wonder if, as you were saying, the priests are again so greedy that they vie with one another, not in virtue and letters—there are few cultured priests, and even fewer honest ones—but in pomp and luxury. Their main desire is to have very fat, richly caparisoned horses, to appear in public with a great following of hangers-on, and they grow more and more slothful, lascivious, insolent and arrogant every day."[67]

"In order to curry favour, they seek out nourishment for each other's vices, so hardened have they become in their filthy, dishonest lives. They surround themselves with most wicked, abandoned accomplices, and are almost constantly inflamed with the desire of some new vice or lechery, which they do not have the money to pay for, since the expense is above their means. Thus they are forced into rapacity."[68]

But this criticism of ecclesiastical corruption must not be mistaken for an attack on religion itself, for religion is one thing and ecclesiastical malpractice another. There is no doubt that in spite of all these contradictions, Alberti remained true to the permanent values of religion over and above its diverse historical and liturgical manifestations. In Alberti's religion there is room for the revival of early Christian practice, for Platonic, hermetic, and pagan ideas, and even for an historicist faith in the permanence of cultural values and the endurance of human thought: "In my opinion, those who are to be most admired are the Indian sages, who affirm that the finest monument a man can have is the memory he leaves behind him."[69]

Whether, like Mancini, one sees the fervour of a practising Catholic in Alberti, or whether one accepts the usual interpretation of an Alberti tied to the neo-paganism of contemporary Florentine culture, one cannot fail to detect the subtle anguish of the man. Deep conflicts between personal conviction and the conventional beliefs of society, between nature and thought, must have troubled his modern conscience, the modernity of which, however, was qualified by its refusal to declare this state of inner crisis openly. He tried, instead, to sublimate or suffocate it in the prudence imposed by his position in society and in the Curia: "Let no one provide for my burial, for I live and hover on the lips of the learned." This epitaph, attributed to the Latin poet Ennius, must have appealed to Alberti, and it hardly seems a coincidence that he should quote it as one of the most significant.[70]

Alberti dictated his will in a house in the parish of S. Celso in the Ponte quarter of Rome on 19 April 1472. It was a modern, middle-class will, quite in keeping with Alberti's principles, especially in the way it provided for the creation of an 'Alberti Foundation'. After commending his soul to God, to the Virgin Mary, to all the saints and the blessed apostles Peter and Paul (the conventional formula used by notaries), Leon Battista Alberti, described as a "litterarum apostolicharum scriptor", chose to be buried next to his father at Padua, and temporarily in the monastery of S. Agostino. He also expressed the desire that provision be made for the completion of the only work of architecture he commissioned, and which he may have designed. This was the tribune in the church of S. Martino a Gangalandi (of which he was prior for more than forty years), described as "incepta et quasi perfecta" at the time.[71] After leaving a sum of money to the person who looked after him in his illness and another to his servant Claudio, and after distributing cloaks of dark or black cloth to various people, including the notary, his first thought was to leave a priceless codex of Pliny's *Natural History* to Giovanni Francesco d'Altobianco Alberti. To his cousin Bernardo he left the so-called Palazzo delle Colonnine in front of the church of S. Jacopo dei Fossi, the house in Via Bologna (which had been let to a spinner), the so-called Alberti orchard, with its adjacent habitation outside the gate of S. Mamolo, the arable lands, vineyards and apple orchards of a farm at Castel dei Britti, about nine kilometres south of Bologna, and all his other goods and properties in the area of the same city. He also established that upon the extinction of the male line of the Alberti family, all the family's goods were to go to the hospital of S. Maria Nuova in Florence.

But the most unusual clause in the will is that whereby he left a thousand ducats for the purchase of a house in Bologna. This was to be used as a college or place of study endowed with its own income, goods and property, where one or two members of the Alberti family wanting to study canon or civil law, or any other subject, could live free of expense. In the event of there being no heirs of the Alberti family, their places were to be taken by two or more poor students in the form of scholarships, but the house and its endowment were not to be transferred on any account. Alberti nominated Cardinal Nicolò Forteguerri of Pistoia, the notary Antonio Grassi of Bologna, and Matteo Palmieri of Pisa, a man of letters and an apostolic abbreviator, as executors of his will. Unfortunately, "they did not fulfil the trust placed in them",[72] and though they saw to the completion of the tribune of S. Martino, they did not see to Battista's final burial in Padua. (His remains were later lost during the re-

67. *I libri della Famiglia*, Book IV, p. 282.
68. *I Libri della Famiglia*, Book IV, p. 283.
69. L.B. Alberti, *L'Architettura*, Book VIII, chap. II, p. 670.
70. L.B. Alberti, *L'Architettura*, Book VIII, chap. IV, p. 694.

71. G. Mancini, *Il testamento di Leon Battista Alberti*, in "Archivio Storico Italiano", Rome, LXXII, 1914, p. 48.
72. G. Mancini, op. cit., p. 28.

construction of S. Agostino.) Grassi took a greater interest in his duties than the others and did in fact buy a house in Bologna. This was in Via Val de la Vesa, now Via di Val Daposa, a part of the building next to the house being added to it. In 1474 a piece of land was bought at Fiesso, seven kilometres from the city, and in November of the same year a statute was drawn up for the "Collegium venerandi viri domini Baptistae de Albertis de Florentia scriptoris apostolici." But when the male branch of the Alberti family became extinct, and sanctions were applied by the Signoria of Florence against students studying at other universities, Sixtus IV was requested to issue a bull distributing the fruits of the Alberti Foundation among ten choirboys between the ages of eight and seventeen, whose obligation was to sing High Mass every Sunday in S. Petronio. Thus, all that remained of Alberti's concern for learning were the voices of ten choirboys singing for his soul on All Souls' Day. All that remained besides this was a commemorative note written by the neo-pagan Humanist, Mattia Palmieri: "1472. Leon Battista Alberti, a man of most refined doctrine and intelligence, and the author of an admirable book on architecture, died in Rome."[73] There was also the gratitude and understanding of his cousin Bernardo, who was responsible for the publication of the first edition of the *De re aedificatoria* in 1485. In his dedication of the work to Lorenzo de' Medici, Politian wrote: "His cousin Bernardo, a wise man and one of his most loyal followers, desiring to honour the memory and wishes of that great man and at the same time manifest his gratitude for the favours you have granted him, now presents you, Lorenzo de' Medici, with those very books, copied from the originals and brought together in a single volume."[74] Thus, Alberti's wishes were ignored, the foundation that was bound up with the hardship and enthusiasm of his formative years in Bologna was never realised, his tomb is unknown, and even his name on the documents relating to his will has disappeared. And yet his fame has survived, intact and mysterious: "I live and hover upon the lips of the learned."

73. G. Mancini, *Vita di Leon Battista Alberti*, cit., p. 495.
74. L.B. Alberti, *L'Architettura*, cit., p. 2.

Already in the "sweet beginnings of Ferrara", at the outset of Alberti's career as an architect, one encounters all those elements that were to characterise the practice of his profession; and not only when he was at the highly qualified, sophisticated court of the Estes, but also later, in other centres of the Renaissance. The dignified attitude he adopted as consultant and expert rather than supervisor, his literary digressions and the treatise that followed his visit to the city, and the absence of documents explaining the specific nature of his employment are all elements which serve to obscure the precise nature and effect of his stay in the city. To this must be added the fact that at Ferrara, as elsewhere, his projects were carried out by local workmen who had no supervisors capable of guiding them in the correct execution of Alberti's ideas.

The Ferrara that greeted Alberti was ruled by the "gentle prince", Lionello d'Este. It had been ruled before him by his father Niccolò, a military man of simple passions, of whom Bandello wrote: "He wanted every woman he saw, and had so many children that he could have made an army with them."[1] It was precisely these passions that provoked something of a Greek tragedy. An illicit relationship grew up between Niccolò's wife, Parisina, and his illegitimate son Ugo. This was discovered through a hole in the ceiling of the room where they used to meet, and in 1425 they were tried and beheaded. But this did not alter Niccolò's love for his 'bastards' or his intention to look after their education: Lionello was entrusted to Guarino, the man who made Ferrara one of the centres of Italian Humanism; Borso was given Giovanni Toscanello as tutor; and Meliaduso was put in the charge of Aurispa.

In 1429 Niccolò married Ricciarda di Saluzzo on the understanding that all sons of the Saluzzo line (the future Ercole and Sigismondo) were to be excluded from the succession. This was reserved for Lionello, who was legitimised by a papal dispensation granted by Martin V in the year of Niccolò's re-marriage, while Meliaduso was forced into holy orders against his will.

When Niccolò died in Ferrara in 1441 and was succeeded by Lionello, the event heralded a great change in the city. The late-Gothic, passionate, full-blooded, feudal court of the old, prolific Niccolò gave way to that of a refined prince, a lover of culture and the arts, and the promoter of a foreign policy that sought to avoid armed conflict (he negotiated peace between Venice and Milan, Milan and Naples, Naples and Venice).

He did not burden his subjects with heavy taxes, but provided for their education by re-opening the university, to which he

---

1. M. Bandello, *Novelliere*, I, 205, in G. Mancini, *Vita di Leon Battista Alberti*, Rome 1967, p. 172.

called Teodoro Gaza for the teaching of Greek, Angelo degli Ubaldi for Civil Law, and Ludovisio Crivelli and Francesco Accolti for Canon Law. Lionello himself corresponded with Humanists such as Ciriacus d'Ancona, Filelfo, Francesco Barbaro, Poggio.

Guarino had gathered together a real Humanist circle at Ferrara, and in Decembrio's *Politia litteraria*, Lionello is presented as the perfect cultured prince who, according to Guarino, had succeeded in integrating his intellectual and physical education. Equal encouragement was given to the arts: one has only to recall the many portraits of Lionello by Pisanello, Jacopo Bellini, and Andrea Mantegna; in the same decade, 1440–1450, Van der Weyden painted the triptych in the study of Belfiore. Piero della Francesca arrived in Ferrara almost immediately after Alberti, with a commission to paint the now destroyed frescoes in the Este castle, frescoes that were to accompany those he had already painted in the church of S. Andrea.[2]

Given the particular atmosphere at the court, it was natural that Alberti should look upon the Este brothers as ideal patrons. He dedicated his "first work", the Latin comedy *Philodoxeus*, which he had previously described as old, to Lionello, and in the year the prince's father died, he sent him the *Theogenius*, expressing his doubt as to whether "it was dignified enough to be read by you, a prince and most cultured man." It was written in the vernacular and dealt with the theme of virtue and fortune in relation to political commitment, a subject that concerned a prince more than anyone else: "But you, Princes and chief citizens, do you not seek great praise, glory, and immortality in this magnanimity of yours? Not with pomp; not with ostentation, nor with crowds of flatterers will you earn real, whole-hearted praise, for this can only be won by virtue."[3]

The prince also runs risks, for "in such a crowd he cannot but be surrounded by hangers-on, spies, flatterers, back-biters, and lascivious, frivolous, immodest, vicious, contaminated men, with whom he must have hateful, shameful dealings at every hour of the day."[4] The atmosphere of conspiracy and scarcely perceptible anxiety that reigned over a principality which, ideally speaking, should be a chaste image of virtue and peace, does not seem to have escaped Alberti's notice, nor did the constant menace of violence, which hangs over the most refined societies. This strictly cultural manner of sensing reality was attributed by Alberti himself, in literary fashion, to his "prophetic soul". In fact, his anonymous biographer writes: "Standing in front of the palace of the Estes, where, in the time of Niccolò the Tyrant, most of the city's youth had been slain, he once said, 'Oh friends,

2. R. Longhi, *Piero della Francesca*, Rome (n.d.), p. 118.
3. L.B. Alberti, *Opere volgari*, II, Bari 1966, p. 71.
4. Ibid.

these pavements must perforce be slippery in the future, when much blood will flow within these walls', for prudent opinion and intelligence combine with the divinatory arts in predicting the future."[5] Alberti was referring here to the coup d'état organised by Lionello's son, Niccolò, against Ercole I; this ended in Niccolò's decapitation, after which, "his neck was washed" and his head "sewn back" on to his body for the State funeral that was held in the Arca Rossa of the Estes in San Francesco.

Alberti believed that the man of culture was not unlike a prince in that he was never alone, a thought that anticipates the famous passage in Macchiavelli about nights spent in conversation with the ancients: "I never have so much company as when I am alone. For then I am surrounded by knowledgeable, eloquent men, with whom I spend the evening and much of the night in discussion."[6] To his friend Meliaduso d'Este, Lionello's restless clerical brother, whom he had met in 1438 when he accompanied Eugenius IV to the Council of the Roman and Byzantine churches, Alberti dedicated his *Ludi Matematici*. This was a collection of scientific, mathematical, and topographical curiosities and problems, which may have been among Meliaduso's favourite subjects, just as it may have had some relation to the role played by certain abbeys, like Pomposa, as "technical centres" or "faculties of agriculture". Alberti took a long time in writing the small volume, aiming to distract the impatient abbot. But Meliaduso never had the time to enjoy it, for he died in 1452, shortly after being dispensed from his vows.[7]

After dedicating the *Theogenius* to Lionello, Leon Battista arrived in Ferrara, where he was made judge of a competition held to choose the best design for an equestrian statue of Niccolò III. That he was an expert horseman is confirmed by the *Anonymous Life*: "He could ride for hours without showing the slightest trace of fatigue, with one end of a rod placed against his foot and the other in his hand, without the slightest movement on the part of the rod. So fine and wonderful a horseman was he, that even the proudest and most mettlesome horses seemed to fear and tremble when he mounted them."[8] It was the right moment to dedicate another book to Lionello, and he wrote the *De equo animante*, in which he describes the atmosphere of the contest: "I find it difficult to describe the joy I felt on my arrival here in Ferrara, for the pleasure of seeing and paying you honour, most illustrious prince, on seeing your most beautiful city, your disciplined citizens, and you, honourable and most human of princes. To this pleasure, which is very great, must be added the opportunity of exercising my talent, which I have, in all truth,

5. Anon., *Vita di Leon Battista Alberti*, trans. by Bonucci, I, p. 91.

6. L.B. Alberti, op. cit., p. 75.

7. On the subject cf. L. Vagnetti, *Considerazioni sui "Ludi mathematici"* in "Studi e documenti di Architettura", 1, December 1972, p. 175 ff.

8. Anon., op. cit., p. 93.

8. *Ferrara, Arco del Cavallo and the Castello Estense.*
9. *Ferrara, the Arco del Cavallo: elevation, side-view, and plans.*

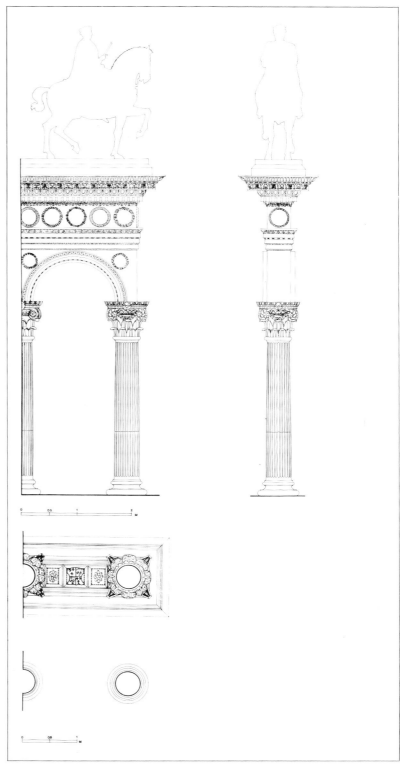

accepted most willingly both for your profit and mine. In fact, after your fellow citizens had decided with great largesse to erect an equestrian statue of your father, many fine artists vied with each other, and I, who take no small pleasure in painting and sculpture, was elected their judge and arbiter. I have looked upon that admirably executed work many times since, and I began to reflect more carefully not upon the beauty and shape, but upon the nature and behaviour of horses. I enquired into all the uses of horses, public and private, in war and in peace. In fact, whether they be brought from the country to the town for the family's education, or whether they contribute to the attainment of glory and the decorum of freedom on the battlefield, these animals are of great use to man, so much so that I doubt whether health or dignity can be had without their help."[9] Here too, Alberti rejected the purely aesthetic approach, preferring to avoid facile judgements based on personal taste, and adopting instead a thoroughly scientific attitude in an attempt to define the best kind of equestrian statue. As for the artists who took part in the competition, Vasari makes a brief reference to the disciples of Brunelleschi, mentioning "the Florentines, Antonio and Niccolò, who made a bronze horse for Duke Borso of Ferrara in 1461."[10] A model of the statue was made by Antonio di Cristoforo of Florence in competition with Niccolò di Giovanni Baroncelli. Later, perhaps as a result of Alberti's arbitration, Antonio di Cristoforo did the horseman, and, with the help of others, the marble pedestal, while the horse was cast by Niccolò Baroncelli, thereafter called Nicholas of the Horse.

One look at the Volta del Cavallo is enough to convince one it is the work of Alberti, though there is no documentary evidence to prove it. Venturi claimed that "the artist responsible, who may have been one of the sculptors who worked on the equestrian statue, did not really succeed in carrying out the Humanist architect's fine design in a dignified manner, though it emerges quite clearly, nevertheless, in this first flower of the Renaissance in Ferrara."[11] There are unmistakable signs of specific Roman influence in its reduced form, which is conditioned by the height of the adjacent portico. These can be seen in the composite capitals, the mouldings, the entablature, the *clipei* (shield-shaped reliefs) on the sides of the arch, and in the coronas of the frieze. These are all characteristics of Alberti's style, even if executed on a reduced scale by unskilled craftsmen, and in spite of the fact that the proportions of the work, which were conditioned by the compressed columns and the reduced span of the arch, give the impression of a classical surface imposed upon a medieval

9. L.B. Alberti, *De equo animante*, in G. Mancini, *Inedita etc.*, Florence 1890, pp. 238–39.
10. Vasari, *Le vite*, ed. Milanesi, II, p. 386.
11. A. Venturi, *Storia dell'Arte italiana, L'architettura nel Quattrocento*, Milan 1923, p. 165. Cf. also A. Venturi, *Un'opera sconosciuta di L.B. Alberti*, in "L'Arte", XVII, Rome 1914, pp. 153–56.

structure. But this may be regarded as emblematic of the cultural atmosphere of the court of Lionello, and is characteristic of the other works that were carried out either under the influence or on the advice of Alberti. As Venturi has pointed out, these include the colonnade in the castle courtyard and the lower part of the bell tower.

The way in which the campanile is reduced to cubic elements by means of square blocks of stone calls to mind Giotto's, as does the more emphatic plastic relief of the corner pillars. The Volta del Cavallo, like everything else Alberti did in the course of his uncertain debut at Ferrara, must be seen as part of a general attempt to impose a classical style on medieval proportions. This being so, the 'button hole' windows, the narrow spaces between the columns, and the heavy arches with their reduced spans may all be explained as the product of a gap between the ideal and its concrete realisation.

Lionello's father, Niccolò d'Este, decided to build the bell tower in 1412, and the foundations were laid according to a plan drawn up by a certain Niccolò da Campo, an official of the Banca dei Soldati. The first order, "from the Evangelists upwards" (the four symbols of the Evangelists are almost at ground level), was begun in 1451, while Alberti was at the court.[12] Later, the project was continued without him, but very slowly. Borso levied various taxes to finance the structure; both the second and third orders were completed in 1464 by stone cutters from Mantua under the direction of Piero Benvenuti, thereafter called Peter of the Orders. The fourth order was completed in the sixteenth century.[13] This doctrinaire manifestation of Renaissance art in Ferrara was typical of the period, but it soon gave way to a revival of the Gothic tradition of the Po area, perhaps because the influence of Alberti was not so decisive. In fact, Alberti found himself having to deal with structures, such as the arch and the bell tower, that had no interiors. Thus he was obliged to express in 'Latin', or decorate in the 'Latin' fashion, two elements that were typical of the medieval 'vernacular' in typology and proportions.

After meditating upon his brief but significant experience in Ferrara, and realizing the fundamental importance of type and proportion while writing his treatise, Alberti concluded that the kind of marriage of styles he had tried to effect was impossible. Later, at Rimini, he was to affirm, in polemical fashion, that the two styles, and the two fields of proportion implicit in them, were incompatible. From an eclecticism in which the two styles were mixed, he was to pass to an eclecticism wherein they ran parallel.

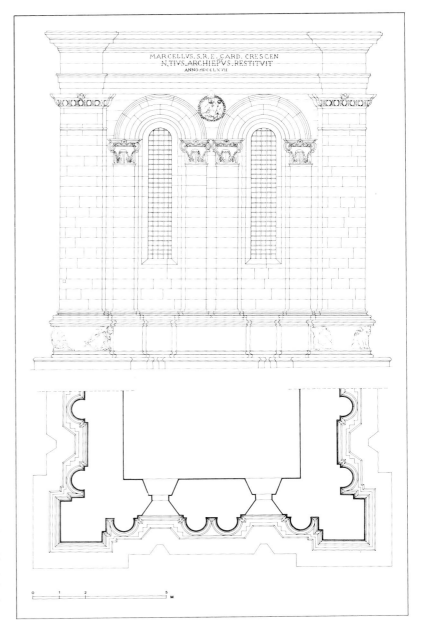

12.   L.N. Cittadella, *Notizie amministrative storico-artistiche relative a Ferrara*, Ferrara 1868, p. 96 ff.
13.   Here is a brief chronology of its construction:
1465 - Benedetto di Rimini, a wood merchant, agreed to provide all the material necessary for the scaffolding of the "campanile novo de marmo, sursum et supra ipsum campanile, junxta designum et edificium ipsum factum ac fabricatum de lignamine". Thus, a model and a design did exist.
1466 - The painter Giovanni Bianchini was paid for "having painted the five shields above the second window of the new bell tower in fine colours, decorating them partly with gold and partly with gold foil". The second order had already been completed.

1493 - The third order had been added, and thought was being given to the fourth and its crowning part. There were continual payments for the paint and gilt lavished on the decoration of the carved inscriptions, garlands, borders, and statues.
1494 - Work was suspended on the fourth order.
1579 - Giambattista Aleotti resumed the work and built the planned fourth order.
1596 - The work was finished.
1790 - A competition was held to choose the best design for the crowning part of the bell tower. Many artists took part in it, and most of them were in favour of a dome.

"Examples of ancient monuments, such as theatres and temples, from which one can learn as much as from famous teachers, have, of course, been preserved. But I have noticed to my sorrow that they are falling into greater ruin every day."[1] "But then there is the damage caused by man. ... By God! I cannot but rebel sometimes when I see monuments, which even the wild barbarians spared for their beauty and splendour, or which even time itself, that tenacious destroyer, would willingly let stand forever, falling into ruin because of the neglect—not to use a stronger word, for I might have said the avarice—of certain men."[2] These complaints are not very different from those voiced by Poggio in his description of Rome and by Biondo in *Roma Instaurata*. But Alberti did not simply protest: he began the collection of all known facts about Rome's monuments and urged their restoration, an undertaking that reached its climax during the Pontificate of Nicholas V, to whom Alberti presented his *De re aedificatoria*.

Tommaso Parentucelli, the future Nicholas V, belonged to the same world as Alberti. He too had studied at Bologna, had been a tutor in the house of Palla Strozzi, Giovanni Rucellai's father-in-law, and had served under Cardinal Albergati, the man Alberti accompanied on his missions beyond the Alps, and whom the future pope was to assist religiously up to his death. When Eugenius IV was in Florence for the Council, with Alberti as one of his abbreviators, Tommaso was in the company of the cardinal of S. Croce. Vespasiano da Bisticci later wrote:

"And since Messer Lionardo d'Arezzo, Messer Giannozzo Manetti, Messer Poggio, Messer Carlo d'Arezzo, Messer Giovanni Aurispa, and Messer Gasparo da Bologna, a very erudite man, and many more learned men used to meet every morning and evening at the corner of the palace to discuss various things, Messer Tommaso, as soon as he had accompanied the cardinal to the palace, would come along on the back of a mule with two men-servants on foot. He was usually dressed in blue, while his servants wore the dress of footmen or long blue cloaks, with berrettas on their heads. There was not the pomp at the court of Rome that there is now. He was always arguing in the above-mentioned place, or talking and discussing at the court of Rome, for he was a most vehement debater."[3]

Vespasiano adds that "he used to say he would like to do two things, if ever he had the money: form a library and build, and he did both during his pontificate."[4] After his unexpected election to the papacy, he once asked Vespasiano during an audience: "Vespasiano, would the people of Florence have ever believed that a priest only good enough for ringing bells would one day

1. L.B. Alberti, *L'Architettura*, V, I, p. 400.
2. Ibid., X, I, pp. 868–70.
3. Vespasiano da Bisticci, *Vite di uomini illustri del secolo XV*, Florence 1938, pp. 32–33.
4. Ibid., p. 35.

16. *View of Rome in a fresco by Masolino da Panicale. Castiglione Olona, Baptistery.*

become Supreme Pontiff?"[5] Vespasiano also writes of Tommaso's affection for the Florentines:

"You know how many favours Cosimo de' Medici did me when I was in need. Now I want to reward him. Tomorrow morning I shall put my money in his bank. One can never be too generous to men who are grateful." At one time during the jubilee the bank of the Medici held more than a hundred thousand florins of the Church's money, according to what I have been told by reliable persons who worked for them. He then told me: "I want to pay the Florentines a great honour. Tomorrow morning I shall grant them an audience in a public consistory, such as is granted to kings and emperors."[6]

The only certain documentary evidence we have of the relations between Alberti and Nicholas V is a passage in Matteo Palmieri's *Cronistoria* entered against the date of 1452: "Since the Pope wanted to build a more beautiful church in honour of Saint Peter, he had huge foundations laid and the walls extended to a height of twenty-six feet (only in the apse of the choir), but the grandiose project, equal to any undertaken by the ancients, was first interrupted on Leon Battista'a advice, and then set aside after the Pope's premature death. Leon Battista Alberti, a man of sharp, penetrating intelligence, and well instructed in the arts and sciences, presented the Pope with his most erudite volumes on architecture."[7]

This, however, was only the final stage in the collaboration between pope and architect, as we may deduce from the reference to St. Peter's—the most difficult problem in the Pope's building programme—and the date of Palmieri's entry, made two years after Nicholas' lavish preparations for the 1450 Jubilee celebrations. This is also confirmed by reference to the treatise, which clearly reflects the experience Alberti had acquired as a restorer of ancient monuments in Rome during this period. There are no other references in the sources, and no hint of Alberti receiving any retribution for the advice he gave, except for the bull of 7 December 1448, issued in the second year of Nicholas's pontificate. This refers to Alberti as the Pope's *familiare*, or servant ("ex familiari experientia"), and granted him the priory of Borgo a S. Lorenzo, which Mancini considers quite out of proportion to the importance of Alberti's position.[8] Recent research in the State Archives in Rome and in the Vatican Archives yielded no further information than that known to Pastor and Mancini.

Opinion differs as to the part played by Alberti in the elaboration of Nicholas's town planning policy. Some, pointing to the lack of evidence, are inclined to believe that his advice counted for

5. Ibid., p. 43.
6. Ibid.
7. L. von Pastor, *Storia dei Papi*, Rome 1942, I, pp. 517–18.
8. G. Mancini, *Vita di Leon Battista Alberti*, p. 277 n. 1, pp. 303–04 n. 5.

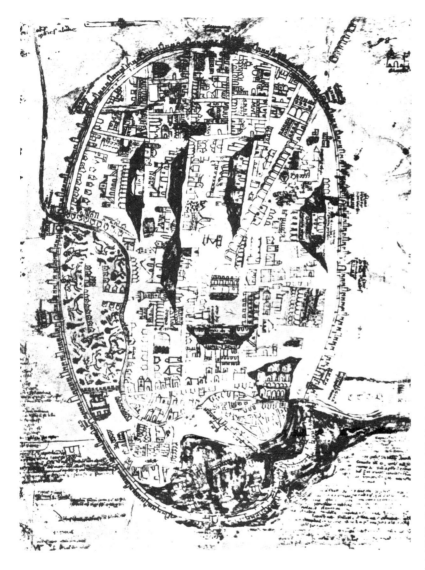

little, while others maintain that he exercised a decisive, if not direct influence on the whole programme of restoration and innovation initiated by the Pope. The latter conclusions are partly based on Vasari's statement that the Pope "had a great, resolute spirit, and knew so much that he was able to guide and direct his artists as much as they did him."[9] The papal treasury of the fifteenth century was not administered with the same order and thoroughness as in later years, and the documents that have survived (many of which have been published by Müntz) are extremely laconic and unsystematic. One must also take into account the Pope's generosity, of which Vespasiano da Bisticci again gives a vivid description: "He used to carry a bag by his side with hundreds of florins in it, handfuls of which he gave away to the deserving out of the love of God."[10] Perhaps it is no coincidence that Vespasiano immediately goes on to speak of building: "Pope Nicholas had many churches built in Rome, besides beginning that wonderful edifice in honour of Saint Peter, which could contain the whole court of Rome. He built wonderful structures in churches throughout the world, according to what Messer Gianozzo Manetti has written in his biography, and the building he raised in honour of Saint Peter would have been enough not only for a pope but for one of those Roman emperors who ruled the whole world. The buildings, together with the decorations he had carried out in honour of the sacred liturgy, cost a fortune. He did well to spend money instead of accumulating it, as so many others have done."[11]

Taking into consideration the unsystematic administration of the papal treasury and the incomplete accounts of the works, it is pointless to try to extract from the documents something that neither Pastor, Müntz, Janitschek, nor Mancini found; that is, evidence of Alberti's active participation in Nicholas's building programme. Insofar as he was a papal abbreviator and the Pope's 'servant', Alberti's function must have been a purely advisory one. At least this would explain Manetti's silence on the matter. For in his hagiographic biography of Nicholas V, Manetti tends to give all the architectural credit to the Pope and none at all to Alberti, his colleague. The reason for this was probably professional jealousy, or Florentine envy provoked by the familiarity with which the Pope must have honoured Alberti. It is Vasari who earns our gratitude for having seen Alberti's contribution in its proper dimensions, and for having laid a sound historical basis for a discussion of the problem:

"Leon Battista happened to arrive in Rome during the pontificate of Nicholas V, who had been turning the city upside down

9.   Vasari, *Le vite*, ed. Milanesi, III, p. 100.
10.   Vespasiano da Bisticci, op. cit., p. 50.
11.   Ibid.

with all his building projects, and through the good offices of his close friend Biondo da Forlì he was befriended by His Holiness. Nicholas had previously sought advice on architectural matters from the Florentine sculptor and architect, Bernardo Rossellino (as I shall mention in my life of his brother Antonio); but after he had started to restore the Vatican and to do some work in S. Maria Maggiore, according to the Pope's wishes, Rossellino always went to Leon Battista for advice. And using one to carry out the ideas of the other, the Pope went ahead with many useful and commendable projects. These included the restoration of the ruined aqueduct of the Acqua Vergine fountain, and the construction of the fountain in the Piazza de' Trievi, with its still surviving marble ornamentation, including the arms of Nicholas V and of the Roman people."[12]

Two events happened at about the beginning of Nicholas's reign that must have been decisive in the growth of Alberti's cultural prestige. The first was the discovery and rescue of a ship from the waters of Lake Nemi, a task entrusted by Cardinal Prospero Colonna to "our Leon Battista Alberti, an excellent geometer and the author of very fine books on the art of building."[13] The incident is described at the end of an important passage in Book Five of the treatise: "Recently, while writing this work, a ship dating from the time of Trajan was lifted out of Lake Nemi, where it had lain for more than 1300 years. Examining it, I was able to observe that its pine and cypress wood was in an excellent state of preservation. On the outside, its wooden planks had been covered with a double layer of linen cloth soaked in tar, and this in turn was protected by a sheet of lead made fast with brass nails."[14]

The second event was the writing of the *Descriptio Urbis Romae*, which, as Vagnetti's recent studies have shown, occurred during Alberti's second stay in Rome, between 1443 and 1455, and not during his first, between 1431 and 1434, when he was secretary to Biagio Molin, bishop of Grado and papal chancellor. This more correct dating is based on the relationship between the *Descriptio* and the *Ludi Matematici* (written between 1443 and 1448).[15] Vagnetti and Frutaz have explained how the importance of the *Descriptio* derives from the fact that no systematic, orthographic plan of Rome had been drawn up during the thousand years that had passed between the marble one of Severius and Leonardo Bufalini's of 1551, which was carried out almost at the same time as Bartoli's translation of the *Architettura* into the vernacular. Vagnetti's reconstruction of Alberti's scientific methods of measurement based on the use of polar co-ordinates

shows how, in spite of a not inconsiderable mistake regarding the city's general orientation and the North pole, the architect arrived at an accurate location of the perimeter of the Aurelian Wall, one that almost coincides with our own idea of its position. But Alberti's scientific methods went beyond the scope of a topographical exercise or mathematical *ludus*, and assumed urbanistic significance. For his description of Rome implied a global concept of the city as an organism, in which the walls and gateways were the first important elements, followed by the Tiber, and finally by the "city's temples and public buildings". Alberti's list includes all the most significant buildings of antiquity, as well as all the Christian churches and places of worship. The occasion for such a map must have been the impending jubilee, an inference confirmed by the fact that Nicholas's first concern was the city walls and gateways. Moreover, there seems to be a very close correspondence between Alberti's list of monuments and the restorations carried out by the Pope.

Some Humanists protested, while others adopted an ambiguous attitude towards Rome's classical remains. There was no better example of this than the Pope himself, who continued to grant special permissions for the use of ancient ruins as quarries for building materials (the construction of the hospice of S. Salvatore di Tutti i Santi, for example, resulted in considerable damage to the Coliseum).[16] Alberti, on the other hand, produced a systematic guide to Rome's monuments. Nothing more than a series of numbers, the *Descriptio* was instrumental in laying the foundations for that organic relationship between pagan and Christian which was to be the key to the *renovatio imperii*, and which explains why the jubilee of 1450 was above all an intellectual, cultural success, rather than a touristic one.

This is borne out by Giovanni Rucellai's enthusiastic descriptions of the classical beauties and ruins of Rome in his *Zibaldone quaresimale*. Giovanni had approached Alberti about 1446 in connection with a house he wanted to build in Florence. In 1450 he left Perugia for Rome, where "in the morning we rode out and visited the four churches mentioned above. Then, after eating, we remounted our horses and went to look at Rome's ancient walls and fine buildings. In the evening, after returning home, I thought over all the things I have noted down in this book."[17] Giovanni's list, like Alberti's, naturally begins with St. Peter's, and continues with S. Maria Maggiore, S. Giovanni in Laterano, and S. Lorenzo. The list of monuments visited by Giovanni Rucellai almost coincides with Alberti's in the *Descriptio* and includes Castel S. Angelo, the tomb of Romulus, and the church of S. Maria Rotonda.

12. Vasari, op. cit., II, "Vita di Leon Battista Alberti", pp. 538–39.
13. G. Mancini, op. cit., p. 278.
14. L.B. Alberti, op. cit., V, 12, p. 388.
15. On this subject see L. Vagnetti, *La "Descriptio urbis Romae" di L.B. Alberti*, in "Università degli Studi di Genova Facoltà di Architettura e Rilievo dei Monumenti", I, October 1968, pp. 68 ff., and L. Vagnetti, *Lo studio di Roma negli scritti albertiani*, contributed to the International Conference on L.B. Alberti, Accademia dei Lincei, April 1972.

16. Müntz, *Les arts à la cour des papes pendant le XV et le XVI s.*, Paris 1878-1882, p. 107.
17. G. Rucellai, *Zibaldone quaresimale*, London 1960, p. 68.

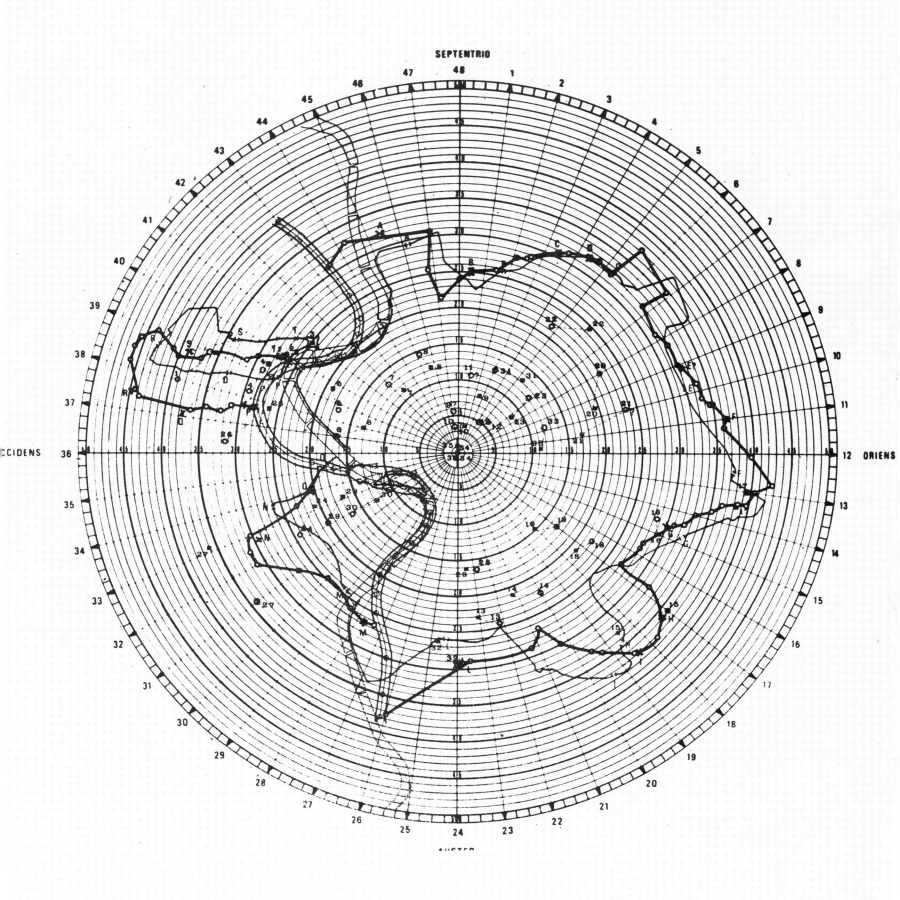

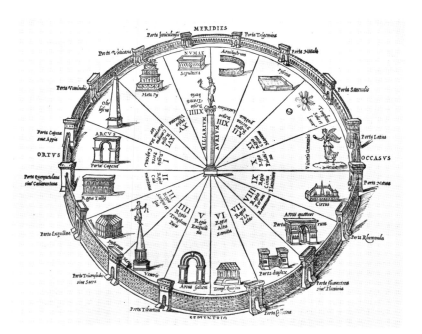

However, this self-confident Florentine merchant finds space to make more ample reference, even in so schematic (one might even say uncritical and gross) a list of "antique bric-à-brac" as his, to two centrally-planned buildings. One is S. Costanza, described as "circular, with coupled columns, beautiful arches, and very beautiful mosaics in the ceiling .... enclosed by a roofed ambulatory with a very pleasant mosaic in the vault."[18] The other is "the church of S. Stefano Rotondo, a circular pagan temple, which stands upon twenty columns with architraves, and is open on all sides, surrounded by an ambulatory with a brick roof. [There is] an ancient chapel on one side with a mosaic, small panels and plaques of porphyry and serpentine, leaf patterns, bunches of grapes, inlays, and other decorations."[19] All this reflects a cultural interest, which, if not developed under the direct guidance of Alberti—who is credited with the restoration of S. Stefano Rotondo—must have been stimulated by him.

Though Giovanni Rucellai makes no explicit reference to Alberti's book, his son Bernardo is lavish in his praise of it. Bernardo was an assiduous member of Careggi's neo-Platonic circle, and he accompanied Lorenzo de' Medici and five other "orators" to Rome for the election of Sixtus IV in 1471. On this occasion, the group was accompanied on its tours of the city by Alberti (in the last year he was still able to ride). The memory of that visit to Rome induced Bernardo to write his own *De Urbe Roma*, a book enriched by the advantage of having had so expert a guide as Alberti to interpret the Latin inscriptions and the various monuments. It was also written in a very different atmosphere from the plague-stricken one in which his father had hurriedly jotted down his sketchy notes: "Nam olim Romae, cum ego atque Donatus Acciaiolus et Laurentius Medices, duce Baptista Alberto, prisca monumenta inviseremus."[20]

His tribute to Alberti takes on a reverential tone from the very first of his concisely written paragraphs: "Nam lateritia ipsa, (Roma) turribus frequens aliisque id genus munimentis, nullum, praeter magnitudinis, decorem retinet aliis alio more, ut tum res erant, Principibus imperantibus; siquidem Baptista Albertus se in vetustis moenibus pavimentata opera, crustisque perornatos parietes vidisse adfirmet, vir sane architecturae peritissimus, ut eius scripta indicant, ut qui in prosequendis antiquitatum monumentis huius aevi omnes facile superaverit."[21]

This is followed by a reference to the Antonine Baths, "visited with Battista Alberti as guide", and to a view of Tarquin's embankment: "Quin etiam perdurasse huiusce aggeris (Tarquini) vestigia usque ad Baptistae Alberti aetatem ex illius de Architectura

18. Ibid., p. 74.

19. Ibid., p. 73.

20. Valentini, Cecchetti, *Codice topografico della città di Roma*, Rome 1953, Bernardo Rucellai, "De Urbe Roma", p. 445.

21. Ibid.

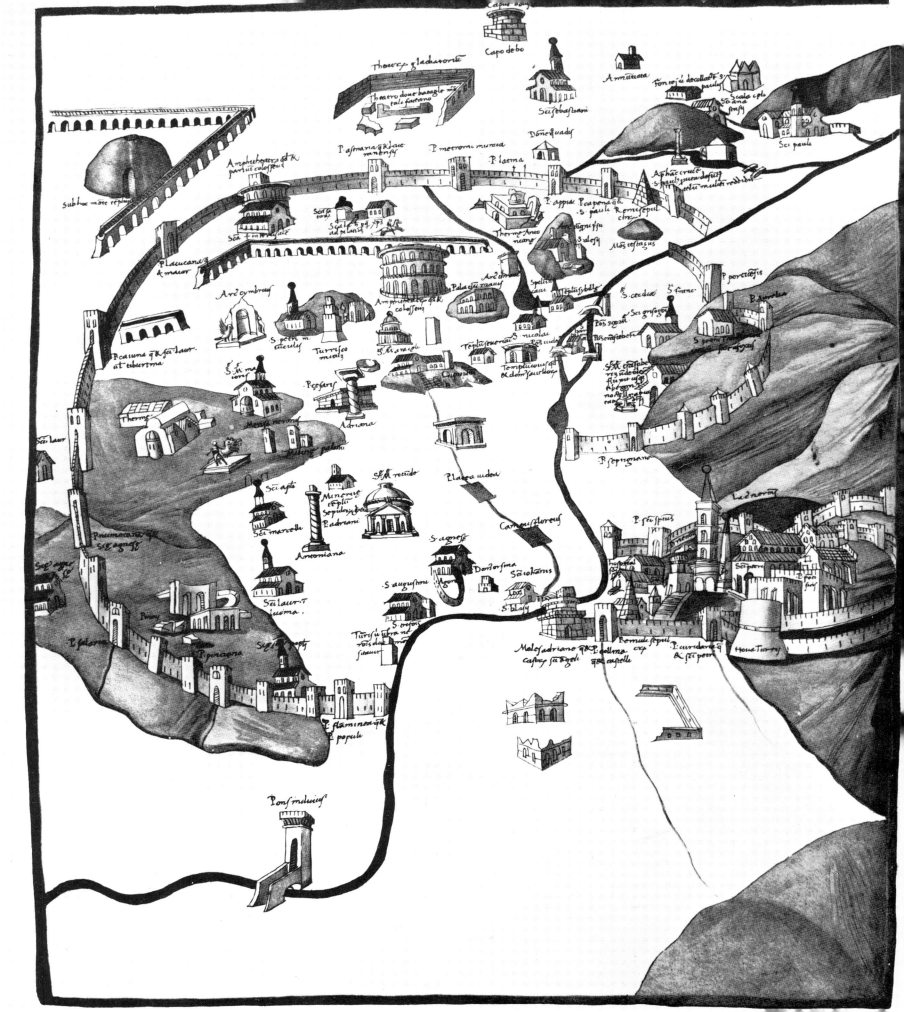

Commentariis conligitur; siquidem dicat a Vitruvio praeceptum quod Romae passim, in Tarquinii praesertim aggere, observaverat, ut anterides substituerentur."[22] He then mentions the Ponte Elio, one of the great projects Alberti designed for Nicholas V: "iuvat referre quod Baptista Albertus in libro *de Architectura* scribit, ponti omnium praestantissimo stetisse tectum suffultum columnis quadraginta duabus marmoreis opere trabeato, tectura aenea, ornatu mirifico. Quod reliquum est, neque indigum quo minus pro nostro in antiquitatem studio prosequamur: Hadriani moles Antoninorum fere omnium sepulcrum fuit, ita ut subsequentibus temporibus Antoninorum monumentum adpellaretur."[23] Finally, he mentions the *Descriptio urbis Romae* itself: "Verum de situ ipso moenium ac mensura Urbis Baptista Albertus scite admodum disseruit, ut qui eam machinis mathematicis summo studio prosequutus sit; vir, ut diximus, prae ceteris huius aevi antiquitatis amator, architecturaeque peritissimus."[24] This shows how, even after twenty years, the *Descriptio* was still a living memory for Bernardo and his companions, especially in the general plan it traced of the city. The works of Giovanni and Bernardo differ not only in the greater cultural refinement of the latter, but also in the reverence Bernardo has for Alberti, whereas his father does not even mention him. But for Giovanni Rucellai Alberti was not so much a figure of history as a familiar contemporary, a fact that may also explain why he, like Giannozzo Manetti, fails to mention Alberti's Florentine works.

As for Nicholas V's building programme, Manetti writes: "The Pope had five great projects firmly in mind: the reconstruction of the city walls, aqueducts, and bridges, the restoration of the forty so-called 'stational' churches, and the construction of the new Vatican quarter, including the papal palace and the church of Saint Peter's."[25] The works of restoration were carried out for the jubilee and financed with its proceeds. We shall now consider these projects one by one in order to determine the part Alberti played in their realization.

Of the walls, Infessura says: "In the year of our Lord 1450, Pope Nicholas set about the decoration and construction of Rome, first of all restoring the walls, towers, and gateways of the city, particularly those in the Testaccio quarter. He also built a big wall with large towers and three small circular ones."[26] This corresponds to what Alberti says in Book Four when, citing certain "visible" walls in Rome, "which have a patrol round about halfway up", he continues: "The walls should be flanked at intervals of fifty cubits by towers in the form of buttresses. These should project outwards according to a circular plan, and should

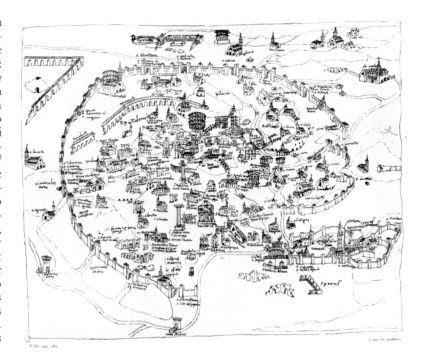

22. Ibid., pp. 447–48.
23. Ibid., p. 456.
24. Ibid., p. 455.
25. L. von Pastor, op. cit., p. 510.
26. Müntz, op. cit., p. 158.

·NICOLAVS·V·PON·MAX.
POST·ILLVSTRATAM·INS!
GNIBVS·MONVM·VRBEM·
DVCTV·AQVÆ·VIRGINIS
·VET·COL·REST·1453·

·FONTANA·DE·TREVE·

be higher than the walls themselves."[27] Nearly all the work was entrusted to Master Beltramo di Martino of Varese,[28] the biggest contractor at the time.

As for the restoration of the Acqua Vergine aqueduct, the part played by Nicholas V is confirmed by an inscription:

NICOLAUS V. P.M. ILLUSTRATAM
INSIGNIBUS MONUMENTIS URBEM
DUCTUM AQUAE VIRGINIS VETUSTATE
COLLAPSUM SUA IMPENSA IN SPLENDIDIOREM
CULTUM RESTITUIT ORNARIQUE MANDAVIT
ANNO DNI. CH. MCDLIII.

He brought it from the direction of the Porta Pinciana along a different course from that which it formerly followed, and got it to issue in a different place from that which we see now. This is told us by two learned contemporary writers who were both witnesses to the deviation of the Acqua Vergine, and whose praise-worthy works, though written in 1430, did not appear until 1471, after the noble invention of printing. One was Biondo, and the other Tortelli. The first describes it thus: "Juturnae Lacus (i.e. Aedes) in Campo Martio, ubi nunc Verginea; et nulla alia Aqua Urbem Roman nunc illabitur." The second provides an even better description: "In Campum Martium, quae nunc Trivii Regio dicitur, constat Aquam Virginem per Quirinalis collis ca-vernas illabi; nam ea sola aqua jam Urbem ex exteris ingreditur."[29] The Acqua Vergine had three outlets "beneath the castle, and the water filled a huge basin of hewn stone built around the three outlets."[30]

Vasari also attributes the work to Rossellino and Alberti: "The Pope went ahead with many useful and commendable projects. These included the restoration of the ruined aqueduct of the Acqua Vergine fountain, and the construction of the fountain in the Piazza de' Trevi, with its still surviving marble ornamen-tation including the arms of Nicholas V and of the Roman peo-ple."[31] Even after the work had been completely altered by Sal-vi,[32] Milizia continued to attribute it to Alberti: "Nicholas V, who had a passion for building, entrusted Alberti with the resto-ration of the Acqua Vergine aqueduct and the construction of the fountain of Trevi, which is now so modernised that not a trace of Alberti's original design remains."[33] Mancini also sup-ported Alberti's authorship: "They say the work was directed by Battista, and I can see a clue to the part he had in the repair of the aqueduct. This is his reference to the use he made in tra-cing an aqueduct with an instrument he employed in measuring Rome. 'With this I was able to discover the old aqueduct, parts

27. L. B. Alberti, op. cit., IV, 4, p. 300.
28. Müntz, op. cit., pp. 158–60. Cf. also: ASR. The administrative account no. I, 1502 for the year 1450 mentions rather modest restorations being carried out on the gateways and mainly on the Porta del Popolo. It is inte-resting to find that some work was done on the roads too, including the paving of those between Porta del Popolo and Ponte Molle, and between S. Celso and Tor di Nona. This register was interrupted as a result of the plague, but it confirms that the programme briefly sketched by Manetti was actually real-ized, and in the order he describes.
29. A. Cassio, *Corso delle acque antiche*, Rome 1756, I, p. 280.

of which appeared in the hillside."[34]

There is no doubt that the most difficult phase in the restoration concerned that part of the aqueduct which passed beneath the Trinità dei Monti, as was proved in the later stages of the operation.[35] Discussing methods of measuring the level of water in the *De re aedificatoria*, Alberti makes specific reference to the use of the circle in calculating radiants. This was a method he invented in the course of writing the *Descriptio*, and he employed it later in the reconstruction of the aqueduct: "I make use of this circle in drawing up maps of towns and regions, and for the digging of underground passages."[36] In the same chapter, Alberti shows such a grasp of the technical aspects of building aqueducts as to convince one that he could hardly have acquired all his knowledge from books, or from Frontinus, and that he must have had first-hand experience of the problems he wrote about. This being the case, and considering his expert knowledge of the classical writers and Roman technology, it is not difficult to credit him with the restoration of the Acqua Vergine aqueduct.[37] The Ponte S. Angelo combined with the plague to cast a shadow over the jubilee festivities of 1450, for it was blocked by a vast crowd of pedestrians, with the result that two hundred people died.[38] However, its importance for Alberti may be judged by the fact that one of the very few drawings by Alberti to be mentioned by Vasari concerns the bridge. Vasari begins by pointing out that Leon Battista "devoted himself more to his studies than to draughtsmanship", and then adds: "All the same he expressed his ideas very ably in his drawings, as can be seen from some sketches of his in our own book, showing the bridge of S. Angelo and the covering he designed for it in the form of a loggia to give protection from the sun in summer and the rain and wind in winter. He was commissioned to do the work by Pope Nicholas, who had intended to carry out many similar projects throughout Rome but was prevented by his death."[39] Though the sketch has since disappeared, there still remains the testimony of Alberti's own words: "Some bridges are also provided with roofs, such as the finest one in Rome, Hadrian's Bridge, a truly memorable work, so much so that its mortal remains—if may I so describe it—have aroused a feeling of reverence in me. It was supported by forty-two marble columns and surmounted by a roof of wooden beams encased in copper and richly decorated."[40] And again:

"In order to reinforce the rail or side wall of a bridge, one should introduce square, horizontally placed pedestals, upon which, if you wish, you may raise columns to support a roof. These pede-

30.   Ibid., p. 281.

31.   Vasari, op. cit., II, pp. 538–39.

32.   N. Salvi worked on the fountain between 1732 and 1751 the year of his death. It was completed by G. Pannini in 1762.

33.   F. Milizia, *Opere complete*, IV, Bologna 1827, "Memorie degli architetti antichi e moderni", I, p. 201.

34.   G. Mancini, op. cit., p. 297.

35.   A. Cassio, op. cit., p. 281.

36.   L. B. Alberti, op. cit., X, 7, p. 924.

37.   The documents published by Müntz (op. cit., p. 157) are extremely laconic: "1453. 18 June, 200 ducats in cash to Pietro di Giuliano da Chona by order of Nello, which His Holiness has paid him for the fountain of Trevi, plus 200 papal ducats His Holiness gave him of his own without writing anything down."

38.   L. von Pastor, op. cit., p. 450 ff.

39.   Vasari, op. cit., II, pp. 546–47. See also L. Collobi Ragghianti, *Vasari, il libro dei disegni*, in "Critica d'arte", XX, Florence 1973, pp. 23–24.

40.   L. B. Alberti, op. cit., VIII, 6, p. 710.

stals should be four feet high, including their plinths and cornices. The spaces between them should be occupied by parapets. The upper part of the pedestals and parapets should consist of either a straight or reverse ogee moulding, extending along the entire length of the bridge. This should be balanced by the plinths below. The height of the columns, including their decorations, should be the same as the width of the bridge."[41]

There is a woodcut of the bridge, as described in the text, among the illustrations to Bartoli's edition of 1550. Palladio returned to the same subject twenty years later, when he wrote of "a stone bridge of my invention" in the *Four Books of Architecture:* "It must not be thought that the building of colonnades on bridges is a new idea, since it has been said that the Ponte Elio [that is, the Ponte Adriano named after Aelius Hadrianus] in Rome was still covered with loggias, bronze columns, statues, and other wonderful decorations in ancient times."[42] Alberti's project, which was thus taken up and reinterpreted many years later, arose out of the need to restore an ancient monument: "I would go so far as to say that the Ponte Adriano is one of the most solid constructions ever built by man. Nevertheless, it has been so badly damaged by floods that I doubt whether it can last much longer."[43] But when he came to restore the bridge, Alberti grafted a design of his own onto the earlier structure, a design born both of history and imagination, and the result was an ideal reconstruction that was the expression of Alberti's own age. In discussing Alberti's activity during the reign of Nicholas V, Zevi has said:

"Alberti performed the function of what we would now call a superintendent and restorer. This enabled him to express his true genius, which was of a critical, largely reflective bent, though informed by direct experience and proven technical skill, and orientated towards the integration of thought and action. The role of a restorer is an eclectic one. A restorer is not a historian pure and simple, since he is committed professionally; he is even less a creative architect, since scientific research is his very point of departure. Good restorers have rarely been genuine artists. Alberti, however, is an exception to this dreary rule, for he retained the characteristic flexibility of all Renaissance culture in spite of his devotion to the ruins of the past."[44]

There remains the third point in the programme Manetti attributes to the Pope, the restoration of the forty 'stational' churches, together with the other works outside the Vatican. The documents published by Müntz enable us to form an idea of the extent of these projects on the basis of the money spent on them.[45] In this respect the most important were those connected with the

41. Ibid., p. 712.
42. A. Palladio, *I quattro libri dell'architettura*, Venice 1570, III, p. 25.
43. L. B. Alberti, op. cit., X, 10, p. 948.
44. B. Zevi, article on Alberti in the EUA, I, pp. 196–97.
45. "1453. 31 December. Payments made for special works outside the palace on this, the last day of December, 25,021 duc. [ducats], 65 b. [bolognini]: 200 duc. for the fountain of Trevi, our own work; 212 duc., 56 b. for the tower on the Campidoglio; 1000 duc. for the paving and gluing of S. Stefano in Celio Monte; 236 duc. for the glass windows of the same; 200 duc. for the

restoration of S. Stefano and S. Teodoro, on which one thousand and two thousand ducats were spent respectively. The work on S. Celso, the parish where Alberti lived in the last years of his life (it is not known whether he was already living there in this period), was limited to clearing up the church's immediate surroundings and carrying out of a few slight alterations to its façade: "Piazza S. Celso required the demolition of a great number of houses."[46] The work at S. Maria Maggiore consisted mainly of the reconstruction of the papal buildings near the basilica, though it is not known whether Alberti had anything to do with this. The roof of the Pantheon was also restored,[47] and work was begun on a large scale on the Campidoglio, the ruinous state of which had been denounced by Poggio. This project was entrusted to Master Pietro di Giovanni of Varese, a nephew of Master Beltramo, the builder of the tribune in St. Peter's, who was probably outside the sphere of Alberti's influence. (This is best demonstrated in the work of Rossellino and the masters of Florence and Settignano who worked with him.)

In his life of Rossellino Vasari sums up these projects:
"The Pope also had in mind, and carried out to a large extent, the restoration and reconstruction, where most necessary, of the forty churches of the stations founded by Saint Gregory I, who was called the Great. Thus he restored S. Maria Trastevere, S. Prasedia, S. Teodoro, S. Pietro in Vincula, and many other lesser churches. He did the same, but on a far grander scale, in six of the seven major or principal churches, such as S. Giovanni in Laterano, S. Maria Maggiore, S. Stefano in Celio Monte, S. Apostolo, S. Paolo, and S. Lorenzo fuori le mura. I shall not mention Saint Peter's, as this was a special project."[48]

S. Teodoro was also involved in an unusual accident. According to Infessura: "Pope Nicholas V rebuilt the Church of S. Teodoro twice. The first time he restored the old building, but after the restoration, its foundations collapsed. He then rebuilt it on a slightly different site, and on a slightly smaller scale."[49] This would seem to imply a scaling down of the church, of which only the ancient apse has survived. The documents probably refer to the second restoration, but there is no mention of Rossellino. The only clear reference is to Master Giovanni di Andrea of Florence, who did "the glass windows". Thus the names of Rossellino and Alberti cannot be connected with this project, though the interest it reflects in the centrally-planned church may have been stimulated by their circle.

There is plenty of evidence as to the state of S. Stefano Rotondo sul Celio. This church was dedicated to St. Stephen by Simpli-

glass windows of St. Peter's; 25 duc. for the glass windows of S. Eusebio; 74 duc., 24 b. for Castel S. Angelo; 14 duc., 28 b. for the fort of Ostia; 445 duc., 12 b. for the work, on the roof of S. Apostolo; 254 duc., 10 b. for the work on S. Maria Rotonda; 2000 duc., for S. Teodoro; 109 duc. 58 b. for the windows in marble and iron of the chapel in S. Maria della Febbre; 64 duc., 43 b. on the Palazzo della Zecca; 267 duc., 68 b. on the restoration of the fort of Castelnuovo; 1700 duc. to Ser Giuliano di Roberto for the wall in Terrioni; 18,000 duc. to Master Beltramo for the tribune and Porta Pertusa; as all set down here in this f. 201, 25,021 florins, 65 b. - T.S. 1453, f. 33' (Müntz, op. cit., p. 139).

46. Müntz, op. cit., p. 140.
47. Ibid., p. 145.
48. Vasari, op. cit., III, pp. 99–100.
49. M. Armellini, *Le chiese di Roma dal sec. IV al XIX*, Roma 1942, p. 1461; Müntz, op. cit., p. 145.

28. *The Holy Sepulchre of Jerusalem, plan of the construction in the fourth century with medieval additions (after Krautheimer).*
29. *Original plan and reconstruction of S. Stefano Rotondo (after Verzone).*
30. *Rome, S. Stefano Rotondo, exterior.*
31. *S. Stefano Rotondo, axiometric section: on the right, in its original state; on the left, after Alberti's re-modelling.*

32-35. *Rome, S. Stefano Rotondo. This church was the most concrete achievement to emerge from the huge programme of restoration and reconstruction planned for Rome by Nicholas V with Alberti's advice; it may even have been restored under his "superintendence".*
The documents say nothing about Alberti's role in the restoration of the church (the same applies to everything he did in Rome in this period). They contain specific references to Bernardo Rossellino and other "specialised" craftsmen such as blacksmiths and glaziers, and refer to the cost and nature of the work. There is nothing else, apart from a clear

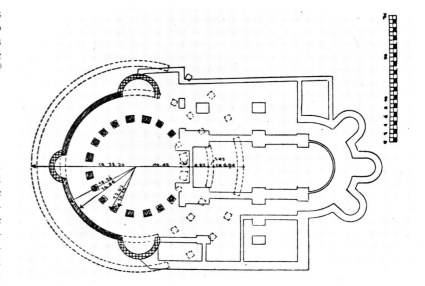

cius I in the fifth century, embellished with marble and mosaics in later years, and remained the object of constant restoration up to 1100. Biondo writes: "quam tecto nunc carentem, marmoreis columnis et crustatis varii coloris marmore parietibus musivoque opere inter primas urbis ecclesias ornatissimam fuisse judicamus."[50]
Michele di Bonaiuto wrote in the time of Martin V:

> "Ipsius paries mansit de marmore cultas
> porfidu simul et variis cum floribus actas
> et fuit intus cum multis ornata columnis.
> Nunc iacet in coeno defracto tegmine tecti.
> Sunt altaria deiectis temerata lapillis."[51]

Many churches were dedicated to this saint in the same period of history, but S. Stefano is undoubtedly one of the most unusual of all early Christian churches. It consists of a vast circular space with a diameter of about twenty-four metres and a high drum supported by twenty columns. Two T-shaped pillars and two large granite columns form a diametrical axis, with three arches supporting the roof. The central space was enclosed by an ambulatory almost as large as the rotunda itself. This too was marked off by a ring of columns, and it opened out into four deep spaces, which lay along the line of the main axes. These were connected by narrow circular ambulatories disposed along the diagonal axes, and formed four open patio-like courtyards surrounded by columns. Krautheimer thought that there was no great space between the outer wall and the first ring of columns of the courtyards whereas Verzone more correctly believes that the space was a large one, and that the rest of it was covered by porticos built in line with the entrances; these porticos prepared one for the entrance into the basilica itself. The entire construction was enclosed by a circular wall, the continuity of which was broken by a single small apse, probably a twelfth-century addition. From the time of the Renaissance this unusual edifice was thought to have been an adaptation of a pagan temple dedicated to the god Faunus, "eaque in Fauni aede prius fundata fuit",[52] or of Nero's "macellum magnum". Indeed, many scholars have argued over this theory, though it has since been disproved both by Krautheimer's exhaustive study[53] and recent restoration.[54]
This time the documents published by Müntz help us to establish beyond all doubt the nature of the restoration work carried out during the pontificate of Nicholas V. Moreover, there are the records of contemporary witnesses. Infessura and Albertini, for example, write that Nicholas V "had a roof put on the church of S. Stefano Rotondo, and restored it together with the buildings of the friars and doctors."[55] Nicholas himself declared in a bull:

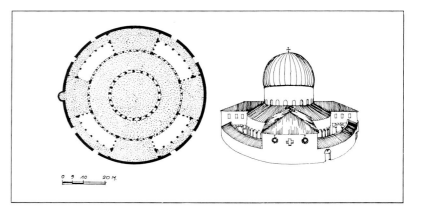

50. F. Biondo, *Roma instaurata*, I, 80, in Müntz, op. cit., p. 141
51. M. Armellini, op. cit., p. 1457.
52. F. Biondo, ibid.
53. R. Krautheimer, *Santo Stefano Rotondo a Roma e la chiesa del San Sepolcro a Gerusalemme*, in "Rivista Archeologica Cristiana", 12, Rome 1935, pp. 51–102.
54. S. Rossi, *Santo Stefano Rotondo a Roma*, in "L'Architettura IV", 1958–69.
55. Muratori, *Scriptores*, III, Part 2, p. 1132, in Müntz, op. cit., p. 141.

indication that the building was reduced in size. Its outer wall was demolished, together with its chapels and ambulatories. This relieved the burden on the respective roofs, which had been complicated by various graftings and intersections.

Once the edifice had been reduced to its inner ring of columns, the spaces between those of its outer ring closed, the inner ring covered with a sloping roof, the central drum surmounted by a complex wooden cone, and the lighting problem solved by means of occhi (circular apertures) and noticeably dated mullioned windows, it became a new spatial structure.

The oriental-like continuum (with its constant interplay between interior and exterior, a relationship made mysterious and variable by the movement of the sun) was transformed into a centrally-planned Renaissance structure detached from its outer environment and volumetrically self-contained. There is a considerable difference between the two structures (one might even consider the second inferior, as Francesco di Giorgio did later). Whatever one's point of view, Alberti's plan involved a decision of fundamental importance that solved many economic, constructional, and stylistic problems. It is difficult to believe Rossellino achieved all this by himself.

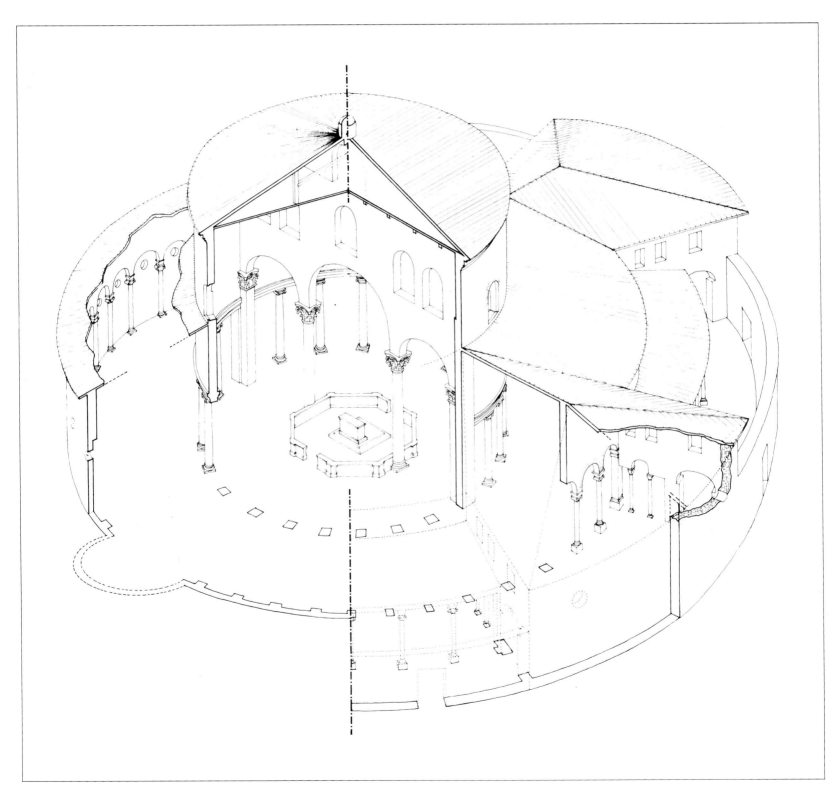

43

"Hinc est quod nos, qui dum miserati deformi ruinae venerabilis ecclesiae sancti Stephani in Coelio monte de Urbe, tamdiu... per multa tempora collapsae, ut divino cultu penitus destitutae, eamdem ecclesiam non sine magnis sumptibus, deo opitulante, instauraverimus, et ad decentem statum reduximus."[56]

The expense involved was considerable—Rossellino received about two thousand florins in 1453—and it is specified in a way that enables us to establish the exact nature of the restoration carried out.[57] This included filling up the spaces between the columns of the outer ring, except for those in line with the chapels, and the construction of a new sloping roof to cover the space between the outer and inner rings of columns, which reinforced the latter. This gave rise to a lighting problem, which was solved by means of the "eight large windows, two large circular windows, two small windows, and thirty-six small circular windows" mentioned in the documents. In this way, the mysterious, exotic building (which may once have had a wooden dome), with its orientalising patios and colonnades, was simplified, and brought almost brutally into line with the canons of a Renaissance centrally-planned church.

The project must have been conditioned by the question of the church's stability, as well as by overriding economic considerations. This is indicated not only by the amount of money it required—a very considerable one compared to the sums spent on other projects in the same period—but also by the phrase "ad decentem statum reduximus" in the Papal bull. Here, the idea of *decus* seems to imply not so much the abandonment of the *ornatus* or *exornatus* that we find in earlier sources as a greater concentration on the essential aspects of the restoration. Commenting upon a drawing of the project, Francesco di Giorgio remarked: "Building ruined, its columns and vaults richly decorated on the outside. Pope Nicholas rebuilt it, but damaged it even more. It is called S. Stefano Rotondo."[58] It may be significant that criticism of the damage done during the restoration of S. Stefano Rotondo was levelled by Francesco di Giorgio, who never missed an opportunity to dissociate himself from the influence of Alberti, even when this was exercised at an advisory level in connection with work carried out by Rossellino.

Yet in spite of the lack of any specific documentary evidence, the date of the church's restoration (which precedes that of the presentation of the *De re aedificatoria* by a year) and the fact that Rossellino worked on it allow us to affirm that Alberti was responsible for the project. Zevi is of the same opinion:

"S. Stefano Rotondo is a particularly significant work. Alberti restored the columns of the inner ring, demolished the outer wall, and enclosed the building within the perimeter of the second ring of columns, walling up the spaces between the latter. Thus, he revolutionised the early Christian structure, at the same time subordinating his respect for the past to the actual needs of the church, and placing creative freedom before his knowledge of the history of early Christian architecture. Since this work was carried out at the time he was writing his treatise, some passages in the latter have something of the importance of a 'poetic testimony'. The reinforcement of the inner ring of columns, the architrave of which is straight, and the walling up of the outer one, where the columns support a series of arches, is the practical realisation of a statement made by Alberti in the *Ten Books*. Alberti considered the space between the arch and its columns to be incongruous; columns should be surmounted by straight entablatures, while arches should rest upon *columnae quadrangulae*, or pillars. Thus, in closing the outer ring of columns, he was only transforming what was for him an unacceptable structure into a decorative element reminiscent of certain classical buildings, and of S. Miniato in particular. But this is not all; with the elimination of its outer ambulatory, the early Christian basilica took on a clearer perspective. In fact, the early outer ring, engirdled by a continuous wall, had no definite spatial value; there were no clear limits to its size, while it was rich in dispersive atmospheric penumbra. In short, it was the antithesis of that thorough geometrical division of space by which every natural irregularity is absorbed into and cancelled out in proportion, circumscribed and framed within that harmonious *finitio* which excludes any addition to, or subtraction from its single parts without causing evident damage."[59]

"All these works," writes von Pastor, "pale before the gigantic plans for the reconstruction of the Leonine city, the Vatican, and the church of Saint Peter's."[60] The restoration and reconstruction of the Vatican palace came first. The work was begun in 1447 and continued up to the Pope's death, under the constant direction of Antonio di Francesco of Florence, the "palace engineer". However, it gathered momentum as it proceeded from the decoration of a few rooms and chapels to a total remodelling of the entire edifice, which was mainly concerned with the construction of a wall of defence, of which a tower still stands;[61] it may be that the project benefitted from Alberti's advice. As for his involvement in the construction of St. Peter's, Manetti is quite explicit, as we have seen already.[62] Alberti mentions St. Peter's twice in his treatise, and it is no accident that he should do so

56. Ibid.
57. "1453. 14 March. Master Bernardo di Matteo of Florence, resident in Rome, to be given this day, the 14 March, 700 ducats from the treasury, which he has received from me in cash through Alessandro Mirabelli and Ambrodio Spanochi in five instalments, between the 14 November 1452 and this present day... the which 700 ducats His Holiness has ordered to be given to the said Master Bernardo for his part of the work on S. Stefano Rotondo". "23 April. 100 florins for the same purpose". "3 June, 200 florins paid with His Holiness' approval for the rest of the work done by the said Master Bernardo in S. Stefano Rotondo. Total, 1000 florins." "To Master Bernardo di Matteo of Florence, mastermason... 1000 ducats from the treasury... for the pavement of S. Stefano Rotondo, its plastering, and the marble altars, doors, and windows he did for the said church, all at his own expense, as agreed with His Holiness. — T.S. 1453, folios 105 and 143 (3)". "6 March. To Giovanni d'Andrea and his fellow glaziers... 40 ducats in cash from the treasury, that is, to the said Master Giovanni for some of the windows in S. Stefano Rotondo...". "10 July. 36 ducats in cash to his companion, Charles, in payment for the rest of the work in S. Stefano, as agreed..." Same date: "To Master Giovanni d'Andrea and companions [or companion], painter of glasswindows, on this day, the 10 July, 236 ducats from the treasury... for 8 small windows and 36 small *occhi*, with and without figures, in S. Stefano Rotondo." Ibid., folios 104, 143, etc. "1454. 27 April. To Master Domenico da Monte-

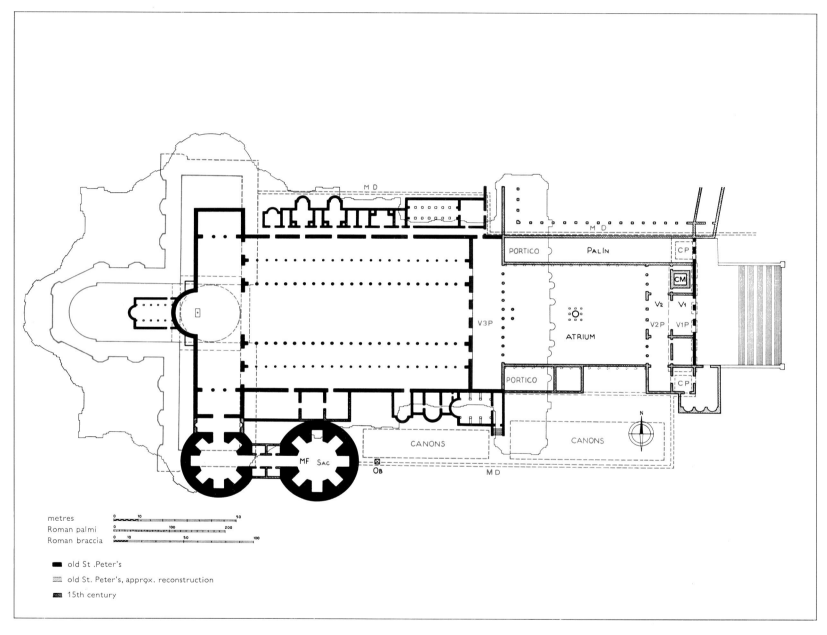

lupo, blacksmith, on this same day, 28 duc., 51 b, in cash for 827 pounds of wrought iron for S. Stefano Rotondo, that is, 4 windows, a chain for the vault, hooks, and cramps, as agreed.

58. Francesco di Giorgio Martini, *Trattati di architettura, ingegneria, e arte militare*, Milan 1967, I, p. 283.

59. B. Zevi, op. cit., p. 197.

60. L. von Pastor, op. cit., p. 514.

61. A. P. Frutaz, *Il Torrione di Niccolò V in Vaticano*, Vatican City, 1956.

62. See note 7 above and T. Magnuson, *Studies in Roman Quattrocento Architecture*, Rome, 1958, p. 168.

at the very beginning of the first book:

"I have noticed one thing about the basilica of Saint Peter's in Rome which is self-evident. A very long, big wall has, very unadvisedly, been built over a number of large voids. This has not been reinforced by being curved at some points, nor is it buttressed with supports of any kind. Moreover—and this is something that should have been taken into consideration—the entire stretch of wall, beneath which there are so many voids, has been built so high and in such a position as to be buffetted by the north winds with extreme violence. The result is that it has already inclined from the vertical by more than six feet on account of the continual pressure of these winds. And there is no doubt that the slightest pressure or movement could bring it down at any moment. It would have fallen already, given its present inclination, were it not held up by the beams of the roof. But the architect's intentions were partly justified, because, conditioned by the particular nature of the site, he probably thought that the church would be sufficiently protected from the winds by the hill above it. Even so, it would have been better to reinforce the wall on both sides."[63]

This fundamentally accurate analysis of the basilica's instability and lack of lateral wind protection, factors which made the structure particularly difficult to restore, is then followed by a plan to reinforce it:

"Since the side walls of the great basilica of Saint Peter's in Rome are inclined from the vertical, and exert pressure on the columns, threatening to bring the roof down, I had thought of the following plan. All the parts that were out of line were supported by a column, and I thought of demolishing these parts and filling up the resultant spaces with ordinary masonry, fixing strong stone clamps and braces into the old wall so as to bind the new masonry to the rest of the restored structure. Finally, I would have supported the beam holding up the roof, beneath which the inclined parts of the wall were to be demolished, by means of certain devices called *capre* (goats). These would have been placed above the roof, with their lower parts fastened to the strongest points of the roof and wall. I would have done the same for all the other columns, wherever necessary. (The *capra* is a naval invention consisting of three beams, the heads of which are tightly bound and braced together, while its lower ends stretch out like a tripod. Together with pulleys and winches, it can be used to lift weights with the greatest ease)."[64] The passage seems to describe an ingenious solution, but one which had already been rejected. The treatise was finished by 1452, but

whereas Müntz's documents mention the work carried out on the large tribune in that same year, the only other work they refer to prior to 1450 is that related to the windows and the portico. One may draw the conclusion that the decision to rebuild St. Peter's had matured in the two years following the financial success of the jubilee, even if Nicholas's first intentions were to restore part of the basilica and rebuild only the choir *ex novo*. Heydenreich writes:

"The huge, unusual plan of what is believed to be Rossellino's choir, which they had started to build behind the apse of the early Christian basilica, remains incomprehensible unless seen as part of a larger design. The considerable extension of the choir involved colossal structures, for which contemporary building techniques, at least those employed in Rome, were quite inadequate, especially if one considers the size of the pillars and vault. Thus, the necessary architectural expertise was sought in the great early Christian churches, and in more recent ones such as the cathedrals of Florence and Milan, S. Petronio at Bologna, and the unfinished cathedral of Siena. Taking into account the site and particular requirements of the basilica of St. Peter's, one realizes that the plan drawn up in 1450 could not have been conceived in any other way, and this is clearly proved by Giannozzo Manetti's description. Some years earlier Urban V had reconstructed it, and very successfully too, in our opinion. But the most surprising aspect of Nicholas's projects, compared with previous attempts at reconstruction, is that it shows an initial desire to preserve the whole of the ancient basilica, just widening and reinforcing it by means of a kind of huge coffer of masonry. The new choir that was to complete the building was begun first. This was because its foundations, which continued to be regarded as unchangeable by all the architects who worked on it, from Bramante to Michelangelo, had already been laid. It is difficult to establish to what extent Alberti's contribution to the construction of St. Peter's was a positive or negative one. According to Matteo Palmieri, the Pope suspended the work on Alberti's advice, which would seem to imply that Alberti was critical of the project. In any case, that he contributed to it is certain, and this means that he had an opportunity to judge all the problems involved in so huge a project for himself."[65] The work was entrusted to Master Beltrame di Martino of Varese, and there is no documentary evidence to support Palmieri's statement that Alberti advised its suspension in 1452. On the contrary, the documents show that payments were made to Beltrame for the tribune in 1454.[66] However, a temporary sus-

63. L. B. Alberti, op. cit., I, 10, p. 74.
64. Ibid., X, 17, p. 998.

65. L. H. Heydenreich, *Il Primo Rinascimento*, Milan 1974, p. 55.
66. Müntz, op. cit., p. 124.

pension may have been ordered to allow certain alterations to be made to the project itself. Such a conclusion seems to be justified by the fact that the payments of 1454 involved large sums of money for "the rest of the foundations of the tribune in Saint Peter's" and "*pianele* made in his kiln", that is, Roman bricks, which may have been used for facing.

Though there is no mention of Rossellino in the treasury accounts, Manetti claims that he supervised the construction of the new tribune: "Nam cum eo solo omnia ad praedictam fabricam pertinentia communicabat."[67] On the other hand, from 31 December 1451 Rossellino appears in the accounts as "palace engineer". Thus Alberti may have become involved in the project in 1452, just as Palmieri says. Or he may have come in on it after the decision was taken to put Rossellino (who was both the Pope's confidant and Alberti's friend) in charge of the work. Nor does this mean that the financial management of the project ceased to be in the hands of the master from Varese.

The complicated history of the construction of St. Peter's lies beyond the scope of this study. The main problem here concerns the nature of the original plan—if such a plan was ever drawn up. Did the planners hesitate between the restoration of the old building and the construction of a new one, as a certain contradictory attitude in Alberti himself would seem to suggest? For in one passage of the *Architettura* he appears to question the stability of the ancient Constantinian basilica outright, while in another he seems to be in favour of partial restoration limited to the choir. The subject must have provoked a lively controversy, for both Grimaldi and Vegio denounced the state of the basilica's foundations. Grimaldi writes: "nec minus parietes ipsi circo inservientes fundati erant supram solidam argillam, sed supra terram motam, ut in fundando novo campanile ad meridiem clare satis apparuit,"[68] while Vegio complains: "nunc omnia (quod non sine dolore magno scribimus)... funditus disjecta sunt."[69] Thus, one can appreciate the enormous responsibility Nicholas took upon himself, and the courage he showed, in his decision to tackle the most audacious architectural project of all times —the rebuilding of the holy sepulchre of St. Peter's. Apparently, the Pope felt the need to sum up his faith in architecture in the spiritual testament he dictated on his deathbed: "Quibus quidem nos caussis, non ambitione, non pompa, non inani gloria, non fama, non diuturniori nominis nostri propagatione, sed majori quadam Romanae Ecclesiae auctoritate, et ampliori Sedis Apostolicae apud cunctos Christianos Populos dignitate, ac certiori usitatarum persecutionum evitatione, talia tantaque aedificia

67. A. P. Frutaz, op. cit., p. 16, n. 2.
68. Müntz, op. cit., p. 118.
69. Ibid.

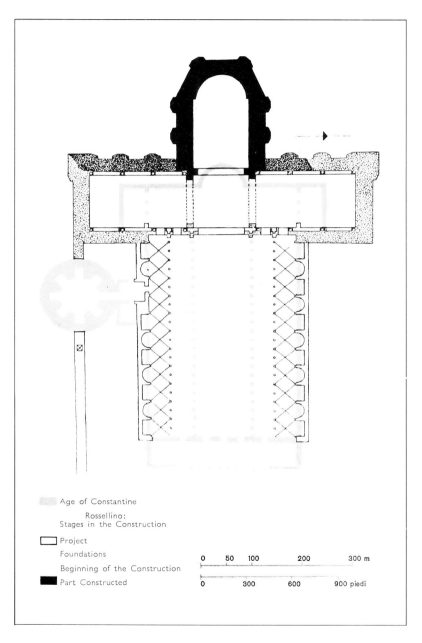

Age of Constantine

Rossellino:
Stages in the Construction

Project

Foundations

Beginning of the Construction

Part Constructed

0	50	100	200	300 m

0	300	600	900 piedi

mente et animo conceperamus."[70]

The most important and the most controversial aspect of Nicholas' town planning scheme and the part Alberti had in it concerns the fortification of the Leonine city and the plans for the Vatican quarter. Secure defences had become essential at the time, with Constantinople falling to the Turks and the outbreak of Porcari's Republican conspiracy in 1453. Castel S. Angelo was to be an outpost in a defensive network built on the lines of a citadel fortress, a characteristic feature of Renaissance town planning.[71] As Gregorovius wrote: "The sight of the Supreme Pontiff walking among the walls, towers, and fire-spitting bombards of the city, can only be understood and explained in the light of the history of Rome, humanity, and the papacy. There is no doubt however, that Nicholas had sufficient priestly diffidence to be fully conscious of the contradictions these temporal needs gave rise to. In fact, he conceived the brilliant idea of combining the Vatican's defence system with the reconstruction of the Leonine city."[72] When Vasari wrote that the Pope "had in mind to turn the whole of the Vatican into a fortress, like a city set apart",[73] he was describing the Vatican's symbolic value as a *civitas Dei*, separated from the secular part of the City, and yet connected to it by the Ponte Adriano and the Castel S. Angelo: "Rome is the symbol of Babylon and the Vatican is the heavenly city. According to St. Augustine, a favourite author of Nicholas, the city of God and the earthly city are united on earth, and will not be separated until the Last Judgement. Only then will Good reign supreme."[74]

The most significant part of Nicholas's programme was the decision to organise the area between Castel S. Angelo and St. Peter's into a network of squares connected by three main streets. The only source we have for the reconstruction of this plan is Manetti, whose description, though fairly accurate, still leaves a number of questions unanswered. However, the problem as to whether Manetti's description corresponds to a plan of Alberti's cannot be broached without taking into account Dehio's fundamental studies on the subject.[75] Dehio concluded that it did, and his deductions were accepted by von Pastor.[76] Magnuson, on the other hand, after making a careful analysis of Manetti's text, adopted a more sceptical attitude to the importance of Alberti's role and influence though his arguments are not wholly convincing.[77] More recent studies have re-confirmed the importance of a general influence exercised by Alberti, but without going any deeper into the matter.[78] In fact, given the total absence of documentary evidence, the only approach to the problem is that

suggested by Dehio, in other words, the comparing of Manetti's description with corresponding passages in the *De re aedificatoria*. However, one may ignore the question as to what extent Nicholas V's project was the expression of the Middle Ages or the Renaissance, a problem that takes up a great part of the German historian's dated, but still fundamental text, since the problem is an artificial one, and represents a defect in what is otherwise a sound work of historical scholarship. It can easily be explained by the fact that the question of historical periods gave Dehio a chance to attack the theories of Burckhardt.[79]

Dehio's reconstruction reveals that at the very centre of the project was a longitudinal axis running from the bridge of Castel S. Angelo to St. Peter's, and that the site of the apostle's tomb was the culminating point both of the spatial perspective and of the design as a whole. The project began with a square: "Ad tertium de vico, ut ita dixerim, curiali, juxta nostrum ordinem procedentes, novam hujus vici constructionem a porta pontis molis Adrianae inchoandam fore cognovimus, ubi magnam quamdam aream, cunctis habitationibus inter moenia Urbis, quae tanto ulterius in latitudinem extendebantur, ut ad perpendiculum magnae turris palatinae ab eo ad hoc ipsum aedificatae dirigerentur, et inter Tiberim consistentibus, funditus demolitis."[80] This square constituted a kind of junction in the system of axes, and provided further security for the castle. Alberti wrote in his treatise: "However one may look at it, as the highest point of the walls or as the key to the city, the castle must have a wild, fierce, threatening aspect."[81] Thus psychological impact is seen as an essential element of architecture.

The square, according to Magnuson's calculations, measured 130 metres,[82] and was the starting-point for three streets which Manetti describes as "ratae et amplae". The streets could hardly have been parallel, though they were lined with arcades and ran into another square in front of St. Peter's. Alberti affirms that "as for the streets of the city, not only will they be finely paved and perfectly clean, but beautifully adorned with two identical rows of arcades or houses of the same height",[83] and he mentions the ancient Theodosian arcade, which started on the left bank of the river and reached the tomb of St. Peter by way of the Ponte Elio: "I find that there were two very beautiful streets of this kind in Rome: one between the gate and church of Saint Paul, which was about 5 *stadia*, or 1400 feet long, and another between the bridge and church of Saint Peter's, which was 2500 feet long and had a colonnade of marble columns and a lead roof."[84] Vasari refers to the same subject: "He designed three streets leading

70. T. Magnuson, *Studies in Roman Quattrocento Architecture*, Rome 1958, p. 16; Matteo Palmieri, *Vita di Niccolò V.* in "Rerum italicarum scriptores", III, 2, col. 950.

71. P. Marconi, *La città come forma simbolica*, Rome 1973.

72. F. Gregorovius, *Storia di Roma nel Medioevo*, Rome 1972, V, p. 328.

73. Vasari, op. cit., III, p. 100.

74. L. Cassanelli, G. Delfini, B. Fonti, *Le Mura di Roma*, Rome 1974, p. 102.

75. G. Dehio, *Die Bauprojekte Nicolaus des Fünften und L. B. Alberti*, in "Repertorium für Kunstwissenschaft", III, 1880, pp. 241–75.

76. L. von Pastor, op. cit., p. 517.

77. T. Magnuson, *The project of Nicholas V for rebuilding the Borgo Leonino in Rome*, in "Art Bulletin", 36, 1954, pp. 91–115 and *Studies in Roman Quattrocento Architecture*, Rome 1958, pp. 68 ff.

78. L. Benevolo, *Storia dell'Architettura del Rinascimento*, Bari 1972, I, p. 213; P. A. Frutaz, op. cit.; and L. Cassinelli, G. Delfini, B. Fonti, op. cit., p. 89 ff. This contains an interesting bibliography on general aspects of the problem.

79. Cf. W. K. Ferguson, *Il Rinascimento nella critica storica*, Bologna 1969, pp. 513–14.

80. T. Magnuson, *Studies*, op. cit., p. 353, par. 31.

38. *Work carried out in the Vatican quarter and the Leonine city in the time of Nicholas V according to Manetti's description (after Magnuson).*

a = *Castel Sant'Angelo with the turrets of Nicholas V* | b = *site of the old church of Santa Maria in Traspontina* | c = *Meta Romuli* | d = *Porta Castello* | e = *Porta Santo Spirito* | f = *Porta S. Pietro (also known as Porta S. Egidi or Porta Viridaria)* | g = *Porta Cavalleggeri (or Porta Torrione)* | h = *Original site of obelisk* | i = *Porta Pertusa.*

MB = *Wall of Boniface IX* | ML = *Leonine walls* | ML (N) = *Leonine walls reconstructed by Nicholas V* | MNIII = *Walls built by Nicholas III around the Pomerium* | TL (N) = *Towers of the Leonine walls reconstructed by Nicholas V* | TG = *Big tower of Nicholas V* | MN = *Defensive walls built by Nicholas V.*

The coloured line indicates the structures planned by Nicholas V.

BasV = *Vatican Basilica* | PP = *East side of the planned square in front of St. Peter's* | EP = *New main entrance* | MD = *Defensive walls.*

Lines and figures indicate the height above sea level in metres.

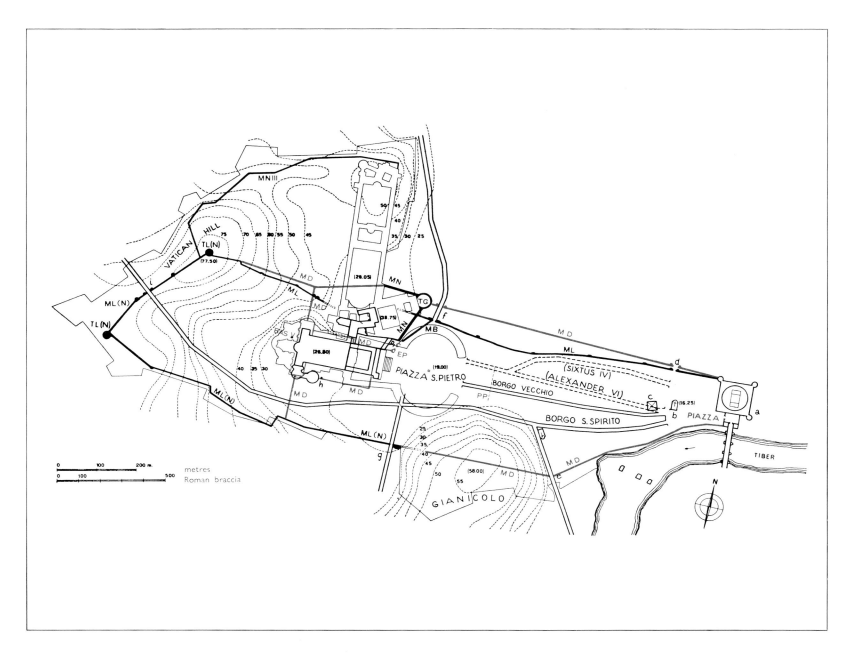

81.   L. B. Alberti, op. cit., V, 4, p. 350.
82.   T. Magnuson, op. cit., p. 72.
83.   L. B. Alberti, op. cit., VIII, 6, p. 710.
84.   Ibid., p. 708.

to Saint Peter's, to where I believe the old and new Vatican quarters are now, covering them on both sides with loggias and excellent shops. He separated the noblest and richest Arts from the lesser, putting each in a street of its own."[85] Manetti says the three streets were meant to have different functions: the inner one was destined "pro mediocribus diversorum exercitiorum artificibus"; the middle one had nobler functions "intermedia vero usque ad laevam similibus nummulariorum, drapporum, pannorumque mensis, et hujusmodi majorum opificum tabernis utrimque institutis"[86]; and the one on the left, nearest the Tiber, was intended "pro infimis opificibus apotecae utrisque pariter lateribus ordinabantur". The upper storeys were to have living accomodations: "Juxta enim variae diversorum opificum tabernae, supra vero domorum habitacula condebantur."[87] Houses in the city, according to the *Ten Books*, should have "large court-yards, a portico, space for the passage of carriages, beautiful gardens, and so forth. If the lack of space makes this impossible, then all that is necessary for a house can be obtained by constructing a building of several storeys on a piece of very level ground."[88] On the other hand, "The dwellings of the poorer people ought to imitate, as far as is economically possible, the elegance of those of the wealthy, though such imitation should be tempered by the thought that thrift takes precedence over beauty."[89] The three streets were to emerge "ad alteram ingentissimam aream ante apostolicam aedem apparentem protendebantur."[90] The square is described:

"Nunc vero ad mirabilem ac profecto magnanimam, et devotissimam apostolici templi designationem deinceps procedamus. Ante primum igitur hujus sacrae aedis vestibulum super scalas prominens maxima quaedam area quingentorum in longitude, centum in latitude cubitorum pulcherrime apparebat. A formosis namque praedicti vestibuli gradibus, quos partim marmoreos partim porphyreis, partim smaragdinorum colorum decoris, gratia interferebat, incipiens, usque ad egregia et nobilitata intercolumnia per quingentos, ut diximus, passus in longum extendebatur, super quibus tres commemorati vici porticus, speciosorum omnium spectaculorum visu pulcherrimum specimen, sustentabantur."[91] As Dehio has pointed out, the 1:2 ratio of width to length corresponds exactly to Alberti's own rules: "the best kind of piazza is that which consists of two squares."[92] According to Manetti, an obelisk was to have stood in the centre of the square. It was to have been decorated with four bronze lions and the statues of the four evangelists, and was to have been surmounted by a statue of Christ the Saviour holding a crucifix.

A long staircase was to have led from the square to a huge vestibule: "In superiori hujus ampli soli parte oblongum vestibulum reperiebatur, quod quinque egregiis portis aequis inter se portionibus distinguebatur: et a primo scalarum grado usque ad praedictas primi vestibuli portas LXXV. Cubitorum latitudo, longitudo vero ultra CXX. passus protendebatur. Atque in utraque hujus vestibuli extremitate singulae turres e pulcris marmoribus in altum ultra centum cubitos erigebantur; quae quidem et ad munitionem templi, et ad opportunam canonicarum horarum pulsationem simul famulabantur."[93]
At this point there were to have been two bell-towers with two stretches of wall leading to the church. Here too, there is a remarkable affinity between these plans and ideas expressed in the *Ten Books*: "In our opinion a portico, and indeed the whole church, should be built on a raised site, higher than the rest of the city, for this adds to the importance of the building."[94] Alberti adds: "Finally, the place where the church is built should be frequented, known to all, and, as they say, prominent. Moreover, it should be cut off from all contact with the profane. For this reason there should be a square in front of the façade, and the size of this square should be worthy of the church. There should be wide, paved streets all around it or, better still, majestic squares, so that the church may be seen on all sides."[95] Finally, there is a warning that the portico "should never be narrower than the entire width of the temple, or wider than a third of its length.[96] Manetti's description of a basilica with a nave and four aisles specifies that the nave should be 320 feet long (240 feet up to the transept), the tribune 80 feet, the choir 80 feet wide and 150 long (the apse taking up 70 feet). With a total length of 480 feet and a total width of 240 feet[97]—which corresponds exactly to Alberti's rule: "A basilica should be twice as long as it is broad."[98] Manetti emphasizes the need for anthropomorphic proportions: "Instar humani corporis futurum videri solet. Nam a thorace ad pedes usque deorsum, oblongo hujus basilicae spatii, quantum a patentibus tertii vestibuli foribus ad magnae crucis initio porrigebatur, persimile apparebat. Alterum deinde illius crucis spatium brachiis utrimque extensis humanis humeris conforme, cunctis diligenter et accurate considerantibus videbitur. Reliquum vero spatium, quod ambitu magnae tribunae continetur, nequaquam humano capiti dissimile censebitur. Atqui ne haec, qualiscumque est, similitudo nostra temere a nobis inducta, et ab ipsa rei veritate longe abhorrere existimetur, constitue quaeso hominem in superiori hujus templi parte, cujus universum corpus humi prosternas velim, ita ut caput ejus ad Occidentem vergat,

85. Vasari, op. cit., III, p. 100.
86. T. Magnuson, *Studies*, p. 354, par. 38.
87. Ibid., p. 354 par. 41.
88. L. B. Alberti, op. cit., V, 18, p. 432.
89. Ibid., p. 434.
90. T. Magnuson, op. cit., p. 71.
91. Ibid., p. 356, pars. 83–85.
92. L. B. Alberti, op. cit., VIII, 6, p. 716.

93. T. Magnuson, op. cit., p. 357, pars. 90–91.
94. L. B. Alberti, op. cit., VII, 5, p. 558.
95. Ibid., VII, 3, p. 548.
96. Ibid., VII, 5, p. 556.
97. On the question of Manetti's mistakes and measurements see Magnuson, op. cit., "Confronto ai disegni del Sangallo" pp. 190–200.
98. L. B. Alberti, op. cit., VII, 14, p. 636.

brachiis in diversa latera utrimque porrectis, altero ad Septemtrionem, altero vero ad Meridiem vergente, pedes autem ad Orientem spectent, atque humano corpore per hunc modum abste constituto, dubitare non poteris, quin hanc nostram similitudinem undique convenire ac quadrare arbitreris.[99]
And again: "Eam quippe ad similitudinem totius mundi fabricatam fuisse nonnulli doctissimi viri putaverunt, unde hominem a Graecis microcosmum appellatum esse existimarunt."[100] This clearly anticipates the whole of later anthropomorphic culture, from the famous designs of Francesco Di Giorgio to St. Peter's, where Bernini's colonnade represents the outstretched arms of a man, and the dome a tiara. The connection with Alberti, however, lies more in his organic system of proportions than in any direct analogy with the human body: "On the other hand, just as the head, feet and each particular part of an animal is connected with all the other parts, so in a building, and especially in a temple, all the individual elements should be made to correspond so exactly that the proportions of each may easily be calculated by measuring one of them."[101]
Such are the affinities between Manetti's description and Alberti's treatise, which Dehio was the first to examine and explain according to a method that may still be considered valid. There are two reasons for the present summary of the German historian's findings. One is that much of Alberti's treatise is autobiographical, the fruit of first-hand experience. This becomes fairly obvious if one looks beyond the classification of his subject matter, which is not particularly systematic. Another is that the real importance of Alberti lies in his cultural influence in general, in the references he made to classical monuments and Latin sources, and in the way he singled out particular problems. If one accepts this, then the entire question of dates raised by Magnuson, which leads him to reject the idea that Alberti contributed to the plan of St. Peter's or that he exercised any general influence in the 1450's, becomes quite marginal.
No other theory is possible, unless one accepts the now largely discredited one of "missing documents" and the evidence of Vasari (though he should certainly not be underrated). Magnuson himself, after skirmishing with Dehio and trying to diminish Alberti's influence, comes to the conclusion that the project must have been approved by a panel of experts headed by the Pope, and that a few Humanists, including Alberti and Rossellino (the chief architect), must have been members of this panel.[102] This much is sufficient for our purposes; it would be pointless to look for more. Alberti took no direct part in the construction of St. Peter's, since the want of time and the nature of things prevented him from doing so.

Gregorovius stressed the ambitious nature of the scheme, attributing to the Pope "the thought that one day he would sit enthroned in that papal cloister like an Eastern prince in his paradise. He was convinced he could better the Seven Wonders of the world and equal the glory of Solomon, who had built both the palace and the temple. His daring plan was conceived on the scale of the great imperial palaces of the Palatine, the Fora, and the Thermae. Unfortunately, it could not be carried out, and its only importance derives from the fact that it is one of the biggest pipe-dreams of the Roman Renaissance."[103]

But the German historian was mistaken, for Nicholas V's project was realized later in all its essentials. Though it did not take shape with the stylistic homogeneity that the Pope and Alberti would have given it, the construction of the Vatican (a whole history of architecture in itself) was completed in accordance with the main features of the project described by Manetti: Castel S. Angelo, the new Vatican basilica and the apostolic palace, the square in front of the basilica, the creation of the various quarters of the city, and the housing of the Curia in the Vatican. The work took five centuries to complete, but Nicholas, Alberti, and all the great minds they gathered round them worked out a plan from which it was impossible to deviate very far. Indeed, it obliged future artists to adopt ideas that had originally been proposed by Alberti. An example of this is the colonnade that surrounds the square of St. Peter's, a revival of Alberti's idea of a continuous portico, even if it was carried out in the Baroque style.

The question as to how much of Nicholas's building programme may be attributed to Alberti is a very nice one. From the foregoing analysis one may conclude that Alberti was more involved in the separate parts of the project than with the plan as a whole. Since the plan was drawn up at the very time Alberti was writing his treatise, curial prudence may have led the architect to allow Nicholas to claim authorship of the main idea for connecting Castel S. Angelo with the tomb of St. Peter. It is equally possible that Alberti knew relatively little about the plan as a whole. There is no doubt, however, that he seems to have shaped its single parts, suggesting the appropriate fortifications, the lay-out of the streets and squares, and the basic elements of the basilica and palace. Manetti's references to the symbolic Jerusalem, the comparison he makes between St. Peter's and the temple of Solomon, and his very anthropomorphic concept of the basilica's proportions suggest that someone other than Alberti was responsible for the

99. T. Magnuson, op. cit., p. 359, pars. 131–35.
100. Ibid., p. 360, par. 136.
101. L. B. Alberti, op. cit., VII, 5, p. 558.
102. T. Magnuson, *The Project of Nicholas V*, p. 115.

103. Gregorovius, op. cit., p. 329.

general design. In fact, there are no corresponding references in this respect in the *Ten Books*, nor is there any mention of the general organisation of the project.

This may appear strange, considering how closely the treatise reflects Alberti's personal experience. But the real reason for his silence may have been that he preferred the circular type of church to the basilica: "Our countrymen very often used the basilicas as places of worship. This was because they had grown used to meeting in private basilicas, and because the altar had a greater dignity when set up in place of the tribunal, while the space around it was perfectly suited to a choir. Moreover, the other parts of the basilica, such as the nave and aisles, could be used by the people either to walk about in, or to attend the religious ceremonies."[104] In the seventh book he insists on the secular nature of the basilica, which he maintains is more suitable for a court of justice.[105] There was also his distrust of huge projects that could rarely be completed in an average man's lifetime: "The greatest projects are hardly ever completed by the men who first conceived them, because life is short and the projects so vast."[106] This seems to reflect a suspicion of megalomania and suggests that Nicholas V was the real driving force behind the whole project. Vasari writes: "The Pope would have completed everything if only he had been allowed to live longer, for he had a great, resolute spirit, and knew so much that he was able to guide and direct his artists as much as they did him. Great enterprises can always be accomplished when this is so, when he who commands can understand for himself and so settle matters on the spot. But if the man in command is irresolute, incompetent, and wavers uncertainly between this plan and that, listening first to one man's opinion and then to another's, he can often waste a lot of time without doing anything. But there is no point in saying anything more about Nicholas's plan, since it was never carried out."[107] One must also take into consideration the influence Palmieri's Platonism and Manetti's diplomatic experience may have had in encouraging the Pope's visions of grandeur.

It was in this atmosphere of learning and art, so conducive to visions of grandeur, that the Porcari conspiracy suddenly exploded in 1453. Inspired by an ideal of republican freedom (there was no want of reference to Brutus), the plot was discovered and crushed by the Pope. Alberti added his own voice to the universal condemnation of the conspiracy pronounced by the Humanists, whose main concern seems to have been that of warding off any suspicions that may have associated Humanism with republicanism. In the *De porcaria conjuratione*,[108] Alberti describes the atmosphere

in which the unforeseen events took place more vividly than Piero de' Godi of Vicenza, Giuseppe Brippi, or Leonardo Dati:[109] "Ager cultus, Urbs facta aurea proximo jubilaeo, civium dignitatis aucta, uti quisque postulandum a pontifice duxerat. Nullae exactiones, nulla nova vectigalia, summa justitia, maxima ornandae Urbis cura. Quid! malum hoc est nimia felicitas?"[110] Alberti's ideas are clear, and mainly inspired by his concern for glory and the dignity of the city: "Inter ceteras urbes italas hanc non in postremis studiis bonarum *artium* esse *deditissimam*."[111] He concludes: "Non ignoro primum, uti ajunt, inter porcos, qui grunnitum sustulerint, hunc futurum principem omnium ad motum. Sed alia ex parte versatur ante oculos pontificis majestatis."[112] Nevertheless, the solidarity that had formerly united men of conscience and culture suffered as a consequence. Some, like Infessura, were even ready to hail the sacrifice of Porcari as that of a man of principle, who had been the friend of liberty and righteousness. The gout-stricken Nicholas gradually changed. As von Pastor says: "His inner peace had gone, for the ghost of the ancient Republic had threatened to annihilate his life, his power, and all his grandiose plans for science and art."[113] He died soon afterwards (1455), but not before he had formulated a justification of his life's work in his testament:

"I have reformed and strengthened the Holy Roman Church, which I found ruined by war and burdened with debts, by uprooting schism and re-conquering the Church's towns and castles. Not only have I freed her from her debts, but I have also built magnificent fortresses for her defence at Gualdo, Assisi, Fabriano, Civita Castellana, Narni, Orvieto, Spoleto, and Viterbo. I have embellished her with the finest, most beautiful buildings that an art of pearls and gems could devise, and I have enriched her with books and carpets, gold and silver, and other precious objects. And all these treasures I have collected, not with avarice and simony, bribes and hard-fistedness. On the contrary, I have been magnanimous in all kinds of ways, in building, in the purchase of many numerous books, in the production of many copies of Latin and Greek texts, and in the payment of learned men of science. All this have I done by the divine grace of our Creator, and for the continuation of peace in the Church during my pontificate."[114]

The death of the Pope was a grievous loss to Alberti. Nicholas V was the only patron he had who could see further than himself, and who did not have to be instructed in the principles of Humanism because he was himself a major figure in the Humanist movement. Even he failed to foresee its dangers.

104. L. B. Alberti, op. cit., VII, 3, p. 548.
105. Ibid., VII, 14, p. 632.
106. Ibid., IX, II, p. 864.
107. Vasari, op. cit., III, p. 100.
108. L. Mancini, *Opera inedita et pauca separatim impressa di L. B. Alberti*, Florence 1890, pp. 257–66.

109. L. von Pastor, op. cit., I, pp. 581–83.
110. L. B. Alberti, *De porcaria coniuratione*, p. 264.
111. Ibid., p. 265.
112. Ibid., p. 266.
113. L. von Pastor, op. cit., I, p. 643.
114. Ibid.

CHAPTER FOUR
In Florence for the Rucellai

GIOVANNI RUCELLAI

After spending some time in the rarified, literary republic of Lionello d'Este and in the chivalrous, superstitious court of Sigismondo Malatesta, Alberti moved to Florence where he found men who corresponded to his ideal of a prudent, civilized middle class, whose business did not prevent them from taking an interest in literature, and who had a deep-rooted faith in Divine Providence. These, of course, were all themes he dealt with in the *Famiglia*.[1] His patron was a characteristic figure of the Florence of Cosimo de' Medici: Giovanni Rucellai, a minor politician who had accepted Cosimo's leadership unquestioningly. Giovanni's *Ricordi* of 1461 and 1473 give us a vivid account of the man's self-esteem. He professes satisfaction with himself, with the good fortune that made him a Florentine, with his good health (he never spent "a day in bed" until he was seventy), and with his good luck in business, or rather, "in the business of commerce and exchange," which brought him riches, honour, and prestige. He is happy to have lived in the time of Cosimo, "who has been, and is, so wealthy, virtuous, gracious, famous and popular that never has there been another who has had, or has, such qualities and capacities either within the city or without, nor in the whole of Christendom."[2] He is satisfied with his wife, the daughter of Palla Strozzi, "a good housewife and housekeeper", and with his Don Bernardo's wife, the daughter of Piero de' Medici and grand-daughter of Cosimo. He is also content with his own political ability: "I have served the state disinterestedly for twenty-seven years, that is, between 1434 and 1461, during which time I have had to manoeuvre very carefully, avoiding mistakes."[3] For Rucellai there was no greater pleasure than making and spending money, and for fifty years he did little else, to the extent that, "it has given me the greatest pleasure and contentment, — and how much more pleasurable it is spending money than making it."[4]

One of his greatest pleasures was building, since this served three purposes; "[it honoured] God, the city, and my own memory." In his memoir of 1473 he draws up a detailed list of his building projects. His own palace is mentioned first: "And still determined to buy land to build on, I was obliged to put out a lot of money, since I had to give 30 soldi to the lira, not to mention the difficulty of getting the owners to sell (which was almost impossible). I then converted eight houses into one: three of them were in Via della Vigna, and five behind." He continues: "I spent a considerable amount of money on my house, the façade of the church of S. Maria Novella, the chapel with my tomb in S. Pancrazio

(the gold brocade alone in this church cost more than a thousand ducats), on the loggia opposite my house, and on my villas and gardens at Quarachi and Poggio a Chaiano."[5] He lists the works of art in his house, including paintings "by Domenico Veneziano, Filippo Lippi, Antonio Pollaiolo, Andrea del Castagno, and Paolo Uccello. There were also sculptures by Desiderio da Settignano, Giovanni di Bertino, and Andrea Verrocchio." He describes Giuliano da Maiano as a "carpenter" and "master of inlays," and mentions Vittorio di Lorenzo Bartolucci the woodcarver and Maso Finiguerra the goldsmith. There is no explicit reference to Alberti; some critics have taken this omission as reason to doubt the authenticity of the attribution of certain works to him. In Florence, as at Rimini, Alberti arrives on the scene on tiptoe as it were, and even the date of his arrival is uncertain, though it may have coincided with his moving from Rome to Rimini.[6] Dezzi believes that Alberti and Rucellai met for the first time in 1450 and that Alberti spent "a second, longer period in Florence towards 1456."

As on other occasions, Alberti's appearance in Florence seems to have stimulated an increase in architectural activity. The building programme of Giovanni Rucellai had three phases. The first may be described as "routine"; it involved the construction of a palace of great prestige, such as would put the Rucellai among the top families of Florence (by adopting a skilful policy of marriage alliances it was already connected with the Pittis and the Medici). The palace was built in accordance with Alberti's idea that palaces could be used as fortresses in times of adversity. The construction of the Palazzo Rucellai necessitated the rebuilding of some earlier structures and the bringing together of a number of separate properties. Giovanni Rucellai's entry in the land register for 1469 mentions "a house for my own use, which in 1427 consisted of a number of houses. These were knocked down and made into one."

Here, Alberti's ideas are particularly relevant: "Everything should be in proportion to one's social importance. Indeed, I believe that it is preferable for the rich to go without certain decorations in their private houses than to be accused in some way of extravagance by the more discreet and frugal." "On the other hand, since we all agree that we should endeavour to leave a reputation for wisdom and power behind us . . ., and since we are accustomed to decorating our houses as much out of love for magnificence as for the honour of our country and families (which no one will deny is every wise man's duty), the best house is undoubtedly the one whose most public parts (which should be designed to

1. L. B. Alberti, *L'Architettura*, I, 4, p. 32.
2. Rucellai, *Zibaldone Quaresimale*, London 1960, p. 118.
3. Ibid., p. 122.
4. Ibid., p. 121.

5. Ibid., p. 121.
6. Cf. M. Dezzi Bardeschi, *Il complesso monumentale di S. Pancrazio a Firenze e il suo restauro*, in " Quaderni dell'Istituto di Storia dell'Architettura ", XIII, 73-79, Rome 1967, p. 17.

give pleasure to guests) are the most decorous. These are the façade, vestibule, etc." He continues: "One thing at least should be quite clear. Whoever seeks to know what true ornament really is should realise that it is not something one can obtain by mere wealth, but that it requires, above all, taste and intelligence"[7]. To this may be added yet another quotation: "In my opinion, no wise man will even want to depart from general usage in the decoration of his house. On the contrary, he will be careful not to provoke envy with too much ostentation. ..."[8]

These words seem to contain an explicit reference to old Cosimo's rejection of a design by Brunelleschi for a palace in Piazza S. Lorenzo, which would have run parallel to the basilica: "thinking it too great an expense, Cosimo cancelled his instructions, though he greatly regretted his decision later."[9] Disappointed by Cosimo's decision, Brunelleschi destroyed the model, saying "that he had always wanted to carry out some rare work, and had thought he had found someone willing and able to do it."[10] Filippo's indignation and Cosimo's regret must have been a subject of discussion in the city for a long time. But Cosimo's behaviour and leadership could hardly be criticized by members of his own party, such as Rucellai. This was the task of ambitious adversaries like the Strozzis, who later took up Brunelleschi's idea of a palace with three sides flanked by streets when Filippo Strozzi built the palace on the Canto dei Tornaquinci. Giovanni Rucellai's prudent behaviour was similar to Cosimo's. Some additions were made to the front of his palace, where the number of windows was increased from five to seven; others too, were to have been made, as the unfinished wall of the façade on the right of the observer clearly shows.

The second stage in Rucellai's building programme had two objectives: his town residence was intended to satisfy the needs of prestige and social intercourse; his country villa was to be a haven of peace and quiet. The first consideration explains the Loggia, which Rucellai tells us was built "for the honour of our family, to be used on occasions of joy and sorrow."[11] When Bernardo married, "the festivities were held outside, upon a platform raised three feet above the ground and covering an area of about 3200 square feet. This occupied the whole of the square in front of our house, the loggia, and the Via della Vigna as far as the walls of our house. It was shaped like a triangle and beautifully decorated with various cloths, tapestries, bench- and seat-covers; there was an awning of deep blue cloth above turned inside out to protect the guests from the sun. The whole of the awning was decorated with garlands and leaves, and there were roses in the centre of the garlands."[12] If one considers that the small square in front of the Palazzo Rucellai forms a kind of tribune, the following passage in the *Ten Books* takes on added interest: "There is no doubt that both squares and crossroads are more attractive when decorated with colonnades, under which the older men can walk, sit, doze, or see to their mutual affairs."[13]

Of villas — such as "the two handsome dwellings, one just outside the city at Quarachi, the other farther away at Poggio a Caiano"[14] mentioned by Rucellai in his memoir of 1473 — Alberti writes that they may have "all the seductions of loveliness and delight,"[15] whereas town houses should be more austere. He pays particular attention to the subject of suburban gardens, affirming that there should be no conflict between the pleasures of country life and "the business of the city," but that the two should be reconciled where possible. This is all the more necessary insofar as the best solution (that is, the free, pure air of a villa built on slightly raised, isolated ground) is not always possible. Of all practical, useful projects "the first and most wholesome is a garden, of the kind that does not impede activities connected with the city, but which at the same time is immune to the impurities of the city atmosphere."[16] The garden at Quarachi, of which Giovanni di Paolo Rucellai has left a loving, detailed description ("it gives great pleasure to the eye and comfort to the body"[17]), was according to its owner, "situated where the air is excellently temperate, where one finds the healthiest people; nor is the air as rarified as in the hills, for it lies on low ground. It may be described as the most beautiful part of the plain, since it is almost halfway between two big castles."[18]

Poggio a Caiano, on the other hand, seems to correspond exactly to Alberti's ideal site for a villa: "Therefore, I would suggest a slightly raised position. Moreover, the road leading up to the villa should have a minimum gradient so that those approaching it will not realise they have climbed a slope until they find themselves on higher ground, with all the surrounding countryside below them. Both pleasure and convenience demand that there be no lack round about of flowery meadows, sunny fields, fresh shady woods, crystal clear streams and fountains, pools to bathe in, and all the other things mentioned previously in connection with villas."[19] But the design of the villa was such as might have aroused envy or questions of prestige, so that Giovanni Rucellai, like the expert 'manoeuvrer' he was, very prudently gave way to the Medicis once more. According to Passerini,[20] it seems that Giovanni had considered building a villa at Poggio a Caiano to a design of Alberti's. But Lorenzo de' Medici took a fancy to

7. L. B. Alberti, op. cit., IX, p. 782.
8. Ibid.
9. C. Frey, *Il libro di Antonio Billi*, Berlin 1892, p. 34.
10. Ibid., p. 35.
11. G. Rucellai, op. cit., p. 20.

12. G. Rucellai, op. cit., p. 28.
13. L. B. Alberti, op. cit., VIII, 6, p. 712.
14. G. Rucellai, op. cit., p. 121.
15. L. B. Alberti, op. cit., IX, 2, p. 788.
16. Ibid., p. 790.
17. G. Rucellai, op. cit., p. 21.
18. Ibid., p. 23.
19. L. B. Alberti, op. cit., IX, 2, p. 792.
20. L. Passerini, *Genealogia e Storia della Famiglia Rucellai*, 1861, p. 120.

the place, and Giovanni was obliged to part with the property, which was part of his wife's dowry.

The third stage in Rucellai's building programme involved religious architecture: his tribute to the church of his quarter and the funeral chapel he had built in his family's parish church. The church of his quarter was no ordinary church but S. Maria Novella, one of the most famous monasteries in the Catholic world, and prominent enough to house Eugenius IV on his flight from Rome during the Council. The completion of its façade was one of the most important projects in Florence, one that offered a man who expressed satisfaction at having paid sixty thousand florins in taxes a golden opportunity to display his wealth and high principles. This too, was a form of voluntary taxation, one that had been practised by Cosimo, who, like all rich Florentines, was eager to dispel the suspicion of usury that accompanied all profitable commercial and banking enterprises. There was no better way of putting one's conscience at rest than to erect a church, for this symbolised one's devotion and gratitude to Providence, the dispenser of that fortune of which economic privilege was the most tangible evidence.

Unlike the inexpert, violent Sigismondo Malatesta, Giovanni Rucellai was well aware of the time building involved and of the brevity of human life. In his memoir of 1471 he claims to have set aside the income from Poggio a Caiano for the construction of the façade of S. Maria Novella, the money being placed in the trust of the consuls of the Arte del Cambio: "... and whether the façade of S. Maria Novella is carried out or not lies within the discretion of the consuls of the said Art ... and should it be decided to do anything to the façade, let the said consuls look into the matter and provide for it with the income from the said property."[21] But the date of the memoir does not tally, for the notarial document published by Dezzi shows that Rucellai had already decided on the religious buildings he was going to construct by 15 November 1440, and that the income from the property, or the proceeds from its eventual sale, was already bound to the construction of a chapel "with a tomb similar to that of Christ our Lord in Jerusalem, which the said Giovanni desires to be built either in the church of S. Maria Novella or, preferably, in that of S. Pancrazio in Florence."[22] Thus the façade of S. Maria Novella, commonly believed to be Alberti's last work in Florence — by Mancini, for example, who stresses the importance of the date (1470) inscribed on the façade, which is not very different from that of the tomb in S. Pancrazio (1467) — was carried out earlier, when Alberti accompanied Eugenius IV to the Council

of Florence in 1439-1442.

In his memoir of 1469 Giovanni Rucellai recalls a conversation he had with the Bishop of Cortona in the cloister of the Annunziata regarding the "beauties" of Florence. He says that "the order of the preaching friars does not have another church or monastery as beautiful as S. Maria Novella of Florence in the whole of Christendom,"[23] and goes on to associate it with the monastery and library of S. Marco, which were financed by Cosimo. Dezzi believes that the idea of a shrine similar to the Holy Sepulchre in Jerusalem was linked with the façade of S. Maria Novella by Alberti, but that his patron changed his mind and the more modest chapel of S. Pancrazio was built. (No further documentary evidence has been found to confirm this.) The fact remains that the idea of a family chapel containing his own tomb represented the climax of Rucellai's religious, propagandistic, architectural ambitions. In a letter to his mother, he writes: "Yesterday I finished organising the expedition to the Holy Land, where I have sent two wood carvers together with engineers and other men at my own expense to get the right design and measurements of the Holy Sepulchre of our Lord Jesus Christ, and to bring them back as quickly as possible, so that I may fulfil my wish to build one like it here in our chapel, which I am having built in our parish church of S. Pancrazio. This has already reached a good point, as you know, and the only thing it needs now to make it perfect is the model of that priceless treasure."[24]

A considerable tradition had grown up around the Holy Sepulchre, nourished by the *novelle* written about the East, the more or less reliable accounts of travellers, and theological tracts. Numerous imitations of the Holy Sepulchre had been constructed throughout Europe. Ferdinand II even considered moving the original from Jerusalem and placing it in the Cappella dei Principi in Florence, while Guarini's chapel of the Holy Shroud in Turin is proof of the fascination it continued to exercise on Italians for centuries.[25] Giovanni Rucellai's Florentine business-sense led him to combine a trade mission with a technical one, the purpose of which was to link the international prestige of his firm with his ambitious religious projects. The latter were justified by his social position: "Perhaps there are not many in the city who can pass before me." In his recollections of Rome and the jubilee, Rucellai mentions "a fine little chapel in S. Giovanni in Laterano decorated with marble, porphyry, and mosaics, which is called the Sancto Sanctorum, for it contains numerous relics of saints. And they say one can obtain the same indulgence there as at the Holy Sepulchre in Jerusalem."[26] This may have given him the idea of emp-

21. G. Rucellai, op. cit., p. 26.
22. M. Dezzi Bardeschi, *La facciata di Santa Maria Novella a Firenze*, Pisa 1970, p. 21.

23. G. Rucellai, op. cit., p. 65.
24. Ibid., p. 136.
25. Cf. E. Battisti, *Schemata nel Guarini*, Turin 1970, p. 136.
26. G. Rucellai, op. cit. p. 70.

loying Alberti, that able functionary of the papal secretariat, to petition the Pope for the same privilege. Though Alberti was no longer a papal abbreviator, Paul II issued a bull of indulgence in 1471, having heard "that our beloved son, Giovanni Rucellai, a citizen of Florence, moved by singular devotion, has founded and endowed a chapel called the Holy Sepulchre in the monastery church of S. Pancrazio, which belongs to the order of Valonbrosa in Florence, and that he has built a solemn sepulchre in it at his own expense, similar to that in Jerusalem."[27]

Rucellai never mentions Alberti. This may be because, though an amateur architect, he was too important an official to be treated as a workshop artist. Giovanni Rucellai may have been naturally inclined to attribute all the merit of his architectural projects to himself. However, the coincidence of certain dates and cultural interests, such as the "right ordering of the family," the significance of private and religious architecture, the love of gardens and villas, his visit to Rome (where he was as interested in Roman monuments as in the jubilee), and his concern with the moral themes of virtue and fortune, makes it impossible to credit Rucellai with so much intellectual originality. One can credit him with a certain measure of cultural independence, once one has understood how profoundly influenced he was by the culture of which Alberti was a major figure and populariser.

It is difficult to believe that Rucellai's building programme was not influenced by Alberti, who reminds the architect (and therefore himself): "You must not go offering your services to every man who says he wants to build, like those superficial, vain artists who compete with each other for commissions. Indeed, I wonder whether it is not better to wait until your client has sought your help more than once, since those who desire your skill must in turn have faith in you. For why should I set about explaining the excellence and usefulness of my ideas when the only recompense I obtain is the confidence of the incompetent? In my opinion, a man who, by means of his skill and knowledge, saves his client considerable expense, while at the same time giving him considerable pleasure and providing for his comfort, deserves no small recompense."[28] This reads like the page of a diary; Alberti seems both to declare his passion for architecture and to assert his professional discretion as an architect who was never paid for any specific work. This explains his avoidance of all specific references to individual buildings and his constant need of others to carry out his designs. However, it has created considerable confusion regarding his different roles as adviser, designer, and director of works. It also indicates why he felt his patrons owed

him a debt of gratitude, the buildings he constructed for them being less important than the fact that he had constructed *them*, by building up their capacity to judge things for themselves.

THE PALAZZO RUCELLAI

Alberti was particularly fond of the compactness that results from the use of the same material for the whole of a building, and this is illustrated in the construction of the Palazzo Rucellai by his use of *pietra forte* (fine grained sandstone). Another favourite device was the use of channels and pilasters to hide the joints in a building, pilasters enabing the architect to eliminate any roughness or irregularity in the joints. In the Palazzo Rucellai, many of the stones of the pilasters, especially those on the ground floor, are *passanti* (in other words, they have the lesser projection of the rustication rather than that of the pilaster itself). The sixth pilaster from the end is an exception, and this has prompted Sanpaolesi's plausible theory that the façade was initially designed with five windows, only to be changed to seven when work was begun on the first floor, a change that may have been conditioned by the width of the square in front of the palace and by the construction of the loggia.[29] The freedom that characterises the articulation of the stone façade, both in the height of its blocks of hewn stone and in their irregular, modern width, seems to question the fixed scheme of the superimposed orders: there seems to be a contrast between the freedom of the execution and the rigidity of the design. To this must be added the subtly doctrinaire introduction of the *opus reticulatum*, which forms a kind of seat with a back in the spaces between the stylobates of the ground-floor pilasters.

The rule laid down by Alberti himself in his treatise,[30] according to which pilasters should not project more than a fourth nor less than a sixth of the side, is disregarded. Instead, they are made to produce a very fine, typically Florentine *stiacciato* effect (one of very low relief, which renders the real volume of bodies in a pictorial way). Even the proportional variations in the height of the pilasters are unusual, for those on the first floor are half a module less than the ones on the ground floor and a whole module higher than those of the second floor (half a module being equal to the width of the pilaster at its base). The order of the first floor may be taken as the building's basic element, with its Corinthian pilasters nine modules high, including base and capital. The pilasters of the ground floor, instead of being more compressed, are nearly nine and a half modules high, while those of the second floor are a little less than nine. These unusual proportions were evidently

27. Ibid., p. 136.
28. L. B. Alberti, op. cit., IX, 11, p. 862.

29. P. Sanpaolesi, *Precisazioni sul Palazzo Rucellai*, in "Palladio" I-IV, January-December 1963, p. 61.
30. L. B. Alberti, op. cit., VI, 12, p. 518.

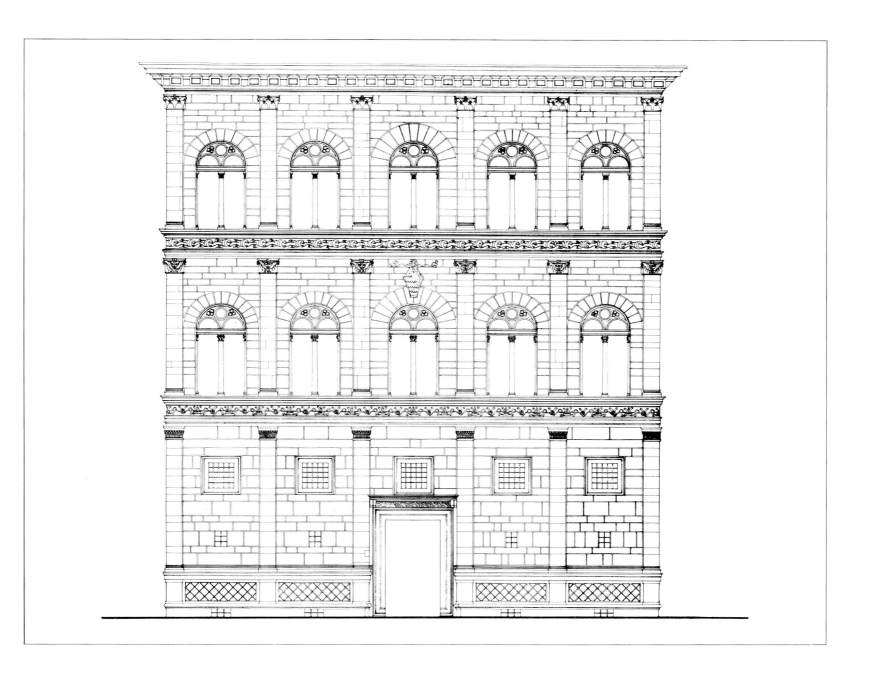

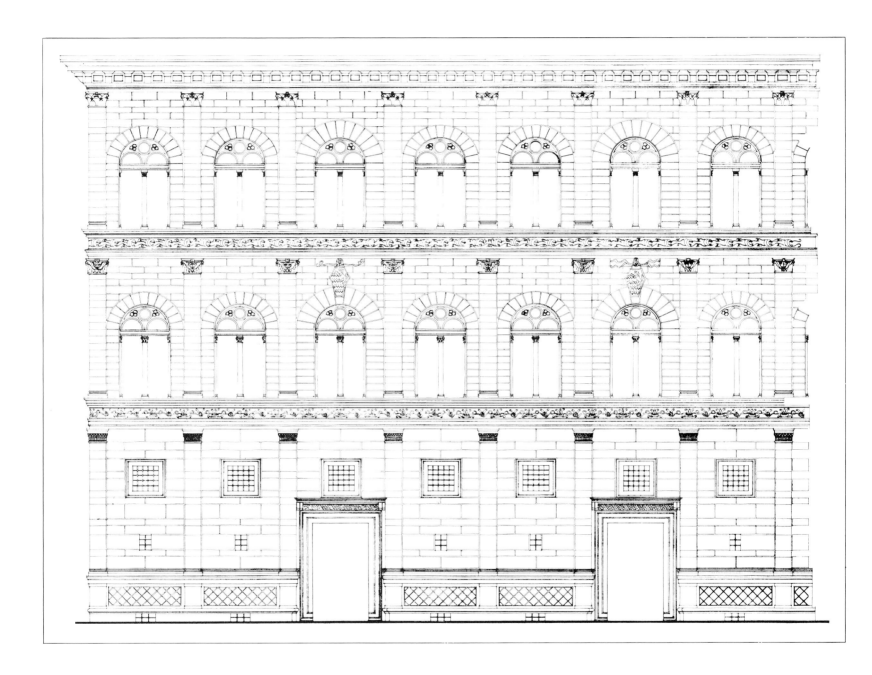

41. *Florence, Palazzo Rucellai. Diagram of the façade.*

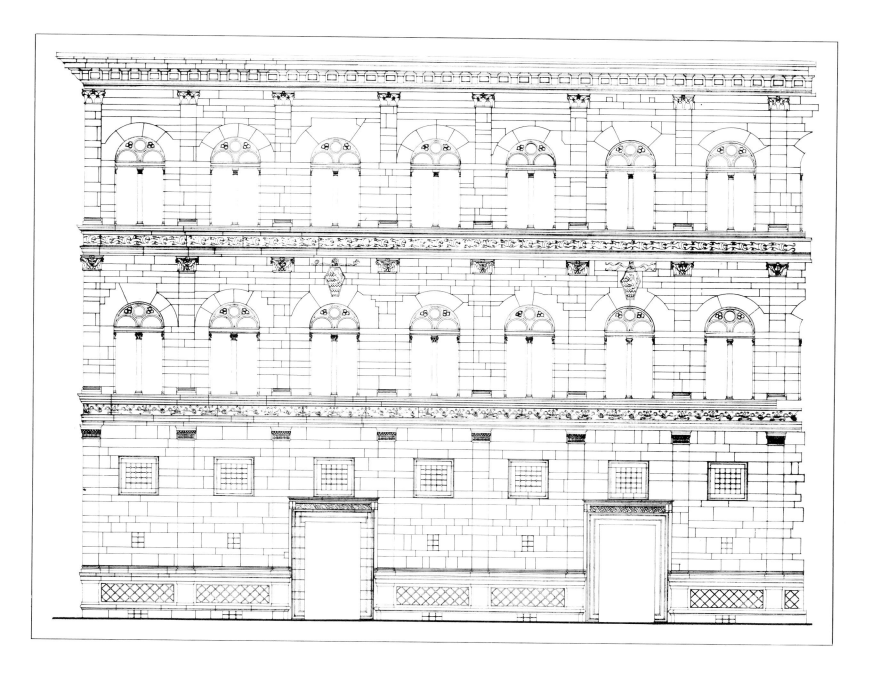

42. Proportions of the order of the Palazzo Rucellai.
43. Proportions of the Rucellai Loggia.

44-50. Florence, Palazzo Rucellai. The palace is a skilful compromise between the patron's wishes, the architect's design, and the constructional techniques of the masons. Giovanni Rucellai does not seem to have saved very much by buying the property piecemeal, and he himself complained about having to pay thirty soldi *to the lira for the houses nearby (i.e., approx. 50% more than their market value).*
Apart from the sentimental and traditional reasons involved, Rucellai's attitude was consistent with the prudence that served to advance the reputation of a commercial enterprise. It was better for the latter to register

a slow, steady growth rather than a rapid, abnormal one — which would have been the case had Rucellai bought the whole area and built a palace ex novo.

Yet the no less urgent demands of a policy of prestige were to be satisfied not so much by temporary solutions of a functional kind as by a definite artistic choice overriding all considerations of cost. For Alberti, the Palazzo Rucellai (or rather the façade of the palace) was an opportunity to adopt certain architectural elements common to many Florentine buildings (roughly-hewn stone, rustication, and large two-lighted windows)

determined by the state of the interiors and the heights imposed by the rebuilding of pre-existent structures. No rules governing the proportions of these elements are set forth even in the treatise, except those regarding the spaces between columns. Alberti says that such spaces should not exceed the width of the column by more than three and three-eigths, which is very close to the proportions of the Rucellai façade. However, any evaluation of the palace must take into consideration the indeterminate contribution of those who executed Alberti's design.

The attribution of this building to Alberti, confirmed by the studies of Sanpaolesi, has met with much opposition, raised many doubts, and has even been rejected. Sanpaolesi has pointed to the differences between the side, courtyard, and interiors, all of which are clearly tied to the Brunelleschian manner, and the façade, which is very inferior artistically. But Ricci, among others, though a sensitive and appreciative scholar of Alberti's work, denies Alberti's authorship: "Both in its general plan and in the plentiful, trite decoration that disfigures every part of it, the palace appears to be the work of some local sculptor such as Rossellino, rather than that of an architect dedicated to Roman grandeur and harmony. The fact that the Palazzo Piccolomini at Pienza, which is an imitation of it, is almost wholly attributable to Rossellino, inclines us to attribute the Palazzo Rucellai to him as well."[31]

The documentary evidence for so categorical a denial consists of one sentence in the *Life* by Antonio Billi: "Bernardo the architect, his brother, made the model of the house of the Rucellai. And Antonio di Migliorino Guidotti made the model of the Rucellai Loggia."[32] There is clearly a misunderstanding here as to the real meaning of the word *modello*, which has been taken to signify 'project' when its correct meaning is 'model' (the wooden model that was made of the project). Alberti urges the architect "to give much thought to the work to be undertaken both as a whole and as regards the measurements of its single parts, making use not only of drawings and sketches, but also of models made of wood and other materials."[33] He writes at length of the importance of such models, which, he declares, are indispensable for the precise ordering of the separate parts of a building, for estimating the cost of a project, and for the elaboration of a clear idea of its structure and decoration. He rejects the use of attractively painted, coloured models: "Plain, simple models are preferable to finely finished ones, for then the idea of the designer will not be lost in admiration of the model."[34] (Here, Alberti clearly has in mind Brunelleschi's models of the dome and lantern.) Given the im-

44. Florence, Piazza Rucellai.

31. C. Ricci, *Il tempio malatestiano*, Milan-Rome 1925, p. 90. The same text as in C. Ricci, *L. B. Alberti*, Turin 1917, p. 22.

32. C. Frey, op. cit., pp. 46-47. Cf. same theory in C. Frey, *Il codice magliabecchiano*, CL. XVII, 17, Berlin 1892, p. 94, and in C. Fabriczy, *Il codice dell'anonimo gaddiano*, Florence 1893, p. 64.

33. L. B. Alberti, op. cit., II, 1, p. 96.

34. Ibid., p. 98.

while introducing the "novelty" of a grid of superimposed orders. This novelty derived from a re-interpretation of certain classical models, and it resulted in the construction of a proportional structure. Both the old and the new had their rules and affirmed the general concept of order. We must not forget that Alberti was working in Florence, where the medieval tradition of improvisation, though slightly modified by fifteenth-century practice, was still strong.

The stone blocks of the façade were not "divided" into two kinds, as the compositional logic of the façade would seem to require. Instead, similar blocks were used both for the pilasters and the bays. Each particular problem was solved as it arose by means of passanti, single blocks of stone forming part both of the pilaster and of the rustication adjacent to it (since they do more work, they were naturally more difficult to place). This proves that Alberti's façade was a mere screen for the men who actually built it (including Rossellino, who made the wooden model of the palace) and that the only rule they followed was the craftsman's "rule of art"; that is, they used well-chosen blocks of sandstone of even grain, with well-made junctures.

The modifications to the design made during the actual construction of the palace must also be taken into consideration, for an analysis of the stone blocks shows that the façade was extended to include seven instead of five windows, which involved the addition of a second doorway. In other words, the façade became "bi-focal" instead of "mono-axial", and its general proportions became fundamentally horizontal instead of vertical. These were important alterations, and they were carried out without damaging or distorting the structure in any visible way. Alberti's "grid" is so flexible an instrument that one can easily imagine a further extension of the façade being planned, a theory that is borne out by the way in which the stone screen is "docked" at its ends. This does not convey the idea of something "unfinished", but of something "indefinite" that can be reproduced on an urban scale.

The suggestion of Roman opus reticulatum in the lower part of the structure (repeated, but no longer visible, in the Loggia opposite) creates the impression of a back of a bench and integrates the bench with the wall behind it. This is a novelty within a novelty, for it represents a departure from the conventional kind of base current at the time. Alberti was able to introduce it because the façade's structural functions (at a visual level) had been transferred to the upper scheme of superimposed orders.

Every detail of the façade was designed and carried out with extraordinary consistency. The only qualities of the stone exploited were its homogeneousness and compactness, while nothing was demanded of the carvings except uniformity and sobriety. What really counted was the design, as well as the subtle counterpoint between the strict, unpretentious definition of the "orders" and the naturalness of the stone blocks.

portance he attached to models, Alberti must have entrusted that of the Palazzo Rucellai to a man of proven ability, such as Rossellino, whom he had probably met already by that time. It seems unlikely he would have given it to the first wood-carver who happened to pass by. Furthermore, the crucial discovery of the relationship between the initial five-window design of the palace and its later seven-window realization, together with the possibility that the project was to have been enlarged still further, suggests that a larger model might have been made of the palace in its final state, as it existed in the mind of its owner.

THE RUCELLAI LOGGIA

The design of the loggia, which was executed by someone who has remained virtually unknown,[35] did not save Alberti from the criticism of Vasari, who was particularly exacting about loggias (see his criticism of Tasso's Mercato Nuovo): "For Cosimo Rucellai, Alberti designed the palace which was being built in the Via della Vigna and also the loggia opposite the palace. In this loggia he turned the arches over the closely spaced columns in the façade and also over the corbels, in order both to have a series of arches on the outside and to follow the same pattern internally. He had to make projections at the inside corners because he had put a space at each corner between the arches. When he came to vault the interior he was unable to use a semicircular barrel-vault, which would have looked mean and awkward, and so he resolved to throw small arches across from corner to corner. Here he showed a lack of judgement and design, demonstrating very clearly that theoretical knowledge must be accompanied by experience: no one can develop perfect judgement unless his learning is tempered by practical application."[36] Vasari seems to anticipate Schlosser's condemnation of Alberti's cultural monumentality in the name of experience, that common denominator in all artistic activity, and the only quality capable of bridging the gap between 'sophisticated' artist and the common wood carver. Vasari wrote his *Life* of Alberti with particular care, even mentioning his relationship with Cosimo Bartoli, but he may have been somewhat ruffled by the simultaneous publication of the vernacular version of the *De re aedificatoria* and the first edition of his own *Lives*. However, his overall judgement of Alberti is that though many architects "have done better work than Alberti, such has been the influence of his writings on the pens and speech of scholarly men that he is commonly believed to be superior to those who were, in fact, superior to him."[37] The constructional problem referred to by Vasari arises out of

the difference in diameter between the outer arches and the perimetral semi-arches of the 'sail' vaults, for since the latter rest on quarter columns placed at right angles to the half columns supporting the former, their spans are different. But whether this is a fault, or a deliberate attempt to give solidity to the upper parts of the structure, is a moot point. The proportions of the loggia are similar to those of the Tempio Malatestiano; there is a ratio of 1 : 2 between the space between the columns and the highest point of the arches, and another of 2 : 3 between the same space and the height of the columns, including the abacus. This compromise between classical theory and local tradition is faithfully reflected in the treatise: "The arches of colonnades should really be supported by square columns. In fact, round ones are defective, since the head of the arch is not perfectly in line with the column beneath it, but overlaps it to the extent to which its square surface exceeds the circular column. In order to remedy this defect, the best classical architects placed another square plinth on top of the capitals of the columns. Sometimes the plinth measured a fourth or a fifth of the column's diameter, and it had a straight ogee moulding. The width of the plinth, at its base, was equal to the widest part of the capital, while the width of the upper projecting parts was equal to the height of the plinth. Thus, the heads and corners of the arch rested on something more solid."[38] This coincides with Alberti's design of the Rucellai loggia, as does a reference to the arches' cornices: "We have already observed that an arch is no more than a curved beam. Therefore, arches should be decorated in the same way as beams whenever they are turned over columns. If one wishes to decorate them even more, one can run an architrave, frieze, and cornice along the whole length of the wall just above the arches, according to the proportions one would apply to columns of the same height."[39] Alberti has thought out here, along more strictly classical lines, the problems Brunelleschi faced in the façade of the Foundling Hospital. Finally, it would appear that the men who actually built the loggia kept very close to Alberti's design — perhaps because the project was so clear and simple — so that the loggia is the most Albertian of all his Florentine works.

THE FAÇADE OF S. MARIA NOVELLA

On the eighth day of the *Decameron*, Boccaccio tells how Buffalmacco plays a trick on a fat-headed doctor from Bologna who suffers from uncontrollable urges at night. He puts him, "just after he had fallen asleep, all wrapped up in one of his finest robes, in the top of one of those high niches that have recently

35. Guidotti appears in Manetti and Gaiole's circle, among the disciples of Brunelleschi working on the completion of S. Lorenzo and S. Spirito (Gaye, op. cit., I, p. 168).
36. Vasari, op. cit., II, pp. 541-542.
37. Ibid., p. 536.

38. L. B. Alberti, op. cit., VII, 15, p. 642.
39. Ibid.

52-55. Florence, Loggia Rucellai. *The loggia was used to celebrate important events in the life of the family. On ordinary days it served as a meeting-place, as well as a private "market" both for the house and the square that eventually took its name from it. Its construction and incorporation within another building was a notable* coup de prestige *on the part of Giovanni Rucellai in the prudent promotion of his family's fortunes.*

Not only did it represent an "opening-out" of a single edifice into the urban texture around it (as in the case of the Palazzo Medici, where the loggia below the palace was later walled up), but a kind of absorption of public life into the private. The entire operation was made possible owing to the scale of the two projects (palace and loggia), for neither is monumental or stylistically obtrusive, while both are in keeping with the size and characteristics of the medieval town.

The Piazza Rucellai may be considered an early example of the "cross-roads" or "market" decorated with colonnades — a feature of the Ideal City described by Alberti in the De re aedificatoria. *It is important, for it shows that Alberti made no distinction between the rational classical city and the city seen as a living organism.*

Not much more can be said about the structure, for it is impossible to examine the original cavities of the arches (now closed by dark glass panels), the carved stone identical to that of the palace opposite, or the complicated vaults criticised by Vasari. (Should they be attributed to Antonio Guidotti, who made the model of the loggia?).

The most significant feature is the compressed plinth over the capitals. This was an experiment to test the validity of a classical device adopted to overcome the difficulty that arose when the square section of an arch was placed upon the circular section of the column beneath it. This problem led Alberti to develop his theory that architraves were best accompanied by columns, and arches by pillars.

The loggia is a sober work, and its sobriety is reflected in its stone-work, capitals, and mouldings. It has none of the artisan excess and the more common exaggerations of fifteenth-century local art. Nor does it have any of the stereotyped features that characterised the craft of the contemporary wood-carver. Alberti may have kept a tighter, more personal control over its actual construction.

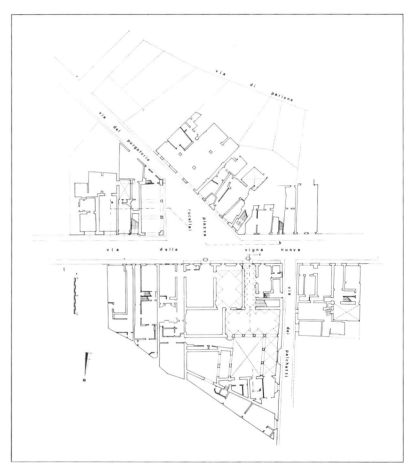

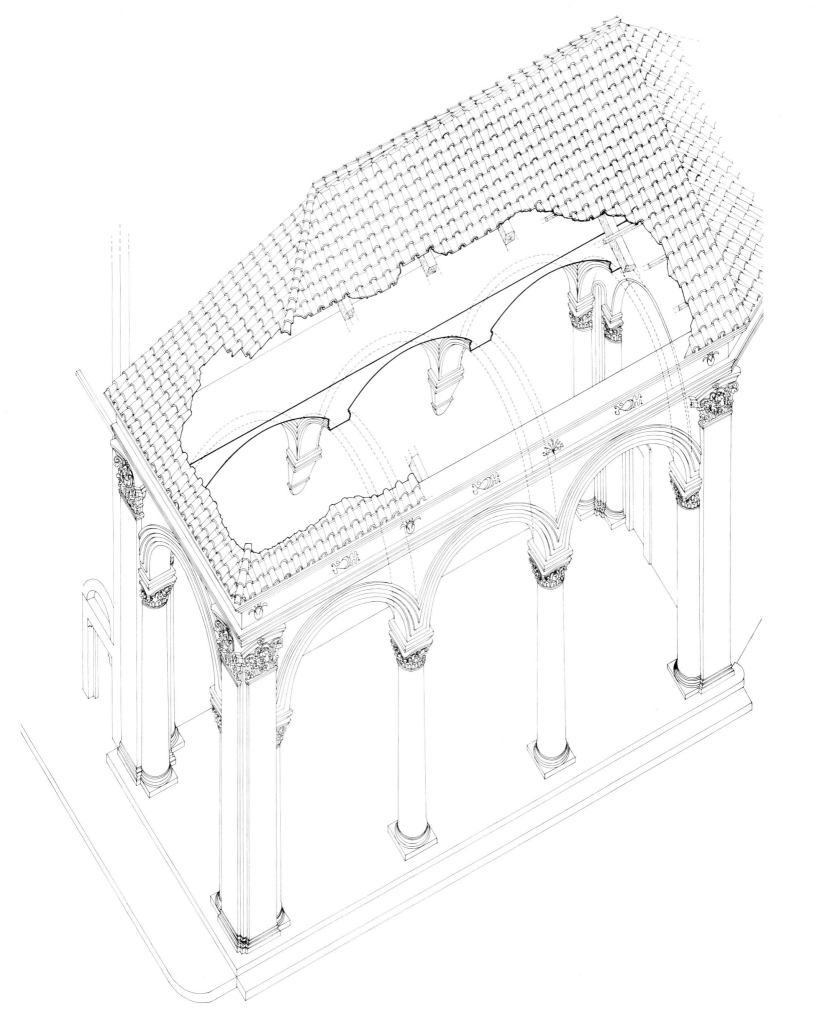

been built outside S. Maria Novella." Then: "Seeing Bruno approach to find out how things were going, Buffalmacco went into the new square of S. Maria Novella."[40] These contemporary references suggest that the project must have caught the imagination of the Florentines from the very beginning, even though it remained unfinished.

The *avelli* (arched niches) were the reason why so much time passed before work was begun on the façade exactly eighteen years from the date Giovanni Rucellai drew up the deed tying the income from the property at Poggio a Caiano. They were probably the reason for Alberti's presence, too. In fact, the delay was caused by the removal of two earlier niches and the claims of the Baldesi family, descendants of a certain Turino. The family had paid for the doors that gave access to the church and now claimed the right to complete the rest of the façade. "But the friars as usual appealed to Rome and obtained certain briefs, so that the quarrel was soon over, the two parties coming to an amicable agreement. Part of the agreement was that the Baldesi should grant the Rucellai the privilege of covering the rest of the rough, whitewashed façade with marble, and that the part that had been done already, from the first cornice down, should be left just as it was when carried out with the bequest left by the aforesaid Turino di Baldese."[41] It was probably Alberti himself, acting discreetly, who helped to settle the dispute in favour of the Rucellai, while the decision to preserve the earlier structures (the object of much later criticism) was the result of the court action.

A kind of no man's land between the old and new parts of the façade has given rise to many theories. One, based on documentary evidence, maintains that the Baldesi family completed the façade up to the level of the arches "in the middle of the façade."[42] Mancini believes that Alberti continued the whole of the part between the arched niches and the entablature, including the slender pillars and round-headed blind arches. In the two editions of his *Architectural Principles in the Age of Humanism*, Wittkower takes up a position halfway between the two. At first, he supported the theory that attributed the blind arches to Alberti, but in the later Italian edition of his book he adopted Paatz's position, accepting "the fact that the Gothic architect had archaizing tendencies and built the arcades in the style of the Florentine proto-Renaissance of the late twelfth century."[43] It is difficult to believe that Alberti, whose principles never allowed him to imitate a style, carried out the small Gothic pillars and capitals. It seems equally improbable that the unfinished façade could have coincided exactly with the very

point at which he fixed the height of the cornice and entablature on the basis of two definite points of reference: the archway of the portal, which was probably pointed and in which he introduced his own fully rounded arch, and the height of the rose-window. On the other hand however, there seems to be a certain homogeneity in the marble used for the entire area of the blind arches, whereas that used for the decoration of the rest of the façade appears to be of a different quality. This suggests that Alberti rounded off the arches in order to establish a logical connection between the earlier part of the façade and the height of the columns already too high with respect to classical canons and to the proportions of the corner pilasters. This identification of Romanesque with Roman was part of the Florentine cultural tradition, and it recurs in much of the architecture of the time, even in Brunelleschi's.

Once he had established a basic height for his design, Alberti could turn to the essential problem of the project: the incompatibility between the classical proportions to which he was instinctively inclined and those parts of the earlier church (especially their height) by which he was conditioned. The upper part of the façade in line with the nave was easily remedied by placing the rose-window at a tangent to the cornice, which partly interrupts its circumference. But the most difficult problems were connected with the lower part, where, in spite of the introduction of stylobates and the disproportionate heightening of the upper parts of the main half-columns (thirteen times their diameter including the capital, while even the upper pilasters are twelve modules), the height was still not sufficient. The architrave does not correspond to the rules laid down by Alberti in his treatise, being a seventeenth of the height of the columns instead of a thirteenth. Even after the addition of the frieze and the cornice, both as high as the architrave, the problem remained.

Alberti's solution was to adopt the obvious, yet ingenious device of an attic interposed between the lower and upper storeys of the façade. This is divided into a series of square panels and framed at both ends by the extremities of the pillars, which are decorated with coats-of-arms. These plastic reliefs also serve to check the upward thrust of the pillars. As Wittkower points out, these devices combine to re-group the general proportions of the façade into the geometrical pattern of a square. Thus it embodies classical and Renaissance ideals of proportion: "Such simple ratios were used by Alberti. The whole façade of S. Maria Novella can be exactly circumscribed by a square. A square of half the side of the large square defines the relationship of the two storeys. The

40. G. Boccaccio, *Decameron*, Day VIII, Novella IX.
41. V. Borghigiani, *Cronaca analitica del Convento di S. Maria Novella*, in M. Dezzi Bardeschi, *La facciata di S. Maria Novella*, Pisa 1969, p. 11.
42. M. Dezzi Bardeschi, op. cit., p. 13.
43. R. Wittkower, *Architectural Principles in the Age of Humanism*, London 1973.

main storey can be divided into two such squares, while one encloses the upper storey. In other words, the whole building is related to its main parts in the proportions of one to two, which is in musical terms an octave, and this proportion is repeated in the ratio of the width of the upper storey to that of the lower storey.

The same ratio of one to two recurs in the sub-units of the single storeys. The central bay of the upper storey forms a perfect square, the sides of which are equal to half the width of the whole storey. Two squares of that same size encase the pediment and upper entablature which together are thus exactly as high as the storey under them. Half the side of this square corresponds to the width of the upper side bays and is also equal to the height of the attic. The same unit defines the proportions of the entrance bay. The height of the entrance bay is one and a half times its width, so that the relation of width to height is here two to three. Finally the dark square encrustations of the attic are one third of the height of the attic, and these squares are related to the diameter of the columns as 2 : 1. Thus the whole façade is geometrically built up of a progressive duplication, or, alternatively, a progressive halving of ratios. It is clear then that Alberti's theoretical precept that the same proportion be kept throughout the building has here been fulfilled. It is the strict application of an unbroken series of ratios that marks the unmedieval character of this pseudo-proto-Renaissance façade and makes it the first great Renaissance example of classical *eurythmia*."[44]

There is no doubt that Alberti was also responsible for two other features of the façade: the central portal (a more concentrated expression of his style) and the volutes that surmount the sloping roofs of the aisles. These structures combine a fifteenth-century sharpness of outline with the deliberate preciousness of their marble inlay, which is so fragmented as to emphasise its independence of the façade's compositional scheme of orders. Thus the two elements are relegated to the function of precious accessories, and are the happy result of a policy intended "to improve what is already built and not to spoil what is yet to be done."

Alberti's real contribution to the façade must have been limited to these essential aspects, for it is difficult to imagine him, in spite of his readiness to compromise with local tradition and his sincere admiration for S. Miniato al Monte, occupying himself with the details of the inlays and of the iconographical composition they probably involved. The iconography is dominated by the name of Jesus in the pediment, where Christ is invoked on behalf of the crusade of S. Bernardino, whose fame as a preacher must certainly have resounded in what was one of Florence's oldest preaching churches. The inlays were carried out by Giovanni Bertino, who has come close to being credited with the whole façade. Expressing his praise of the "templum" of S. Maria Novella, Fra Domenico Giovanni da Corella (who was at Dicomano near Florence) wrote that Giovanni Bertini "fabricavit opus":

"Sed licet ipsa foret specie formata decenti
Equa sibi facies non tamen ante fuit
Quam proprio nunc recellarius ere Johannes
Precipuo tante matris amore calens.
Exornat tabulis vario de marmore sectis
Et frontis spatium perficit ipse novum.
Hinc populi pleno semper laudabitur ore
Et merces dabitur centupla iure sibi.
Hic quoque pre lucet bertini fama johannis
Arte sua tantum qui fabricavit opus.
Undique pomiferis complectens hostia ramis
Nudaque sub vario marmora flore tegens."[45]

This is contradicted by the testimony of another friar, Giovanni di Carlo, who, in dedicating his *Lives* of some of the friars of the monastery to Alberti's friend Landino, wrote of the façade: "opera L. B. Alberti celeberrimi architecti marmoreo tabulato et monumentorum insigni vallo contenta."[46] But Alberti's part in the design of the façade was really clarified by Vasari when he wrote: "In Leon Battista's time, meanwhile, Giovanni di Paolo Rucellai wished to build in marble, at his own expense, the principal façade of S. Maria Novella. He consulted Alberti, who was a close friend of his, and receiving not only advice but a model as well, Rucellai finally determined to have the work done as a memorial for himself."[47]

Dezzi, meanwhile, has demonstrated that Giovanni di Bertino was responsible for covering the façade with marble between 1458 and 1470.[48] He has also shown that Giovanni took part in all the major works of that period where marble was used. In 1448 he was at S. Lorenzo: "Giovanni di Bertino, stone-cutter, L. 70 for a capital carved out of stone."[49] He is mentioned in the accounts of the monastery of the Servite friars as having carried out the Cappella dell'Annunziata,[50] and he appears at S. Miniato al Monte and S. Marco; finally, in 1467, he was working on the chapel of S. Pancrazio for the Rucellai. He is also included in Rucellai's list of painters and inlay-workers who decorated his house. Giovanni di Bertino's presence in Michelozzo's circle has even given rise to the theory (for which there is no documentary

44. Ibid.

45. S. Orlandi, *Necrologio di Santa Maria Novella*, Florence 1955, p. 307.
46. G. Mancini, *Vita di L. B. Alberti*, Rome 1967, p. 461.
47. Vasari, op. cit., II, p. 541.
48. M. Dezzi Bardeschi, op. cit., pp. 18-19.
49. G. Mancini, op. cit., p. 460, n. 2.
50. Vasari, op. cit. II, p. 444, n. 5.

59-75. *Florence, Façade of Santa Maria Novella. There are two interpretations of the relationship of old to new in this work, that is of the connection between the earlier structure and Alberti's design. There is the added problem of Alberti's actual contribution to the work carried out by the "marble-cutter", Giovanni di Bertino. One interpretation emphasises the façade's "novelty" and points to the courageous inclusion of the avelli (arches) and portals in the Renaissance design, the firmness with which "classical" features have been combined with Gothic ones (in spite of the impossibility of merging them into a homogeneous style), the*

independence of the façade with respect to the main body of the church, and the new typology it inaugurated. Other considerations favour an altogether different point of view: the respect shown by the architect for the earlier structure, the harmony achieved through the use of the same marble, and the derivation of the façade's classicism from an apparent identification of Roman and Romanesque (or from a belief that the two styles were closely related). This last factor had an important bearing on the acceptance of the façade's "novelty" by the city and those who had commissioned it, for there were earlier Florentine façades of a similar style to justify

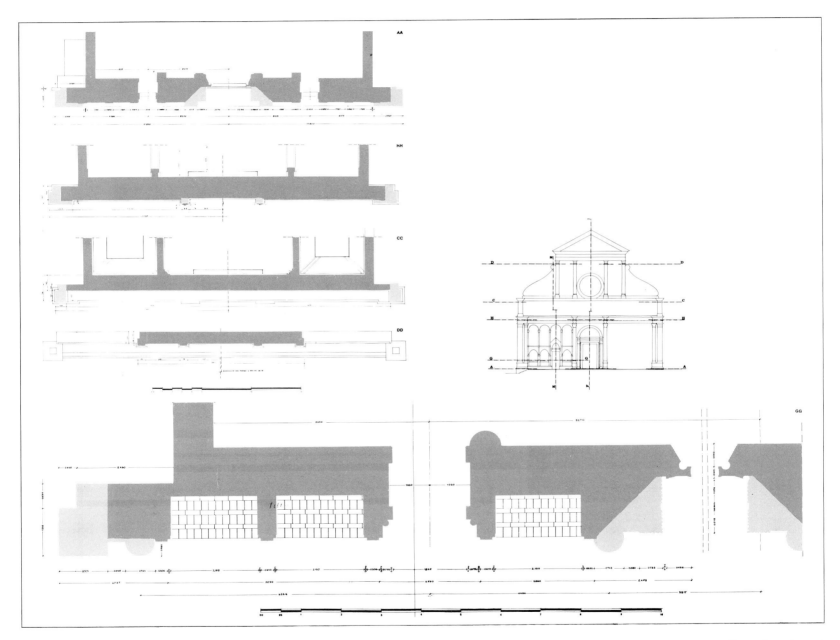

56. *Florence, S. Maria Novella. Horizontal sections of the façade at various heights (after Dezzi Bardeschi).*

57. *Marble facing of the façade of S. Maria Novella (after Dezzi Bardeschi).*

it — that of S. Miniato in particular. Alberti was wholly consistent with his principles when he drew up his plan of the façade. He was also prudent and willing enough to compromise with local taste, and much of his design is concealed by the bravura of the craftsmen who carried it out.

Both interpretations are valid, but in order to reconcile them one must pay particular attention to the structure's proportions. Only by adopting such courageous solutions as the vertical prolongation of the orders and the interruption of the circumference of the rose-window by the upper cornice of the attic was Alberti able to reduce the area of the predominantly

vertical old façade to a field of commensuration corresponding to a square, that is, to an area governed by the simple ratios of a square.

Once this grid had been established, all its single parts fell into place in a way that permitted decorative liberties, artisan preciosities, and stylistic excess.

At this point an iconological plan was drawn up. This expresses the popular taste for clear geometrical patterns elaborated in marble inlay, and it is only very remotely connected with the geometry of Alberti's design. Where the passage from the old to the new might have been more

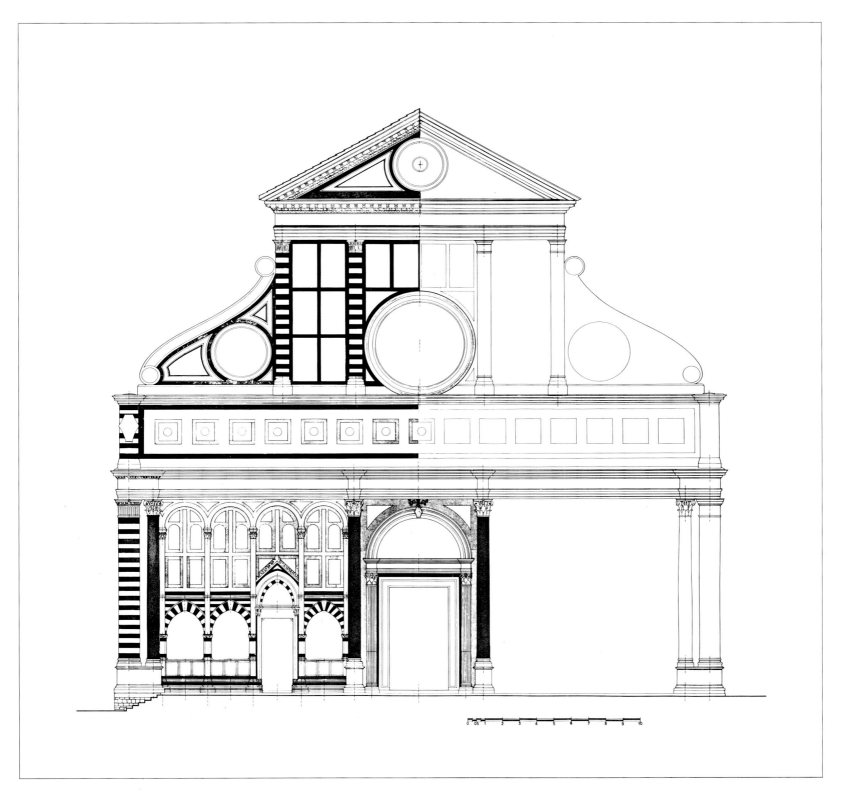

glaring, the transition was subtly effected by means of the round-headed blind arches, whose junctures allow us to attribute them to Alberti. The solemn inscriptions in the friezes of the entablatures are also typical of Alberti, both in their sense of history and graphic style. There is also the detailed embroidery of the volutes and the mythical sun of St. Bernardino's monogram in the pediment. But these are pretexts for refined design and accurate craftsmanship, and it is difficult to imagine Alberti applying himself to work of this kind.

58. Diagram illustrating the proportions of the façade of S. Maria Novella.

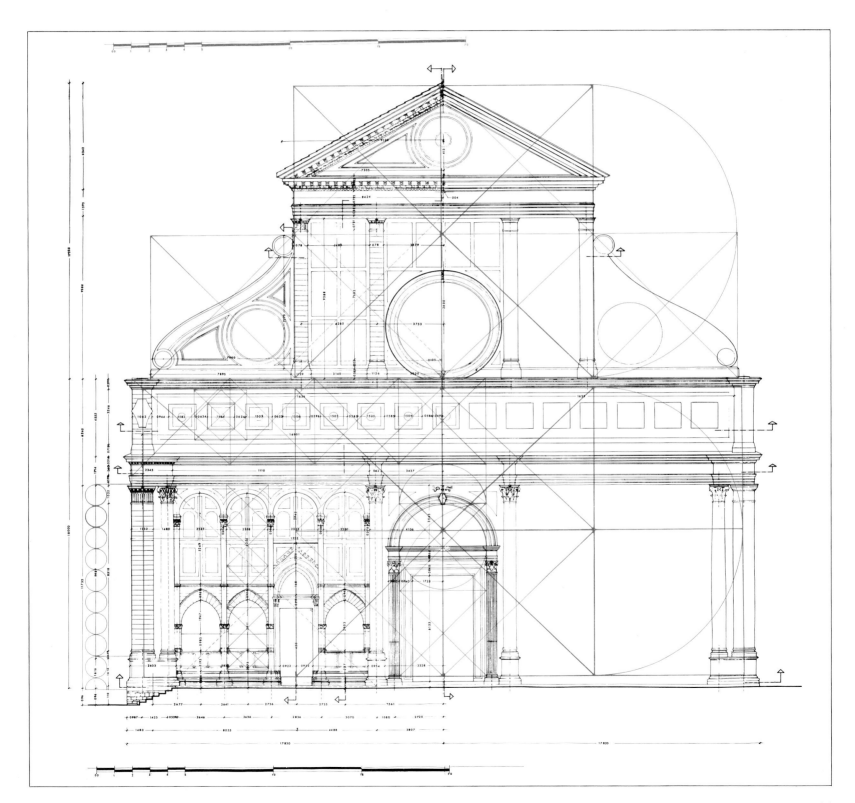

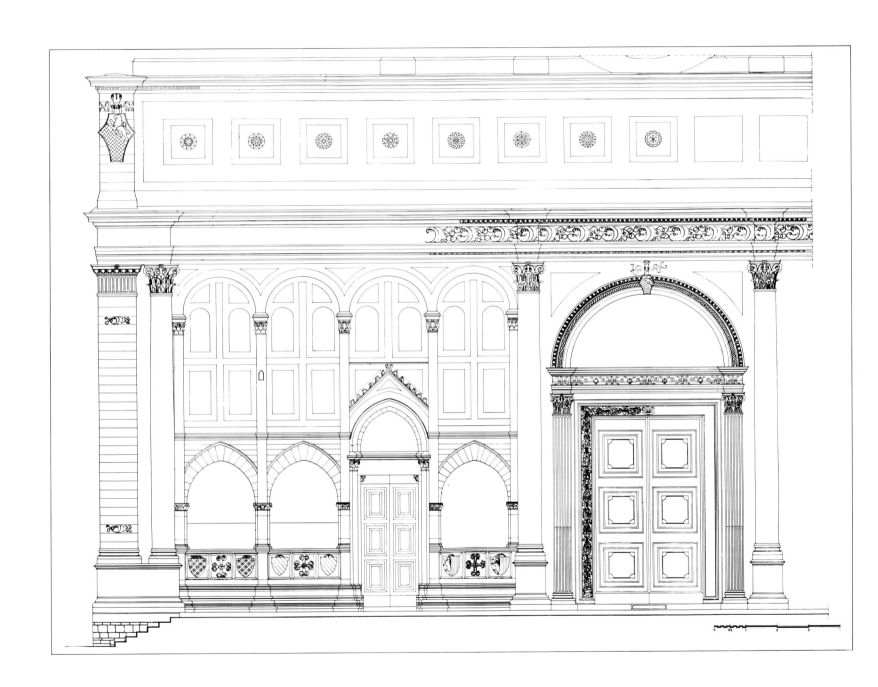

88

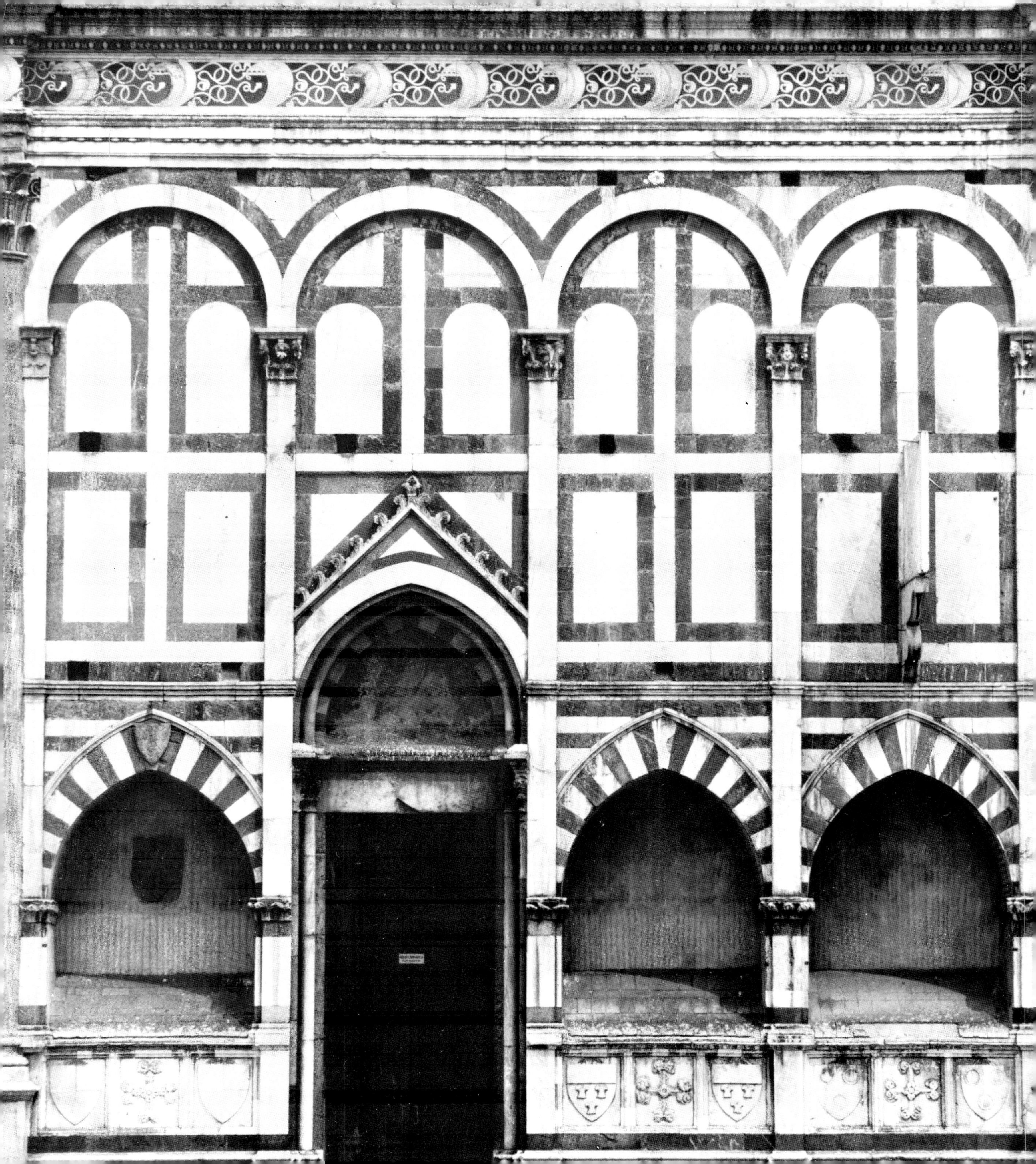

proof as yet), that Michelozzo himself may have directed the work at S. Maria Novella.[51] And if Michelozzo was too old at the time of the Annunziata, and Giovanni di Bertino was a sufficiently capable organiser and director to substitute for him, then he may well have done the same at S. Maria Novella, which only involved carrying out a plan already drawn up by Alberti.

In any case, it was Giovanni di Bertino who achieved that balance between local tradition and fifteenth-century art which did so much to dilute Alberti's intellectualistic message, while at the same time serving to introduce his ideas into the main stream of contemporary Florentine art. Alberti never went beyond a certain point in encouraging this process, nor could he have achieved it by himself, since his position as a 'civil servant' prevented him from frequenting building sites. But he must have regarded it, if not favourably, at least with detachment, given the respect local tradition enjoyed and the general readiness to compromise with it. This attitude was already emerging as the distinctive characteristic of Florentine art after the first burst of creativity had passed with Brunelleschi's generation; it was also the reason for Florence's being cut off from the cultural debate on classicism, and from the Baroque to which the latter gave birth.

THE CHAPEL OF S. PANCRAZIO

A rectangular, rather irregular hall (the height of the walls varies between 12.20 and 12.30 metres, and its width between 6.15 and 6.40 metres), with its smaller sides half the size of its larger ones, was the point of departure for Alberti's design of the Rucellai chapel. The design is interesting on account of its vaulted roof, which necessitated the raising of the main supporting-walls (as one can see on close examination)[52] and the somewhat courageous demolition of one of the longer walls of the rectangle and its replacement with two architraved columns. This idea was praised by Vasari: "For the Rucellai family Alberti also made, in a similar style, a chapel in S. Pancrazio which rests on great architraves supported by two columns and two pilasters piercing the wall of the church below; this was a difficult but sound piece of work and one of the best that Alberti ever did."[53] Both columns and architraves were later used in the early nineteenth-century, neo-Classical restoration of the façade carried out by Benini, who also added the large rose-window and the lions. D'Agincourt's study of the chapel, made in 1779, when he did his drawings of the monuments of Tuscany,[54] gives a fairly accurate idea of the original structure, whose fluid lines must have been dictated by liturgical motives and by the beautiful marble shrine it houses.

On the other hand, the formal style of its stone decorations, especially those on the inside of the arches, on the architraves with their strigilated friezes, and on the columns surmounted by Corinthian capitals, must be seen in terms of the dense, turgid style of fifteenth-century sculpture, with its distinct, yet interpenetrative light and shade. This sculpture was characterised by the restrained rhetoric one finds in the vestibule of the Cappella de' Pazzi,[55] a very common characteristic of Florentine art in this period, at least as far as stone carvings and mouldings are concerned.

Once he had settled the question of the outer shell of the chapel, Alberti proceeded to design the jewel it was to contain: the imitation of the Holy Sepulchre. The relative proportions of the shell and its content have been analysed in detail by Bruschi and Dezzi, who have found them to be 'golden', especially those regarding the elevation. There is no mention of such proportions in the treatise, where Alberti is more concerned with eliminating the irrational and calculating approximate values on the basis of round figures.[56] The outstanding inventiveness of the project is confirmed not only by Vasari, but also by the fact that the scaffolding used to construct the shrine is even mentioned by Richa in the seventeenth century: "And after Giovanni had obtained the exact measurements of the Holy Sepulchre in Jerusalem, he got Leon Battista Alberti, a very famous architect, to draw up a design of the exterior decorations.

Alberti then built a device fifteen feet high and five feet wide, after he had decided to follow the dangerous course of making various holes in the ceiling of the church below."[57] Richa gives the measurements of the tomb as being "six feet wide, nearly ten feet long, and nine feet high from the centre of the vault to the floor,"[58] which indicates that the scaffolding he refers to was that used for putting the marble blocks of the shrine in place with the help of winches. Once the right scaffolding had been designed, work on the tomb could begin. There is no documentary evidence on the subject, but the tomb's striking resemblance to S. Maria Novella (one need only consider the rosettes) points to Giovanni di Bertino as the author (see Paatz, Stegmann-Geymüller, Dezzi). Richa writes: "The tomb consists entirely of different coloured marble divided into panels by grooved pilasters, between which are rosettes and vague symbolic patterns. A frieze runs round the top, and it is surmounted by a cornice and a crown of lilies. The frieze contains these letters:
YHESUM QUERITIS NAZARENUM CRUCIFIXUM.
SURREXIT NON EST HIC. ECCE LOCUS UBI
POSUERUNT EUM."[59]

51. M. Dezzi Bardeschi, op. cit., p. 19.
52. M. Dezzi Bardeschi, *Il complesso monumentale di San Pancrazio e il suo restauro*, in "Quaderni dell'Istituto di Storia dell'Architettura", XIII, 73-79, Rome 1967, p. 19 ff.
53. Vasari, op. cit., II, p. 543.
54. G. B. L. G. Seroux D'Agincourt, *Storia dell'Arte*, Prato 1826, I, p. 17.
55. M. Dezzi Bardeschi, op. cit., p. 24.
56. Ibid., p. 21.
57. G. Richa, *Notizie istoriche delle Chiese fiorentine*, Florence 1755, Pt. I, p. 314.
58. Ibid., p. 315.
59. G. Richa, op. cit., p. 314.

"Above the little door that provides access to the tomb on its west side is the inscription:

JOHANNES RUCELLARIUS PAULI FIL. UT INDE SALUTEM SUAM PRECARETUR UNDE OMNIUM CUM CHRISTO FACTA EST RESURECTIO SACELLUM HOC AD INSTAR IHEROSOLIMITANI SEPULCHRI FACIUNDUM CURAVIT MCCCCLXVII."[60]

The object of paying homage both to the family tomb and to that of Christ was enhanced by the papal indulgence. The entire project was realized through the Money-lenders Guild, of which Rucellai had been a member, and to which he left a number of farms on condition that "the said Consul visit the chapel every year in procession on the Sunday after the feast of Saint Pancras."[61] Richa describes the ceremony: "On the Saturday prior to the Sunday, written invitations were sent out to all the members of the guild and to relatives and friends of the Rucellai family. On the following morning everyone gathered in the hall of the guild and then proceeded in procession to Or San Michele, where the image of Mary was uncovered and worshipped for six minutes. The procession then continued on its way to S. Pancrazio, where the four Consuls were immediately followed by the members of the Rucellai family, of which there were sometimes as many as eighteen couples. After reaching the chapel and receiving the usual honours paid them by the monks, they all attended mass in the chapel of the Holy Sepulchre, holding lighted candles in their hands. After this, they made their offerings at the high altar, receiving a little bunch of flowers from the monks in return."[62] Setting aside the questions regarding the nature of the information Rucellai's men brought back from Jerusalem and the appearance of the Holy Sepulchre in the fifteenth century (it was constantly being altered right up to the nineteenth century), it may be affirmed that the chapel was principally modelled on S. Costanza and S. Stefano. The first was the mausoleum built by Constantine's family to receive the body of Christ; the second was an Eastern Roman construction,[63] whose measurements accorded very closely with those of the Holy Sepulchre. Alberti knew both of these Roman buildings well, and was personally involved in the restoration of the second. It is not known, however, whether he was aware of the similarity in the proportions of the two structures or whether, according to legendary tradition, it was he who suggested the idea of checking the measurements of the Holy Sepulchre on the spot. Further evidence that the chapel was inspired by models derived from the Holy Sepulchre is Alberti's knowledge of the church of S. Stefano in Bologna, where he had been a student.

60. Ibid., pp. 314-315.

61. Ibid., p. 315.

62. Ibid., pp. 315-316.

63. R. Krautheimer, *S. Stefano Rotondo a Roma e la Chiesa del S. Sepolcro, Gerusalemme*, in "Rivista di Archeologia Cristiana", Rome XII, 1935, p. 85 ff. See also L. H. Heydenreich, *Die Capella Rucellai von San Pancrazio in Florenz*, in "De Artibus opuscula XL: Essays in honour of E. Panofsky", ed. by M. Meiss, New York 1961, pp. 219-229.

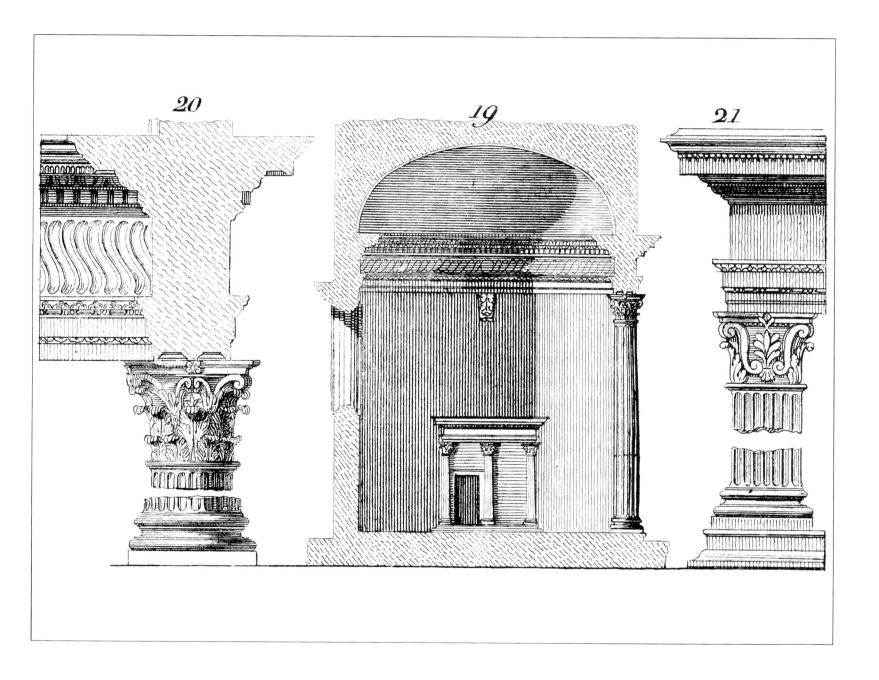

77. *Details of S. Pancrazio in Florence from an engraving by D'Agin-court.*

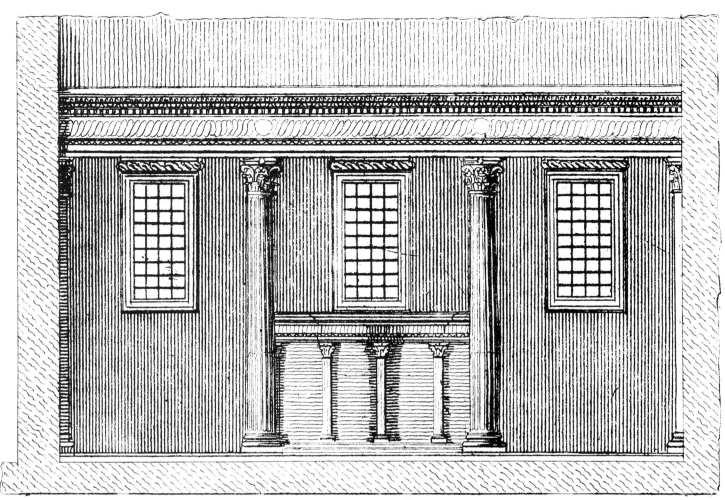

18

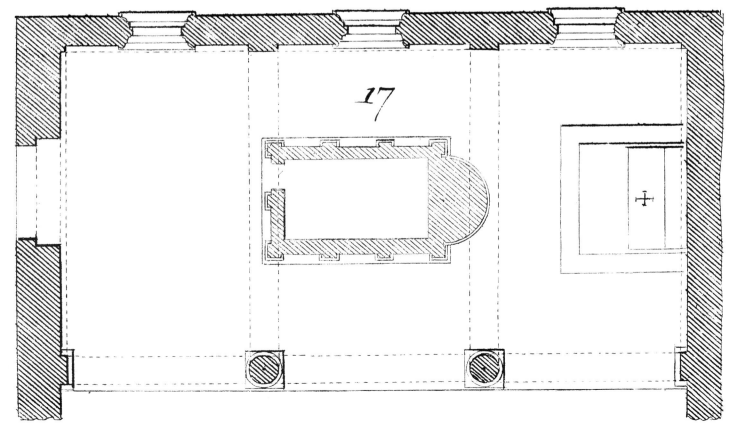

17

This was a sixth-century church that had been rebuilt in the twelfth with an ambulatory and a small central shrine supported by columns, known as the tomb of S. Petronio, or S. Sepolcro. In any event, the Rucellai tomb is no pedestrian imitation of the Holy Sepulchre. Alberti had never been to Jerusalem, nor did his *forma mentis* incline him to mere imitation. However, certain features of the original that had been recorded by eye-witnesses were actually adopted in the construction of the new tomb: the division of the sides into four sections, the high-domed ciborium, and the proportional ratios (it seems that the measurements are half those of the original). But the most important feature is Alberti's transformation of the medieval, oriental style of the original edifice in accordance with the classical canons that were more congenial to him.

Dezzi remarks that the astonishing thing about Alberti's shrine is the effective expressiveness of the structure, which derives from the creation of a deliberate contrast between the uncompromising, Cartesian rationality of its design and the freedom of its decorations. The fantastic exuberance of the coloured patterns that fill the circles in the centre of the square panels of white marble has its roots in a thorough assimilation of the Tuscan-Romanesque tradition. Here, the study of the inlays of the façade of S. Miniato, of the abbey of Fiesole, and of the cathedral of Pisa, has combined with classical Humanism to produce an indirect kind of creative art.[64]

This must have corresponded to Alberti's own wishes, and cannot be attributed to the men who carried out his design, for he urges: "In all our mosaics we should avoid using the same colours and patterns too frequently, too rigidly or too freely. One should avoid leaving gaps in the mosaic, for all the parts should be fitted and connected with the greatest precision, in such a way that the work is perfect in all its parts."[65] After demonstrating a thorough grasp of the techniques involved in cutting, polishing, and putting strips or pieces of marble together by means of gluey substances made of wax, pitch and resin, he adds: "In putting the pieces together you should arrange them in a way that is harmonious and pleasing to the eye. The stones must be in harmony with each other, the colours also; and you should be careful to contrast different colours, so that one sets off the other."[66]

His ideal of harmony is particularly evident in the little apse. Here he has avoided using pilasters, which would have created problems in following the curve of the wall, making it more difficult to connect the architrave with the rest of the structure.

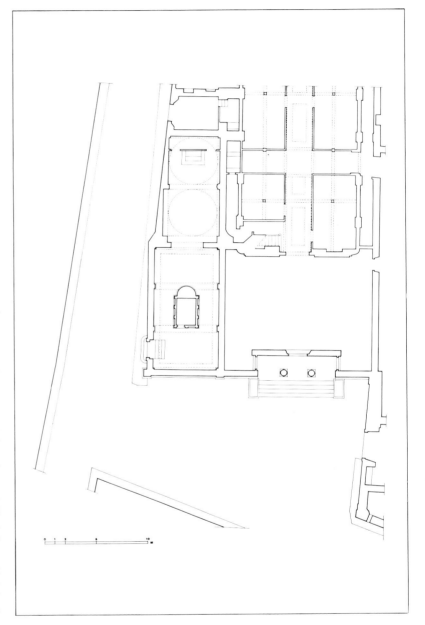

64. M. Dezzi Bardeschi, op. cit., p. 25.
65. L. B. Alberti, op. cit., VI, 10, p. 510.
66. Ibid., p. 506.

80-129. Florence, Cappella Rucellai in S. Pancrazio. In carrying out the most ambitious part of Giovanni Rucellai's building programme — the construction of his tomb in the form of the Holy Sepulchre — Alberti realized one of his finest achievements. He devised a purely architectural solution for a problem that would normally have required the highly skilled craftsmanship that lay half-way between sculpture and architecture (but which was more sculptural than architectural) of which the Rossellinos were masters. His recourse to the collaboration of Giovanni di Bertino confirms his penchant for the "geometry" of inlay-work. Much of the inlay of the tomb is either similar to, or repeats, decorative patterns that embellish the façade of S. Maria Novella. (This predilection also marks the point beyond which he refused to comply with the demands of local tradition and his patron's wishes). Though many details of the work lie hidden beneath later restoration, one can still follow the interplay of its horizontal and vertical lines, and perceive how these "variations" co-exist with the fixity of the shrine's geometrical design. The shrine is bound to the structure that contains it by the geometrical division of the pavement, to which it is also connected by complex and obscure proportional

80. Front of S. Pancrazio with Alberti's columns and frieze (present state).

ratios. It seems improbable that after elaborating a system of simple ratios in his treatise and experimenting with them in his works, Alberti then fell back upon irrational ones.

However, there does seem to be a kind of **concordia discors** between the marble work of the accurately proportioned tomb (which reproduces the characteristic features of its revered model in Jerusalem) and the stone work of the chapel, where Alberti's treatment of space cannot be assessed in any way, since the wall facing the entrance has been closed and its columns and frieze incorporated in the façade of the church.

The ovuli, mouldings, and the decorative reliefs of the façade are in the skilful, but conventional, turgid style of the Florentine Quattrocento — the Cappella dei Pazzi was completed in a similar fashion — which was fundamentally alien to Alberti's spirit. Justified as an essential part of Brunelleschi's heritage, this style was the expression of a local humus and later formed the basis for the rejection of Alberti's Romanitas.

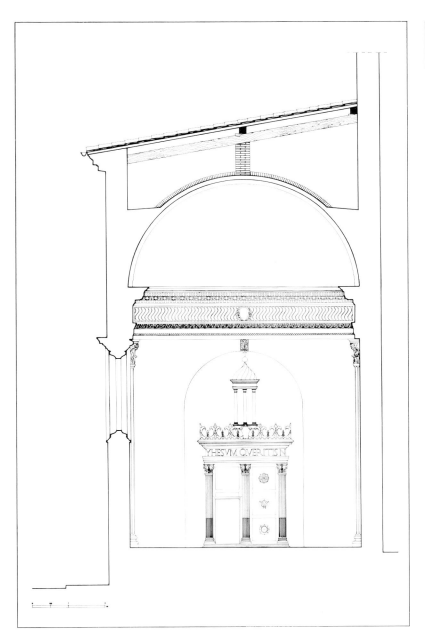

81. *Transverse section of the Cappella Rucellai.*

82. *Cappella Rucellai, plan.*

Instead, he has introduced two simple strips of white marble (of the same width as the pilasters) into the panels divided into squares. The skilful division of the floor anchors the shrine to the space it occupies, while the delicate but pronounced frieze of lilies surmounting the cornice, though typically Florentine, conveys a hint of that interest in the east which was an aspect of the cultural atmosphere of the time. This last quality gave the whole project its significance from the point of view of the prestige of the man who commissioned it.

The inscription, its Roman letters finely carved in marble, is extremely important. The letters are 16.8 cm. high, the same height as those in the inscriptions of Cæcilia Metella in Rome and of the Porta dei Leoni in Verona, two of the most classic examples of the lapidary letters of antiquity.[67] Alberti's letters are slightly narrower than those of ancient Rome (the ratio of width to height is 1 : 12 rather than 1 : 10). But his attempt to vary the width of the letters, the so-called "graces", never strays beyond the limits inherent in the technique of inlay-work, which excludes anything too narrow or sharply angled. He also revived the use of the Roman capital, theorized later by Pacioli in his *Divina proportione*. ("I was a guest of our fellow citizen Leon Battista Alberti for many months in his house in our beloved Rome in the time of Pope Paul, and he always treated me well. He was undoubtedly a man of very great intelligence and learning in the humanities and rhetoric.")[68] Alberti's love of inscriptions, which he urged Pacioli to rationalise by tracing proportional diagrams based on the fundamental forms of the circle and square, was born of his familiarity with those of antiquity. (The same love is expressed in Giuliano da Sangallo's notebooks, particularly in the thirteenth table of the "Sienese Notebook", where the "graces" of carved inscriptions become so refined as to look like punctuation marks, radiolaria, or mono-cellular bodies; some even seem to anticipate the refinements of art nouveau.)

Inscriptions are to be found in all Alberti's works; at S. Maria Novella, where the letters had to be slightly larger (a 1 : 10.5 ratio) because of their height and distance from the observer, and in the Tempio Malatestiano, where the inscription in the frieze of the façade differs from those inside the church on account of its barely suggested, tightly controlled "graces". If one considers for how long Roman inscriptions continued to be used in Florentine Romanesque architecture,[69] one may consider them as yet another element in the continuation of the Roman-Romanesque tradition and in that Renaissance fusion of the Romanesque and classicism which was Alberti's goal, and which

finds one of its finest expressions in S. Pancrazio. It is not surprising, therefore, that Alberti should have made a study of the stylistic and proportional aspects of inscriptions or that he should so frequently urge their use in churches to eliminate pictorial decoration and promote "philosophical wisdom."

In writing of inscriptions on the pediments of classical temples, he says: "It used to be the custom in our country to inscribe on chapels the date of consecration and the name of the person to whom they were dedicated. In my opinion, such a custom ought to be approved unconditionally."[70] Elsewhere he writes: "For our part, we consider written maxims to be fitting, their purpose being to make men more just, moderate, thrifty, virtuous, and more acceptable to God. For example, ones like 'be as you would like to appear' or 'love and you will be loved', and others of the same kind. Above all, the whole pavement should be taken up with lines and figures pertaining to music and geometry so that the minds of all present may be drawn towards culture."[71] The declaration that "the most suitable material for the interior decoration of a covered space is marble or glass in the form of strips or inlay"[72] is further confirmation that S. Pancrazio was one of the few works to receive Alberti's constant personal attention.

67. On this subject, see G. Mardersteig, *L. B. Alberti e la rinascita del carattere lapidario romano nel '400*, in "Italia medievale-umanistica", 1959, II, pp. 285-307.

68. L. Pacioli, *Divina proportione*, Venice 1509, Pt. I, 8, c. 29v.

69. P. Sanpaolesi, *Sulla cronologia dell'architettura Romanica fiorentina*, in "Studi di Storia dell'Arte in onore di Valerio Mariani", Naples 1972.

70. L. B. Alberti, op. cit., VIII, 6, p. 694.

71. Ibid., VII, 10, p. 610.

72. Ibid., p. 608.

94. *Shrine of the Holy Sepulchre, left side.*
95-103. *Shrine of the Holy Sepulchre, marble inlays on the left side.*

IOHANNES RVCELLARIVS
PAVLI·F· VTINDE SALVTEM SVAM
PRECARETVR VNDE OMNIVM CVM
CHRISTO FACTA EST RESVRECTIO
SACELLVM HOC
ADĪSTAR IHEROSOLIMITANI SEPVL
CHRI FACIVNDVM CVRAVIT
MCCCCLXVII

121-124. *Florence, Chapel of S. Pancrazio, details of the frieze.*

125. *Chapel of S. Pancrazio, the ceiling.*
126. *Chapel of S. Pancrazio, the entablature and cornice above the window.*
127. *Chapel of S. Pancrazio, detail of the order.*

128. *Chapel of S. Pancrazio, detail of the frieze.*
129. *Chapel of S. Pancrazio, detail of corner.*

130. Sigismondo Pandolfo Malatesta, detail of a medal by Pisanello. Florence, Museo del Bargello.

131. Sigismondo Pandolfo Malatesta, detail of a medal by Pisanello. Brescia, Museo Cristiano.

SIGISMONDO AND THE TEMPLE OF RIMINI

The very name of the Tempio Malatestiano is symbolic of a concept of architecture that bound architect and patron together. The church, formerly dedicated to St. Francis, was called a temple and rebuilt to celebrate the deeds and splendour of a "new prince". This was a new phenomenon, and one that reflected both the classical origins of Alberti's culture (wherein temple and church were synonymous) and the concept of the patron as the central figure in all architectural enterprises. Hence the ambiguity of the building, which has been regarded as both sacred and pagan ever since, a quality that also struck Von Pastor as being "strange".

The first to pronounce this judgement was Pius II, Aeneas Sylvius Piccolomini, the Humanist Pope who defeated the intrepid Sigismondo Malatesta. After referring to the wickedness of the man, to his hatred of priests and his disbelief in the immortality of the soul, Piccolomini adds: "aedificavit tamen nobile templum a Rimini in honorem Divi Francisci verum ita gentilibus operibus implevit ut non tam cristianorum quam infidelium daemones adorantium templum esse videretur, atque in eo concubinae suae tumulum erexit et artificio et lapide pulcherrimum adiecto titulo gentili mori in hunc modum: Divae Isottae sacrum."[1]

Pius's praise of the temple's nobility was probably motivated by his esteem for Alberti. Nevertheless, he raised the critical problem of the relationship between the building's interior and its exterior, besides pointing out the ambiguity of the *domina-diva* in the inscription of Isotta's tomb. As for Sigismondo, there is no more hostile portrait than that drawn by Pius II, his Pope and enemy: "Sigismondo Malatesta was an illegitimate member of the noble family of the Malatestas, and had a great spirit and a powerful body. He was an eloquent and skilful captain. He had studied history and had more than an amateur's knowledge of philosophy. He seemed born to do whatever he put his hand to. But he was so ruled by his passions, and abandoned himself to such an uncontrollable greed for money, that he became a plunderer and a thief to boot. He was so dissolute that he raped his daughters and sons-in-law. When a boy, he often acted as the female partner in shameful loves, and later forced men to act as women. He had no respect for the sanctity of marriage. He raped virgins who had vowed themselves to God as well as jewesses, killed young girls, and had young boys who rebelled against his will brutally whipped. He committed adultery with many women whose children he had held at baptism, and murdered their husbands. His cruelty was greater than any barbarian's, and he inflicted fearful tortures on guilty and innocent alike with his own bloody hands. He

1. E. Garin, *Pio II*, in "Storia della Letteratura Italiana", Milan 1965, III, p. 194.

rarely told the truth, was a master of pretence and dissimulation, a traitor and a perjurer who never kept his word. ... When his subjects finally beseeched him to pursue a policy of peace and to have pity on a country that was constantly exposed to pillage for his sake, he replied: "Go, be of good cheer, for you will never have peace as long as I live". This was Sigismondo, a restless, sensual man and a tireless warmonger, one of the worst men that have ever lived or will live, the shame of Italy and the disgrace of our generation."[2]

The tone of the hagiographic Greek inscription on the first side pillar of the church, attributed to Basinio of Parma, is not very different: "Sigismondo Pandolfo Malatesta, the son of Pandolfo — having survived many grievous dangers in the Italic war — a bringer of victory — in thanksgiving for the deeds he performed with valour and fortune, to God the Everlasting and to the city has dedicated this temple — having in his magnanimity built it at his own expense — leaving a noble, holy monument."[3] This echoes more than one Albertian theme, from the reference to valour and fortune to that of the temple dedicated to God and the city, which reappears in the *De re aedificatoria*: "No work of architecture requires greater thought, attention, and precision than does the construction and decoration of a temple. For it is unnecessary to remind you that a well-built, finely decorated temple is the greatest and noblest ornament a city can have."[4] As one can see, the adjective 'noble' occurs in Piccolomini, Alberti, and in Basinio's commemorative plaque.

Pius II's severe condemnation was not provoked by any rejection of Humanism on the part of Sigismondo. The man who commissioned the Castel Sismondo had a fair smattering of Humanist culture; indeed, this constitutes one of the most suggestive elements of the Tempio. Castel Sismondo was an engine of war that reflected the ideals of the adventurous, courtly, neofeudal, late Gothic knight who built it. Sigismondo's Humanism, on the other hand, is reflected in his idea of death, which he saw as a drawing together of the privileged court of the learned, including Basinio, the poet who had sung Isotta's praises, and the philosopher Gemistos Plethon, whose remains Sigismondo brought back as a trophy of war from the campaign in the Morea so that they might be buried near his own in San Francesco. Documentary evidence and the remains of the walls of the chapels prove that the church had every right to be called Malatestiano, for all the Malatestas, beginning with Malatesta da Verucchio, the founder of the family, had been buried either in the church or in the monastery.[5]

Sigismondo's transformation of the church of S. Francesco went through three phases, which corresponded to three distinct stages in his cultural formation and in the development of his political ambitions. At first he was just a local warlord with the idea of building a chapel. In 1447 Nicholas V issued a bull authorising Isotta to restore the Cappella degli Angeli, at a time when Sigismondo was thinking of dedicating a chapel to his patron saint. A year later, Sigismondo received Isotta's promised dowry, and on 7 April 1449 he wrote from the Venetian camp at Cremona to Giovanni de' Medici in Florence, asking for a "master painter, though the chapels are still fresh and cannot be painted at the moment, since it would be a waste of time. After he has painted these chapels, I shall want him to paint other things, such as will give both him and me great pleasure ... and since you write that you need money, it is my intention to draw up an agreement with him, whereby he shall receive so much a year as shall give him security, wherever he wishes to be paid what is promised him."[6] We do not know whether the painter was Filippo Lippi or Gentile da Fabriano, but the idea of pictorial decoration was eventually abandoned. When Piero della Francesca arrived in Rimini about 1450, he only did the frescoes in the sacristy and his famous portrait of Sigismondo. (This is particularly surprising when one considers that Piero had already reached his maturity and was associated with Alberti, the nightly vigils at Urbino, and the art circles of Ferrara.) In Piero's painting, the kneeling Sigismondo "adores his good-natured, naturally portrayed patron, Sigismund, the saint-king, with a cool self-confidence, and, to the great scandal of the Romantic, pietistic art historians, accompanied by his greyhounds. He is even covered from behind by the threatening military architecture of the Castellum Sismundum Ariminense."[7] But something must have happened to lead Sigismondo to prefer sculpture to frescoes as the principal means for decorating his temple.

Alberti later wrote. "It seems to me that the great gods love purity and simplicity in colour just as they love them in life."[8] He continues: "In my opinion, paintings on wooden panels are preferable to frescoes on the walls of temples, but I would prefer reliefs even more."[9] A selection of such paintings can be found at Pienza, protected from the common people's superstitious love of *ex voto* plaques by a severe bull of Pius II. Alberti is not altogether clear about the nature of the reliefs he mentions. On the one hand he affirms that "everything on the floors and walls of the temple should inspire philosophical wisdom."[10] (Nor does it seem that the latter can only be inspired by inscriptions.) On

2. Pius II, *I Commentarii*, Siena 1972, I, pp. 186-187.

3. I. Pasini, *Il Tempio Malatestiano*, Exhibition catalogue, "Sigismondo Malatesta e il suo tempo", Rimini 1970, p. 134.

4. L. B. Alberti, *L'Architettura*, Milano 1966, VII, p. 542.

5. C. Ricci, *Il tempio malatestiano*, Milan 1925, pp. 166-199. See also, for an analytical reconstruction of the evidence, A. Campana, *Per la storia delle cappelle trecentesche della chiesa malatestiana di San Francesco*, in "Studi Romagnoli", 1951, II.

6. G. Gaye, *Carteggio inedito d'artisti*, Florence 1839, I, p. 159.

7. R. Longhi, *Piero della Francesca*, Rome (n.d.), p. 119.

8. L. B. Alberti, op. cit., p. 608.

9. Ibid.

10. Ibid., p. 610.

the other, he adds: "Nor is it fitting that there be objects in the temple capable of distracting the minds of the faithful from religious thoughts with their charms and allurements." (This seems to be the opposite of what happens in the Tempio Malatestiano.) Alberti insists that "that man is right who affirms that the roof, walls and floor of a temple ought to be decorated with artistic, elegant, and above all enduring ornaments, provided these be austere as well."[11] "Therefore, the best interior decoration for a covered space should be of marble, glass, mosaic, or inlay-work. As for the outside, the ancients' custom of decorating their buildings with stucco reliefs is preferable. In both cases it should be seen that the pictures and reliefs are placed in the right position."[12] In addition to the general rules formulated in the treatise, there are direct references to his own work: "There is a kind of chalk near Rimini, which is so compact that it looks like marble or alabaster. With the help of a saw, I cut some very fine leaf patterns out of it, which I used to decorate the walls."[13] And concerning statuary: "Others were of the opinion that statues ought to be raised in public places of worship of those who had benefited mankind, and whose memory they held to be as worthy of veneration as that of the gods, so that posterity in worshipping them might be moved to imitate their virtue."[14]

It is not known when Alberti appeared on the scene at Rimini; his arrival is not connected with any particular event. However, the passages suggest that Matteo dei Pasti and Agostino di Duccio were chosen to carry out the decorations through his influence. Matteo's medals date from 1446, but the documentary evidence concerning him precedes Sigismondo's letter to Giovanni de' Medici. In June 1449 Matteo made out a letter of attorney for the sale of a house in Verona, and in August 1449 he received a farm together with a sum of money as part of his wife's dowry. He is described as "Concivis hornatissimus meus, qui a Rimini inter priores apud Sigismundum Malatestam habetur."[15] In another document he is referred to as "Aulico del Magnifico Signore", while the Florentine sculptor Masaccio di Bartolomeo calls him "Sigismondo's companion" in his memoirs.

Matteo dei Pasti must have felt free to carry on his own activity as an architect in this period, for he drew up a completely new organic architectural design for Sigismondo, besides the pictorial one he had been asked to do. This is confirmed not only by the inscription discovered by Ricci — "MATTHEI VS. D.P. (Veronesis de Pastis) ILLUSTRIS · ARIMINI · DOMINI · NOBILISS · ARCHITECTI OPUS"[16] — but above all by the fact that the Romanesque oculus of the façade is nearly half a metre out

of line with Alberti's portal. This indicates that the whole of the nave was enlarged and that the entire outer wall to the left (looking at the façade) was demolished and rebuilt.[17] Thus, working along essentially Gothic lines, Pasti carried out a radical transformation of the earlier structure which consisted of five funerary chapels of different sizes with walls of varying thickness. This is confirmed by the regular measurements of the two coupled chapels, which are narrower than the first two adjacent to the façade. The result is an abcc(ba) scheme, in which the last two (hypothetical) terms were to have re-established the symmetry of the inner front of the nave. (These alterations led to the destruction of the tombs of many of Sigismondo's ancestors.)[18]

The iconological plan of the sculptural decorations of the chapels is a homogeneous one and has a number of points in common with the text of Basinio's *Liber Isotteus*, where the poet writes of the inseparability of love and death. This is precisely the main theme of the decorations in the Tempio Malatestiano: "Corpore frigida mors moribunda per obsoluto regnat at in gelido pectore fervet amor."[19] Basinio also includes a laudatory description of the temple:

"Hinc ad Arimineam fertur laetissimus Urbem
Victor ubi Superis votum dum solvit honorem
Ipse Deo reddens summo mirabile templum
marmore de Pario construxit et Urbe locavit
in media, quod dura Jovis non ulla moverent
fulmina, non Saevos queis dejicit ille Gigantas.
Porta aeterna ingens nigro durissima saxo
Vestibulo posita est *pulchro* quam candida circum
quatuor in caelum Capita arrexere columnae
Candida praeterea muri latera undique magni;
Sex intus late Signis fulgentibus Aedes
Hinc, atque hinc pulchra testudine ad aethera missae
Marmora tum partim fulvo conduntur in auro,
ostentant nudas partim sua signa figuras.
Parte alia ingenti surgit testudine templum
Aetheris in morem, magnumque imitatus Olimpum
Ille labor manuum *Signisque ingentibus altum*
ardet opus, fulgentque poli viventia monstra."[20]

Such was the Platonic atmosphere of the court of Rimini, which forms a strange contrast with the violence and aggressiveness of Malatesta himself. However, it explains his lack of moral inhibitions and suggests the philosophical origins of an attitude that saw no contradiction between the holy and the pagan. This contradiction has attracted the attention of many pious critics,

11. Ibid., p. 608.
12. Ibid.
13. Ibid., II, 2, p. 154. Cf. also Pasini, *Il Tempio Malatestiano*, p. 131.
14. L. B. Alberti, op. cit., VII, p. 658.
15. G. Grigioni, *I Costruttori del Tempio Malatestiano in Rimini*, in "Rassegna bibliografica dell'arte italiana", Ascoli Piceno 1908, II, 7-8, p. 121.
16. A. Campana, op. cit., p. 18.
17. G. Ravaioli, *La facciata romanica del S. Francesco di Rimini sotto i marmi albertiani*, in "Studi Romagnoli", 1950, I.
18. A. Campana, op. cit., p. 37.
19. E. Garin, op. cit., p. 288.
20. G. Del Piano, *L'enigma filosofico del Tempio Malatestiano*, Forlì 1928, p. 14.

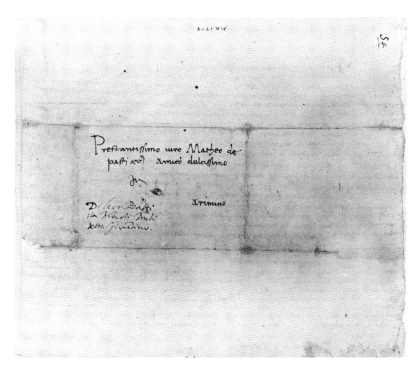

but for Malatesta and his court it was resolved in the Idea as form, and in the forms of the Idea that lay beyond sensory phenomena. In the words of Garin: "The taste for mythological preciosities, often connected with astrology, became more marked; the personal allusions, the use of symbolism, and the artificial compositions increasingly obscure. Natural magic tended to assume the thoroughness of a science, while the ambiguity that had its roots in a certain kind of literary occultism grew in popularity. There is complacency in the increasingly courtly praise of noblemen, and in the recourse to pagan gods. This last is sometimes expressed in subtly ambiguous ways, and at others quite openly."[21]

Valturius attributes the decorations of the interior of the temple to Sigismondo himself: "amplissimis praesertim parietibus, permultisque altissimis arcubus, peregrino marmore exedificatis, quibus lapideae tabulae vestiuntur, quibus pulcherrime sculptae inspiciuntur, unaque sanctorum patrum, virtutum quatuor, ac caelestis zodiaci signorum, errantiumque syderum, sibyllarum deinde musarumque et aliarum permultarum nobilium rerum imagines, quae nedum praeclaro lapicidae ac sculptoris artificio, sed etiam cognitione formarum, liniamentis abs te acutissimo et sine ulla dubitatione clarissimo huius seculi principe ex abditis philosophiae penetralibus sumptis, intuentes literarum peritos, et a vulgo fere penitus alienos, maxime possint allicere."[22] It is difficult to say whether this is courtly homage or historical fact. Sigismondo apparently liked to think of himself as being descended from the Scipios. (Paul II later asked him: "How could you ever appeal to the most illustrious, worthy house of the Scipios, good Romans all, who never did anything to taint their honour?"[23]) The commentaries of the *Somnium Scipionis* were written by Macrobius: they contained Pythagorean and Platonic ideas on death and immortality, described sun-worship, and emphasized the efficacy of the constellation of Cancer. Thus the reference to sun-worship in the inscription that runs round the Chapel of St. Sigismund may not be just a coincidence: "SANCTE DICATA TIBI HAEC AEDES ET CONDITA SOLI."[24] Sigismondo himself is the sun, "dux et moderator luminum reliquorum." The *Somnium Scipionis* also says: "Omnibus qui patriam conservaverint adiuverint auxerint certum esse in caelo definitum locum ubi beati aevo sempiterno fruantur."[25] This was precisely the kind of paradise for heroes that Sigismondo believed in — and the reason why Pius II rebuked him for his faith, or lack of it. It certainly helps us to understand the chapels in the Tempio Malatestiano.

The Cappella dei Pianeti is decorated with the signs of the zodiac

21. E. Garin, op. cit., p. 287.
22. R. Valturio, *De re militari*, XII, 13.
23. C. Mitchell, *The Imagery of the Tempio Malatestiano*, in "Studi Romagnoli", 1951, II, p. 77.
24. Ibid., p. 83.
25. Ibid., p. 84.

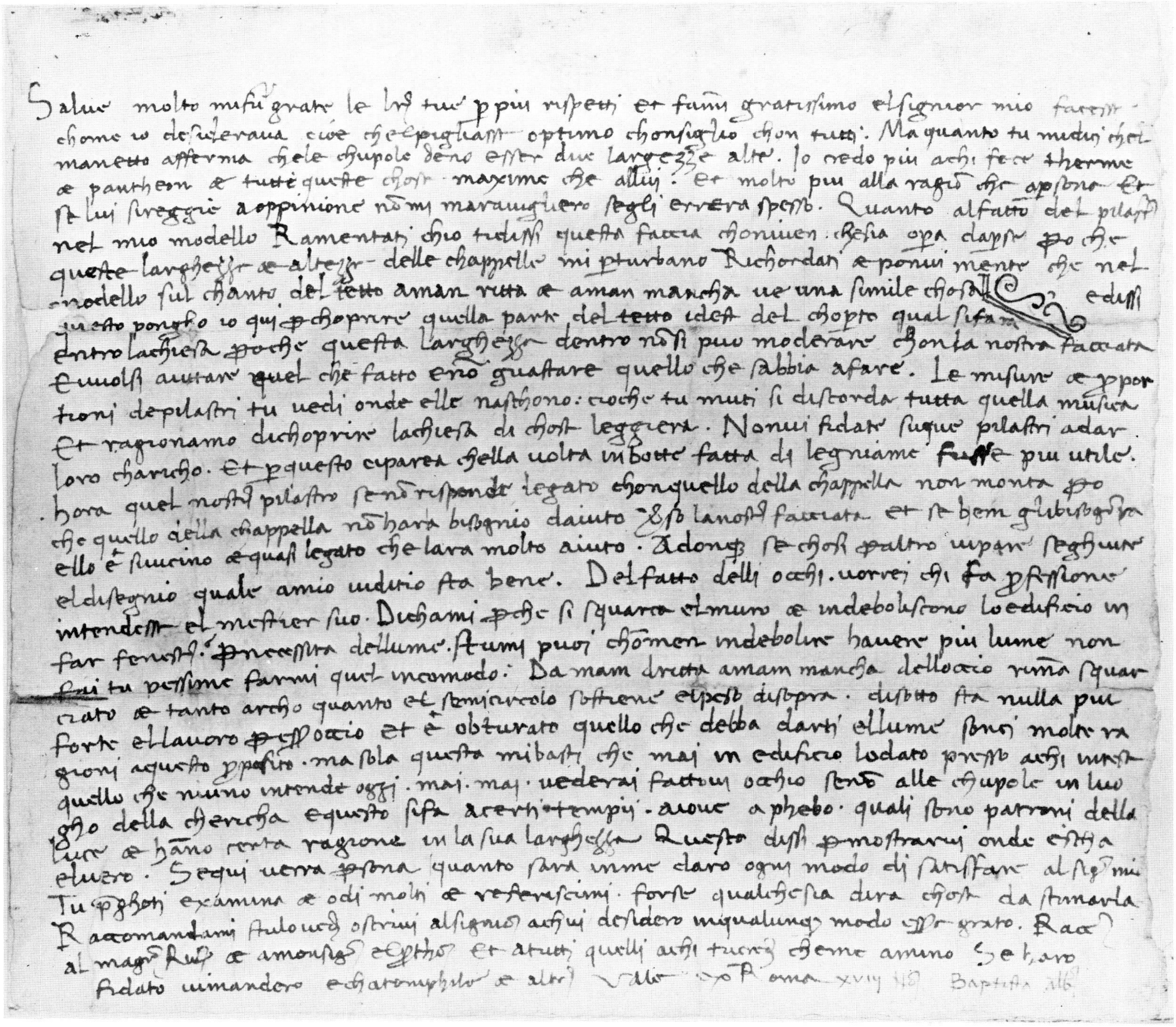

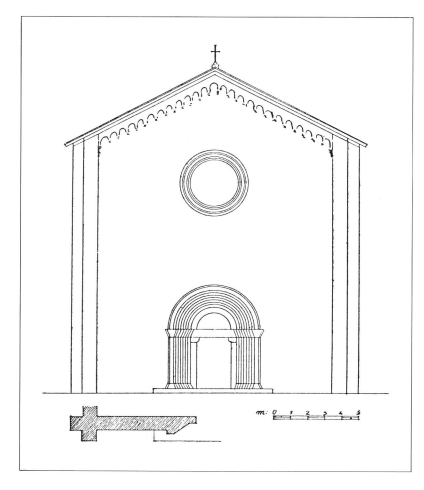

and other symbols from the Egyptian theology of sun-worship. The walls of the Cappella delle Arti Liberali are covered with the subject matter of Greek theogony, including the Muses, together with the arts and sciences they protect and Apollo enlightens. The Cappella degli Antenati is decorated with the symbols of the Hebrew faith, of Mosaic monotheism, with the judges and kings of Israel, and with sibyls and prophets announcing the advent of Christianity. Finally, in the Cappella di Sigismondo one encounters the radiant sun, symbol of the light of Christ, together with statues of the virtues representing a summary of Christian theology.[26]

The details of this iconological programme[27] may have been elaborated by Basinio, together with Valturius the military adviser, who was also a refined Humanist.[28] But it is inconceivable that Alberti did not know of it or exercise some influence upon it. Alberti was a member of the Roman Academy at the time, together with Pomponio Leto and Platina, and while in Florence for the Council he may have met Gemistos Plethon, who had considerable influence over Cosimo and the cultural world of contemporary Florence.

In short, Alberti may have been no stranger to hermetic culture, and he may have inspired a series of decorations for a court that stood halfway between Florence and Venice, the corresponding centres of Platonism and Orientalism the cultural elements that inform the decorations of the Tempio Malatestiano. In spite of Pius II's condemnation of Sigismondo and the charge of ambiguity brought against him during the Counter-Reformation, his cultural heterogeneity may be taken as evidence of his good faith. For he was no mere dabbler in a culture whose contradictions have been pointed out by later generations, but of which he himself was unaware. On the contrary, his life exemplifies these contradictions, and he paraded them openly. He even defended them, however wrong-headedly, as capable of effecting a theological synthesis of human knowledge and bridging the gap between reason, magic, and religion.

Agostino di Duccio carried out his reliefs in that "delicate manner" of his (to use Vasari's words), with the gracious facility for illustration that is the distinctive characteristic of his art.[29] The result is a shy, graceful ballet of stylized drapery and musical instruments. Rimini is shown too, protected by Venetian galleys in the harbour, its Roman landmarks — the old bridge and the new temple — standing out against the magnificent background of Castel Sismondo, beneath the sign of Cancer.

The third phase in Malatesta's programme began just as his power

26. G. Del Piano, op. cit.

27. Valturius writes that it is inspired by "the most hidden secrets of philosophy", op. cit., XII, p. 13.

28. I. Pasini, op. cit., p. 135. There is also documentary evidence that Poggio Bracciolini worked on it, for he wrote to Valturius about the sibyls.

29. C. Ravaioli, *Agostino di Duccio a Rimini*, in "Studi Romagnoli", 1951, II, p. 113 ff.

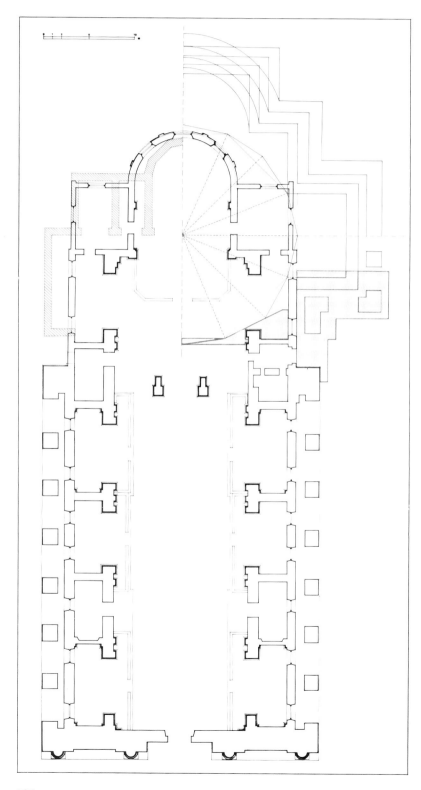

was reaching its zenith, and this time Alberti was directly involved in the decision to re-model the Tempio according to the principle that "sometimes a wall can be built on top of another, just as a fur coat can be worn on top of a suit of clothes."[30] If, from a practical point of view, Alberti's freedom of action was limited by the existence of the foundations and by his respect for the earlier structures, his plan went well beyond the collage of late-Gothic and early-Renaissance ideas that had characterized Pasti's eclectic design. His letter to Pasti suggests a controversy that must have arisen from the criticism and incomprehension with which his plan was received. But his tone reflects his self-confidence: "I believe far more in reason than in people"; "Remember what I told you"; "Remember and be careful to follow my design"; "I wish everyone who did a job knew what he was doing"; "There are many reasons for doing this, but this one is enough for me"; "I said this to show you where the truth lay."

First Alberti established his field of action: "This façade must stand on its own, since I don't trust the width and height of the chapels." He made no bones about the incompatibility between the proportions implied in his own classical style and those of the earlier Gothic building. This clarity of vision led him to make several decisions: the roof of the church had to be a light one ("Don't trust those columns") and the new columns on the sides could do without the help of the old ones, while if the latter needed any support, the new columns "are so close and almost connected that they will be greatly helped by them." As for the adoption of a tripartite window instead of a rose-window and the probable objection that this would weaken the façade, Alberti maintained that what counted was the hole in the wall and the upper half of the semi-circle. The lower half was nothing but a filling-in that cut off a source of light, without making any contribution at all to the stability of the structure.

Alberti's design was radical enough to provide the old church with a completely new wrapping, but it did not mark a complete break with the earlier style. The resemblance of the façade to the Roman arch at Rimini (the diameter of the columns is the same in both structures: three Roman feet) showed that is was not necessary to go beyond the Po valley to find examples of ancient Roman art. The idea of placing sarcophagi beneath the lateral arches and the façade (a feature of the first plan that was drawn up) must have been derived from S. Maria Novella and its niches, though there was the mausoleum of Theodoric nearby at Ravenna, with its powerfully compact lower order (it was probably thought to be Roman at the time). As for the roof of the nave, Alberti

30. L. B. Alberti, op. cit., VI, 12, p. 514.

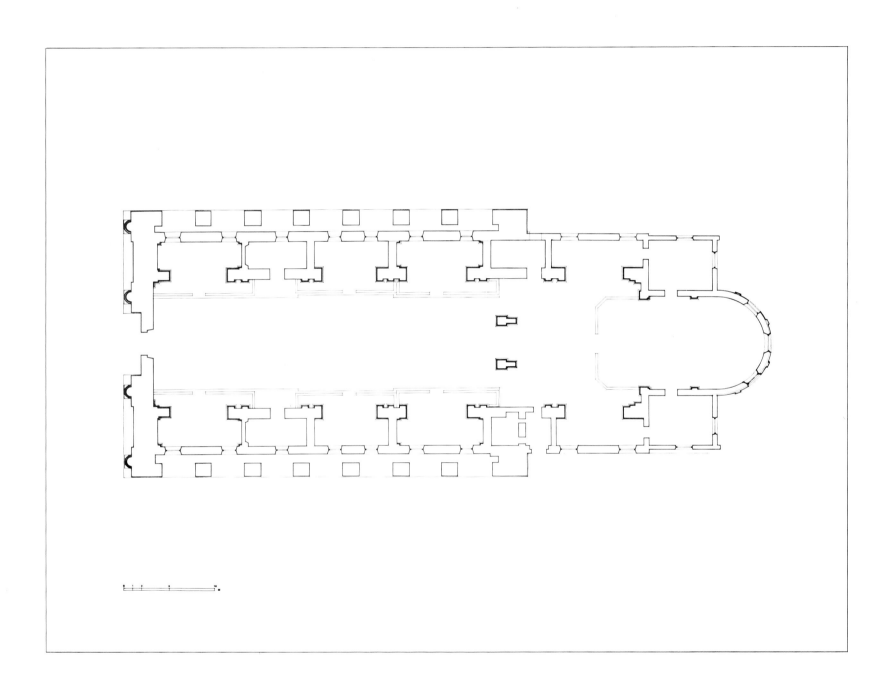

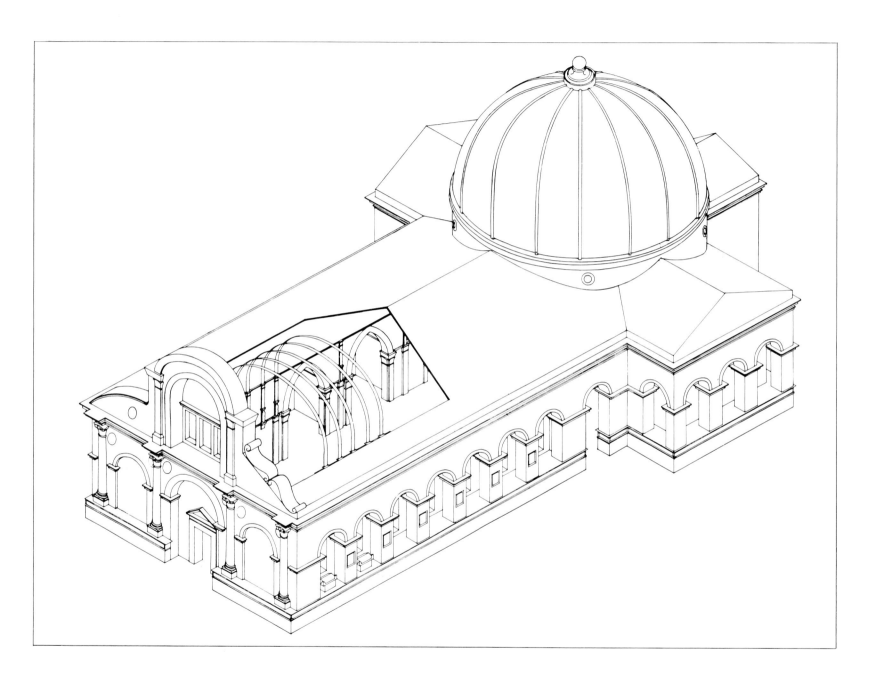

140-201. *Rimini, Tempio Malatestiano. The church testifies to two important stages in the expansion of Sigismondo's programme, decided on the advice of Alberti. The first regards the interior, which reflects Alberti's preference for sculptural rather than pictorial decoration. Matteo de' Pasti and Agostino di Duccio's reliefs suggest that Alberti provided them with general instructions, which they then interpreted rather freely. The illustrations below analyse them in detail, for their complex sculptural imagery (at times Gothic, at others more quattrocentesque) is the expression of a cultural world in which religious and pagan values "merge in the fog of a single primordial Christian-philosophical revelation" (Cassirer).*

Hence the repeated accusations of ambiguity levelled at Sigismondo ever since Pius II's first j'accuse. But Sigismondo's confused, violent predilections, like those of the intellectuals and artists of his court, were motivated by a relish for life, a taste for the rational and the irrational, and admiration for the ancient religio *that had preceded Christianity and which the latter had absorbed and granted the charisma of truth. All the dangers of Platonism, the suggestiveness of oriental culture, and*

140. Rimini, Tempio Malatestiano, sketch of the façade.

the subtle, unresolved cultural allusions Alberti himself gave cautious expression to in his writings, explode visually in the iconology of Rimini. The ingenuity of these reliefs was typical of the man who commissioned them, and it was inevitable that Sigismondo should become the target of fierce criticism.

Alberti took a more personal, direct interest in the second stage of the project: the reconstruction of the exterior. This is confirmed by the firm, threatening tone of his famous letter to Matteo de' Pasti. However, one has to make one's way carefully through the remote and recent history of the edifice before one can understand the controlled "music" of its proportions and the value of its individual parts. The use of Roman stone and Byzantine marble figures largely in the structure, though the beautiful doorway is more closely related to the world of Venice than to that of Rome. Every detail confirms that the church's classicism is that which was current in the area of the Po valley. Sometimes it takes the form of direct imitation, as proved by the exact correspondence between the form and size of the façade and those of the Roman arch in Rimini. At others, the influence is more subtle and indirect, as in the case of the twisted pink

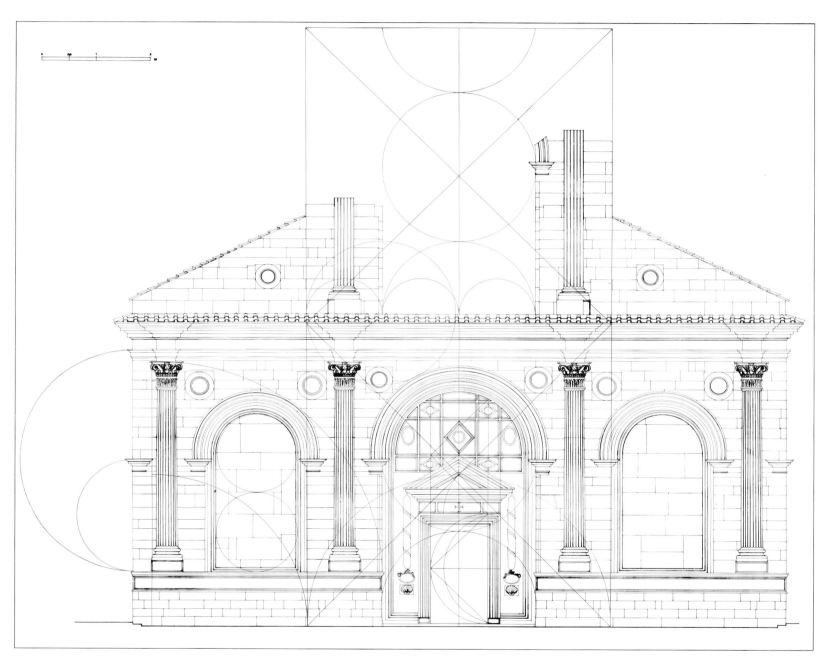

141. Rimini, Tempio Malatestiano, diagram illustrating the proportions of the façade.

marble torus of the stylobate. Alberti's padanitas *can be understood in the light of his formation and travels, and it explains why his ideas were more readily accepted in the area of the Po valley than anywhere else. These are subtleties which make a stone-by-stone examination of the façade and sides of the church even more exciting. In spite of the fragmentary, glaringly incomplete character of the structure, it is the expression of Alberti's full maturity and his finest achievement.*

142. Rimini, Tempio Malatestiano, the side.

143. Rimini, Tempio Malatestiano, diagram illustrating proportions of the side.

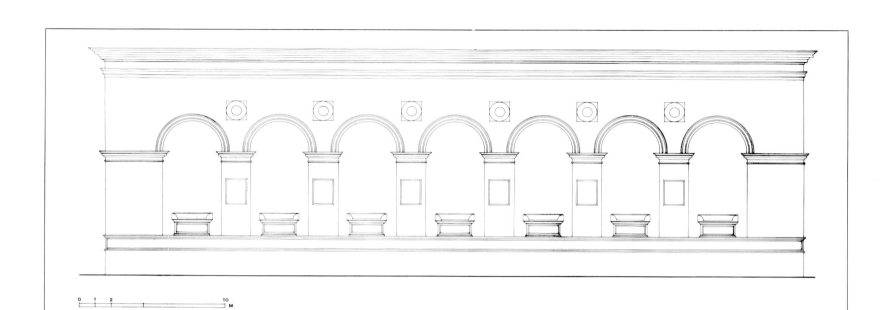

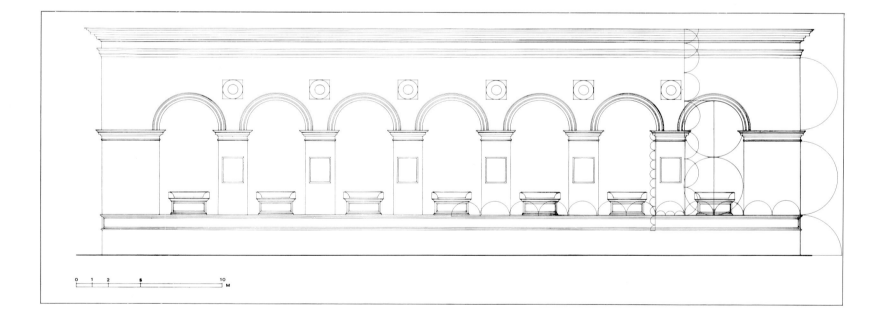

thought of constructing a barrel-vault, but not trusting the stability of the earlier structure, he wrote to Matteo dei Pasti: "We thought the church needed some kind of light roof ... which is why a timber barrel-vault seemed to be the best solution". (This was the kind of ceiling built in Venice.)

If the dome had as many ribs as shown in Pasti's medal, it would have had sixteen segments and large round-headed arches radiating from a central element that would have been neither a lantern, nor an aperture (as in the Pantheon): "only cupolas should have apertures in the form of a priest's tonsure, as in certain temples dedicated to Jove and Apollo, who are guardians of the light". The baptistery of Parma provides an example of a dome with sixteen segments based on an octagonal plan, without a lantern in the middle. The medal also shows curved elements over the side bays screening the roofs of the aisles, a motif later introduced into Venetian architecture by Codussi. However, this is contradicted by the drawing in Alberti's letter to Matteo dei Pasti (the only autograph drawing that has survived), which shows straight sloping walls decorated with a kind of volute connecting the nave and aisles.

Other elements, such as the twisted torus in Veronese marble that tops the church's high base (a refined, plastic, chromatic device borrowed from Venetian architecture) and the triumphant polychrome central portal of porphyry and green marble, which combines Roman dignity with a certain Byzantine quality, show that in the very development of his great classical project, Alberti expressed what may be called *padanitas* (a quality characteristic of the Po valley). His education in Padua and Bologna and his visits to Ferrara account for this. In comparison, his contacts with the Renaissance world of Florence were sporadic. What is quite evident is the eclecticism of his art: "We shall collect and transcribe into this work all the most valid, useful observations that can be gleaned from the writings of the greatest architects of the past, as well as those rules they actually applied in the execution of their works. We shall also mention certain discoveries we have made in the course of our studies, and which we believe may be of some use."[31]

Vasari writes: "In brief, so well and so solidly did he build the church of S. Francesco that it now ranks as one of the foremost temples in Italy."[32] The main reason for this solidity is that the façade has no organic relationship to the interior of the church, the width of the nave, or the width of the chapels. On the contrary, its tripartite division and two storeys make it a completely independent unit. This is true even from a vertical point of view,

31. Ibid., 1, p. 18.
32. Vasari, op. cit., II, p. 539.

that is, when one relates the façade to the wooden barrel-vault that was to have covered the nave, and which would have been protected by a saddleback roof. Portoghesi maintains that Alberti had S. Miniato in mind when he thought of the two superimposed storeys of different width connected by sloping walls.[33] But Alberti wanted to create something different from a Basilican church with a nave higher than its aisles. Moreover, he rejected the idea of a single triangular pediment, which would have suited his classical design.

Alberti's real intentions are revealed in Matteo dei Pasti's medal and in the existing fragments of the second storey (greatly altered by restoration). These show that he was thinking along the lines of a round arched *edicola* containing an arch with an architraved tripartite window, which would have been more Paduan and Venetian than Renaissance. The window — Matteo de' Pasti must have been worried by the problem of light — could not be architraved in relation to the development of the vault: "The windows of temples must be decorated in the same way as their doors. But since their apertures are in the upper part of the wall, near the point where the latter joins with the roof, and since their corners come close to the curvature of the roof, they are designed differently from doors; in other words, their width is twice their height. The whole width of a window is divided by two colonettes, which are introduced in the same way as in a portico, though they are nearly always square." This clearly refers to the tripartite window he had designed for the Tempio Malatestiano, and to its position in relation to the barrel-vault of the interior.[34] The compact nature of the façade had led Alberti to consider how to let as much light into the church as possible.

There are very close affinities between the façade and the Arch of Augustus at Rimini; in the building material used for both edifices, in the way the columns thicken in the middle, and in the diameter of the columns, which is the same in both structures. In fact, the façade is related to the most complex kind of tripartite triumphal arch. According to one unconfirmed theory, the two lateral arches were to have contained the tombs of Sigismondo and Isotta. Another theory, based on Pasti's medal, maintains that the three arches were of equal depth, but the two illustrations of the temple under construction in Basinio's *Esperide* show no trace at all of splay in the lateral arches;[35] on the contrary, the cornice is carefully and heavily pencilled over. This was further confirmed in the course of restorations carried out after World War II, when the whole façade was dismantled and rebuilt.[36] Alberti's façade was so well joined to the Gothic one behind it

33. P. Portoghesi, *Il tempio malatestiano*, Florence 1965.
34. L. B. Alberti, op. cit., VII, 12, p. 626.
35. Cod. Osbon. f. 137 v.; Vat. f. 133 v. Cf. C. Pächt, *Giovanni da Fano's Illustrations for Basinio's Epos Hesperis*, in "Studi Romagnoli", 1951, II. "In the first place, after removing the marble covering that filled the two lateral arches, it was possible to establish without a shadow of doubt that

that when one of them moved slightly during the wartime bombing, the other moved with it. This necessitated a complicated work of restoration and dismantling. As for the width of the façade, Alberti adopted the following rule: "I have found that the width of the façades of temples in ancient times was divided into twelve parts (or nine, where the buildings had to be particularly strong), one part corresponding to the width of the wall."[37] In fact, the façade is approximately thirty metres wide, whereas the total thickness of the two façades (the Gothic one and Alberti's) is 2.50 m., a twelfth of the width.

In his letter to Matteo, Alberti describes the capitals as being very beautiful.[38] However, they do not correspond to the ideal expressed in the *De re aedificatoria*, where capitals which differ from those normally used "are not recommended by the experts." Alberti may have written this in a revised version of the text, or the capitals at Rimini may be intended to prepare one for the decoration of the interior. The fact remains that the ones he adopted are atypical, and their sibyls' heads call to mind certain Etruscan capitals.

Analysis of the façade and sides of the building reveals the constant application of a module of about 59-60 centimetres (the equivalent of two Roman feet). Thus Alberti's measurements are consistent with his design. As for the now famous words in the letter to Pasti, "you can see where the size and proportions of the columns come from; if you alter anything you will spoil all that harmony ...", the reference to music denotes a specific field of measurement, according to which both architecture and music were based on the same series of proportional ratios.

Matteo must have been worried by the position of the chapel windows and their risky alignment with the newly constructed arches. Alberti, on the other hand, was more concerned with maintaining a specific system of proportions, and his strong words to Matteo must have had the desired effect, for the measurements throughout the edifice are unusually consistent. "All ornament is more beautiful when what lies beneath it is made entirely of one kind of stone, and when all its parts are so well joined that the joints cannot be seen."[39]

The basic 1 : 2 ratio, Alberti's diapason, is calculated on the width of the columns in relation to the span of the arches.[40] The ratio between the span of the arches and the height of the architrave is 2 : 3, a sesquialtera. With the introduction of the arch, one has to take into account the optical effect produced by the piers, which, according to Alberti's own theory, should extend as high as the corresponding projection of the cornice: "In vaults

those two cornices could never have bordered large arches of the same depth as those in the sides, as those who have studied the ideal reconstruction of the church on the basis of Matteo de' Pasti's medal have often concluded. On the contrary, the façade was conceived like that from the beginning".
36. E. Lavagnino, *Restauro del Tempio Malatestiano*, in "Bollettino d'Arte", April-June 1950, XXV, 4, pp. 176-177.

37. L. B. Alberti, op. cit., VII, 10, p. 606.
38. I. Pasini, op. cit., p. 136.
39. L. B. Alberti, op. cit., IV, 12, p. 516.
40. Ibid., IX, 5, p. 824.

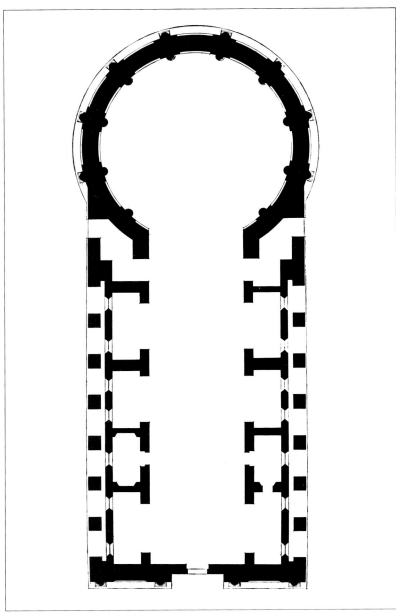

the springs of the arches should be high enough to prevent the projection of the cornices from concealing any part of the arch from anyone standing in the middle of the temple."[41] Another modular element is introduced with the radius of the arch, which results in the total void being inscribed within a 2 : 4 rectangle, that is, a 1 : 2 ratio. Even the plaques on the pillars are rectangles based on a 2 : 3 ratio, while the frieze that runs along the stylobate (including the twisted torus) is half as high as the width of the pillars: another 1 : 2 ratio. The more solid end pillars, both those near the façade and those in the opposite direction towards the tribune, are about twice as wide as the others. But here, the slight proportional difference (about 15 centimetres) must have been caused by the line of the pre-existent windows, and by the most important one near the tomb of Sigismondo.[42]

On the whole, the ratios are very simple ones. According to Alberti, the fifth and the diapason are preferable, because of their simplicity and rationality: "In colonnades where the columns are set close together, the space between the columns must not be less than one and a half times the column's diameter. In colonnades where the columns are spaced out, the space must not be three and three eighth more than the column's diameter. In colonnades of the intermediate kind, the proper ratio will be two and a fourth. In the closer kind, it will be two, which is precisely that of the sides of the Tempio Malatestiano."[43]

It might seem surprising that, in spite of all the intricate diagrams drawn up to explain the ratios of his buildings, a "sophisticated" artist such as Alberti — the adjective is Vasari's — should choose fundamental ratios. But it was precisely these that transformed the individual elements of his designs into logical structures. Most important was the relationship between module and measurement and its use in defining the essential ratios of structures. One must concentrate on the fundamental; one must avoid taking any particular structural detail (a cornice, for example) as a point of reference, and consider instead the precise field of commensuration that is being applied. Looking at the shell of the Tempio Malatestiano, one can see that the same module measurement and the same system of proportions have been applied to its façade and sides. One may suppose, therefore, that they would also have been applied to the construction of the tribune and the dome.

Alberti wrote later: "Finally, an architect must never embark on unusual projects that have never been attempted before out of an inordinate desire for glory."[44] There was nothing that had never been attempted before in the Tempio Malatestiano. Ne-

41. Ibid., VII, 11, p. 612.
42. Cf. Ibid., IX, 5, p. 822.
43. Ibid., VII, 6, p. 562.
44. Ibid., IX, 11, p. 864.
45. C. Ricci, op. cit., p. 212.
46. Ibid., p. 217.

vertheless, the project proved too much for the man who commissioned it. One of the greatest difficulties from the beginning had been obtaining sufficient supplies of stone and marble. The monument that suffered most as a consequence was the basilica of S. Apollinare in Classe at Ravenna, from which "marmora et tabulas porphireas ac serpentinas"[45] were taken on payment of sums of money to the abbot; it is precisely this marble that gives the façade its slightly Roman-Oriental aspect. A lot of material was taken from the Roman port of Rimini and from many other buildings in the city, "wherever there was some noble stone that could be used for decorations or inscriptions, to the great detriment of the city's ancient monuments."[46] Supplies of Istrian stone were ordered from Giorgio di Sebenico, but he failed to honour his commitments; other material was sought at Verona and even Ferrara, perhaps on Alberti's advice.[47]

The delay that plagued the construction of the church was paralleled by the rapid decline in Sigismondo's fortunes. In 1460 Valturius could still compare Sigismondo to the "divine Vespasian who built and completed the Temple of Concord and Peace", but in 1461 the friars were compelled to sell a house to pay for repairs to the roof and chapels. Thus, with the site almost deserted and Matteo de' Pasti sent off to Mahomet II, the workmen left for Urbino, where "the bastard"[48] who had brought Sigismondo to heel employed them (and possibly Alberti in the capacity of adviser) in the construction of his own new palace. Work on the church came to an abrupt halt; there was no suggestion of a temporary solution to the problem, a revision of its design, or a continuation of the work on a smaller scale. Perhaps Sigismondo thought he would be able to resume building once the squall that had shaken his regime had passed. But this was not to be. Paul II, the persecutor of the Humanists, gave the defeated Sigismondo the towns of Foligno and Spoleto in exchange for Rimini, and the ephemeral, hermetical world of Sigismondo's former possession was subjected to a kind of ideological purge, both culturally and politically.

THE PROBLEM OF THE TRIBUNE

In 1475, at a banquet celebrating the marriage of Roberto Malatesta, the guests were served a cake "made of fine sugar" and shaped just as "the church of S. Francesco should have been."[49] Thus a model of Alberti's design must have existed, or at least been known to exist twenty years later or the court pastry-cooks could hardly have made their cake. The fame of the project must have been still very much alive at the time, particularly with

respect to its most controversial feature, the dome, which we find illustrated in Matteo de' Pasti's medal.

The resumption of work on the church involved a departure from its original design. An apse with five chapels was added in the sixteenth century,[50] though the chapels were demolished in the eighteenth century, when the chancel was re-designed and a semicircular apse built in their place. Such was the plan of the church when it was completely rebuilt after World War II.

Ragghianti deserves credit for being the only person who has tried to reconstruct the church according to Alberti's original design. Unfortunately, led astray perhaps by the drawings of the architect who helped him, Donati, he arrived at a reconstruction that seems to be on a different scale from the rest of the structure and which is spoilt by a tendency to add unlikely elements to the present building, whether they are compatible with it or not. Moreover, his concept of Alberti's design rests on the belief that the dome was based on the Pantheon. Consequently, he ignores the hemispherical, ribbed dome we find in de' Pasti's commemorative medal. (Alberti's well-known letter to de' Pasti concerning the proportions of the dome, in which he makes specific mention of the "therme and Pantheon", apparently misled Ragghianti.) More important still is Ragghianti's argument that, since Alberti had to add a new tribune to a nave that already existed, he would have dealt with the problem in the same way as he did when he designed the tribune for the Annunziata in Florence much later. He points out that "the architect was inevitably less clear about his aims regarding both structure and form.

However, the later example of the Annunziata, together with Pasti's medal, tend to exclude the possibility that Alberti planned to introduce a transept or some kind of larger element which would have stood further back with respect to the façade and sides."[51]

Quite apart from the comparison with the Annunziata, which is pure conjecture, the fact remains that a deep, L-shaped foundation was discovered in the course of excavations carried out in 1926-27 near the small side-door of the church. This continues the line of the side arches at first, then turns perpendicularly and terminates on a line with the sewer beneath the road. Tosi has left a number of drawings of these excavations.[52] Pasini's analysis, on the other hand, draws attention to the remains of walls discovered beneath the pavement of the church in 1895 (at which time the remains were measured for accountancy purposes, not for their historical value.) Pasini observes: "They

47. "Permission given to the Magnificent Sigismondo da Malatesti of Rimini to extract 100,000 stones from Argenta and from the coast of Filo".

48. "Indeed, you are wicked and do ill to offend me", Pandolfo wrote, challenging him to a duel, and adding: "Should you not accept, which I doubt, I warn you that I shall proceed against you in a way that seems to me most fitting to my honour". No duel took place, but there was a war instead, and Sigismondo paid dearly for it.

49. I. Pasini, *Vicende e frammenti del Tempio Malatestiano in Rimini*, in "Storia Arte e Cultura", Rimini, July-December 1969.

50. G. Ravaioli, *Il Malatestiano: studi, proposte e realizzazioni*, in "Studi Romagnoli", Faenza 1951, II.

51. C. L. Raggianti, *Il Tempio Malatestiano*, II, in "Critica d'Arte", 1965, 71 and 74, p. 31.

52. A. Tosi, *Alcune Note sul Tempio Malatestiano*, in "La Romagna", Imola 1927, XVI, 2, pp. 214-35. Ravaioli questions the validity of this finding and argues that there should have been a bend in this part of the original fifteenth-century foundations "much earlier, that is, at the very point where the outer marble facing at the end of the last large space between the pillars after the seven arches now finishes". He concludes rather vaguely: "Those he (Tosi) discovered closer to the apse, though connected with the former, may be related to earlier structures." But it is difficult to see what theory he is trying to put forward, since there seems to be no trace of any earlier project in the form of a Latin cross.

were probably seen again when the same pavement was restored after the war, but it doesn't seem as if anyone took any notice of them, and the plan we publish here is based solely on the data of 1895."[53] The plan shows "two large foundations, which appear in the plan as triangular surfaces in the western part of the two eighteenth-century chapels, and whose purpose we are unable to explain, since they do not seem to have any connection with the walls built in the fourteenth, sixteenth, or eighteenth centuries. These are the remains, which, as we have said, might give further support to Ragghianti's reconstruction, since they may be connected with the sketch of the foundations of the domed chapel that was to complete the temple."[54]

We have tried to draw a diagram of the plan of the church showing the foundations discovered by Tosi together with the walls referred to by Pasini. Allowing for an adequate offset in the foundation wall, and extending the line of this wall within the church as far as that of the wall of the chapels, one can connect the point thus obtained with that where the wall in the centre of the church begins to form a triangle. The result is a straight line inclined at an angle of 45° and measuring about nine and a half metres, the equivalent of sixteen modules. The length of this line is the same as that perpendicular to the axis of the nave, and is a clear indication that the tribune was to have been built according to an octagonal plan.

If this were so, it would explain the ribs of the dome in Pasti's medal. There are precisely seven of these, and each section of the octagonal dome would have been divided by a central rib, unlike Brunelleschi's prototype, where the ribs merely separate the various segments of the octagon. A closer study of the actual angulation of the wall reveals, in spite of the medal's lack of detail, that the design had not eight but sixteen sides inscribed within a circle. This explains the sixteen ribs, of which seven are visible in perspective in the medal. Such a design would have been more consistent with Alberti's principle that "what has a structural function must also be visible."

Such a structure would have been very similar to the ribbed dome of the baptistery at Parma, which is of a radial nature and has no ring for a lantern; both characteristics seem to be reflected in the termination of the dome in Pasti's medal, where there is no sign at all of a lantern. This is a significant confirmation of the *padanità* of Alberti's dome, which, though clearly hemispherical, had nothing to do with the Pantheon. Alberti's more fragmented, ribbed structure was better suited to the regular rhythm of the pilasters in the interior, which are arranged in line with the beams of the

53. I. Pasini, op. cit., p. 224.
54. Ibid., p. 226.

wooden ceiling, while the small impost arches on the walls of the tribune would have introduced a more openly Byzantine and Gothic note.

Alberti's idea that the area of the altar should be the darkest and most mysterious part of the church explains the small circular windows of the tribune (as seen in the medal) and the absence of a lantern: "The sense of awe that darkness provokes is of a kind that helps to incline the mind to veneration, in the same way that there is much severity in majesty."[55] But a domed structure must have adequate lateral support (one recalls the earlier incident involving the "dead tribunes" Brunelleschi designed for S. Maria del Fiore), and Alberti must have been induced, as the discovered foundation demonstrates, to introduce the necessary supporting elements: two chapels in the transept, another chapel in the apse, and a triumphal arch, or screen, between the tribune and the main body of the church. This is confirmed in the plan of the church's walls drawn up by Pasini and completed when the pavement was restored, though there are some doubts about the manner in which he traced some of the axes. Even the depth of these spaces seems to be right. The thickness of the wall that would have acted as a filter between the nave and the tribune seems to be the same as that of the chapels in the transept (providing one removes a sufficient amount of masonry from the arm of the L-shaped foundation).

Finally, the most difficult problem of all: what would the exterior of this part of the building have looked like? According to Ragghianti, who gives no support for his theory, it would have continued themes already expressed in the façade. However, the uncovered foundation is thicker than the corresponding foundation for the side arches. This is understandable enough, since the tribune was to have been higher than the lateral orders and the façade by about a third, as Pasti's medal shows. Moreover, the foundations have a particular outer offset which must have had some purpose, perhaps to serve for another wall. If one disregards the offset, the thickness of the foundation corresponds to the rules laid down by Alberti: "The solid part of the walls, or the framework of the building which separates the apertures of the temple's various apses should never be less than a fifth of the thickness of the empty space between them."[56] This is exactly the case at Rimini.

It seems reasonable to suppose, therefore, that the idea of a double shell of continuous brick masonry and rhythmical rows of marble columns would have been extended to the tribune and apse. In fact, the rhythmical progress of the colonnade, where

55. L. B. Alberti, op. cit., VII, 12, p. 616. He later adds: "As far as the light is concerned, I prefer to see the entrance of the church well lighted, and the nave not too dark. But I think it is better for the area of the altar to be more solemn than elegant" (p. 618).

56. Ibid., VII, 4, p. 554.

184-201. Rimini, Tempio Malatestiano. Marble decorations by Ago-stino di Duccio and others.

The church's complex sculptural iconology was devised by Basinio and Valturius. One of the most significant images is that of the boatman in the Chapel of the Planets. He looks back over his shoulder like Benjamin's Angelus Novus, who was driven towards the future as he looked back at the past. The boatman's progress towards regeneration is barred by monsters. The moon, whose fabulous landscape is also depicted, represents the first stage of the soul in its ascent towards a higher state; the thin crescent can be seen in the form of a veiled shape fading into the sky. Rimini is depicted at the height of its splendour, with its numerous towers, its Roman bridge, and the Tempio Malatestiano surmounted by a classical pediment. The sun can be seen moving from Cancer towards its highest point in the summer solstice, an allusion to the ephemeral summer of Sigismondo's rule. Mercury, with his long caduceus entwined with serpents (the symbols of science), points the way for the souls of the dead — winged figures that move up or down. In the the Chapel of Isotta, beneath the ambiguous motto "Tempus loquendi tempus tacendi", is a crowd of angels playing musical instruments and putti riding in couples on the backs of dolphins.

184

the arches have a span of approximately 3.60 metres and the pillars are approximately 1.78 metres wide, corresponds exactly to the outer shell of the chapel, that is, to one side of the octagonal tribune, which is 9.60 metres wide. Looking at the building, one can easily imagine the classicism of its exterior embracing the whole of the structure, from the façade to the sides, to the tribune, to the apse. (The grafting of a new classical element on to a Gothic interior had an illustrious precedent in the tribune of S. Maria del Fiore.) Alberti's point of reference might easily have been the cathedral of Florence rather than the later, more thoroughly Roman rotonda of the Annunziata, for the former also involved reconciling Gothic with Renaissance elements. Moreover, it was a building he had studied and whose importance he emphasized in his treatise.

This plan, apart from reconciling the church with the Riminese tradition (which demanded that it be in the form of a Latin cross), has found critical support in Ricci, who believes it would have been necessary either to introduce a transept or to reinforce the apses to provide support for the dome.[57] The plan would also have met the general static requirements of the building, its stylistic characteristics, the scale of its planimetry, and even the pattern of voids and solids of the sides, which could thus have been extended to all the visible parts of the exterior. It would also have solved the strictly practical problem of the side entrance, which Ragghianti shows was necessary. The marble scarf-joints on the façade on the right might have been intended for "a continuation of the wall, and have been predisposed to form either an outer or inner angle."[58] However, an examination of the heads of the joints shows that any turning inwards of the wall would have been impossible, since this would have altered the width of the pillar and this was determined by obvious symmetrical reasons and the position of the plaque. Thus, there seems to have been some uncertainty as to whether the wall was to continue with the introduction of a side door, or whether it was to turn outwards at an angle of 45º to link up with the terminal parts of the foundations discovered by Tosi (both points lie along a straight line at an angle of 45º). The second hypothesis finds some support in the fact that the joints are slightly out of line. But if this were the case, another foundation should have been found lying in this direction, which is quite different from that of the foundation actually found. The joints must have been connected with the introduction of a side door, for in this event the span of the doorway would still have been about 3.55 metres, equal to that of the side arches, even though its height would

57. See I. Pasini, op. cit., p. 223.
58. C. L. Ragghianti, op. cit., p. 33.

have differed as a result of the inevitable interruption of the high stylobate to provide access to the church.

There is a certain logical relationship between the scale, structure, and proportions of our ideal reconstruction and the church as we know it, so that our theory may appear more plausible than some of those advanced so far. But our theory can be confirmed or corrected only by a systematic plan of excavation, which now seems necessary if we are to clarify the history of Alberti's design beyond all doubt.

202. *Giovanni Angelo di Antonio: detail of the Nativity of the Virgin.*
New York, Metropolitan Museum.
203. *Piero della Francesca: Federico da Montefeltro. Florence, Uffizi.*

Alberti always worked cautiously and indirectly, in the manner of a diplomatic official of the Curia. Even so, his connections with Urbino are even more difficult to establish. With Sigismondo his relations were fairly direct and open, to the extent that he came near to being considered ideologically suspect during Pius II's violent campaign against the lord of Rimini. His relationship with Federico da Montefeltro, on the other hand, must have been strictly cultural and intellectual. In Sigismondo Malatesta, Alberti had had to deal with a cavalier figure fascinated by the images of Platonic classicism and suspected of paganism. But in Federico he found a man of systematic learning, whose prudent diplomacy provided far less scope for the art of war. Their relationship was probably closer than has been supposed, though not close enough to allow Federico to interfere in Alberti's work, for, as the architect writes in his treatise, "omni materia seclusa." The facts are sufficiently well documented. In 1475, three years after Alberti's death, Federico da Montefeltro wrote to Landino thanking him for a copy of the *Disputazioni Camaldolesi*: "nihil fuit familiarius neque amantius amicitia qua Batista et ego eramus coniuncti."[1] In one of Landino's dialogues Alberti is made to say: "I have often had occasion to remark Federico's goodness by virtues of our long friendship and the hospitality he has shown me. Every year I leave Rome in the autumn and seek health and rest at his court. At such times I feel as if I have left the suppers of Sardanapalus for the banquets of Alcinous, and have met a Socratic host."[2] Alberti's firsthand experience of Urbino, acquired at the very time Federico was engaged on his great building projects, is confirmed in the *De re aedificatoria*: "There is plenty of water at Fiesole and Urbino, in spite of their being mountain towns, since the ground there is stony and held together by clay. Moreover, it appears there are clods of earth which contain the purest water within their cavities."[3]

As for Federico, there is no better account of him in the role of patron than the hagiographic one of Vespasiano da Bisticci: His lordship had studied architecture in such a way that no lord or gentleman of his own day knew as much about it as he did. This is confirmed by all the edifices he built, whose large orders and measurements he planned down to the smallest detail. The greatest of these is his own palace, of which this age has not seen the like, so well planned is it, and so many fine views does it command. Though he employed architects, to whose opinions he listened, he calculated the measurements and disposed of even the smallest details himself. And when he spoke about architecture, it seemed as if it were the only thing he had ever done

1. Federico da Montefeltro, *Lettere di Stato e d'Arte*, ed. by P. Alatri, Rome 1949, p. 102.
2. G. Mancini, op. cit., p. 479.
3. L. B. Alberti, *L'Architettura*, X, 3, p. 890.

OPVS·PETRI·DE·BVRGO·SCI·SEPVLCRI

204. *Piero della Francesca: the Flagellation of Christ. Urbino, Galleria Nazionale delle Marche.*

in his life, so that he could explain it and see that everything was carried out as he advised.[4] Federico's secretary, Francesco Galli, compared him with Vitruvius himself.[5]

In general culture, there were even closer affinities between Federico and Alberti. Bernardino Baldi describes the duke's library: "The bookcases were arranged beautifully against the walls, while the frieze·that ran round the room contained a Latin inscription in verse."[6] This last detail must have pleased Alberti very much. The books were "all written by hand, and not one printed, for he would have been ashamed to own such a thing."[7] There were 772 different titles, and the following were grouped together: "Vitellonis Prospectiva. Liber rarissimus; Prospectiva communis, sine auctoris nomine; Vitruvius, De Architectura. Codex vetustus; Leonis Baptistae Alberti, De Architectura, Libri X."[8]

If to these we add the *Petri Burgensis pictoris Libellus de quinque corporibus regularibus, ad illustrissimum ducem Federicum et Guidonem filium*, Gianozzo Manetti's *De Vita Nicolai V summi pontificis*, Frontinus's *De acquaeductibus*, and Flavio Biondo's *Roma illustrata*, we have a complete bibliography, one in which Alberti is given pride of place. In 1480 Federico wrote to the Duke of Ferrara asking him for a copy of the *De architectura*, for "I have heard that your Lordship has the originals,"[9] while the "Codice Vaticano urbinate latino 264" of the *De re aedificatoria*, dated Padua 1483, bears the coat-of-arms of Federico da Montefeltro, Duke of Urbino.[10] Thus Federico's interest in Alberti's treatise continued even after the architect's death.

Baldi believes that Alberti was on such good terms with the Duke that "he intended dedicating to him the ten books on architecture that he had written with so much care and knowledge. But after his death, his brother Bernardo was persuaded by Angelo Poliziano to make a gift of them to Lorenzo de' Medici."[11] This was the same Bernardino Baldi who wrote the first philological commentary on Vitruvius, the *De verborum vitruvianorum significatione*, inspired to do so by Alberti's famous passage on Vitruvius's obscurity.[12] The coupling of Vitruvius with Alberti, that is, the simultaneous interest in the ancient Roman author and the "new Vitruvius" (an interest that was later extended to Frontinus) was a particular feature of the cultural world of Urbino, and probably resulted from Federico's encounter with Alberti. Francesco di Giorgio, who was directly involved in the planning of architectural projects, wrote his own treatise immediately after Alberti's, and his book is included in Federico's list: "Francisci Georgii senensis Architectura, cum picturis, ad illustrissimum ducem Federicum (280)."[13]

4. Vespasiano da Bisticci, *Vite di uomini illustri*, Florence 1938, pp. 102-103.

5. M. Dezzi Bardeschi, *Gli architetti dalmati e il ricorso all'antico nel Rinascimento italiano*, in "Bollettino degli Ingegneri", 1968, II, p. 7.

6. C. Guasti, *Inventario della libreria urbinate*, in "Giornale storico degli archivi toscani", VI, 1862, p. 128.

7. Ibid., p. 129.

8. Ibid., p. 55. Besides the numerous Scholastic, Latin, and Greek texts, there are others related to the rival culture of which Malatesta was the chief exponent. Against no. 226 one finds: "Mercurius Trismegistus de potestate

As Maltese has pointed out: "Francesco wanted to make Vitruvius more relevant than Alberti had done, not just because he wrote in the vernacular, but also because his whole art was informed by classicism, which he went into thoroughly, checking and defending the monuments personally, and attributing decisive importance to direct experience. Alberti also examined, studied, and reconstructed the monuments of antiquity from the buildings themselves, especially during his stay in Rome, and certainly more systematically and consistently than Francesco did. But he does not seem to have left any drawings behind him, none that can stand comparison with his literary work. Instead, Francesco considered drawings to be essential, and illustration formed the very basis of his attempt to resurrect the classical past. Alberti regarded Vitruvius's work as unsound, but offered no evidence that he had checked it point by point, whereas Francesco took meticulous care in checking it against the monuments themselves before correcting or rejecting it."[14] But Francesco was not merely concerned with the correct method of approaching the principal authority of antiquity, but with actual experience and the practice of design. In speaking of stables, for example, he refers to what "I have designed for the most illustrious Duke of Urbino, which is nearly finished, and throughout which may be seen all those parts that are fitting in a well designed, perfect stable."[15] He then gives the correct measurements, the layout of the services, and the description of a "spiral staircase reserved for his Lordship when he goes riding."[16] Alberti's treatise is more detached and formal than Francesco Di Giorgio's, but no less precise.

Castiglione's description of Urbino as a "palace in the form of a city" calls to mind Alberti's concepts of the city as a large house and the house as a small city, ideas that must have influenced the construction of Urbino's private and ducal dwellings. "The hall, main room, and other public parts of a house ought to be set out like the square and thoroughfares of a city, not in any out-of-the-way, secret, narrow corner, but where they are clearly visible and easily accessible in relation to the rest of the building. It is here that the staircases and lobbies should terminate, here where your guests take their leave and thank you."[17] Alberti maintains that there are elements common to both private houses and princely dwellings, but in the latter, which will differ in the number and size of their rooms, "even the private apartments should have an air of majesty, because the houses of kings are always crowded."[18] The passage that follows contains precise references to the Ducal Palace of Urbino: "In royal palaces the rooms reserved for the wife, the husband, and the servants should be set well apart and furnished in such a way that each has not only what is necessary to fulfil its functions, but grandeur as well; nor must the number of servants lead to any confusion. Such a division is very difficult, and cannot be effected under a single roof. Therefore, every quarter must have its own space, area, and roof." And again: "The prince's council chamber and the dining-rooms should be in the noblest part of the palace, situated higher than the rest and commanding a fine view of the sea and hills around."[19] One can almost see the countryside around Urbino in these words. Alberti continues: "The wife's rooms should be set quite apart from those of the prince, her husband, except for their inner room, which they will share together, since it will contain the marriage-bed. The two apartments will be connected on the outside by a single door, guarded by a single porter."[20] He adds that the building "should have a watch-tower, so that eventual disorders in the town may be reported immediately."[21] Alberti explains how the plan of a town reflects the fundamental distinction between a wise prince and a tyrant: "First of all, one must discover what kind of man he is, whether he rules with justice and righteousness, respecting the wishes of his subjects, and guided not so much by self-interest as by a desire to benefit his fellow citizens, or whether he rules in such a way that the people must obey him 'volente-nolente'. Nearly all buildings, and towns too, vary according to whether power is exercised by a tyrant (as the latter is called) or by one who acquires and conserves his power as a magistrature granted him by others."[22] (This seems to allude to the differences between Sigismondo and Federico, between the fortress of Castel Sismondo and the Ducal Palace of Urbino.) "The palace of a king ought to be situated in the very middle of the town, and should be easily accessible and richly decorated, more elegant and refined than imposing. That of a tyrant, on the other hand, will be built like a fortress; as such it will be neither inside nor outside the town. The buildings adjacent to a royal palace will form a worthy setting for it, being public places for shows, the temple, and the houses of the principal citizens. But the dwelling of a tyrant will stand apart from the rest of the town."[23] The greater desirability of elegance and refinement with respect to grandeur is a particular characteristic of the Ducal Palace, which is a fortress on the outside and a palace within.[24] Where else could Alberti have come across a problem of this kind? Certainly not in Florence, where Cosimo's palace suited the kind of life that "its master intended to lead," neither that of a king nor a tyrant, but that of a private citizen. Nor can the problem be connected with Mantua; Alberti did not go there

et sapientia Dei, e greco in latinum traductus a Marsilio Ficino". There is also a copy of Macrobius' "Somnium Scipionis", while no. 414 is "Robertus Valturius de re militari, ad illustrissimum Sigismundum Pandulfum Ariminensem principem, cum instrumentis bellicis depictis".

9. M. Dezzi Bardeschi, op. cit., p. 7.
10. Cf. Orlandi's note in L. B. Alberti, *L'Architettura*, II, p. 1005.
11. G. Mancini, op. cit., pp. 482-83.
12. B. Baldi, *De verborum vitruvianorum significatione*, Augusta 1612, pp. 104-05.
13. C. Guasti, op. cit., p. 55.

14. Francesco di Giorgio Martini, *Trattati di architettura, ingegneria e arte militare*, Milan 1967, pp. 18-19.
15. Ibid., II, p. 339.
16. Ibid., II, p. 340.
17. L. B. Alberti, op. cit., V, 2, pp. 338-40.
18. Ibid., p. 342.

206. *Piero della Francesca: Virgin and Child with Saints and Federico da Montefeltro. Milan, Brera.*

until 1459, and the treatise was finished by 1452. Only at Urbino could Alberti have developed such ideas, and the treatise, despite its courtly manner of expression, is the diary of that experience. Alberti's experiences at Urbino led him to conclusions that were to have a direct influence on the work carried out by Laurana much later (however difficult it may be to trace its chronology). Laurana was in Mantua in 1465, when Alberti's influence in the city was at its highest, and the patent letter of 1467 nominating him "engineer and superintendent of all the masons" at Urbino is so elegantly written that it might well have been dictated by Alberti himself.[25]

The theory that Piero della Francesca introduced Laurana to Federico da Montefeltro after meeting him at Pesaro brings us to the last of those mutual cultural influences centred upon Alberti. Alberti's influence on Piero della Francesca is confirmed by the fact that they always seemed to take the same roads and to end up in the same places, as Longhi has observed[26] (in 1447 they were at Urbino, in 1449 in Ferrara, in 1451 in Rimini, while they both worked for Pius II in Rome), and by certain stylistic affinities. The architecture in Piero's paintings, and even his paintings themselves, seem to observe the principles laid down by Alberti in his *Della pittura*. Particularly Albertian is the hall in the *Flagellation of Christ* (Urbino), the temple in the *Proof of the true Cross*, the portico in the *Visit to the Queen of Sheba*, the cloister in the *Annunciation* (Arezzo), the pilasters and architraves in the *St. Sigismund* (Rimini), the sepulchre in the *Resurrection* and S. Pancrazio, the cloister of the *Annunciation* in the polyptych in Perugia, and the background of the *Urbino altar-piece* in the Brera, where the coffered barrel-vault recalls the one in the contemporary church of S. Andrea. A close resemblance has been found between the position of the angels assisting at Christ's baptism in the painting in London and that of the three Graces in Alberti's drawing in the *De pictura*. Moreover, the entire cycle of frescoes at Arezzo adheres, in a general way, to Alberti's pictorial principles as expressed in his treatise on the subject.[27]

A more subtle theory claims that the enamelled, ethereal landscape in the background of the portraits of Federico da Montefeltro and Battista Sforza was influenced by those "demonstrations" of Alberti mentioned in the *Anonymous Life*: "He then put these remarkable things in a box, where they could be seen through a little hole. And then appeared vast plains engirdling an immense ocean, and more remote regions still, stretching farther than the eye could see."[28]

A mutual exchange of ideas certainly took place between the two (it continued at Urbino with Alberti's offering hospitality to Luca Pacioli), and this is an important factor for the correct interpretation of their artistic personalities. The work of the two great artists found a common point of reference in the myth that culminated in Pius II's pathetic crusade. This inspired the images of the Holy Land in Piero's paintings, the concern with the Holy Sepulchre that runs from S. Stefano Rotondo to S. Pancrazio, the brutal, triumphal manner in which the body of Gemistos Plethon was taken back to Rimini, and the attempt to create a Venetian form of classicism through real and painted architecture. The very ambiguity of a culture that lay beneath the weight of a dual classical heritage, that of the east and that of the west, brought both these great artists together within a precarious equilibrium that has outlasted the passage of time.

19. Ibid.
20. Ibid.
21. Ibid., V, 3, p. 344.
22. Ibid., V, 1, p. 332.
23. Ibid., V, 3, p. 346.
24. The chromatic themes of the small Cappella del Perdono, which is richly decorated in marble and geometrical patterns, are very Albertian, as are the big coffered arches supported by the pillars of the loggias between the little towers.

25. M. Salmi, *Piero della Francesca e il Palazzo Ducale di Urbino*, Florence 1945, pp. 39, 100-04.
26. R. Longhi, *Piero della Francesca*, Florence 1963, p. 84.
27. E. Battisti, *Piero della Francesca*, Milan 1971, pp. 116, 145, 168, 484, and notes 197-203.
28. Anonymous, *Vita di L. B. Alberti*, pp. 102, 105.

LUDOVICO II GONZAGA

Giovan Francesco Gonzaga, first Marquis of Mantua, died on 23 September 1444. "He made a will leaving Lodovico, his eldest son, the marquisate of Mantua, Goito and Marcaria, and all the territory that lay in the direction of Verona."[1] The nineteenth-century edition of Mainardi describes Ludovico thus: "Ludovico Gonzaga became the Marquis of Mantua at the age of thirty-two. He fought his brother Carlo for the succession for a long time and finally defeated him. He was a loyal, affable, generous man who practised his faith, and deserved to be called the 'Turk' on account of his prudence and courage."[2] Some sources attribute his nickname to the courage and ferocity he showed in battle; others claim it was given him by his mother, who, seeing him wear a certain kind of beard, told him jokingly that he looked like a Turk.[3] The military experience he acquired with Piccinino before becoming marquis became the foundation of a policy aimed at setting up Mantua as a buffer-state between Venice, Milan, and the Papacy. His activity as a supplier of arms and men, and as a military commander, was one of the principal sources of his economic strength. As "Captain General of the community of Florence" he accumulated the financial credit that was to serve later for the construction of the tribune in the Annunziata.

But Ludovico was no mere soldier. His education had been entrusted to Vittorino da Feltre, who had been called to Mantua by Gian Francesco Gonzaga. According to Platina, Vittorino undertook "the difficult enterprise in the interests of the commonwealth, for, as he used to say, the education of a good prince would benefit the people he ruled."[4] Compared with that of his contemporaries, Vittorino's teaching was markedly moral and religious, and contained "a vein of laical asceticism almost."[5] This explains Ludovico's religious faith, the sincere Catholicism that led him to found churches and to behave as he did at the time of Pius II's Council. It also accounts for his Humanistic culture, his concern with the greatness of the state, and his identification of the splendour of his house with that of Mantua.

Ludovico undertook a number of building and town planning schemes in his native city, from the paving of the streets to the organisation of the city centre. "The Marquis Luigi also wanted to enlarge the Palazzo della Ragione, which, as we have said, was begun in the days of his father Giovanfrancesco. The public clock-tower was built near the palace, Luigi commissioning Professor Bartolomeo de' Manfredi, a Mantuan, to build it. So our chroniclers say."[6] Ludovico is mentioned again in the *Fioretto*:

"He built many beautiful buildings in the city: he began the church of S. Sebastiano to the design of the famous Florentine architect, Leon Battista Alberti, and completed the ingenious clock-tower, the work of the expert Mantua astronomer and mathematician, Bartolomeo Manfredi. He did the same with the dyke between Goito and Mapello, along which runs a part of the Mincio, and which serves to water the fields. He also gave a magnificent welcome to the Emperor Frederick III and the King of Denmark when they visited the city."[7] Ludovico levied special taxes for works that would benefit the whole territory, and he was able to do so regularly thanks to the agricultural wealth of the region he ruled. He also made use of forced labour, and by applying a system of demographic proportion, he obliged the peasants to dedicate a certain number of days to the construction of public works, using their own carts and cattle. He also levied corvees for the cultivation of his own lands.

Yet in spite of this economic wealth — even greater here than in Rimini — the treasury was occasionally lacking in funds, as Mantegna's complaints show. The trimming policy adopted by Ludovico in the war between the Viscontis and the Sforzas, between the anti-Viscontean league and Milan, did nothing to help him realize his twofold ambition: to turn Mantua into a neutral *force de frappe* with which alliance would be indispensable, and to make it the Catholic centre of affairs not only in the Po valley but in Europe, with Ludovico himself assuming an important role in international politics as a contadino, Humanist and soldier. The holding of the Council in Mantua created problems of organisation — such as providing lodging for the twenty-six cardinals and "other archbishops, bishops, abbots, generals of religious orders, prelates, and ambassadors of kings, princes and republics throughout Christendom, who were all lodged in the city. The Marquis had given the nobles Baldassare Castiglione and Carlo Agnelli the special task of seeing to the comfort and needs of so many important people. The Marquis had also given orders that there should be no lack of food supplies, with the result that the roads and rivers were crammed with carts and barges night and day."[8]

Pius II arrived by boat: "As we sailed down the Po, the two fleets met, the duke's and the marquis'. The first escorted Pius, and the second wanted to escort him too. All the valleys round echoed to the sound of trumpets."[9] On 26 May the Pontiff entered Mantua, dressed "in priestly vestments, with a sparkling mitre on his head, studded with precious stones,"[10] and was presented with the keys of the city by Ludovico. The Pope wrote later:

1. S. Gionta, *Il Fioretto delle Cronache di Mantova*, Mantua 1844, p. 85.
2. Ibid.
3. F. Amadei, *Cronaca Universale di Mantova*, Mantua 1955, II, p. 50.
4. E. Garin, "La Letteratura degli Umanisti", in *Storia della Letteratura Italiana*, III, Milan 1966, p. 134.
5. Ibid., p. 132.
6. F. Tonelli, *Ricerche Storiche di Mantova*, Mantua 1797, p. 369.

7. S. Gionta, op. cit., pp. 85-86; Cf. also G. Coniglio, *I Gonzaga*, Varese 1967, pp. 53-54.
8. F. Amadei, op. cit., p. 99.
9. E. S. Piccolomini, *I commentari*, Siena 1972, I, p. 207.
10. Ibid., p. 211.

"All the cities where Pius stayed had done the same, except Siena and Florence. These, oppressed by the tyranny of the people, did not do so in order to show that they were free."[11] Disappointed by the lack of attendance and tormented by attacks of gout, the Pope decided to stay in Mantua "just long enough to see what the princes' intentions really were"[12] and to launch his pathetic appeal for a crusade, an idea that was to be the dominant motif of his pontificate.

Mantua must have seemed like a prison to the officials of the Curia. The Pope himself wrote: "The place was marshy and unhealthy, and the heat burnt up everything; the wine was unpalatable and the food unpleasant. Many people fell sick, and many caught the fever. The only sound was the croaking of frogs."[13] The cardinals spent their time boating, not without causing the Pope some alarm. They also went hunting, this time causing the Marquis some worry, since he was afraid Cardinal Borgia (the future Alexander VI) would ruin his hunting reserves. In a letter to one of his gamekeepers, he complains that the Cardinal hunts "with so many dogs dragging nets that he will ruin the whole countryside within a few days."[14]

The Council ended on 14 January 1460 with the platonic proclamation of a crusade, which the princes were left free to join or not. The Pope left Mantua five days later, a sick and disappointed man. Though the Council cost Ludovico a lot of money, it ended on a note of great personal prestige with the elevation of his son Francesco to the purple. Thus he could take a period of rest at the health resort of Petriolo, near Siena, and stop at Florence on the way to settle the question of the tribune in the Annunziata. While at Mantua, the Pope had looked into the matter of the authenticity of the sample of Christ's blood that was kept in the basilica of S. Andrea. (This led to the church's reconstruction some years later.) Pius was accompanied to Mantua by Alberti, now an old official of the Curia, whom the Pope knew and admired, having read his *De re aedificatoria* (amongst other things): "Alberti the Florentine wrote some excellent volumes on architecture."[15] He too, had been guided by Alberti on his archaeological walks in the surroundings of Rome: "There are still many big cisterns at Albano. Battista, of the Florentine family of the Albertis, a learned and very zealous scholar of antique monuments, told me he had discovered more than thirty hidden among the thorns and brambles. Pius visited four huge ones that had survived."[16] The Marquis Ludovico must also have known Alberti, since the Latin edition of the *De pictura* had been dedicated to his father in about 1438, when Giovan Francesco visited Eugenius IV in

Ferrara at the time of the Council. Alberti had written in the dedication: "You govern a peaceful, well-ordered city by virtue of your prudence, and when you rest from public duties, you find the time, as is your habit, to study letters. Therefore, considering your customary humanity, which is far greater than any other prince's, not only in the glory of your military deeds, but also in your knowledge of letters, I hope you will not disdain to look upon these books."[17] The Marquis Ludovico obtained two very important briefs from Pope Nicholas V. The first concerned the foundation of a big hospital and the abolition "of all smaller ones, except that of Saint Anthony (because of its religious function, which it fulfils so diligently), their incomes to be brought together under the administration of the diocesan bishop and set apart for the big hospital."[18] The second, a *motu proprio* of 1452, took the church of Mantua (its clergy, bishop, and property) out of the hands of the patriarch of Aquileia and placed it under the direct jurisdiction of Rome.[19] Alberti himself might have had some part in carrying through these important matters, in view of the special relations that existed between Mantua and Florence. The first evidence of Alberti's presence in Mantua before 1459 is contained in a letter written by the Marquis which mentions his being in the city for the Council: "since His Holiness has asked for the loan of a copy of Vitruvius, we have sent you this messenger of ours for the purpose, begging you to be so kind as to send it to us through him. And should you not have taken it with you but have left it here in the city, be so kind as to write to whoever has it, so that we may procure it for His Holiness. You will do me a great favour if you do this."[20] The letter is important not only because it leads one to suppose Alberti must have visited the city before 1459, but also because it suggests that he may have revised the *De re aedificatoria*, which he continued to work on after 1452. The letter does not say where Alberti was, but he could not have been very far from Mantua, for when the Pope left for Rome in February 1460, he seems to have remained in the city, where the Marquis wrote to him from Milan: "Honourable Lord. Should we delay our return to Mantua, we beg you to excuse us, and to await our arrival in any case, for we hope to return within a few days. Milan, 22 February 1460."[21] Thus, the Marquis Ludovico had a copy of Vitruvius; in addition, he had many manuscripts copied and illuminated, besides encouraging tapestry and pottery.[22]

Alberti found a stimulating environment in Mantua. Luciano Laurana was there at the time; in 1465, however, Barbara the Marchioness of Brandenburg was urging him to return from

11. Ibid.
12. Ibid., p. 217.
13. Ibid., p. 218.
14. G. Coniglio, op. cit., p. 63.
15. G. Mancini, op. cit., p. 386.
16. Ibid.

17. Ibid., p. 388.
18. I. Donesmondi, *Dell'Istoria Ecclesiastica di Mantova*, Mantua 1612, p. 38.
19. F. Amadei, *Cronaca Universale della Città di Mantova*, Mantua 1955, I, p. 73.
20. W. Braghirolli, *Archivio Storico Italiano*, Florence 1869, 3rd series, vol. IX, p. 6, Mantua, 13 December 1459.
21. Ibid., p. 7, Mediolani 22 February 1460.
22. G. Mancini, op. cit., p. 390.

Pesaro, and in 1468 he moved to Urbino.[23] Above all, there was Luca Fancelli, who, though still little known, had the same importance for Mantua that Biagio Rossetti had for Ferrara. Luca was no mere director of plans drawn up by Alberti, but an artist with a distinct personality of his own. He had been formed in the school of Michelozzo, and had been sent to Mantua by Cosimo il Vecchio on Ludovico's request. He had already given tangible proof of his talent in the design of the palace at Revere, the place where Pius II stopped for the first time in Mantuan territory: "They spent the next night at Revere, where the palace, though unfinished, reflects the singular genius of its architect in its structure and ornaments."[24] Luca's artistic prestige is further borne out by the fact that it was he who approached Mantegna in 1458 to persuade him to leave Padua for Mantua.[25] The painter finally settled down in the city after 1459, at the time of the Council. The relationship between Mantegna and Alberti was a very close one: both grew up in the cultural atmosphere of Padua, both were inspired by classical antiquity, and an element of classicism is common to all their works. Mantegna's paintings may even have been directly influenced by the *De pictura*.[26]

At about this time, when this particular cultural climate prevailed, Ludovico suddenly decided to build the church of S. Sebastiano: "After returning to Mantua from Milan, the Marquis Ludovico had a very mysterious dream (Schivenoglia does not describe it for us). On waking up, he thought it over until he felt an inner voice urging him to build a church. At the time the Marquis had ordered work to be carried out on the fort at Porta Pradella (on the left as one enters) because he wanted to reinforce the gateway, which, as yet, did not have the outer bulwark that covers and defends it now. He suspended the work on the fort, and had all the material that was to have served for its construction transported to a place near Porta Pusterla, which was still uninhabited at the time, being little more than a field called Redevalle. And so, thus inspired, he began this year to lay the foundations of a church dedicated to Saint Sebastian the Martyr on this very spot.[27] Mancini writes: "The Marquis's impatience to start building and the long-standing friendship that bound the Gonzagas to Alberti may have influenced Ludovico when he came to choose an architect. The Marquis may also have been impressed by the praise lavished on the architect of the magnificent church of Rimini by Sigismondo Malatesta, who happened to be in Mantua at the time."[28] Replying to the Marquis's letter on 27 February 1460, Alberti assures him that he will wait for him in Mantua. He also informs him that he has moved to the villa at Cavriana

"for a change of air for a few days" (he was a health and hygiene fanatic), and adds: "The mouldings of S. Sebastiano, S. Lorenzo, and the loggia are now finished, and I don't think you will dislike them."[29] This raises the still unsolved, still unstudied problem of the possible restoration of the eleventh-century rotunda of S. Lorenzo. Nor has the loggia mentioned in the letter been identified in any convincing manner, though it may be the one in front of the Palazzo della Ragione. There may also be a reference to the clock-tower in a request made by Luca Tagliapietra when he was restoring S. Andrea in 1470: "He showed me a letter from Your Lordship on the subject of the tower etc. But for the moment I have decided to do what is mentioned in your letters. We shall think about the other things afterwards."[30] If this supposition is correct, then the idea that the whole complex of S. Lorenzo, the clock-tower and the Palazzo della Ragione was planned according to Alberti's advice becomes more credible. Another letter refers to the "painting" of the tower, "with its inscription referring to you", while the Marquis urged Fancelli to get in touch with Alberti so that "he may design the same lettering for you, which, according to us, was: Johannes Franciscus primus Marchio Mantue etc. If he too is of the opinion they should be designed in any other way, let us know."[31]

This is a further example of Alberti's fondness for Roman inscriptions, of which those in the friezes of the Tempio Malatestiano, S. Maria Novella, S. Pancrazio, and S. Martino a Gangalandi, bear constant witness. Alberti's penchant for, and competence in such matters must have been known to the Marquis, who attributed considerable importance to the commemoration of his deeds in stone.

The quadrant of the clock-tower and the inscription in the frieze, though simplified and abandoned later, may have been designed by Alberti. They re-appeared later in Codussi's clock-tower in Piazza S. Marco in Venice.

SAN SEBASTIANO

San Sebastiano may be considered one of the earliest and most significant examples of the Renaissance centrally-planned church. A number of references in the *De re aedificatoria* help to clarify its unique nature: a temple consists of a portico and a cella; the quadrilateral church comes immediately after the central one; a temple can have apses, though "quadrangular temples usually have only one, situated at the far end of the interior, immediately facing the entrance. But if one wants to add others to the sides, this may easily be done with rectangular plans, where the church

23. For the presence of Luciano Laurana in Mantua, see also Filarete, *Trattato di Architettura*, p. 173, the article on Laurana in the DAU and E. Marani, in *Mantova*, *Le arti*, Mantua 1961, II, 2, "Esordio del Rinascimento", passim.

24. E. S. Piccolomini, op. cit., I, p. 207.

25. W. Braghirolli, "Luca Fancelli, scultore, architetto, idraulico del sec. XV", *Archivio Storico Lombardo*, Milan 1876, III, p. 612.

26. This is the main point of discussion in the article by M. Muraro, "Mantegna e Alberti", *VI° International Conference on Renaissance Studies*, Florence 1961, pp. 103-132.

27. F. Amadei, op. cit., p. 119.

28. G. Mancini, op. cit., p. 392.

29. W. Braghirolli, op. cit., p. 8, 27 February 1460.

30. Ibid., p. 14.

31. Ibid., p. 13, 19 October 1470.

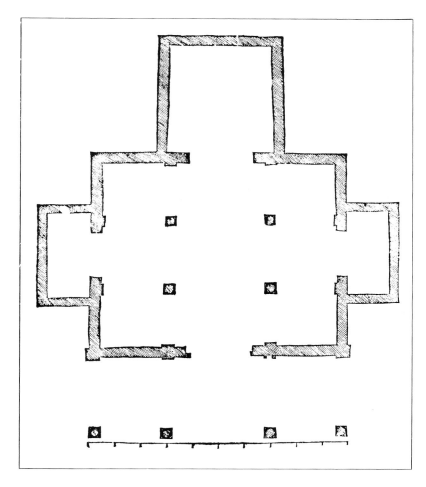

is twice as long as it is wide, bearing in mind that not more than one should be placed in each side."[32] Alberti adds that an apse can be rectangular or semicircular, and if there is only one, it may have an entrance. This is done by dividing the width of the temple into four parts, two of which will be equal to the width of the apse: "But if you wish to make it larger, this division may consist of six parts, of which the aperture of the apse will occupy four."[33]

This corresponds roughly to the ratio between the width of the apses in S. Sebastiano (9.45 metres) and the side of the church's central square (16.15 metres). The rule according to which the side apses must have the proportions of a double square was not observed in S. Sebastiano; the apses have a depth of 5.15 metres and a width of 9.45 metres. The reason for this is that the planimetry of the church was based on the construction of a central square space covered by a cross-vault, and of a diagonal square which is double the first one. This geometric design clearly reveals how the sides, or corners, of this second square are made to converge upon the centre of the niches in the three apses. The result is a 1 : 2 ratio governing the edifice's surfaces and lengths. The double square of a square is a concept of fundamental importance in the history of thought and architecture; it establishes the primacy of geometry. Plato, in a famous passage in his *Menon* (a dialogue known to Alberti),[34] after rejecting various arithmetical possibilities, declares geometry to be superior to all forms of measurement.[35] (The construction of the double square was also an essential feature of the Gothic tradition,[36] but Alberti had nothing in common with this.) Thus the revival of a method of constructing the square along its diagonals, explicitly mentioned in the treatise, could be supported by quotations from Plato. It is also connected with the subtle analysis of the relationship between the whole and its half, or *diapason*, which occurs in the ninth book[37] and which Alberti applied experimentally in so many of his works.

The proportions of the areas of a building, Alberti says, must harmonise with its upper parts: "The roots are the sides of the squares of the numbers: the powers are the areas of those same squares. The multiplication of the areas produces cubes. The first of all cubes, whose root is 1, is itself 1 in its entirety. Moreover, they affirm that it alone is, has all the forms, is perfectly stable, and can rest upon any base of any kind with equal safety."[38] Since Alberti discusses the doubling of the square and the irrationality of the diagonal immediately after praising the cube, the whole passage appears to be relevant to S. Sebastiano: "A line

32. L. B. Alberti, op. cit., VII, 4, p. 552.
33. Ibid.
34. G. Mancini, op. cit., p. 356.
35. Cf. A. Frajese, *Platone e la Matematica del Mondo Antico*, Rome 1963, pp. 99-110.
36. F. Borsi, *Per una Storia della Teoria delle Proporzioni*, Florence 1967.
37. L. B. Alberti, op. cit., IX, 6, pp. 824, 826, 828.
38. Ibid., p. 830.

drawn from one angle of a square to another opposite it divides the square into two equal parts, and is called the diagonal. What its measurement is in terms of numbers is not known, but we do know that it is the root of a square measuring 8."[39] (In other words, the double of a square that is 4 on each side: "the first number is 2.")

The volume of S. Sebastiano is basically that of a cube, while the height of the imposts of the arches in the apses is equal to their width, making a 2 : 3 ratio between the width of the apses and the spring of the relative arches. The huge vault too, with its massive, broad bases, creates a 1 : 1 ratio between the height of its imposts and the walls beneath, and a 1 : 2 ratio between the space covered and the total volume. Similar simple ratios govern the planimetry of the crypt, which clearly conditions, and is conditioned by, the general plan of the church. In fact, the modular element consists of a cross-vault covering a square space with sides measuring 2.40 metres and supported by columns measuring 0.90 x 1.20 metres. Thus the sides of the columns are half the size of those of the vault, which results in a ratio of 1 : 2: Alberti's *diapason*. The construction of the square along its diagonal produces a square that is double the first, if one considers the general square as made up by the four columns and their relative archivolts. The height of the imposts of the vaults is about 2.40 metres (disregarding the question of the present level of the church's pavement), which means that the width of the pillar is half that of its height, while the spring of the arch is about 3.60 metres high. In other words, there is a 2 : 3 ratio between the height of the spring of the arch and its width, and the same ratio (adopted by Alberti at Rimini as well) also applies to the upper part of the church. In accordance with the rule laid down in the treatise ("To the celestial gods they raised temples above the ground"[40]), the total volume of the crypt (the cause of the church's raised pavement) is about 4 metres, or a fourth of the total height of the temple above it, when the latter is considered as a cube with sides measuring about 16 metres.

The present-day visitor is likely to be led astray by the church's cold, aggressive, modern restorations, though the overall impression is of a hall in one of the Roman baths, similar to that of Nero's for example, as it appears in the drawings of Palladio-Scamozzi.[41] The arched openings, for which Alberti showed little sympathy, were added by the restorers. The fragmented outer walls were clearly filled in the middle, and a large window like those used in Roman baths would probably have blended with the rest of the structure better than the arched aperture introduced

39. Ibid.

40. Ibid., VII, 3, p. 546.

41. V. Scamozzi, *Le Fabbriche di Andrea Palladio*, I, "Le Terme dei Romani", Plate V.

LATESTA DELARCHO DISEGNIATO ARICONTRO

later.[42] The restoration of the church as a whole, including its wall texture, is questionable. Its most controversial aspect, however, are the two side staircases. These cannot be reconciled either with Wittkower's theory, according to which Alberti planned one large staircase stretching along the whole width of the façade, nor with any practical plan (whether of Alberti's invention or not) providing access to the church by means of side loggias; one of the latter still exists, and is clearly fifteenth-century in style. Labacco's plan, which specifies the edifice's measurements and may therefore be granted a certain credibility, clearly shows that the entrances were at the ends of the portico, and that the niches on the sides of the three entrances were balanced by other niches on the sides of the three corresponding entrances in the centre of the portico.

The crypt is abnormal, partly because its pilasters are much narrower than the ones above it. This caused later architects to adopt solutions incompatible with Alberti's principles, and one can only suppose that the pilasters were introduced when the building was continued in the sixteenth century.

The basic design of the façade, its broken entablature and central arched window of classical derivation, has been thoroughly analysed by Wittkower: "There is still one element which seems to disturb the classical harmony, namely the break in the entablature and the connection of its two halves by an arch in the pediment. There existed any number of combinations of the straight entablature with the arch. Brunelleschi had introduced the motif into Renaissance architecture in his Cappella Pazzi, following such pseudo-classical medieval works as the façade of the cathedral of Civita Castellana near Rome. But one hesitates to accept a dependence of Alberti's severe temple front on such prototypes. On the other hand, the motif occurs frequently in Hellenistic temples and tombs in Asia Minor. Although the idea is very tempting, it cannot be assumed that Alberti had any knowledge of these faraway places. The only building that could have influenced him is a monument well known to artists of the Quattrocento, namely the arch at Orange, the side fronts of which show the motif together with an articulation similar to our reconstruction of Alberti's S. Sebastiano."[43]

Work on the project was far from continuous, in itself a sufficiently valid reason for its various inconsistencies. After beginning construction in 1460, Fancelli left for Florence, where he remained in 1461, writing to the Duke: "And I shall have to return soon to see to S. Sebastiano as well."[44] Alberti apparently returned to Mantua in 1463, since the "engineer" Giovan Antonio d'Arezzo

42. See the restorer's plans: "Once the apertures in the walls and apses have been walled up, the mullioned windows above them changed to circular ones, and the sixteenth-century marble tribune which was taken from the church when the latter was used as a storeroom, and which is now in the "garden of honour" in the Palazzo Ducale, is put back in its original position, the hall will reacquire that severity which is in keeping with its patriotic function". In A. Schiavi, "Il Famedio di S. Sebastiano", in *Bollettino del Collegio degli Ingegneri e Architetti di Mantova*, March 1924, p. 7.

43. R. Wittkower, *Architectural Principles in the Age of Humanism*, London 1973.

wrote to the Marquis: "I have seen that Messer Battista has everything he needs, for he asked me to do so, and I have placed myself at his disposal."[45] The Marquis also wrote, asking how the various works were proceeding, and was told as regards S. Sebastiano: "I am waiting to start the construction of a great part of the church, from the halfway mark upwards."[46]

There is abundant evidence of the good relations that existed between Ludovico and Alberti (including a basket of four quails the Marquis sent him in September[47]). In December, "Messer Battista is very anxious to lay down the whole pavement (of S. Sebastiano), and has told me more than once that we had better get a supply of stone."[48] A document of the same year mentions certain difficulties that had arisen due either to technical reasons or to the fact that the project had not been respected. Fancelli writes: "We have repaired the walls since their bark had been ruined and a large part of them had to be pulled down from the ground level upwards."[49] The "bark" was probably their outer surface, and the damage may have been caused by the weather of the previous year. The lack of stone (of which there was very little in the area) is mentioned in documents dating from 1464 to 1466.

In 1464 the persecution of the Humanists began, and Alberti left Mantua. Work proceeded under the direction of Fancelli, who, in a letter of 1466, seems to refer to it: "I have started work on many different parts of the said building. We are now working on the cornice of the vault above the door of the portico."[50] There is no doubt that the vault of the portico, with its cappuccine is much closer to Fancelli's fifteenth-century style than to the severe Roman manner of Alberti's arch. Yet a letter from the Marquis proves that Alberti was present on the building-site in 1470: "We have read what you say as to Battista degli Alberti's opinion regarding the reduction of the pillars of the portico etc., and we assure you that whatever seems fitting to him has our approval."[51]

This reduction of the pilasters could refer as much to their number as to their size. In the first case, considering the almost quattro-centesque, non-Albertian character of the vault of the portico, the intention may have been to eliminate the double narthex so as to conform to the Etruscan temple scheme proposed by Vitruvius. But the size of the space (16.60 metres by 4.55 metres) would have made it difficult to introduce a row of pilasters in the centre; they would have had to be about 60 centimetres wide, leaving two arches with vaults measuring 2 metres, which would have been too small with respect to the cross-vaults of the crypt.

44. W. Braghirolli, "Luca Fancelli", in *Archivio Storico Lombardo*, Milan 1876, III, p. 615, note 15, 31 March 1460.

45. W. Braghirolli, "Leon Battista Alberti a Mantova", in *Archivio Storico Italiano*, Florence 1869, 3rd series, vol. IX, I, Pt. p. 11, 24 January 1463.

46. Ibid., 27 August 1463.

47. Ibid., 20 September 1463.

48. Ibid., 27 December 1463.

49. Ibid., p. 20, 27 August 1463.

50. Ibid., p. 21, 12 December 1466.

51. Ibid., p. 13, 13 October 1470.

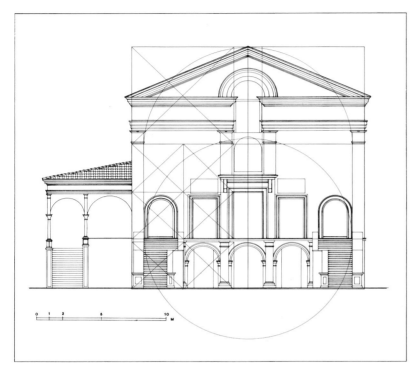

214. *Diagram illustrating proportions of the façade of S. Sebastiano.*

Wittkower argues that the original façade may have had six large pilasters[52] and that the reference in the Marquis's letter is to the elimination of the two that would have divided the present outer bays. If, however, the reference was to a reduction in size, then it is interesting to observe how the two pilasters measure 1.25 metres, while those between the side doors and the arches are 1.50 metres. Such a reduction would have been necessary to make the central portal wider with respect to its height, thereby giving it more prominence — a theory confirmed by the bold cornices that surmount the big central pilasters.

Thus, a number of questions remain unanswered, but the second, simpler theory appears more plausible than Wittkower's, especially when one considers the volume of the portico from the side and the position of the pilasters along the edges of the two full volumes, which are separated by the central aperture and connected by the pediment above. The central pilasters suggested by Wittkower could not have been repeated on the side, where they would have prevented access to the end of the portico. Even if they had been introduced into the façade, they would have been more decorative than anything else, and have made the composition obtrusive and academic. These, in fact, are the qualities that characterise the reconstruction proposed by Wittkower, who, in spite of his masterly analysis of Alberti's works, is over-inclined to consider his façades as separate, independent units.

The later chronology of the church's construction does not help in any way. The only evidence one can gather from the documents in support of the slight alteration suggested above is the rarity of stone buildings[53] in the area of Mantua and the need to order supplies of stone in time. On 25 November 1470 the Marquis wrote once more: "We have taken note of what you write regarding the work on the portico of S. Sebastiano, and since you on your part have taken the trouble to inform us of the measurements and methods of work, for which we thank you exceedingly, so we in turn are sending you our engineer to provide for everything that has to be done. And you must inform him of everything you need, for we are really very eager to see this front portico built before anything else is done."[54] The uncertainty remains as to which portico is being referred to — that of the crypt or the one above it — even though the rustication of the latter must have been finished by that time, since the cornice of its roof was mentioned four years earlier. In 1475 there is further mention of the need of stone for S. Sebastiano,[55] which shows how slowly the work proceeded. In the same period Luca Fancelli talks of

52. R. Wittkower, op. cit.

53. Braghirolli is right when he says the stone could not have come from Tuscany, but that it may have come from Verona (there is the greyish or blackish limestone of S. Sebastiano and at the base of the clock-tower). See F. Rodolico, *Le Pietre delle Città d'Italia*, Florence 1965, pp. 146-147, note A.

54. W. Braghirolli, op. cit., p. 16, 25 November 1470.

55. Ibid., p. 25, 28 June 1475.

215-235. *Mantua, S. Sebastiano. This church poses more problems than any other work of Alberti's. It has suffered most from damage and apocryphal additions, and it remains a kind of huge, blurred "fragment". Its construction was tortured and laborious.*
After getting off to a rapid start, it encountered numerous difficulties, work being frequently held up by the lack of stone, the vagaries of the weather, Fancelli's frequent absences from Mantua, and his limited availability when present owing to his numerous other projects. The originality of its design was not understood; if Cardinal Gonzaga could consider it more of a "mosque, or synagogue" than a Christian church, *one wonders what the ordinary common people must have thought of it. Little remains of Alberti's work, apart from the plan. This conveys the impression of a large hall in a Roman thermae, an impression which not even Schiavi's ponderous restoration succeeds in destroying. The two outer staircases (added in the same period) are abominable, the problem of the front of the crypt (fifteenth-century?) has been avoided, the scheme of the façade is suspect as a result of alterations made during Alberti's lifetime, the various heights of the construction — and consequently that*

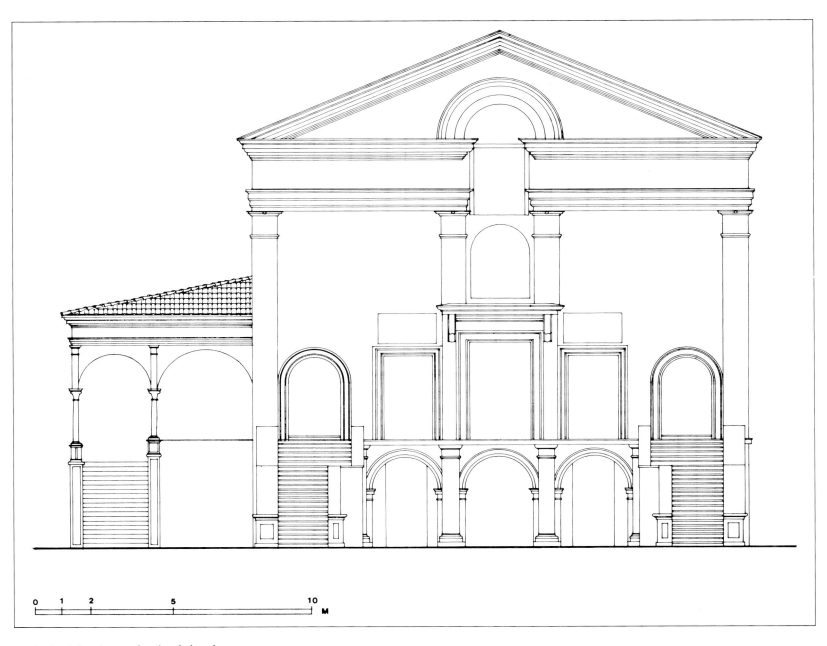

215. S. Sebastiano, sketch of façade.

of the façade — are open to question, the central apertures are incomplete, while there is no doubt that the lateral ones have been distorted, with the result that the distribution of light in the interior is far from Alberti's original intentions. Even the crossvault roof is questionable, for the original plan may have included a dome.

The church is an example of Alberti's style at its most intransigent, of Alberti's classicism at its most dogmatic, when he seized the opportunity local tradition offered him of building in brick, a material he was to use more organically in S. Andrea. Worn by time, restored with cement,

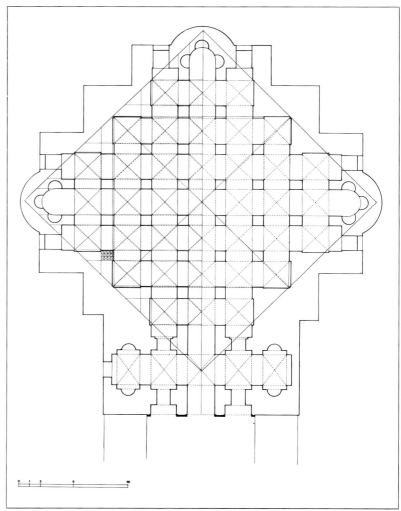

and completed with conventional occhi, the huge brick walls have lost all their grain and authenticity — not to mention their patina.
The edifice is disappointing in its present state, and the observer naturally fastens upon a number of still valid details. These include the more Fancellian than Albertian volticciole a cappuccina (small leaf shaped vaults), the uneven stone moulding, the cornices above the doorways, and the beautiful, fluent carving of the plutei, which testifies to the considerable skill of the men who worked in Fancelli's workshop. This style must have been far more congenial to Alberti than that of the masons of Settignano and Fiesole.

218-219. Mantua, S. Sebastiano. Plan and proportional diagram.

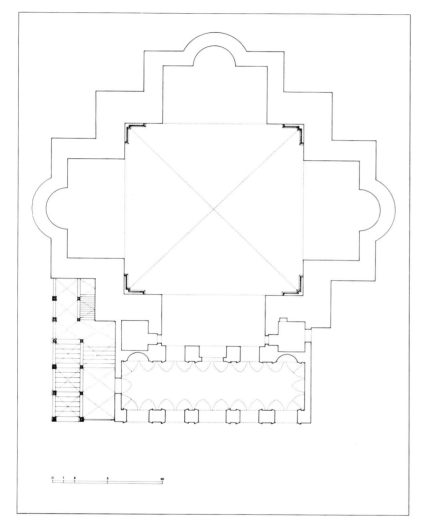

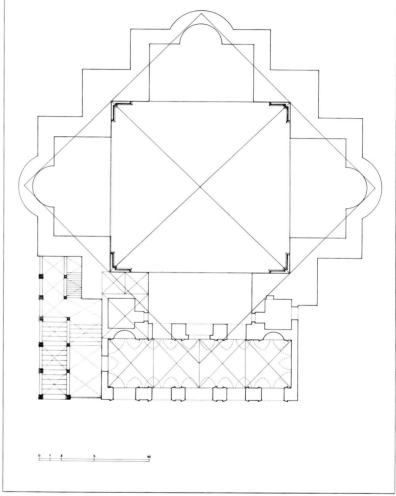

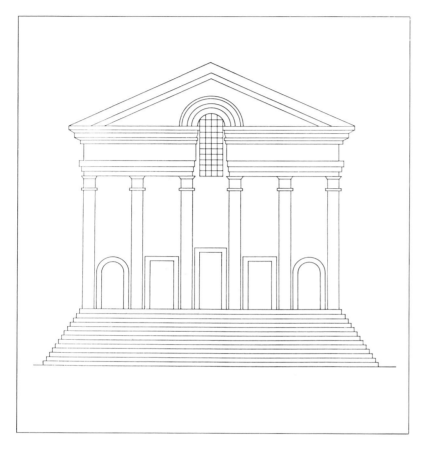

having "walled up two arches, the one in the middle and another on the right of the entrance. There remain two parts of the vault, or of the arch rather, to be walled up with stone, though some time must pass before the work can be done."[56] In 1478 there is another reference to stone being needed for the portico.[57] In a letter of 1477 Luca Fancelli asks to be paid for his work "at S. Sebastiano, on the clock-tower, and on works in wood."[58]

If one considers this delay in relation to Ludovico's building programme as a whole, and to the rather modest scale of this particular project, one can only conclude that Ludovico must have lost interest in the church. There seems to be no other explanation, unless it be the church itself. Pevsner calls it "original, austere and remote."[59] It must have appeared very avant garde and quite incompatible with local taste for Cardinal Francesco Gonzaga to write a year after Alberti's death: "Though the edifice is built in the classical manner and not so very different from Messer Battista Alberti's fantastic style, I still haven't understood whether it is supposed to be a church, a mosque, or a synagogue."[60] However, the inconsistencies that characterise the execution of S. Sebastiano can all be explained by a failure to understand Alberti's message. The problems they create do not only concern the church's entrance and the outer archways with the three carved plutei, which served as a pretext for Schiavi's two ponderous staircases. There is also the question of the façade of the crypt, if one takes it to be a feature of Alberti's original design and not a part of Ardizzoni's sixteenth-century continuation of the building, begun in 1499. There are two other problems as well: whether the façade was raised to a height superior to Alberti's usual proportions for a square because of the need to cover the visible part of the roof behind; and more important still, whether the cross-vault was Alberti's idea, or whether he had planned a dome with two bell towers. The planimetry[61] of the latter had already been elaborated, as one can see in a sketch which the not altogether reliable Antonio Labacco drew beside a plan of S. Sebastiano (now in the Uffizi). If this were so, then the typology of the edifice would be more closely related to certain sixteenth-century constructions than to the hall of a Roman thermae, and Alberti's work would appear to anticipate problems dealt with by later architects, from Bramante to Philibert de l'Orme (the architect of the chapel at Anet).

Alberti was profoundly impressed by Brunelleschi's masterpiece at S. Maria del Fiore, but he has little to say on the subject of domes. He never saw a roof of his own design actually built, nor did he leave a trace of his ideas on this aspect of his work

56. Ibid., p. 25, 24 June 1475.
57. Ibid., p. 28, 26 May 1478.
58. W. Braghirolli, "Luca Fancelli", op. cit., p. 628, 22 February 1477.
59. M. Pevsner, *Storia dell'Architettura Europea*, Bari 1959, p. 146.
60. S. Davari, "Ancora della chiesa di S. Sebastiano in Mantova e Luca Fancelli", in *Rassegna d'Arte*, Milan, 1901, no. 6; C. Fabriczy, "Die Baugeschichte von S. Sebastiano in Mantua", in *Repertorium für Kunstwissenschaft*, Berlin 1904 p. 84, 16 March 1473.
61. See E. Marani, "Leon Battista Alberti", in *Mantova, Le Arti*, Mantua 1961, II, p. 127 and note 51, p. 137.

SOLDATI A VOI LA GLORIA DI PIANTARE IL
TRICOLORE D'ITALIA SVI TERMINI SACRI
CHE NATVRA POSE A CONFINE DELLA
PATRIA NOSTRA; A VOI LA GLORIA DI
COMPIERE FINALMENTE L'OPERA CON
TANTO EROISMO INIZIATA DAI NOSTRI PADRI
XXXI MAGGIO MCMXV
VITTORIO EMANVELE

I RESTI DI QVELLO CHE FV VNO DEI PIV
POTENTI ESERCITI DEL MONDO, RISAL
GONO IN DISORDINE E SENZA SPERAN
ZA LE VALLI CHE AVEVANO DISCESO,
CON ORGOGLIOSA SICVREZZA
DAL COMANDO SVPREMO
IV NOVEMBRE MCMXVIII ORE XII
ARMANDO DIAZ

behind him. This might lend support to the theory that he never planned the roof of a project in advance, but was content to postpone a decision on the matter until a later stage in the project's realisation, when new possibilities might have arisen out of the actual work of construction.

PAUL II AND THE 'PURGE' OF THE HUMANISTS

At the end of 1463 Alberti was busy superintending the construction of S. Sebastiano with "great enthusiasm". In August 1464, however, Paul II succeeded to the throne of St Peter, and shortly after his coronation proceeded to suppress the college of apostolic abbreviators, of which Alberti was one of the oldest members. Apart from the Pope's desire to bring Cardinal Lanso back into the Curia (Pius II had removed him from the department of Briefs), the Pope's action was motivated ideologically, as von Pastor's conservative account of the episode illustrates only too clearly. The main accusation against the Roman Academy was that of paganism. It was also accused of holding secret rites in the catacombs, of which traces were said to have been found. There is no evidence that Leon Battista Alberti took any direct part in these.[62] The suspicion of Republicanism nourished by classical culture, a suspicion that had grown after the outbreak of Porcari's conspiracy, now re-appeared, masked in the form of a concern for law and order. To the marketing of favours and concessions and the doctrinal intrigues of officials and Humanists the Pope added the accusation of redundancy. Platina, whose protests landed him in jail, later wrote: "He dismissed all the abbreviators, calling them useless and ignorant."[63] But the dismissed officials protested by staging a kind of sit-in: "For twenty nights in succession they besieged the entrance to the Papal Palace, without once being received by Paul II."[64] We do not know whether Alberti was among those who vainly sought audience. It is difficult to imagine him doing so, given his keen insight into the power game and human nature, which he portrays so tellingly in *Momus*: "Jove decided he would build another world for the gods and men. His plan was approved unanimously by both the more and less important of his subjects. In fact, as always happens, each one was thinking of himself, believing that the impending change would be to his own advantage."[65]

Feeling himself Mantuan by adoption (a few years earlier he had considered buying some land near the city), Alberti appealed to the Marquis Ludovico, who promptly wrote to the Pope on New Year's Day 1465, praising Alberti: "In the last few years the venerable, most excellent Messer Battista degli Alberti has

been on very familiar terms with me, has often stayed at my court, and has never failed to offer me his labour and services, so that I must profess myself greatly bounden to him."[66] Nor did the Marquis stop there; five days later he wrote to his son, Cardinal Francesco: "We are sure you are aware of how much Messer Battista has done for us in the past in providing the plans and supervising the construction of our S. Sebastiano, for which we are obliged to him. Now he has written to us, begging us to be so kind as to recommend him to His Holiness and to you in his present situation. We have been only too happy to help him in every way possible, and so we have written, recommending him to His Holiness. Now it is our concern that you too, out of the respect you bear us, take it upon yourself to recommend him and to do everything in your power to help him, doing which, you will give us singular pleasure."[67]

The cardinal lived in the Vatican in great splendour, surrounded by antique trinkets, "with the sole defect of being as avid for young girls as he was for young boys. But this is not considered a very great vice in so handsome a man adorned with so many fine qualities, and is considered altogether pardonable. He sees Paul nearly every day."[68] We do not know with what enthusiasm he carried out his father's recommendations; not with very much perhaps. Nor do we know whether he influenced the Venetian Pope in any way, though he enjoyed His Holiness' favour. He certainly did not succeed in getting him to rescind his decision. But he may have got him to provide Alberti with work, for he was retained in Rome because of his architectural merits, and he certainly influenced, even if he did not take any direct part in the design of Palazzo Venezia.

THE BASILICA OF SANT'ANDREA

The re-modelling of the church of S. Andrea was bound up with the much larger problems of reorganising the city's religious life and providing it with a town planning scheme. This resulted in the collaboration between Alberti and Fancelli, whereby one designed and the other executed the Rotonda of S. Lorenzo, the Palazzo del Podestà, and the clock-tower — the civic centre, as it were. The re-structuring of the city's ecclesiastical organisation was a consequence of the crisis that followed the death of the Provost Guido Gonzaga. The family's desire to re-assert its power over the Mantuan clergy on a more permanent footing was fulfilled by Sixtus IV in 1472, with the abolition of the abbey and the foundation of a collegiate church, of which Cardinal Francesco Gonzaga was made the head with the title of *primicerio*

62. L. von Pastor, op. cit., p. 308 ff.
63. G. Mancini, op. cit., p. 409.
64. L. von Pastor, op. cit., p. 305.
65. L. B. Alberti, *Momo o del Principe*, op. cit., p. 249.

66. G. Mancini, op. cit., p. 410, Latin text in Braghirolli, op. cit., p. 12.
67. W. Braghirolli, op. cit., pp. 12-13.
68. G. Mancini, op. cit., pp. 410-11.

and the faculty to use a ring, mitre, and crook.

As for the town plan, Fancelli altered the Palazzo del Podestà in such a way that its façade was made to face the Piazza del Mercato. His style is evident in the houses overlooking the square and in those in the area around the basilica. The novelty of the tower lies in the treatment of its surfaces; it is the first example of a pictorial element introduced into a city built entirely of brick, and the classical elegance of its inscription could only have been achieved by an artist like Alberti. The first suggestion of a plan for S. Andrea occurs in a letter from the Marquis to Alberti concerning the tower: "We have just seen the design you have sent us of the temple, and our first impressions were favourable. But since it is not fully clear to our understanding, we shall wait until our return to Mantua. Then, after talking it over with you, and after explaining our ideas and listening to yours, we shall do what seems best."[69] The correspondence between them shows how much more available Alberti was for eventual commissions in Mantua after his unhappy experience in Rome.[70]

The phrase "it is not wholly clear to our understanding" suggests that the project must have contained some novelty if Ludovico, who understood architecture and later described himself as a disciple of Fancelli's, needed clarification from Alberti. Alberti had sent a general outline of the plan to the Marquis together with a letter containing the usual discussion about the clock-tower: "I have recently been told that Your Lordship and the citizens of Mantua intend building here at S. Andrea, with the prime object of having a large edifice where many people might come and see the blood of Christ. I have seen Manetti's model, and I like it. But it doesn't seem to me to suit your requirements. I have thought up the one I am sending you now, which would be much larger, more durable, worthier, and more cheerful. It would also cost much less. This kind of temple was called *Etruscum sacrum* by the ancients. If you like it, I shall draw up a plan with its proportions."[71]

This suggests that the Marquis must have had a model of the church made by the same Antonio di Tuccio Manetti with whom he had discussed the choir of the Annunziata in Florence; Manetti represented the Brunelleschian tradition, as can be seen in his work at S. Lorenzo. Nor can we disregard the ties that bound Fancelli to the world of Florence, where he had even kept his residence for tax purposes. (The Marquis later tried to persuade Lorenzo de' Medici to reduce the taxes claimed from "our engineer, whom we took into our care in consideration of the memory of Messer Cosimo, so that he may be said to have been brought

up by us."[72]) Though Fancelli himself practised an experimental kind of architecture, he was a great admirer of Alberti, and when he received the final design ("in proportion", since the first was probably drawn up without a scale), he wrote in admiration: "I am delighted with the design of the church you have sent me, because first of all, it helps me to understand the work, and secondly, because ambassadors and noblemen often pass by and we are obliged to render them homage by showing them some fine work. Now I can show them this wonderful design, the like of which does not exist, in my opinion, for which I thank Your Lordship."[73]

Thus the design had something "wonderful" or unusual about it, which was probably what the Marquis couldn't understand. Alberti's plan was based on the functional consideration of size ("a large space where many people might gather"; "this would be bigger") for he had in mind the deeply-felt Mantuan cult of the "most precious blood" (the legend that the legionary who pierced Christ's side with his lance, later brought back to Mantua the sponge soaked in vinegar together with a piece of earth splashed with Christ's blood). Alberti's consideration of size led him to think of a large hall, bigger than the usual basilica with chapels, which, according to fifteenth-century tradition, inspired Manetti's model.

Alberti's estimate of the cost of his project proved optimistic once the final project was drawn up, so much so that the Marquis wrote to his son, the cardinal: "according to the model that has been made, it will require more money and time than were estimated. But this does not concern you, who are young, so much as us."[74] The letter in which Alberti presents his candidature for the project also sums up the church's aesthetic features in the phrase, "more durable, worthier, and more cheerful." The enduring qualities in the work are easily discovered (no wood at all was used in its construction); its dignity is the result of its classicism; and its cheerfulness (in spite of its dull, pedantic, almost macabre sixteenth-century decorations) is a consequence of the distribution of light and, above all, of its size, which implies spatial vitality and a large congregation.

But the subtlest problems are contained in the almost slangy term, *Etruscum sacrum*.[75] Two passages in the treatise mention Etruscan temples. In the first Alberti says: "In various temples, according to a Tuscan custom (Etruscorum more), tiny chapels were built in the sides instead of apses (pro lateribus non tribunal sed cellae minuscolae) in the way we shall now describe. A type of plan was adopted whose width was five sixths of its length."[76]

69. W. Braghirolli, op. cit., p. 14, 12 October 1470.

70. Ibid., p. 16, 25 November 1470.

71. Ibid., pp. 14-15.

72. W. Braghirolli, "Luca Fancelli", op. cit., pp. 626-27, 17 December 1474.

73. W. Braghirolli, op. cit., pp. 21-22, 27 April 1472.

74. Gaye, op. cit., I, and W. Braghirolli, op. cit., pp. 21-22, note 4.

75. See R. Krautheimer, "Alberti's Templum Etruscum", in *Münchner Jahrbuch der Bildenden Kunst*, Munich 1961, XII, pp. 65-74.

76. L. B. Alberti, op. cit., VII, 4, pp. 554-57.

240-276. *Mantua, S. Andrea. Though a posthumous project, the church is perhaps Alberti's most complete work. Its construction proceeded very slowly — only the nave had been finished by the end of the century, after thirty years' work. There is also the fundamental problem as to whether it was originally planned as a Latin cross or in the form of a basilica (an analysis of the documents would seem to indicate the latter). Fancelli described its original design (now lost) as "wonderful". Even now, in spite of its heavy, dark interior (the result of its nineteenth-century mock Renaissance style and the replacement of its excellent original lighting system with conventional* occhi) *one can still feel its power, and enjoy its spatial harmony (governed by simple ratios) and the organic conception of its various parts. Here, Alberti was completely successful in his attempt to construct an organism of "pure" masonry unsupported by wooden elements or metal tie-rods, that is, a structure as lasting as*

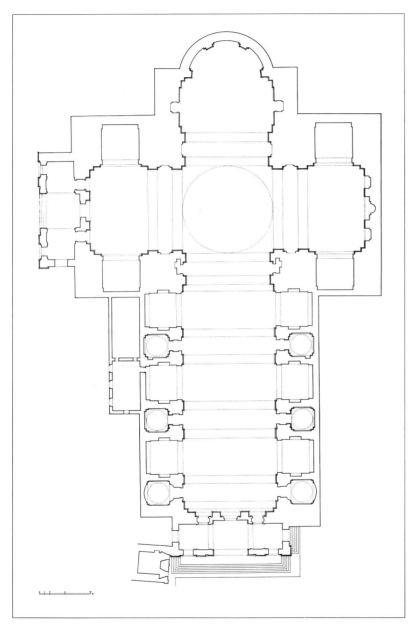

240. Mantua, S. Andrea. Plan.

241. Mantua, S. Andrea. Diagram of proportions.

the monuments of antiquity. One can still see (in the sides of the church) the niches hollowed out in the top of the wall of the barrel-vaulted nave and the buttresses that counter the thrust of the vault. Also visible in the containing wall of the chapels are the wall sections of masonry surmounted by large semi-circular windows (later closed), which alternated with arches in the manner of an amphitheatre. Thus "chambers of light" were created for the illumination of the nave, into which light filtered through the circular apertures and the vaults or small domes of the side chapels.

The intensity of the light varied in accordance with the small and large volumes as these were related to the nave. The result was a synthesis of structure, volume, and light reduced to their essentials. This shows that Alberti had grasped the fundamental values of architecture. He had succeeded in creating the etruscum sacrum he aspired to.

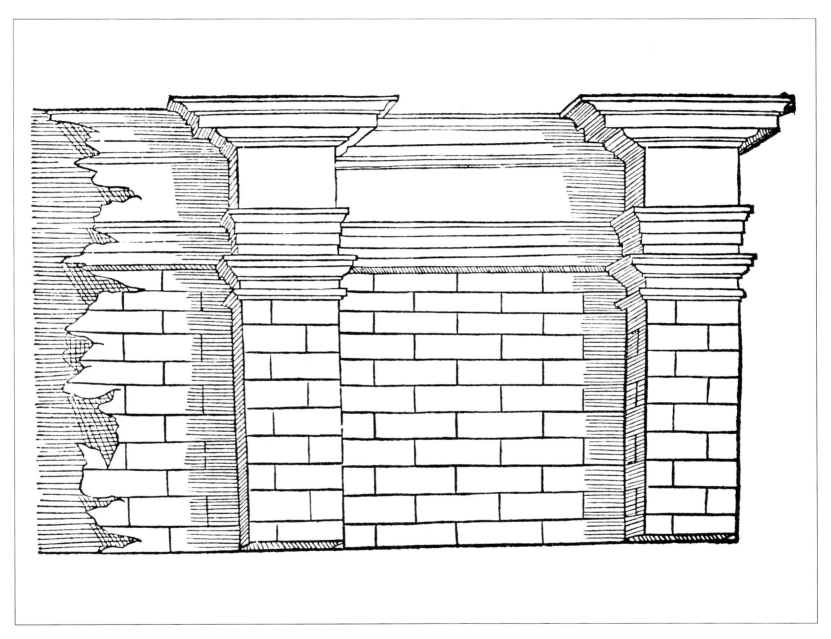

242. Mantua, S. Andrea. Relationship between the order and wall in a woodcut from Bartoli's edition of the De re aedificatoria, 1550.

243. *Mantua, S. Andrea. Façade.*

244. *Mantua, S. Andrea. Diagram of proportions of façade.*

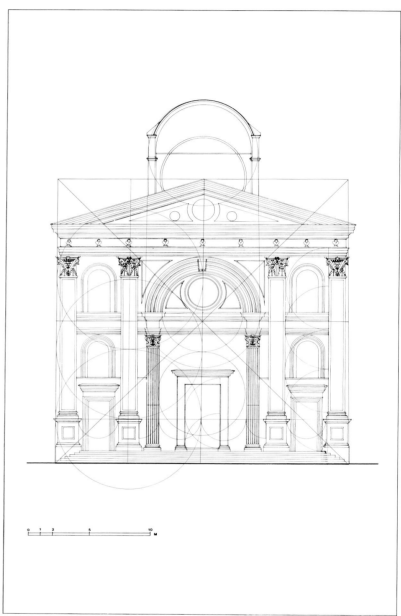

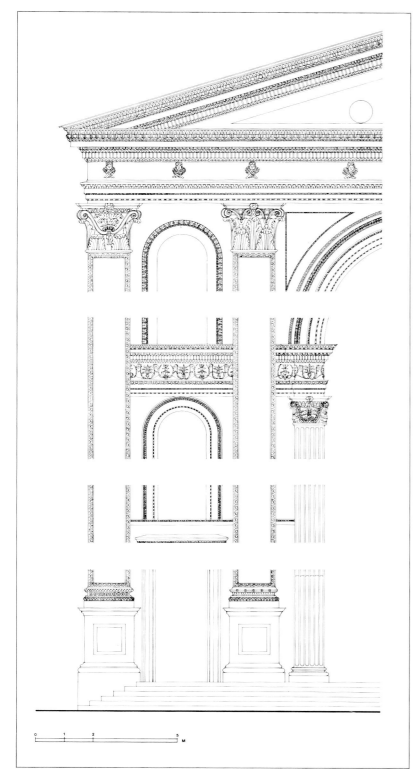

In the nave of S. Andrea, "tribunalia", or open chapels, are alternated with "cellae", or smaller chapels.

Another important aspect of the plan is the question of its proportions. The size of the open chapels has been taken as a surface module, and this corresponds to what fills the solids (including the walls) of the small chapels. The result is a modular length of six elements, whereas the width is subdivided into two parts by the chapels, and into three by the width of the nave. This measures 18.60 metres, three times the depth of the side chapels, which is 6.20 metres. Thus, the entire edifice is governed by a proportional ratio of 6 : 5 between length and width, which is the same as that of an Etruscan temple.

The second passage in the treatise deals with thermae, which had "a vast, solemn hall in the middle, as if to single out the centre of the edifice. This had a roof and was divided into rooms built" like the chapels in what we call an Etruscan temple ("atrium amplissimum et dignissimum cum cellis ex lineamento templi, quod esse Etruscum diximus"[77]). Alberti, then, was led to compare the large halls of the thermae with the typology of the Etruscan temple, and it was in a synthesis of the two that he saw the possibility of creating a huge space, "a vast, solemn hall." This is what he must have had in mind when he undertook the design of S. Andrea.

In another relevant passage Alberti writes: "But where there were to be chapels on each side of the wall, they sometimes built the walls as high as the width of the church in order to make the apertures appear larger."[78] This is precisely the solution he adopted for the elevation of the basilica's interior order.

Such are the points of correspondence between the edifice and the treatise. Alberti's reference to the *Etruscum Sacrum* in his letter implies either that the person he was writing to could understand the allusion or that he intended to clarify the concept further by word of mouth. His main concern was the vindication of an autochthonous Etruscan-Latin tradition as opposed to the Hellenic one that predominates in Vitruvius. Alberti realised there was no point in going any further into the ambiguity of the word "sacrum". That the place of worship was equally a place of ritual and revelation in both pagan and Christian practice was well-known, and the subject could not be clarified by any simple reference to Vitruvius. What was really needed was a broader concept of the term 'Etruscan' than that formulated by the Latin theorist; this was barely tolerant and vitiated by the idea of historical progress. Alberti's respect for the Tuscan order, his insistence on an Italic style of orders, and his efforts to substitute their

77. Ibid., VIII, 10, pp. 768-69; see also Krautheimer, op. cit., p. 71.
78. L. B. Alberti, op. cit., VII, 10, p. 606.

246. *Mantua, S. Andrea. Axiometric section and reconstruction of the original sources of light.*

247. *Mantua, S. Andrea. Axiometric diagram.*

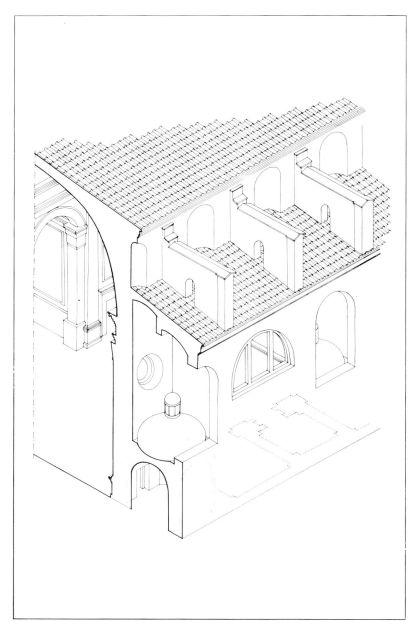

Greek names with Latin ones,[79] convey some idea of the range of his interests. These embraced semeiological problems as well as historical ones, and they could not fail to have some practical outcome in the culminating years of his life. It was inevitable that he should try to produce some concrete exemplification of these ideas, just as he had exemplified the centrally-planned church with S. Sebastiano. Naturally, this future work was certain to have a basilican scheme, though not necessarily of the Latin kind, as Krautheimer has observed. S. Andrea finally ended up this way after work was suspended on the church at the end of the fifteenth century, though the basic elements of Alberti's nave were retained.

The central problem is whether the entire transept and dome were an integral part of Alberti's original design, or whether they were added in the course of the complete reconstruction of the church carried out in the sixteenth century; even then Alberti's modules and heights were retained. (Juvara's dome, successful in itself, does not enter into this discussion.) As in Rimini, the most controversial parts are the transept, the tribune and the dome, though they were later completed in such ways as to avoid the fragmentary, temporary look that characterises the later work on the Tempio. To a certain extent this completion represents a Baroque interpretation of Alberti's architectural heritage, and deserves to be considered as an independent work of art. The unfinished side of S. Andrea, with its superimposed and unexpressed motifs, has the look of a ruin on to which various parts have been added; it has the same fascination as a view by Piranesi, and it sums up the whole history of the church. (This is particularly true when the building is seen in relation to the medieval ruins of the Benedictine abbey.)

The first offerings for the new church were made on Ascension Day in 1471. Ludovico gave 300 ducats and his cardinal son 200. Schivenoglia's chronicle records that on 6 February 1472 they began "to demolish the church of S. Andrea in Mantua in order to rebuild a more beautiful one."[80] On 12 June the foundation-stone was laid and a ceremony held to celebrate the event.[81] In July 1472 the Marquis wrote to Fancelli about the problem of the foundations: "for the love of God take great care to see that the foundations are sound, since one must give much thought and importance to such matters. Measure them three or four times before building them, and take care for the love of God."[82] The Marquis did not limit himself to exhortations but interfered personally on the building-site, issuing instructions of his own. At one point Fancelli had to write to him about an order he had

79. See F. Borsi, "L'Alberti e gli ordini architettonici", in *Studi e documenti d'architettura*, Florence 1972.

80. W. Braghirolli, op. cit., p. 18.

81. F. Torelli, *Ricerche Storiche di Mantova*, Mantua 1797, p. 388, and F. Amadei, *Cronaca Universale della Città di Mantova*, Mantua 1955, II, p. 174.

82. W. Braghirolli, op. cit., p. 18, 22 July 1472.

83. Ibid., pp. 22-23, 6 July 1472.

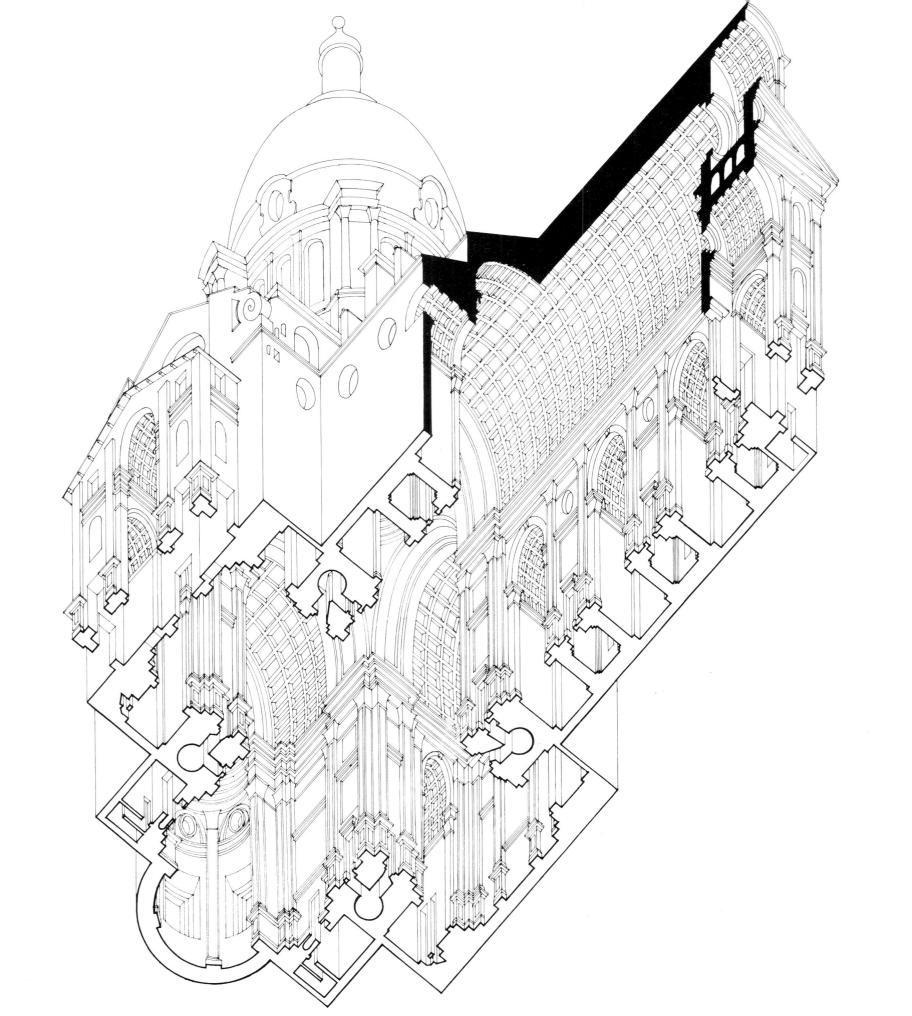

given concerning the construction of a "wall from the floor of the choir upwards", and though Fancelli considered the order to be mistaken, he was obliged to avoid contradicting his patron: "I have ordered certain works to be done out of respect as well."[83] A letter of August 1472 confirms the logic of the design and execution of the project. The bell tower was to be taken as the main point of reference and work was to begin on that side of the edifice, as far as alignments and foundations were concerned: "Half the building is completed on the monastery side, beginning at the bell tower and proceeding towards the sacristy, while it has been raised on the opposite side towards the shops."[84] Deeper foundations had to be laid on the side of the shops. Earlier foundations were discovered, so the walls had to be propped up and precautions taken to prevent subsidence: "Everything will turn out all right providing the work is done well."[85] Alberti died on the eve of the Feast of the Ascension, just before a platform was raised to enable the priests "to prolong the exposure of the relic of Christ's blood."[86]

By the first of September financial difficulties had arisen. After being approached for a loan of mortar and stone, the Marquis asked Fancelli to submit a report on the matter. In May 1473 Fancelli informed him that "all the chapels will be raised to the level of the scaffolding according to the order given ... even if I have only twenty-seven trowels to work with. The only thing left after that will be the main entrance-door of the church."[87] By 1477 the entire project was in jeopardy. Luca had sacked the masons, the authorities had not bothered to replace them, and "in this way the construction of S. Andrea has been suspended, which is very unfortunate." In addition, a difference of opinion had arisen between Giovannino di Bardelone and Luca regarding the direction of the works. The Marquis, however, insisted that "the project cannot be done without Luca, for there is no one who understands it as he does." He points out that Giovannino is a sensible person, but that he does not understand "such subtle projects, since he is used to building houses and haystacks for villas. He is always counting the cost, but beautiful things cannot be made without great expense."[88] In view of the approaching winter, it was better to suspend the work, provide for adequate supplies of material, and wait for Luca, rather than take rash decisions. The same plan is repeated in a letter to "Luca Lapicida," which informs him of the problem of the cold, and of the difficulty in getting the wall to dry in time.[89] Further evidence of the same period shows that work was being done on the ceiling of the third chapel: "on Monday we started work on the third

chapel in S. Andrea."[90] This must have been on the bell tower side of the church. The Marquis duly remarked: "We are glad that the third chapel in S. Andrea is being provided with a ceiling" for the beams had already been put into place, and might have been damaged if left in that state.[91]

In 1480 the Marquis wrote to his son once more about the difficulties encountered in the construction: "These intrigues can only result in damage to the church." He enclosed a letter from Fancelli, in which mention is made of "my building", so that his son might "see everything that has been written to us in the original itself."[92] Two days later he returned to the subject, hoping they would "put an end to their mutual distrust, which was harmful to the building" (probably a reference to the usual differences between the administrators and Fancelli). In 1481 the crisis grew worse. The Pope was asking for money for the crusade, and the whole operation was in danger of coming to a halt: "The edifice of S. Andrea will require a great sum of money, since a fairly large sum will be necessary for its roof at the same time."[93] Ludovico had died in 1478 and had been succeeded by the Marquis Federico I, while Fancelli had carried on as court engineer in charge of numerous projects.[94] In 1484 Federico died and was succeeded by Francesco II, who, "distracted by military enterprises, gave no thought to works of art at the beginning of his rule."[95] It is thought that Fancelli ceased to superintend the construction of S. Andrea after 1485.[96] The roof of the nave was built between 1490 and 1494,[97] whereas Fancelli, after working on the drum of Milan Cathedral from 1487 onwards, was in Florence in 1490 and in Naples in 1492 (where he replaced the recently deceased Giuliano da Maiano). He visited Mantua in 1489 to finish the tomb of the Marchesa Barbara of Brandenburg, and he returned in 1490. In 1493 he was in the city once more, busy paving some of its streets; he had sold his house in Mantua to provide his daughter with a dowry and was in financial straits.[98] It seems unlikely that he took actual charge of the construction of S. Andrea again, though he had plenty of opportunity to give advice, and he seems to have inspired the idea of building a barrel-vault with gravel and mortar in the Florentine manner.[99]

Was it the scarcity of wood or Fancelli's absence that led to the construction of the uncoffered barrel-vault? Presumably, Alberti had intended it to have a more Roman aspect, and his intentions have since been partly (and pedantically) realized in the painted coffer-work. Amadei wrote in the eighteenth century: "This church has the form of a cross, the largest part of which consists of a single arch, or vault rather, which is not held together or

84. Ibid., 6 August 1472.

85. Ibid.

86. Ibid., p. 22, 30 April 1472.

87. Ibid., p. 24, 13 May 1473.

88. Ibid., pp. 26-27, 20 September 1477.

89. Ibid., pp. 27-28, 20 September 1477.

90. Ibid., 24 September 1477.

91. Ibid., 27 September 1477.

92. Ibid., p. 29, 10 September 1480.

93. Ibid., p. 30, 22 June 1481.

94. W. Braghirolli, *Luca Fancelli*, op. cit., p. 619.

95. Ibid., p. 620.

96. E. Marani, op. cit., p. 128.

97. Ibid. Cf. also Dell'Arco, *Delle arti e degli artefici di Mantova*, II, doc. 30 and pp. 30-31, doc. 39.

98. W. Braghirolli, *Luca Fancelli*, op. cit., pp. 622-23.

99. See Federico Gonzaga's letter to Margherita di Baviera Gonzaga, dated 25 September 1479; "We would like you to send us Master Luca Fancelli, our engineer, because we want to show him a method of building roofs with gravel and mortar which is now used in Florence. It is very beautiful, and not very expensive." in W. Braghirolli, op. cit., p. 619, note 35.

supported by the usual large iron keys. Nor are there wooden beams above it so that it might be covered with tiles. Instead, the exterior of the vault, which is exposed to the rainwater, has a sharp outline, so that its back serves as a bed for the tiles that protect it from the rain. Thus, there is no danger of the wood being corroded or rotted by woodworms or rain in the course of time, such as happens in other buildings unfortunately."[100] This last point corresponds to the desire expressed by Alberti in his first letter to the Marquis to build an "eternal" temple, and it also reflects the close relationship between the ideas of Alberti, already dead twenty-two years earlier, and those of Fancelli, about to be dismissed as director of works if not already relieved of direct executive responsibility.

Schivenoglia's chronicle confirms that the church was finished in 1494. Later events may be summarized briefly: between 1597 and 1600 Antonio Maria Viani added the lateral arms, the chancel, and the crypt; between 1697 and 1710 Giuseppe, or Giulio Torre submitted a Baroque project judged to be too expensive, though he built the vaults of the transverse section of the chancel and choir in the same period;[101] between 1732 and 1782 the dome was built to a design of Filippo Juvara; and the final decorations were added under the direction of Paolo Pozzo.[102] The construction of the church, which continued for three hundred years, confirms the theory that the present structure is the result of a continual re-thinking and reinterpretation of Alberti's original design. However, it provides no clue as to what the original tribune and transept would have been like.

Marani writes: "Thus, the idea of the transept may have been formulated in the late sixteenth century, while it is uncertain whether the fifteenth-century plan of S. Andrea provided for a dome at the end of the nave in front of the apse or not. It should be remembered, however, that a closure of the apse, probably unlike the present one, had been traced even in the days of Fancelli."[103] In the letter of July 1472 (which refers to the Marquis' interference in Fancelli's work), a choir is being discussed where mention is made of building "a scaffold from the pavement of the choir upwards," though one can see that its shape had not been decided upon or clearly worked out: "I doubt whether they will be able to decide how to continue the walls upward from the pavement without my help. But it seems to me that they were not to be built higher than they are already."[104] This refers to a difficulty involving the base of the structure and implies adherence to a definite plan; there is no mention at all of a cross, cross-vault, or transept. The idea of a choir was certainly appro-

priate, given the importance of the relic that was kept in the church and shown to the faithful. It might also have represented a compromise in view of the importance of the financial difficulties that had arisen. The time factor, too, must be taken into consideration, for the size of the foundations of the present transept convinces one it could not have reached such a point by then. The planimetry of the church had two basic points of reference: the earlier bell tower and the group of houses (later rebuilt) along the street and market-square. The latter created problems as regards lighting the sides of the church, for one of these sides must have rested against the other buildings from the earliest times (we have already seen how this caused difficulties in the laying of the foundations). The existence of the bell tower must have resulted in the façade being narrower than the rest of the edifice, with consequences we shall examine later. The extreme simplicity of Alberti's proportions (we disagree with Sanpaolesi's theories to the contrary[105]) were those of an "Etruscan temple", with a 6 : 5 ratio between the church's length and width. The basic module of the basilica's plan and elevation is the square, and the void squares of the large chapels correspond exactly, from a volumetric point of view, to the solid squares of the small chapels with their relative piers. The nave is three times as wide as the large chapels, and thus establishes a 2 : 3 ratio. The square module of the large chapels has also been applied to the central arch of the façade, so that the internal system of volumetric values is repeated on the outside of the church. As far as the section is concerned, the width of the nave corresponds to the height of its wall up to the point where the barrel-vault begins; in other words, the basic module has also been applied to the nave. Here too, we have a 2 : 3 ratio, if one considers the width of the semi-nave and the consequent development of the barrel-vault. The ratio between the width and height of the open chapels (as far as the spring of the vault) is 1 : 2, Alberti's diapason, while a suitable stylobate, similar to those adopted by Alberti elsewhere, ensures a 1 : 7 ratio between the width and height of the pilasters from their base to the top. Similar ratios govern the portico, whose size in relation to the main body of the basilica was conditioned by the existence of the bell tower, and which is really an exterior repetition of themes developed in the interior (as regards both the central arch and the arrangement of the pilasters). These themes include the extension of the pilasters as far as the high stylobate of the ceiling, the entablature, and the minor entablatures above the small *cellae*, which are paralleled by the side entrances of the exterior. As Wittkower has observed, though Alberti was probably inspired

100. F. Amadei, op. cit., p. 175.

101. Cf. R. Bellodi, "Arte retrospettiva: la Basilica di S. Andrea in Mantova", in *Emporium*, Bergamo, XIV, p. 351. "The vaults of the transept and chancel were then built, according to the old design." But there is no evidence to prove this.

102. G. B. Intra, "La Basilica di Sant'Andrea in Mantova", in *Arte e Storia*, Florence, January 1902, XXI, 3rd series, p. 104. For a more complete bibliography on the subject, see "La Basilica di Sant'Andrea di Mantova", in *Quaderni di Storia e di Arte Mantovana*, Mantua 1965.

103. E. Marani, op. cit., p. 130.

104. W. Braghirolli, op. cit., pp. 22-23.

105. P. Sanpaolesi, "Il tracciamento modulare e armonico del Sant'Andrea di Mantova", in *Atti del convegno internazionale di studi sul Rinascimento*, Florence 1961, pp. 95-101.

by the Arch of Titus or the Arch of Trajan in Ancona, one should not underestimate this close relationship between the exterior and interior of S. Andrea, which results in one seeing the interior as a development of the triumphal arch motif. Not only do the general proportions of the basilica strictly adhere to the simple ratios laid down by Alberti in the *De re aedificatoria*, but they also constitute a kind of guarantee of the building's stability, which must have been secured in the Roman fashion, without tie-beams or chains of any kind. The side chapels, with their barrel-vaults placed at right angles to the vault of the nave, provide adequate buttressing and counter-thrust. The same effect has been obtained by means of the smaller *cellae*, where the walls between the *cellae* and the nave have been thickened. Above the level of the chapels, a series of niches breaks up and lightens the effect of the masonry, while suitable, basically square buttresses have been placed in the wall sections between the *cellae* and the chapels, or along the axis of the roof of the chapels, so as to counter the thrust of the central barrel-vault more directly.

This system of spatial shells, motivated by considerations of proportion and stability, is also related to the lighting of the church. This must have been something of a problem, since the long central barrel-vault cuts off all source of light from above, while the low houses on the side of the church prevent light from entering from that direction. The problem must have been solved by concentrating on the upper part of the chapels and alternating large lunettes at the ends of the edifice (later bricked up) with large arched apertures. In this way a kind of reservoir of light was created, which illuminated the lanterns and small vaults of the *cellae*, and from which light filtered through round windows into the nave. The only source of light that relieves the present gloom of the church comes from the eighteenth-century dome; but this situation was created when the building was re-modelled in the Baroque style of the Counter Reformation. The circular windows of the chapels, like the modifications that prevented light entering from the outside, were introduced later, as an analysis of the outer masonry clearly shows.

Stripped of its pedantic interior decoration and seen in the essentiality of its volumetric structure, S. Andrea, more than any other work of Alberti's, marks a return to the ancient brick architecture of late Roman times. As Wittkower says, S. Andrea marks the last stage in Alberti's development, after he had experimented with the entire range of ancient styles applicable in the Renaissance: "He developed from an emotional to an archaeological outlook. Next he subordinated classical authority to the logic of the wall structure. And finally he repudiated archaeology and objectivity and used classical architecture as a storehouse which supplied him with the material for a free and subjective planning of wall architecture."[106] This is more apparent in the lateral pronaos of Piazza Leon Battista Alberti, which was built in 1550 and bears the signature of an obscure mason or master-mason, Bernardino Gilberto, precisely because it is uncontaminated by any nineteenth-century decoration. This structure gives one a taste of really great brick architecture. Here one can appreciate the technical mastery of the coffered panels of the vaults and the way in which bands, cornices, and pilasters have been enhanced by the simplicity of certain decorative devices, such as capitals or terracotta ovoli and dentils. The latter add a refined touch of chiaroscuro and an artisan polish to the simple incompleteness of the rusticated brick structure. These are all aspects that facilitated the completion of the church in the Mannerist style, which Alberti anticipated to a certain extent. The transept was probably added in the middle of the sixteenth century, when Mantua was once more dominated by Roman culture in the person of Giulio Romano (though he does not seem to have played any direct part in the project).

The solution of the problem awaits a more systematic investigation of the church's archives, which have been undergoing reorganisation for many years now. What the question really amounts to is this: was the transept an integral part of the original model, or was it built to harmonise with the already existing nave? The latter solution would not have been difficult; the large sections of wall where the *cellae* are completely saturated with masonry and have no spiral staircases would have provided adequate support for the dome. The uncertainty with which Vincenzo Fasolo presents his hypothetical reconstruction of the building[107] leads one to doubt whether the original plan included a dome, even a low one unlike Juvara's slender creation. It also leads one to question the theory that Alberti's project was quite unrelated to the Madonna del Calcinaio or the Annunziata at Arezzo.

S. Andrea marks a decisive turning away from the 'vernacular' to the 'Latin'. This does not mean that Alberti merely imitated some classical model, but that he reinterpreted the classical past in the light of contemporary needs. This gave him greater freedom of action in the organisation of space, which he employed in an attempt to construct a solid, consistent "Etruscan temple" (basilica or Roman hall) devoid of artifice. Given the organic continuity between the pronaos and the rest of the basilica, the apse would also have had to harmonise with the size and structural characte-

106. R. Wittkower.
107. V. Fasolo, "Osservazioni su Sant'Andrea di Mantova", in *Atti del Congresso internazionale di studi sul Rinascimento*, Florence 1961, pp. 207-17.

ristics of the sides, with their *tribunalia* and *cellae*. It might have been conceived as an inversion of the symmetry of the front portico: "Temples may have one or more apses according to their particular requirements. Quadrangular temples usually have one, situated at the far end of the interior, immediately facing the entrance. But if one wants to add others to the sides, this may easily be done with rectangular plans, where the church is twice as long as it is wide, providing one bears in mind that not more than one should be placed in each side. If there has to be more than one, then it is better to have an odd number than an even one."[108]

Portoghesi believes that these words contain a clear rejection of the basilican scheme, even in its most up-to-date form, such as Brunelleschi's S. Spirito. He proposes the alternative of a rectangular hall with three apses, which anticipates the characteristic confusion between centrally — and longitudinally — planned churches so often found in early seventeenth-century Roman architecture (S. Salvatore in Corte, S. Francesco di Paola, and even Borromini's S. Maria dei Sette Dolori). Alberti writes: "The apse in its turn may be either rectangular or semicircular. If there is just one apse placed at the far end of the church, then a semicircular one is preferable; otherwise, it may be square. If, on the other hand, there are a number of apses, then it is aesthetically advisable to combine both kinds, alternating square apses with semicircular ones and arranging them so that those of the same kind face each other."[109] Given the importance of the relic it was to contain, the apse may even have been semicircular. One document relates that "a 'basin' was to have been built where the arms of the cross meet, as a fitting crown for the relic's place of custody."[110] This "basin" suggests a parallel between some kind of central element and the apse in the background, a kind of void and solid concentricity of the building's terminal elements. As in Rimini, one can only formulate conjectures as to the real nature of Alberti's design of S. Andrea, conjectures which excavations alone may prove right or wrong. In the meantime, their validity rests upon logical arguments of a strictly cultural nature, which view the different phases of Alberti's development within a historical perspective. Later, the building was de-structured and modified to the extent in which Alberti's message had been understood and incorporated into general practice. Thus the false idea of Alberti as a fifteenth-century architect who created a style that was described (by Milizia) as "not the most exquisite and impregnated with the undefinable musty smell of dark temples" led to an interpretation of his work in many buildings which Alberti himself would have considered insignificant. Alberti never tried to conceal or to mitigate his detachment from the world he lived in, a detachment he maintained in his personal, moral, and political life. At the same time he was torn by the desire to restore to architecture the characteristic essentiality of all great monuments that have survived the ravages of time. Faced with his last opportunity at S. Andrea, Alberti introduced a greater measure of architectural syncretism into his work than anywhere else. He was well aware that architecture "had been welcomed in Italy from the earliest times, especially by the Etruscans,"[111] who not only built tombs and labyrinths, but also left "those very ancient, illustrious rules that have come down to us in writing as to the way temples used to be built in Etruria."[112] But apart from the 6 : 5 ratios that characterise both, there is a considerable difference between Vitruvius's description of an Etruscan temple and Alberti's design of S. Andrea. Nevertheless, Alberti must have been particularly struck by the passage in Book IV of Vitruvius, in which the "Etruscan temple" is associated with the privileged land of his ancestors, where "the art of building had had its old home among the Etruscans." At the end of his Mantuan labours and of his career as an architect, Alberti, too, could look back upon Brunelleschi's achievement and at the treatise he had dedicated to Messer Filippo in his youth, and feel proud that he had carried out a work "without using beams or wooden supports, a building which I am certain must have been as inconceivable to the ancients as it seems incredible in our own times."[113]

108. L. B. Alberti, *L'Architettura*, VII, 4, pp. 552-53.
109. Ibid.
110. C. D'Arco, in *Delle Arti e degli Artefici di Mantova*, Mantua 1859, II, p. 208, in V. Fasolo, op. cit., p. 216.
111. L. B. Alberti, op. cit., VI, 3, p. 454.
112. Ibid.
113. L. B. Alberti, *Della pittura*, *Dedica*, ed. Janitschek, p. 49.

275. *Mantua, S. Andrea. View into the ceiling of Mantegna's chapel.*
276. *Mantua, S. Andrea. Tombstone in Mantegna's chapel.*

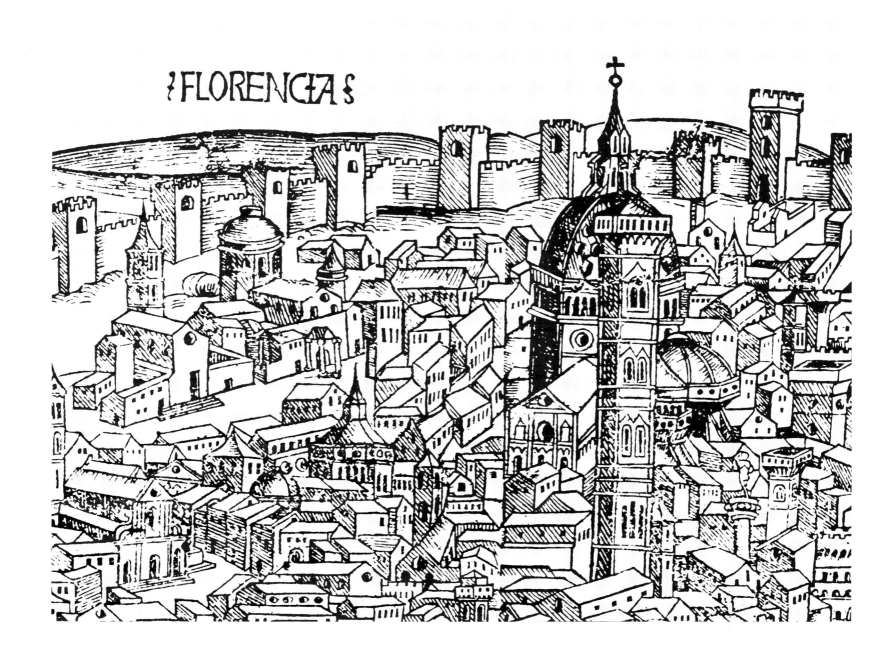

FLORENCIA

A PROJECT FOR THE GONZAGAS:
THE TRIBUNE OF THE ANNUNZIATA

Pietro Roselli[1] made the first systematic study of this work after assembling the many documents concerning its construction. However, he has not established the real nature of Michelozzo's plan or the part Alberti played in the project.

Vasari was the first to attribute the "design and model" to Leon Battista: "He carried out the ... tribune, a very ingenious and difficult structure, taking the form of a circular temple with a ring of nine chapels on the circumference which opened off like niches; this meant that the entrance arches over the pilasters of these chapels, which ornament the walls, have to adapt themselves to the concave shape of the tribune as a whole, curving — as it does — in a different plane. In turn, this means that if you look sideways at the entrance arches they seem to lean forward and they look awkward, as indeed they are."[2] This criticism and that of the arch connecting the tribune with the nave, which "is splendid from the nave, but on the inner side, where it has to follow the curve of the tribune wall, it appears to lean and looks extremely clumsy,"[3] led Vasari to harbour substantial reservations as far as Alberti was concerned. Juxtaposing "knowledge and theory" with "practice and experience", he nevertheless concedes that "Alberti showed great courage for his time in raising the tribune in the way he did."[4] In other words, the times were unprepared for so bold an experiment.

But was Alberti really responsible for the work, and does he deserve the credit for having done it? No longer apostolic abbreviator at the time, he was more available for architectural commissions. He also had, as we have seen, the complete confidence of the man who commissioned the work, Ludovico Gonzaga. And yet, according to the documents, he seems to have had a purely advisory role in the matter, and to have acted as a kind of go-between in an intricate dispute which involved Ludovico Gonzaga, the Signoria of Florence, and the Servite friars. The first step in commissioning the work was taken by Ludovico's father, Gian Francesco, the first Marquis of Mantua, who left a legacy to the church of the Annunziata. Michelozzo took the project up between 1444 and 1453, and immediately the idea of a curved tribune took shape: "The round building that is being built anew."[5] In 1460 Antonio Manetti appears on the scene as the "architect of the curved part at the back where there is to be a choir and a large chapel."[6] But Antonio disappears almost as quickly as he came, leaving "a curved chapel in the workshop to Giovanni Zati,"[7] together with tools and other equipment.

Other documents of the period testify to the rapid completion of foundations outside the church, near those Michelozzo had started to lay, but which had been interrupted five years earlier. No further work was done for nearly a decade, until Ludovico Gonzaga visited Florence twice in 1469 on his way to the baths at Petriolo near Siena. The visits led to a considerable amount of correspondence between the Marquis and the prior of the Annunziata. In one letter the prior refers to a visit of the Marquis's and to the church,[8] where a discussion seems to have taken place "about the money the community owes our church by order of Your Lordship."[9] A sum of money that the Signoria of Florence owed Ludovico for military services had been assigned by the latter to the Servite friars, but bureaucratic delays on the part of the Signoria had prevented its payment. Ludovico wrote to Pietro del Tovaglia, a Florentine merchant who was more or less the Marquis's agent in Florence, that the credit amounted to ten thousand ducats, two thousand of which had been paid and two thousand promised to the friars, and that he was going to add another thousand, partly out of his father's legacy and partly out of his own pocket. On the same day he wrote to the Signoria, urging the authorities to pay the friars so that "they may receive the money and spend it on the main chapel of the building."[10] Documents confirm that in 1470 the friars conceded all their rights to the main chapel to the Marquis of Mantua, who undertook to complete it, together with the tribune, through his representative Pietro di Lapo del Tovaglia; the corresponding deeds were drawn up by the notary Piero da Vinci, Leonardo's father.

On 25 October 1469 Pietro del Tovaglia wrote to the Marquis informing him that the work had begun: "I have begun to work on the Annunziata and have provided all the stone necessary." All the evidence suggests that it proceeded according to Manetti's old plan on the foundations that had already been laid. The same letter contains the first signs of a controversy that was to assume major proportions: "If I were to listen to everything they tell me, then ten thousand florins wouldn't be enough. So I assume an honourable attitude and say Your Lordship does not want to spoil what has already been built so as not to displease those who did it. But they reply that Your Lordship will not count the cost providing what is done is magnificent, to which I answer that that is true, but that Your Lordship does not wish to spend so much so as not to displease those who ordered what has been built already." He then adds, in the Marquis's interests, that in this way the work will cost five thousand florins and that "done in

---

1. P. Roselli, *Coro e Cupola della SS. Annunziata a Firenze*, Istituto di Restauro dei Monumenti di Firenze, Pisa 1971.
2. Vasari, op. cit., II, p. 543.
3. Ibid., p. 544.
4. Ibid., p. 545.
5. P. Roselli, op. cit.
6. Ibid., Doc. 23, p. 27.
7. Ibid., Doc. 25.

8. G. Mancini, op. cit., p. 469.
9. P. Roselli, op. cit., Doc. 29, p. 27.
10. Ibid., Doc. 31, p. 28.

any other way," it would either cost more or remain unfinished.[11] A letter from Giovanni Aldobrandini to Ludovico Gonzaga, dated 2 February 1470, says that "If the project is continued in the way it began, it will not please Your Lordship". He continues: "I met Piero del Tovaglia recently and told him my opinion. And since I thought the design had been drawn up by our herald, I told him I wanted to meet the herald one day there where we were talking. Piero replied that the design was not the herald's but Messer Baptista degli Alberti's, which quite astonished me. Though it is not for me to question the designs of the said Messer Baptista, at the same time I want to preserve what has already been done. So I urge Your Illustrious Lordship to have all the chapels that are being built around the tribune closed and to make a main chapel and choir out of them, for this tribune can be of no use as far as the choir and chapels are concerned."[12] The herald may have been a certain Francesco, who was the herald of the Signoria.[13] The letter clearly attributes the project to Alberti; this seems to have taken into consideration the foundations that already existed, increasing the number of chapels to replace those that were being demolished with a view to connecting the church with the tribune.

Less than a month later, Aldobrandini returned to the attack with a long letter to the Marquis listing all the project's defects: the chapels were too small and very few people would be able to get into them to listen to mass (they would be forced to stand in the choir); "the tribune will be vaulted, and is so small that when the friars sing in the choir (and there are nearly always about sixty of them) they will make such a noise with their singing that they will disturb the celebration of mass in the chapels, while the people attending mass in the chapels will greatly disturb the friars."[14] Nor was it fitting that "the laywomen, being so close to the friars as to be almost shut in with them, should distract them in any way."[15] The choir was inadequate and would be made even smaller by the altar. Aldobrandini then proposes a completely different project. This had a cruciform instead of a circular plan, as in S. Maria Novella and S. Croce, and the added advantage of making use of the old foundations. Aldobrandini adds: "I have shown this new design to Messer Baptista degli Alberti and Piero del Tovaglia. Messer Baptista made some objections, for he thinks it would cost five thousand ducats more."

In his next letter Aldobrandini suggests sending the Marquis a model of the new project, and clearly anticipates the objections Alberti was likely to raise: "I am convinced that whoever advised Your Illustrious Lordship to follow the old design had good intentions. Nevertheless, to whoever urges this, saying that there were buildings of this kind in Rome, my reply is that those in Rome were built as tombs for emperors and had four or six priests, not for a monastery like this. Moreover, they were decorated with mosaics and other such expensive ornaments, while the tribune, if built all in white without any other ornament, will look very bare and sad, apart from the fact that the church could never be restored again afterwards."[16] This is a complete rejection of the classical Albertian style in favour of the Florentine, which combined the sobriety of the plastered wall ("all in white") with the decorative needs of the classical style. But Pietro del Tovaglia stuck to the old project, and on the following day clearly stated his position as regards those who wanted "to demolish what has been done and start again from scratch". He also invited the Marquis to clarify his own position, urging him to hold fast to what had already been decided and to take comfort in the thought that the expense would be less and that "Messer Battista says it will be very beautiful."[17] In another letter, however, Piero vacillates slightly, recommending an unknown master-mason (perhaps Gaiole), "a master of building walls and highly esteemed by Messer Battista degli Alberti." This person wanted to visit Mantua to see S. Sebastiano in particular, and he had a project for the tribune that was similar to Aldobrandini's. Pietro del Tovaglia goes on: "Messer Battista continues to say that it will be the most beautiful construction ever built, and that the others can't understand it because they are not used to seeing such things, but that when they see it built, they will say it is much more beautiful than a cruciform building."[18]

The friars adopted a rather ambiguous attitude. According to Aldobrandini, "they were very attached to the old design, but when they saw the new one, they all changed their minds."[19] Later, they seemed to regret the situation and supported a new project which Giovanni da Gaiole had sent to the Gonzagas on his own initiative.[20] Naturally, the carpenter-architect who now appeared on the scene professed his complete impartiality in the matter, affirming that his only regret was that a decision should have been taken to construct "a building that had been designed by Michelozzo, but which Filippo our master has spoilt in many ways. First of all, because he has built it so close to the church that the nave, or main body of the church, cannot be developed in the form of a cross. There is no room for an altar or choir, nor can the chapel be used, so the project is useless both in itself and as a whole, for it is completely spoilt."[21]

Alberti took little notice of this Florentine busybody, who was

11. Ibid., Doc. 34.
12. Ibid., Doc. 38, p. 30.
13. Cf. G. Mancini, op. cit., pp. 473-474, note 4, and P. Roselli, op. cit., p. 30.
14. P. Roselli, op. cit., Doc. 39, p. 30.
15. Ibid.
16. Ibid., Doc. 39, p. 31.
17. Ibid., Doc. 40.

18. Ibid., Doc. 45, 27 April 1471, p. 33.
19. Giovanni Aldobrandini's letter to the Marquis of Mantua, 23 March 1470, in P. Roselli, p. 31.
20. Giovanni da Gaiole, master wood-carver and architect (1408-79). He worked with Giuliano da Maiano on the Palazzo Vecchio and made some furniture for the Canons of the cathedral. He also worked on the choir of S. Pancrazio. Cf. documents in G. Milanesi, *Nuovi documenti per la storia dell'arte toscana*, Florence 1901, pp. 114-15; testament in Gaye, pp. 172 ff. For his intrusive, quarrelsome character, see his letter to Giovanni de' Medici about the tribune of S. Lorenzo, in Gaye, op. cit., I, pp. 167-69. Cf. also E. H. Gombrich, *Norm and Form*, London 1966.

Gaiole writes about how he was assaulted publicly in Via Larga by a certain Barnabo, an assistant of Antonio Manetti the "wood-carver", for supporting Cosimo il Vecchio's criticisms of Manetti's design for S. Lorenzo. He defended himself against the accusation of not minding his own business by saying that "since we are in the pay of Cosimo and his family, it is our duty to inform him of everything we hear about his affairs, so that he may act accordingly".

Antonio Guidotti, who, as we have seen, did the model of the Rucellai Loggia, was also involved in the controversy, and on the side of Giovanni da Gaiole if anything. The whole controversy revolved around the construction of the tribune "in the manner of Filippo, that is, airy, strong, well-lighted and proportioned". The historical problem regarding Brunelleschi's followers is still an open one, and it remains to be seen whether they continued both his technical methods and his style.

A whole generation of craftsmen, who were either wood- or stone-cutters originally, claimed to be his true heirs; even the amateur Cosimo was involved in the dispute. The first group diluted his concept of space, completing S. Lorenzo somewhat anonymously, and "regularising" S. Spirito. The second reduced his style and sense of structure to the banality of that skilful, facile 'quattrocentesquism' which was to be so popular later. But all betrayed his real heritage, just as they closed their ranks against the art of Alberti, whom they were culturally incapable of understanding. Instead, they took refuge in technicalities, and sought protection in a post-medieval guild *ésprit de corps*.

21. P. Roselli, op. cit., Doc. 46, p. 33.

just a simple artisan claiming to be the guardian and heir of the Brunelleschian tradition. Giovanni failed to realize that Alberti was playing up to him and wrote to Ludovico Gonzaga in all seriousness: "I have shown the model to Messer Battista, who seemed to think it was the only thing to be done. He used these very words, saying that he had intended doing the same thing himself. And so, as Your Lordship knows, experience is the mother of knowledge." One can almost sense Alberti's snobbish disdain and see him rather wearily nodding his assent: "He seemed to think it was the only thing to be done." The letter also contains something like Vasari's contrast between theory and practice and his later division of architects into sophisticated artists and carvers. Never was there so symbolic an encounter as that between Alberti and Giovanni da Gaiole.

Meanwhile, Aldobrandini had taken up his pen once more and had written to the Marquis in defence of the new project. Ludovico now decided to settle the interminable dispute by bringing the whole weight of his martial authority to bear upon the Florentines. After all, the city owed him money, thereby preventing him from using it in a work intended for the benefit of Florence, not his own. He replied to Aldobrandini, telling him "our intention was not to build the most beautiful monument in Florence,"[22] but simply to carry out his father's will. If they wanted to return the money, all the better: "We would willingly transfer the money to prevent the construction of so beautiful a work", especially as he would be much happier building in Mantua than in Florence. Then, the question becoming increasingly complicated and public opinion growing more and more hostile, Ludovico wrote to the Signoria of Florence on 27 May 1471, reminding the Council of Cosimo de' Medici of the credit due to the Annunziata, of the time that had elapsed since the money should have been paid, and of his decision to add another two thousand ducats to the sum owed: "But where I thought to do good, I have found only difficulties. Since this work began I have received a flood of letters, designs, models, and delegations. I have also been made to understand that what I have done does not satisfy either the friars or the large majority of the principal citizens and people."[23] He points out that he had undertaken to build a chapel, not a church: "I did not take it upon me to build this church, nor do I intend doing so." Since no one likes the work, he says, he is going to abandon it. However, he has no intention of dishonouring his commitment; he will credit the friars with two thousand ducats, which they may spend as they please. At the same time he asks for the restitution of his own three thousand ducats, which he

will spend as he pleases.

Ludovico's firmness turned an artistic dispute into a diplomatic incident. "Many citizens were assembled and the letters were read in public so that everyone might express an opinion on the matter. Finally, the reply enclosed was drafted and approved unanimously."[24] The Signoria replied very courteously. It stressed the good relations between the two cities and confirmed that everyone was pleased with what was being built: "quod in aede dive Annuntiatae tam magnifice et tam docte edificas." (*Docte* implies a clear recognition of the merits of Alberti's plan.) The Marquis was made to understand that the letters written to him were the fruit of irresponsibility and envy, and were best ignored. He was reminded of what he, in his wisdom, already knew, that envy and avarice always played a considerable part in great enterprises. The Signoria ended on a note of instinctive Republican pride: "in libera civitate saepe major licentia est."[25] The incident was over, the money promptly paid, and Tovaglia instructed to continue the building "in the way it had been begun." Five years later he was able to write: "The chapel of the Annunziata is now wholly covered and is a worthy structure praised by all."[26]

It is easy to establish the part Alberti had in the construction. It is a posthumous work begun at the outset of Alberti's last year of life, when he was either in Rome or absorbed with the plans for S. Andrea. Once the Marquis had finally settled the economic complications in 1469, he entrusted the work to Alberti, who revised Manetti's project in an attempt to make use of the foundations. The dome, with its broad calotte (made out of a concrete-like mixture of mortar and stone shavings) and its weight distributed evenly upon the drum, recalls certain Roman models and so must have had Alberti's approval. We do not know how far he was responsible for the irregularity of the walls of the exedrae of the chapels in relation to the supporting pilasters. This is believed to be the result of his attempt to solve the problem of the two smaller chapels adjacent to the large central arch, which were to replace the two that were to be pulled down to make way for the arch, and which he designed in such a way as to create as large a space as possible between the tribune and the nave. The solution must have been a compromise intended to take into account the earlier foundations, which had been laid by boring holes in the already existing chapels and "sending down gravel into the bases of the pillars."[27] This was the only point Manetti's work and the earlier church had in common, so the two pillars in question must have been those of the large central arch. Gravel could only have been transmitted to the latter through

22. Ibid., Doc. 41, p. 32.
23. Ibid., Doc. 48, p. 34.

24. Ibid., Doc. 50, p. 35.
25. Ibid., Doc. 49, p. 34, Cf. also Gaye, I, p. 236 ff.
26. Ibid., Doc. 54, p. 35.
27. Ibid., Doc. 24 May 1460, p. 27.

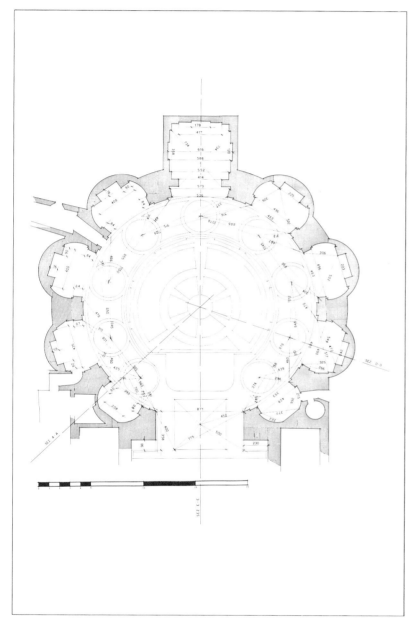

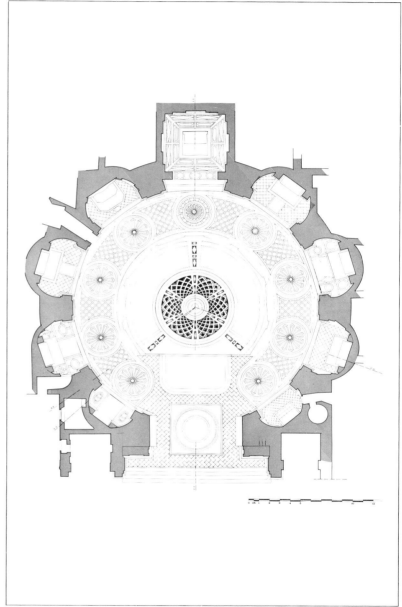

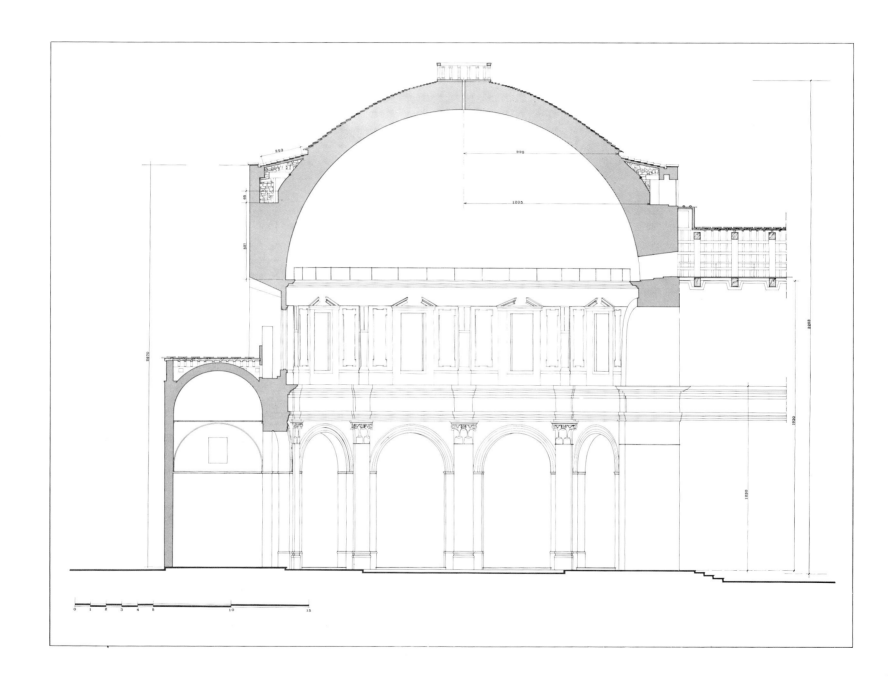

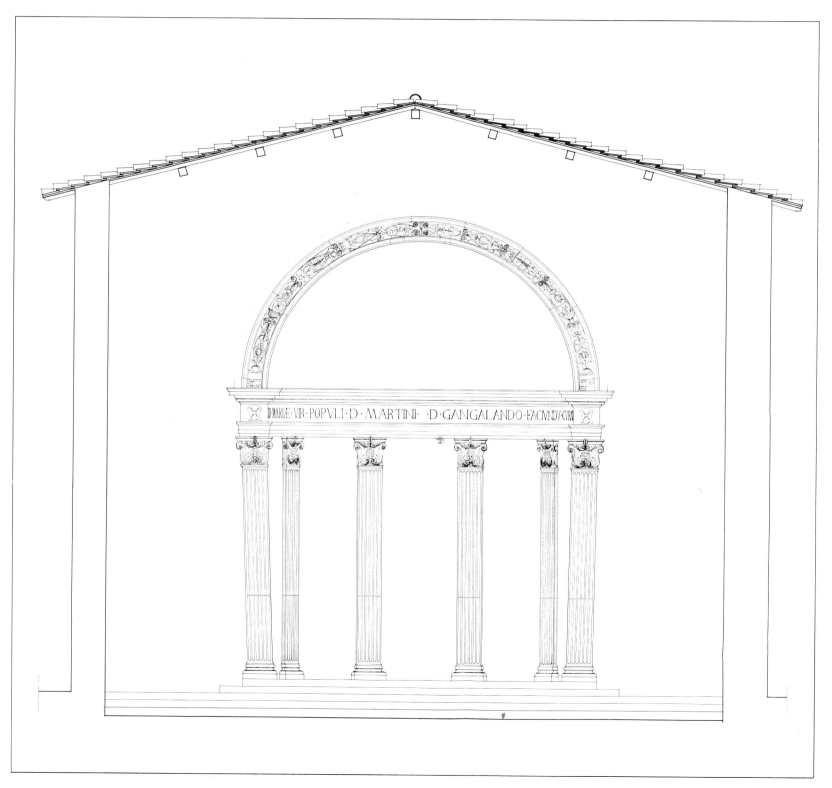

D·MARIÆ·VIR·POPVLI·D·MARTINI·D·GANGALANDO·FACIVNDV·CVR

the nearby chapels, whose area was partly taken up by the pillars. But Alberti's task may have been limited to simply checking the structure and planimetry of Manetti's plan, especially as Ludovico Gonzaga was under no obligation regarding the tribune's decoration and had only undertaken to erect its bare structure. Alberti may not have been aware even of the problem of the intersection of the chapels and the large cylindrical space of the tribune; he may have been equally unaware of that of the relationship between the tribune and the large central arch. In both cases he was to be rebuked by Vasari. On the other hand, he may have intended solving them by introducing ribs and cornices, perhaps according to a polyhedric plan.

In short, nothing more was expected of Alberti than a confirmation of the validity of the old plan, but it was an important confirmation, given the circumstances in which it took place and Ludovico's firm decision to put an end to the controversy raging in Florence. On the other hand, the Florence of 1470 was not the city Alberti had known forty years earlier, nor could it have fascinated and stimulated him as it had when its first generation of architects and artists succeeded in reviving the splendour of the past through its own efforts alone. On the contrary, contemporary Florentine art was hardening into a rigid, artisan neo-Brunelleschianism, which Alberti must have found extremely uninteresting, even though he was occasionally forced to come to terms with it on a practical level, as at S. Pancrazio. The Florentine objections to Roman art, of which we find a significant example in Aldobrandini's letter, must have left him quite indifferent. Alberti was hardly likely to become involved in controversies of this kind at the very time S. Andrea had given him a last final chance to tackle the great theme of the basilica. This was the task he had always avoided, but which fate had now offered him so that he might express his ultimate vision. And since the man who commissioned the tribune in the Annunziata was the same for whom Alberti was building S. Andrea, he must have been particularly eager to retain Ludovico's trust and friendship — and getting Florence to pay its debt could hardly have been very pleasant.

Perhaps Alberti's real contribution to the tribune in the Annunziata may be summed up in the words of Giovanni da Gaiole: "He seemed to think it was the only thing to be done."

SAN MARTINO A GANGALANDI

"Nosti mihi fortunam esse aliunde satis opulentam et honestam."[28] Alberti, denying authorship of certain anonymous letters he was accused of having written, addressed these words to a colleague at the apostolic chancery. Never again was he to complain about economic hardship, so recurrent a motif in the writings of his youth. In 1432 he had obtained a bull from Eugenius IV granting him the priorate of S. Martino a Gangalandi at Lastra di Signa in the diocese of Florence; this is supposed to have provided him with an income of 160 gold florins a year.[29] The church is of medieval origin,[30] but the apse was designed by Alberti, if his testament is anything to go by.[31] It describes the apse as "started and almost complete" and the desire is expressed that it be brought to completion ("perficeatur et compleatur"), so there can be no doubt of its authorship. There remains the problem of its date or at least of when it was begun. Sanpaolesi, whose Institute of Restoration has made a study of the work, says: "... it is impossible at present to say whether there was an earlier apse or not. One can see, however, that the longitudinal axis of the apse is not in line with that of the church; this is apparent at first sight. From the left-hand wall to the base of the corresponding pillar there is a space of 2.78 metres, while the corresponding space on the right is 2.51 metres.

There is no doubt that the present apse was added to the church later, as one can clearly see by examining the masonry. For whereas the bottom wall of the church is built like the rest of it, with small regular blocks of hard stone, the masonry of the apse is of a mixed, very irregular kind.

The round-headed arch in the centre is decorated frontally with a recurrent motif consisting of small candlesticks set within a frame. A simple, elegant entablature runs round the base of the calotte, and the frieze contains an inscription in Roman lettering: 'OPA D. MARIAE VIR POPULI D MARTINI D GANGALANDO FACIUNDU CURAVIT'. Both ends of the frieze are decorated with the Alberti coat-of-arms. The two corner pilasters do not develop vertically but diverge towards the top. If one drops a plumb-line along the inside of the apse wall from the top of a pilaster (below its capital) to the bottom, one discovers a difference of 0.10 metres compared with the pillar on the left, and one of just 0.05 metres with the pillar on the right."[32]

There seems to be no precise reason for the apse's lack of symmetry with the rest of the church. It may be attributable to the particularly long time it took the unskilled, undirected workmen to build it, or the error may have been caused by the introduction of the stone finishings, and of the pilasters in particular, both those of the outer and inner wall.

But it is difficult to believe that the imperfect verticality of the

28.   L. B. Alberti, *Opera inedita et pauca separatim impressa*, op. cit., Florence 1890, p. 275; see also, G. Mancini, op. cit., p. 90.

29.   G. Mancini, op. cit., p. 89.

30.   G. Carocci, *Il comune di Lastra a Signa*, Florence 1895, pp. 10-12.

31.   G. Mancini, "Il Testamento di L. B. Alberti", in *Archivio Storico Italiano*, Rome 1914, LXXII, p. 47 ff.

32.   Accademia Nazionale di San Luca, *Celebrazioni di Leon Battista Alberti*, Rome 1972, p. 23.

pilasters was not intentional, no matter how asymmetrical the assembly of their stones might have made them, and given the unusual nature of the edifice, it may be regarded as an experiment in perspective. In his treatise on painting Alberti defines the mechanism of sight by means of "rays", which are "very fine threads gathered tightly in a bunch at one end, going back together inside the eye where lies the sense of sight."[33] Not all the rays are equal, "for some reach to the outlines of surfaces and measure all their dimensions. Let us call these extrinsic rays, since they fly out to touch the outer parts of the surface."[34] Thus Alberti's attention was drawn to the outer frame of the space formed by the introduction of a new element into the church's design, where the pilasters tend to create an optical effect. The extrinsic rays "form an enclosure around the entire surface like a cage. This is why they say that vision takes place by means of a pyramid of rays. We must, therefore, explain what a pyramid is, and how it is made up of rays. Let us describe it in our own rough terms. A pyramid is a form of oblong body from whose base all straight lines, prolonged upwards, meet at one and the same point. The base of the pyramid is the surface seen, and the sides are the visual rays we said are called extrinsic. The vertex of the pyramid resides within the eye, where the angles of the quantities in the various triangles meet together."[35] Thus the edges of the pilasters are also the sides of a pyramid and are determined by "extrinsic rays". But if one considers that the apex of this pyramid is not in the centre of the figure (the human eye having its 'horizon' on a lower level with respect to the height of the building), then one may suppose Alberti thought that the base of the pyramid should be variable, and that consequently it was to be reproduced not in its true dimensions but according to its "optical size", that is to say, convergent upon a point lower down. Thus the divergence of the two pilasters can be explained as a device intended to correct the opposite effect of a falling inwards (an inherent tendency of perspective). The device is also a rather ingenuous application of those *temperaturae* of Vitruvius's, executed in a rather hesitant manner by the only men Alberti had at his disposal in the small village of Lastra a Signa. Nevertheless, it was an attempt to approach architecture in the light of the poetic ideals of space expressed in the treatise on painting; an attempt that was to have no future sequel. Thus, if the treatise on painting was written in 1435, just a few years after Alberti had obtained the priorate of S. Martino, he must have approached this work as something of a first experiment and may have planned the structure on the basis of the divergence described above.

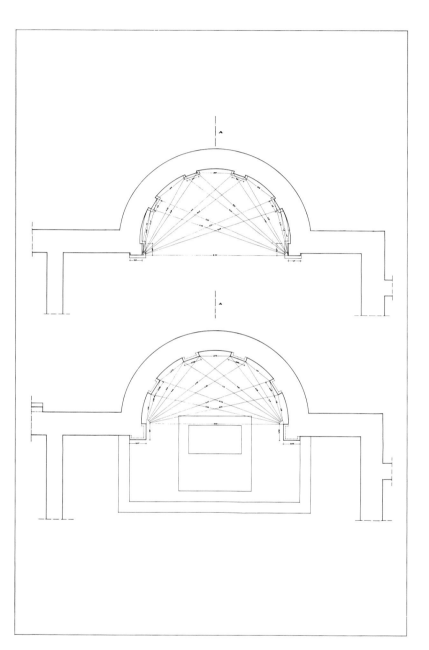

33. L. B. Alberti, *Della pittura*, ed. Janitschek, p. 57.
34. Ibid.
35 Ibid., p. 61.

The logic of the structure, however, indicates that its stone parts, especially those in the upper sections of the building, must have been added last and that the pilasters must have been introduced at an earlier date. The masonry and Alberti's penchant for inscriptions anticipate the characteristics of the chapel of S. Pancrazio, though expressed here with less refinement, the work of unskilled local craftsmen who reduced Alberti's intentions to the level of their own quattrocentesque art. The work was financed with the meagre income of the church and of the farms that went with it, so that it also suffered from the vagaries of good and bad years. Yet the spirit of Quattrocento craftsmanship could be reconciled with the original project far more easily than with any other of Alberti's designs. This was because the work coincided with Alberti's debut as an architect and so concurred with his search for spatial alternatives and optical effects rather than with his analysis of structure.

This little Tuscan country church adds a rustic, almost 'vernacular' touch (emphasised by the usual restoration) to the monumental Albertian canon. Nevertheless, the geometrical exercise that lies behind the division of the apse wall by means of pilasters, the above-mentioned divergence, and the idea of an architectural background as an end in itself surmounted by a Latin inscription together provide a brief, yet adequate introduction to the consistency of Alberti's thought and style. In this case, he also chose the cloak of anonymity, for the inscription says that the work was carried out for the Opera di S. Maria (a confraternity founded in 1463) by a "vir populi", one of the people of Gangalandi.

DELLA PITTURA

Alberti wrote in the margin of his copy of Cicero's *Brutus*: "Die Veneris ora XXa e tre quarti quae fuit dies augusti 1435 complevi opus de pictura Florentiae."[1] The manuscript of the vernacular version of the *Della pittura* in the Magliabechi library ends: "Finis laus Deo die diciassettesimo mensi Iulii MCCCC 36." The first date is irrefutable; the second might be that of a copy. But the problem of which came first, the Latin or Italian text, is really insoluble.[2] These quotations merely underline the self-confidence and conviction that must have motivated so precise a note, and they illustrate the decisive importance Alberti himself attributed to the work.

The two versions have rather different histories. They were written in relative independence of each other, and this resulted in two discrete manuscripts intended for two quite different publics. The Latin version was dedicated to Giovan Francesco, Prince of Mantua; it contains the usual reference to the literary pastimes of the wise prince and another allusion to the "novelty" of the book's subject. The far more well-known dedication of the vernacular version to Brunelleschi is fundamental to an understanding of Alberti's relationship to classical art, and it provides a clear indication of his generation's awareness of the artistic renewal they were effecting: "Without guides or models to follow, we have achieved things unseen and unheard of in the arts and sciences."[3] Alberti sees himself, on a theoretical level, as the heir to the incomparable works of Filippo and "the others", from Donatello to Masaccio. It is an attitude he adopts with pride and a due sense of proportion, and his acknowledgement of Brunelleschi's primacy (that is, of a genius that did not so much seek as 'discover') is consistent with his idea of the primacy of architecture, which is already implied in the rational, geometrical character of this study of painting. In a sense, Alberti's whole life and art developed in the shadow of the dome of S. Maria del Fiore, "which rises up into the sky, casting its shadow over the whole of Florence,"[4] and it is curious that his death should actually coincide with its completion.[5]

The young Alberti had very little personal experience to draw upon when he began to write this treatise.[6] He himself, in fact, laid the basis for the traditional belief that he was a mere dilettante in matters of painting and sculpture. This was seized upon by Vasari,[7] who began a long critical tradition that lasted until the time of Schlosser. Attempts to establish the chronology of Alberti's paintings and sculptures have not led to very different conclusions. These works include the two bronze self-portraits

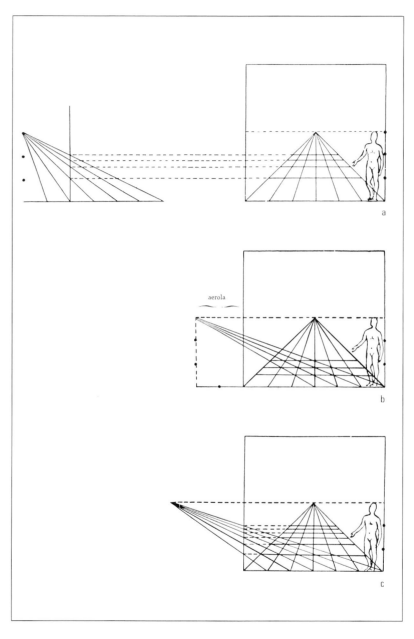

a

aerola

b

c

1. P. Michel, "Le traité de la peinture de Leon Baptiste Alberti: version latine et version vulgaire", in *Revue des Etudes Italiennes*, 1961, p. 83. Cf. also, C. Grayson, *Opere Volgari di Leon Battista Alberti*, III, Bari 1973, p. 305.

2. Cf. Grayson, op. cit., pp. 304-07.

3. Ibid., p. 7.

4. Ibid., p. 8.

5. According to a note of the diarist Landucci: "On Monday, 27 May 1471, a gilt ball of bronze was raised to the top of the lantern of the dome of Santa Maria del Fiore". *Diario*, Florence 1969, p. 10.

6. Alberti says: "Whenever I devote myself to painting for pleasure, which I very often do when I have leisure from other affairs, I persevere with such pleasure in finishing my work, that I can hardly believe later on that three or even four hours have gone by." L. B. Alberti, op. cit., pp. 50-52.

7. "In painting Alberti achieved nothing of any great importance or beauty. The very few paintings of his that are extant are far from perfect, but this is not surprising since he devoted himself more to his studies than to draughtsmanship". Vasari, op. cit., II, p. 546.

8. K. Badt, "Drei plastische Arbeiten von Leone Battista Alberti", in *Mitteilungen des Kunsthistorischen Institutes in Florenz*, VIII, 1957-59, pp. 78-87.

9. C. Grayson, "A Portrait of L. B. Alberti", in *Burlington Magazine*, XCVI, 1954, pp. 177-78, fig. 21.

10. Cf. F. Zeri, *Due dipinti, la filologia e un nome: il Maestro delle tavole Bar-*

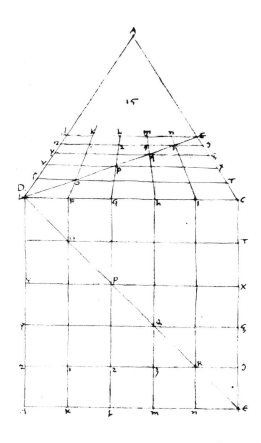

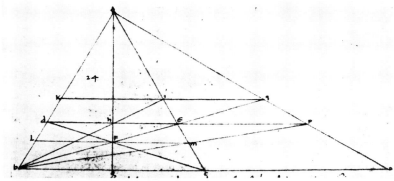

in the Washington Gallery and the Louvre, the bust of Ludovico II Gonzaga in Berlin[8] (attributed to him by Badt), the drawing of another self-portrait in the Codex 738 of the Rome National Library[9] (attributed to him by Grayson), as well as the *Nativity* and the *Presentation of the Virgin*, whose author is known as the Master of the Barberini Panels,[10] but which Parronchi would attribute to him on the basis of a statement by Vasari.[11]

Alberti's treatise was based not so much on direct experience (though he did have some knowledge of technical and figurative problems), as on aesthetic theory, and the people he wrote for were the learned scholars of Ferrara; the same people to whom he dedicated the *Philodoxeus*, the *De equo animante*, the *Theogenius*, and the *Ludi Matematici*. It is no surprise, therefore, to find echoes of his treatise in Decembrio's *Politia letteraria*.[12]

Panofsky's analogy[13] between the categories of classical rhetoric and those of painting is very pertinent. He shows how the 'invention' and 'disposition' of the former became *circoscriptione* and *compositione* (*disegno* nearly a century later) in painting, while elocution became *receptione de lume* (replaced by *colorito* about a hundred years later). This was consistent with the tradition that bound all the arts together, and according to which a painter was expected to know poetry and rhetoric. This tradition was based on the aesthetic theories of Aristotle and Plotinus, and it led to the concept of painting as *istoria* (narrative): "The most important part of a painter's work is the istoria."[14]

Beauty itself is based upon the concept of *convenienza* (harmony): "The painter must take pains, above all, that all the parts agree with each other: and they will do so if in quantity, in function, in kind, in colour, and in all other respects they harmonise into one beauty."[15] (This is clearly indebted to Plotinus.)[16] Painting must strive to achieve a noble, dignified style, but it is also an eclectic, realistic process: "Therefore, excellent parts should all be selected from the most beautiful bodies, and every effort should be made to perceive, understand and express beauty. ... this is the most difficult thing of all, because the merits of beauty are not all to be found in one place, but are dispersed here and there in many [bodies]."[17] Painting is founded above all on realism, however qualified this may be by the Idea: "The idea of beauty, which the most expert have difficulty in discerning, eludes the ignorant."[18] As Panofsky says: "This only means that Renaissance theory, unwilling and unable to sacrifice the concept of Idea, had transformed the realistic doctrine it had developed with so much difficulty in such a way that not only could it be reconciled with the former, but it could even be reinforced by it."[19]

berini, Turin 1961; and A. Parronchi, in *Studi sulla dolce prospettiva*, Milan 1964, pp. 438-67.

11. "There is a work by Alberti in a little chapel dedicated to Our Lady on the abutment on the Ponte alla Carraia in Florence, namely, an altar-predella containing three little scenes with some perspectives which he described (with his pen) much better than he painted them with his brush". Vasari, op. cit., II, p. 547.

12. M. Baxandall, "A Dialogue on Art from the Court of Lionello d'Este", in *Journal of the Warburg Institute*, XXVI, 1963, pp. 304-26.

13. E. Panofsky, *Renaissance and Renascences in Western Art*, London 1970, p. 26.

14. L. B. Alberti, *Della Pittura*, ed. Janitscheck, p. 105.

15. Ibid., p. 111.

16. "The idea, therefore, first co-ordinates the future object composed of many parts into unity, reduces it to a coherent whole, and finally creates the unity by means of correspondences. Since the idea is one, so must the object informed by it be so too, as far as this is possible, for it consists of a multiplicity. And thus, beauty resides in the summit of this object reduced to unity, and overflows into its single parts and the whole". Plotinus, *Enneadi*, Bari 1947, I, Enneade I, 11-12, p. 100.

17. L. B. Alberti, op. cit., p. 151.

18. Ibid.

19. E. Panofsky, *Idea*, Florence 1952, p. 43.

This embraces the whole of Renaissance aesthetic theory, into which Alberti introduced a pagan note with his "abundance and variety of things", which gives "delight" to "istoria" above all else: "I would say a picture was richly varied if it contained a properly arranged mixture of old men, youths, boys, matrons, maidens, children, domestic animals, dogs, birds, horses, sheep, buildings and provinces."[20] This calls to mind the paintings of Pisanello and Jacopo Bellini, and Jacopo may well have collaborated in that "picture of Venice in perspective showing Saint Mark's" mentioned by Vasari.[21] This, then, is the theoretical basis of the treatise, or of what we may call its Ferrarese part; the initial Florentine section is largely based on Brunelleschi's spatial experiments in architecture and perspective. It also makes the treatise a primary source for all Alberti's work, architectural and pictorial.

Leon Battista speaks of painting in general terms as the mechanism of sight: "Is it not true that painting is the mistress of all the arts or their principal ornament? If I am not mistaken, the architect took from the painter architraves, capitals, bases, columns and pediments, and all the other fine features of buildings. The stonemason, the sculptor and all the workshops and crafts of artificers are guided by the rule and art of the painter."[22] Here Alberti digresses, drawing a magnificent, almost poetic comparison between the painter and Narcissus, a metaphor of Plotinian origin[23] which Alberti claims as his own: "Consequently I used to tell my friends that the inventor of painting, according to the poets, was Narcissus, who was turned into a flower; for, as painting is the flower of all the arts, so the tale of Narcissus fits our purpose perfectly. What is painting but the act of embracing by means of art the surface of the pool?"[24] Panofsky observes that whereas Plotinus cites the myth of Narcissus as a warning against losing oneself in purely sensual beauty, Alberti uses it to show that painting has its origins in the love of the beautiful, and above all to explain the genesis of sight.[25]

Alberti affirms that geometry is an essential component of painting,[26] and this is the subject (together with the mechanism of sight) of the first book, which has a popularising, explanatory nature. It discusses the visual pyramid, and painting itself is defined as "the intersection of the pyramid" in the famous passage that begins: "Leaving aside all other things, I shall now describe what I do when I paint."[27] This is the passage that has provoked so much controversy about Alberti's notion of perspective. Indeed, the subject has become a kind of hunting-ground for historians, from Panofsky (whose fundamental essays have restored the Renaissance concept of perspective to its real structural and symbolic meaning)[28] to White,[29] Gioseffi,[30] Sanpaolesi,[31] Grayson,[32] Parronchi,[33] and Edgerton.[34]

Brunelleschi's famous two panels implied two different concepts of perspective — frontal perspective with a single point of convergence, and inclined square perspective with two points of convergence. The controversy regarding Alberti is concerned only with the first concept and may be summed up in the question, was Alberti aware of the point of distance? Steigmuller, Panofsky, Kern, and, more recently, Klein,[35] are of the opinion that he was not, whereas Parronchi believes he was.[36] We agree with Parronchi, for Alberti explicitly states that "no objects in a painting can appear like real objects unless they stand to each other in a determined relationship."[37] And again: "Then I determine the distance I want between the eye of the spectator and the painting, and, having established the position of the intersection at this distance, I effect the intersection with what the mathematicians call a perpendicular."[38]

Alberti professed his real aim to be the popularisation of Brunelleschi's method.[39] Questions remain as to whether the convergence ought to be calculated separately from the main construction, or whether the point of distance should be located between the eye and the plane of the picture. There is no word of this in the passage in which Alberti states that the point lies along the line of horizon. Alberti's main concern seems to be the distance of the straight line (which is perpendicular to the horizon where the measurements are taken) from the painting, and not the point of distance from the rectangle of the figure. The position of the straight line may be moved from where it coincides with the point of distance (without any consequent intersection with the lines convergent upon it, which is a characteristic of infinite vision) to a position where it coincides with one of the sides of the rectangle (thus creating the greatest distances possible between the intersections with the other convergent line, which is characteristic of finite vision). This explains the practicality of Alberti's construction, its utility even "in a small space,"[40] and finally its synoptic value. Once this is recognised, the whole controversy becomes less important, and one realizes that though the theory of perspective is a fundamental part of Alberti's treatise, it does contain other things of interest. If, on the other hand, one exaggerates it, then one may be led to consider it as the sole source of his ideas on figurative art -- and perhaps draw illuminating but captious and narrow-minded conclusions about its importance with respect to his architecture.

20. L. B. Alberti, op. cit., p. 117.

21. Vasari observes: ". . . although the figures were done by other artists". Vasari, op. cit., II, p. 517.

22. L. B. Alberti, op. cit., p. 91.

23. "In fact, whoever throws himself upon them (beautiful simulacra) urged by the desire to touch real things, is like him who wanted to seize his beautiful reflection floating on the water and — this is what the legend means in my opinion — fell into the profound abyss and disappeared". Plotinus, *Enneadi*, op. cit., p. 107.

24. L. B. Alberti, op. cit., pp. 91-93.

25. E. Panofsky, *Idea*, p. 128.

26. L. B. Alberti, op. cit., p. 92.

27. Ibid., p. 36.

28. E. Panofsky, *La prospettiva come forma simbolica*, Milan 1961, p. 68 ff. Cf. also by the same author, *Renaissance and Renascences*, op. cit., pp. 118-27, and R. Beltrame, "Gli esperimenti prospettici del Brunelleschi", in *Atti della Accademia Nazionale dei Lincei*, 1973, XXVIII, 8, fasc. 3-4.

29. J. White, *The Birth and Rebirth of Pictorial Space*, London 1957.

30. D. Gioseffi, "Perspectiva Artificialis", in *Istituto di Storia dell'Arte Antica e Moderna*, Trieste 1957.

292. The "costruzione legittima" in Filarete's Trattato di Architettura. Cod. Magl. f. v. 177. Florence, Biblioteca Nazionale.
293. Leonardo: the "camera ottica". Ms. D, f.r. 8. Paris, Institut de France.

294. Leonardo: the human eye. Ms. D, f.r. 8. Paris, Institut de France.

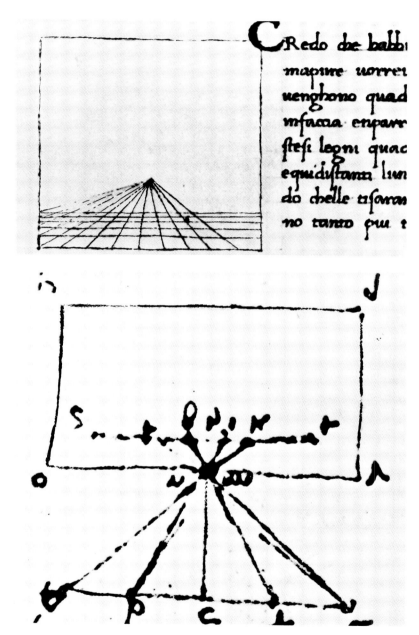

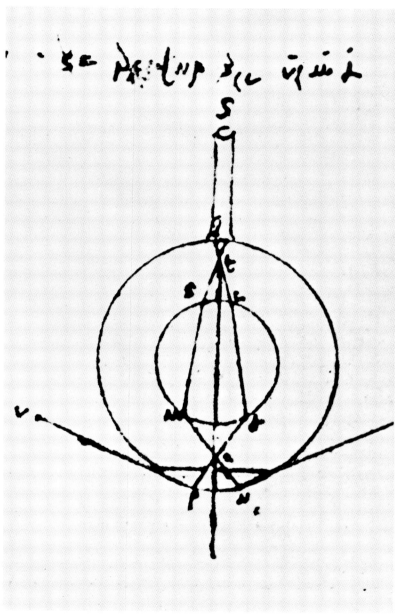

31. P. Sanpaolesi, "Studi di Prospettiva", in *Raccolta Vinciana*, Milan 1960, XVIII, pp. 188-202.

32. C. Grayson, "L. B. Alberti's Costruzione Legittima", in *Italian Studies*, 1964, XIX, p. 14.

33. A. Parronchi, "Il punctum dolens della costruzione legittima", in *Studi sulla dolce prospettiva*, op. cit., pp. 296-312.

34. S. Y. Edgerton, "Alberti's Perspective: a new Discovery and a new Evaluation", in *Art Bulletin*, 1966, XLVIII, pp. 367-78.

35. On this subject, see A. Parronchi's bibliography, op. cit., p. 299. For Klein, see R. Klein, "Pomponius Gauricus on Perspective", in *Art Bulletin*, 1961, XLIII, pp. 211-30.

36. See also T. K. Kitao, "Prejudice in Perspective: a Study of Vignola's Perspective Treatise", in *Art Bulletin*, XLIII, pp. 173-95.

37. L. B. Alberti, op. cit., p. 38.

38. Ibid.

39. "I have set out the foregoing briefly and, I believe, in a not altogether obscure fashion ..." Ibid., p. 40.

40. Ibid., p. 38.

295. The "velo" in the "Due Regole di Prospettiva Pratica" by Vignola. Rome, 1583.
296. The "velo" in the "Artist drawing a Lute" by Albrecht Dürer, 1525.
297. The "velo" with the "quadratura" in the "Artist drawing a reclining Woman" by Albrecht Dürer, c. 1525.

The treatise proposes other ideas that have received less attention, but which must have had considerable influence on the man who, more than anyone else, put them into practice: Piero della Francesca. "Therefore, circumscription, composition, and reception of light make up painting."[41] "Circumscription is the process of tracing the outlines in the painting", and "is simply the recording of the outlines, and if it is done with a very visible line, they will look in the painting, not like the edges of surfaces, but like cracks. I want only the outlines to be sketched in circumscription."[42] Alberti is urging a proper balance between colour and line — exactly what we find in the fluid, regular lines of Piero della Francesca's painting, where one can also see the concrete realisation of the Albertian ideal of the harmony of colour and chiaroscuro,[43] which is summed up in the magnificent words: "we all by nature love things that are open and bright."[44] In one passage his words provide an accurate description of the colours of the *History of the True Cross*,[45] and describe certain carefully observed effects of nature: "For we see verdant leaves gradually lose their greenness until they become white."[46] Of reflected light, Alberti writes: "we see this happen when the faces of people walking about in the meadows appear to have a greenish tinge."[47] This sophisticated realism is accompanied by the rejection of works in gold, which are regarded as an "artisan" residue.

A complex, systematic body of theory, the prudent use of "aids" such as the perspective construction and the *velo* (a device greatly developed by Dürer later), and the cautious acceptance of all that culture had to offer painting in the way of practical help, together gave Alberti complete confidence in himself and in the originality of his treatise. This is expressed in the dedication to Brunelleschi, the tone of which is more historical than laudatory. Alberti's self-confidence led him to draw up a brief outline of certain geometrical exercises to help the painter understand the principles of perspective (there is no doubt that he wrote the vernacular version before the Latin in this case.)[48] It included definitions of elementary geometrical propositions and dealt with problems of representation in two fundamental situations involving geometrical figures: when the design coincides with the plane of projection, in which case the figures are described as *concentriche*; and when it does not, which involves *comminute*[49] (foreshortening). In these exercises Alberti attempts to refine the "cruder terms" he mentions in the *De Pictura* and to give the exercises a more specifically mathematical character; "ex fontibus certitudinis", as he says in the dedication.

It is essential to recognise this self-confidence of Alberti's and

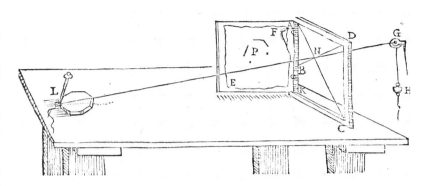

41. Ibid., p. 52.

42. Ibid., p. 44.

43. "But you have to remember that no surface should be made so white that you cannot make it a great deal whiter still. Even in representing snow-white clothing you should stop well on this side of the brightest white. For the painter has no other means than white to express the brightest gleams of the most polished surfaces, and only black to represent the deepest shadows of the night". Ibid., p. 84.

44. Ibid.

45. "If red stands between blue and green, it somehow enhances their beauty as well as its own. White lends gaiety, not only when placed between gray and yellow, but almost to any colour. But dark colours acquire a certain dignity when between light colours, and similarly light colours may be placed with good effect among dark". Ibid., p. 86.

46. Ibid., p. 24.

47. Ibid., p. 26.

48. As he writes in the dedication to Teodoro Gaza: "Elementa haec quae a me pridem etrusca essent lingua eorum civium gratia edita facerem latina tibique visenda mitterem." L. B. Alberti, Opere Volgari, III, p. 113.

49. Cf. the essay with graphic reconstructions of the exercises by A. Gambuti, "Nuove Ricerche sugli Elementa Picturae", in *Studi e Documenti di Architettura*, I, December 1972, pp. 133-72.

to compare the writings on painting with his earlier works in order to appreciate their profound originality. In Theophilus Presbiter's *Schedula Diversarum Artium*, the formulation of artisan rules excludes all possibility of achieving a direct, global vision of painting.[50] Vincent of Beauvais has a more ambitious definition: "Pictura autem est imago exprimens speciem alicuius rei quasi fictura."[51] Still more important is Cennino Cennini's *Libro dell'Arte*, written only thirty years before Alberti's treatise, for it provided the theoretical basis for the whole of Giotto's world and the Tuscan Trecento. Yet this work, apart from its technical rules and a tendency to concentrate on materials, insists that the foundation of painting is *disegno* and *colorito*.[52] Cennini was an empiricist urging the artist to lead a regular life and to take care of the steadiness of his hand, whereas Alberti had a geometrical vision of painting and was concerned with the cultural formation of the painter as a "good man learned in letters." The difference between the two was vast. For Alberti, the artist (and later the architect) takes a central position within an independent, privileged intelligentsia, and is thereby superior to the humbler artisan. Yet the latter was to continue a tradition that lasted well beyond Alberti's time. This is apparent in the medieval elements contained in the manual written by Dionisio da Furnà, who simply recommends that the painter "learn proportion and the characters of figures with precision, so that he may dedicate his labours to working out the calculations of his design"[53] (an example of Byzantine technique and iconography surviving as late as the nineteenth century).

Once Alberti's great originality is recognised, one may consider him from a historical point of view and determine his debt to the Florentine culture of the 1430's, particularly to Brunelleschi. On the subject of perspective, Alberti merely popularised Brunelleschi's ideas; the obscurity of part of his text makes one wonder whether he even fully understood the subject. Manetti's testimony is of decisive importance;[54] speaking of Brunelleschi and perspective, he says: "Those who could have taught it him had been dead for hundreds of years, and it was not to be found in writing. Or if it was, no one could understand it. But by diligence and perception, he either rediscovered it or invented it." This recognition is faithfully echoed in Alberti's dedication of the *De Pictura*. Manetti's words also call to mind Biagio Pelacani, who died in 1416, and who defined the optical ray or visual line as *species mathematicae*; the manuscript copy of his *Questiones Perspectivae* in the Laurenziana was transcribed in 1428, only a few years before Alberti wrote his own treatise.[55] Alhazen, on the other hand,

50. Theophilus Presbiter, *Schedula Diversarum Artium*, ed. Ilg, Osnabrück 1970.
51. A. Pellizzari, *I trattati intorno alle arti figurative*, Naples 1915, p. 440.
52. C. Cennini, *Trattato della Pittura*, Rome 1821, pp. 21-22.
53. Dionisio da Furnà, *Ermeneutica della Pittura*, Naples 1971, p. 8.
54. "Thus, even in those times he [Brunelleschi] taught and practised what painters nowadays call perspective. This is a part of that science which aims at the correct representation of the diminutions and enlargements of distant and near objects as they appear to the human eye, including houses, plains, mountains, landscapes of every region and place, figures, and other objects according to their size at a certain distance. Everything that has been done

hit upon the importance of the perpendicularity of an object with respect to the eye; he was amply quoted by Ghiberti and his ideas have many points in common with the *De statua*. No less important were Ibn Firnass' optical box[56] and the *Della prospettiva* in the Ricciardi Library (2110). Bonucci included the latter among Alberti's works, but it is now believed to have been written by Toscanelli before the *De pictura*,[57] the same Toscanelli who was a friend of Cusanus and to whom Alberti dedicated his *Intercoenales*. All these inter-related influences[58] prove that Florence was a cultural centre to which Alberti made a fitting and opportune contribution. In addition to these references, which illustrate the Florentine character of the treatise, and the previously mentioned Aristotle and Plotinus, there are still other sources: Alberti may even have been influenced by some of the religious literature of his day, that of St. Thomas Aquinas for example.[59]

What kind of influence did Alberti's writings on painting have on his contemporaries? The first indication appears in Ghiberti, who wrote his *Commentarii* with the purpose of re-establishing his prestige as a theorist on art and the mechanism of sight (at the expense of Brunelleschi, who had left no written works at all). His first commentary contains an indirect criticism of Alberti,[60] whom he attacks openly in the third: "One should not write of sculpture and painting as one does of poetry."[61] This implies the rejection of any analogy between the figurative arts and rhetoric, and it foreshadows the subordination of "literature" to "experience", that animates Vasari's judgement of Alberti. Ghiberti's general, inconclusive rejection of Alberti was followed by Manetti's favourable comments in his biography of Brunelleschi and Landino's encomiastic approval, which preceded the most serious and empathic appraisal of Alberti's pictorial theories ever made: Piero della Francesca's *De prospectiva pingendi*.

Piero checked Alberti's theories experimentally and arrived at a new definition of painting and its component parts, substituting the concept of *disegno, commensuratio et colorare* for that of *circoscrizione, composizione e ricezione di lumi*. In this case, though *disegno* may correspond to *circoscrizione* to a certain extent, *commensuratio* is very different from the idea of *composizione*, for it refers mainly to the concept of proportion, whereas *composizione* was more concerned with content and included the narrative aspects of painting. *Colorito* was a broader concept (Piero does not explain it) than Alberti's *ricezione di lumi*, which meant relief and was concerned with the question of blacks and whites mainly. Piero is much clearer than Alberti about the relationship between the distance and proportions "of graded things", though he uses Alberti's

in this field since his day is indebted to him". A Manetti, *Vita di Filippo di Ser Brunelleschi*, Florence 1947, p. 9.

55. G. Federici Vescovini, *Studi sulla Prospettiva Medioevale*, Turin 1965, p. 242.

56. Cf. Schlosser, *Letteratura Artistica*, p. 124 and J. Burckhardt, *Civiltà del Rinascimento in Italia*, Florence 1952, p. 133, note 1.

57. A. Parronchi, *Studi della Prospettiva di Paolo dal Pozzo Toscanelli*, p. 583 ff.

58. P. Sanpaolesi, "Ipotesi sulle conoscenze matematiche statiche e meccaniche del Brunelleschi", in *Belle Arti*, II, 1951, pp. 25-30.

59. "Ad pulchritudinem tria requiruntur. Primo quidem integritas sive perfectio que enim diminuta sunt hoc ipso turpia sunt. Et debita proportio,

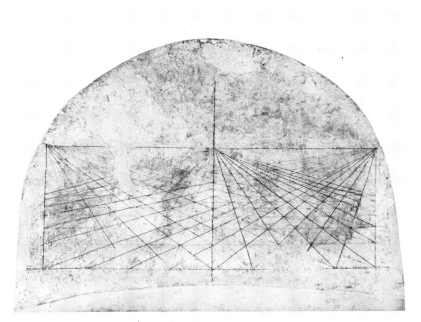

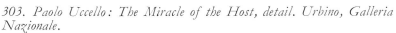

303. *Paolo Uccello: The Miracle of the Host, detail. Urbino, Galleria Nazionale.*
304. *Domenico Veneziano: Sacra Conversazione. Florence, Uffizi.*
305. *Donatello: Miracle of St. Antony. Padua, Basilica di S. Antonio.*
306. *Donatello: Martyrdom of St. Lawrence, panel of the second pulpit. Florence, S. Lorenzo.*

sive consonantia. Et iterum claritas unde quae habeant colorem nitidum pulcra esse dicuntur". A. Pellizzari, op. cit., p. 303.

60. "It is best to be brief and open like a painter or sculptor in everything that is taught about this art, for it has nothing to do with the rules of rhetoric". L. Ghiberti, *I Commentarii*, Naples 1947, p. 2.

61. Ibid., p. 48.

62. P. della Francesca, *De prospectiva pingendi*, Florence rep. 1974, p. 129.

63. As regards Leonardo's ignorance of Alberti's text, which did not appear until the publication of Bartoli's translation in 1546, see Richter, op. cit., p. 33, note 5. But Luca Pacioli, who had been a guest of Alberti's when the latter was an old man, might have been a link between the two. Mallé

terminology in defining proportional ratios: dupla, sesquialtera, and sesquiterza. The first book, which is propaedeutic in character, follows the logical process traced in the *Elementa picturae*; it begins with the definition of geometrical entities, and then goes on to experimentation with figures, whose construction is demonstrated step by step. Piero is chiefly concerned with guiding the hand of his pupil and controlling his movements in the smallest detail: "take the ruler", "remove the ruler", "continue", "guide". His book deals with a number of figurative problems ranging from the drawing of simple polygons to the representation of the human head. All is based on a general definition of painting as the representation "of the of foreshortened or elongated bodies arranged in such a way that real objects seen with the eye from different angles look like depicted objects."[62] The only real advance this represents with respect to Alberti is its emphasis on proportionality regarding the *certa distanzia*. But it was Leonardo, who, proceeding independently and without ever setting eyes on Alberti's manuscript,[63] was to insist upon the universality of painting in the Albertian sense of the word.[64]

The writer most influenced by Alberti's treatise was Filarete. At the very beginning of his book, Alberti is compared with Vitruvius: "For he [Alberti] is, for these times of ours, a most learned man in various subjects, and very skilful in painting, especially in design, which is the foundation of all the arts practised by man. He understands this perfectly and knows a great deal about geometry and other sciences. He has also written a most elegant work."[65] Filarete's "most elegant" suggests he had some knowledge of Latin, which would explain the affinities between his own text and the Latin *De pictura*. There are explicit references to Alberti's work in Book XXII of Filarete's treatise on architecture,[66] but there is an even greater resemblance in the general contents of the two books. In particular, as Gambuti has pointed out,[67] there are similarities in the two authors' definitions of line, point, angle, and surface (or area), while the terms *lembo* and *discrimen* are taken from the *Elementi di pittura*.[68] Moreover, their concepts of the visual pyramid, the nature of visual rays, and perspective construction are very alike. Alberti writes: "First of all, on the surface on which I am going to paint, I draw a rectangle of whatever size I want, which I regard as an open window through which the subject to be painted is seen."[69] There is a very similar passage in Filarete: "First of all we must imagine we are standing before a window through which we can see everything we want to depict in the foreground. Then, using a compass, one must determine four equidistant points and connect

disagrees with this theory (without giving any reasons) in his critical edition of the work, p. 123.

64. "The deity of the science of painting considers those works that are defined by their planes, that is, by the lines of the edges of bodies, to be both human and divine. By means of these lines he guides the sculptor in the perfection of his statues, and imposing the principle of design, he teaches the architect to build beautiful edifices, the potter to mould vases, the goldsmith, weavers and embroiderers in their various arts, all of whom follow the same principle, though expressing themselves in different ways". Leonardo Da Vinci, Literary Works, ed. Richter, London 1938, I, p. 63.

307. *Tarsia with landscape. Urbino, Palazzo Ducale, Studiolo.*
308. *Tarsia with view in perspective. Urbino, Palazzo Ducale, Studiolo.*

309. *Filippo Lippi: Funeral of St. Stephen, detail of the* architecture. *Prato, Cathedral.*
310. *Melozzo da Forlì: Sixtus IV* receiving *Platina, detail of the* architecture. *Rome, Pinacoteca Vaticana.*

65. A. Averlino, called Filarete, *Trattato di Architettura*, Milan 1962, I, pp. 10-11.
66. Ibid., II, p. 641: "This division of bodies and planes is described by the above-mentioned Battista Alberti in his Elements". And on the subject of the fundamental figures of geometry: "If you want to go into these matters in greater detail, read the mathematicians and Battista Alberti in his books on painting." p. 646.
67. A. Gambuti, op. cit., pp. 164-71. And also A. Gambuti, "I libri del disegno: Filarete e l'educazione artistica di Galeazzo Maria Sforza", in *Arte Lombarda*, 1973, pp. 133-43.

311. *Andrea Mantegna: St. James before Herod Agrippa, detail. Padua, Chiesa degli Eremitani.*

312. *Andrea Mantegna: St. James being led to his Execution, detail. Padua, Chiesa degli Eremitani.*

313. *Andrea Mantegna: Execution and Death of St. Christopher, detail. Padua, Chiesa degli Eremitani.*

them by means of straight lines so as to form a square. However, one can do the same using a set square."[70] They share the same views with regard to establishing the "centric point": both profess a preference for central perspective as opposed to a more general frontal perspective. However, Filarete realized that he was indebted to Brunelleschi above all[71] and confessed he had discovered this "most worthy architect of our times"[72] through "my Battista Alberti."[73]

Filarete readily acknowledged his debt to Alberti's treatise; Francesco di Giorgio ignored it completely. Indeed, Filarete's praise was the highest accorded to the *De Pictura* during Alberti's lifetime. It was not until the sixteenth century that Alberti's theories were re-considered: Dürer acknowledged them indirectly, Rivius plagiarised them, the Basle edition of the *De pictura* was published in 1540, and Vasari pronounced his reserved, almost Ghibertian judgement on Alberti in 1568, at the time of the publication of Cosimo Bartoli's edition of the *Opuscoli morali*.[74]

Vasari wrote rather acidly: "Leon Battista Alberti devoted himself to the study of Latin and the practice of architecture, perspective, and painting, and he left to posterity a number of books which he wrote himself. Now none of our modern craftsmen has known how to write about these subjects, and so even though very many of them have done better work than Alberti, such has been the influence of his writings on the pens and speech of scholarly men that he is commonly believed to be superior to those who were, in fact, superior to him."[75]

Alberti's treatise continued to exercise an influence on the cultural world of Florence: Borghini, apart from his reference to the tribune in the Annunziata, felt obliged to counter his arguments in putting forward his theory of the supremacy of sculpture,[76] and Doni[77] also felt his influence. Alberti's fundamental theory of proportion was found to be particularly useful in the course of the debate as to which art was supreme, for it considered all the arts as one. In his *Idea del Tempio della Pittura*, Lomazzo writes: "It is true, as Leon Battista Alberti says, that the painter has greater dignity insofar as he considers it (proportion) more perfectly in connection with the human body, so that the ancients accorded the highest honour to painting as the mistress of proportion. Indeed, they considered all artists to be false, the painter alone being excluded from their general censure."[78]

Even Venice, which was at loggerheads with Florence, owed much to Alberti. In his *Dialogo di Pittura* (in which Leon Battista is said to have "dared, with reason, to oppose Vitruvius's ideas on perspective"),[79] Pino returns to the concept of *circoscrizione*

68. Emphasis is placed on the purpose and usefulness of these studies. As Filarete says: "... in order to establish the first principles of design and to adopt them in the drawing of useful designs, and in carrying out everything else one wishes to design". This is a gloss on Alberti's last definition in his *Elements*: "Here follows what must be remembered about the true nature of design". Cf. also A. Gambuti, op. cit., in *Arte Lombarda*, p. 138.

69. L. B. Alberti, op. cit., p. 36.

70. Filarete, op. cit., XXIII, pp. 650-51.

71. "Therefore, I believe Pippo di Ser Brunelleschi succeeded in making this plane, which was a very subtle, beautiful invention indeed, and that he discovered what is reflected in the mirror when the eye, though watching at-

314. *"Lesson, or advice on how a father should behave". Perspective framework of the ceiling in a fifteenth-century Florentine woodcut, from M. Zanobi dalla Barba's edition of the "Flores Poetarum".*

315. *Christ before Pilate, Florentine engraving, c. 1460. Boston Museum.*

316. *Jacopo Bellini: Christ led before Pilate. Paris, Louvre.*

tentively, sees distortions and diminutions". Ibid., p. 653. And again (p. 657): "I really believe that in this way Filippo Brunelleschi discovered perspective, which was not known in earlier times. For the ancients, in spite of their intelligence and subtlety, had never understood or adopted this concept". Cf. also A. Parronchi, *Studi etc.*, op. cit., pp. 291-93.

72. Ibid., p. 693.

73. Ibid., p. 640.

74. "The moral writings of Leon Battista Alberti, a Florentine gentleman, which contain many rules necessary for the right conduct of men both in public and private life, translated and corrected by Cosimo Bartoli, in Venice, for Francesco Franceschi, Sanese, 1568".

317. Frontispiece of Bartoli's edition of the "Opuscoli Morali", printed in the same year as the second edition of Vasari's "Lives", 1568.

which binds painting, architecture, and perspective together, even though he describes Alberti's *velo aver quadratura* (veil and square frame) as "an insignificant, useless thing."[80] He is in favour of "depicting landscapes in a mirror, as the Germans do,"[81] and takes up Alberti's broader concept, according to which "things painted from nature can be rectified by means of a mirror." Of course, Pino is concerned with painting from a practical point of view, not with theory. Though fascinated by Alberti's culture, there is none of the scientific enthusiasm of Dürer or Alberti in his warning to the reader: "Leon Battista Alberti, who was also a painter, wrote a treatise on painting in Latin, which is more about mathematics than painting, even though he promised the contrary."[82] In spite of the refusal to accept ready-made rules that was characteristic of the fifteenth-century spirit, and in spite of the *contaminatio* of Mannerism and the relegation of perspective to the role of an auxiliary technique, Alberti's ideal of the cultural and moral importance of the painter continued to exercise an influence for a long time.

DE STATUA

The *De statua* is the least known of all Alberti's writings on art,[83] and the date of its composition is uncertain.[84] One argument for an early date, prior to the treatise on painting, is that it was written only in Latin; the *Anonymous Life* mentions the difficulty Alberti had in writing the *Libri della Famiglia* in the vernacular between 1432 and 1434.[85] Parronchi has found[86] a passage in Ghiberti's third commentary that contrasts personal experience with mere book-learning;[87] this may be a sarcastic allusion to Alberti's *De statua*, which would have preceded the writing of Ghiberti's third commentary were this the case. Further evidence may lie in the similarity between the instrument Alberti used to establish the points of a statue (the *definitore*) and that he used to compile the *Descriptio urbis Romae* (the so-called *orizzonte*), written between 1443 and 1455.[88] This instrument may have been tried out first on the human figure and then used in establishing the city's planimetry which would have been quite consistent with Alberti's concept of the close relationship between man and city. The problem becomes more difficult with the points of the statue—those points in space that require three co-ordinates; the planimetry of a city requires only polar co-ordinates.

The components of these rudimentary instruments were basically the same; they consisted of a circle, a rotatory arm (*linda*) in the centre of the circle, and a plumb-line to ensure that the circle was horizontal. The fundamental terms are the same in both

75. Vasari, op. cit., II, p. 536.

76. R. Borghini, *Il Riposo*, ed. Rosci, Milan 1967, p. 298.

77. A. F. Doni, *Il disegno*, Milan 1974, p. 54 verso. In his letter to Salviati of 3 June 1447. Doni writes: "In this great city, where all the beautiful things of the world arrive, I have also seen the book on painting by L. B. Alberti translated by Domenichi". op. cit., p. 109.

78. G. P. Lomazzo, in P. Barocchi, *Scritti d'arte, etc.*, op. cit., Naples 1973, II, p. 1845.

79. Ibid., I, p. 135.

80. Ibid., p. 116.

81. Ibid., pp. 134-428.

82. Ibid., p. 96.

83. There are only four Latin manuscripts and no generally accepted authentic Italian version (see Grayson, in Alberti, *Opere Volgari*, Vol. III, p. 429). There is Janitschek's 1877 edition of the Latin text (*L.B. Albertis Kleinere.. Schriften*, 1877, rep. Osnabrück 1970), and only one translation in the vernacular, Bartoli's of 1568. This was done from a partly corrupt manuscript, re-issued in Milan in 1804 and included by Bonucci as an original work in his 1843 edition of the "Opere Volgari". Cf. G. Flaccavento, "Per una moderna traduzione del De Statua di L. B. Alberti", in *Cronache di Archeologia e Storia dell'Arte*, I, 1962, pp. 50-59.

318-319. *Illustrations from "Leon Baptista Alberti, Of Statues",
London, 1664 (Appendix to R. Fréart's "A Parallel of the Ancient
Architecture with the Modern").*

320. *Illustration from the "Della Pittura e della Statua", edition of 1804.*

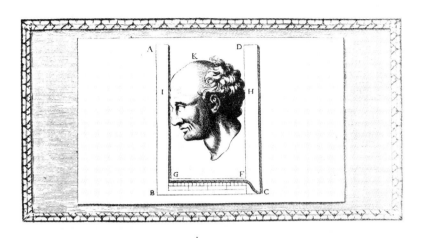

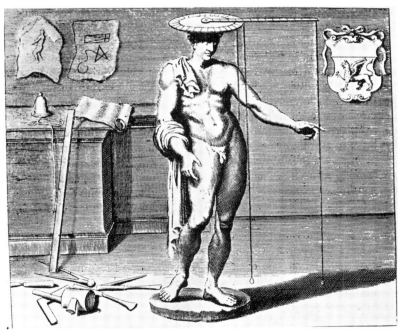

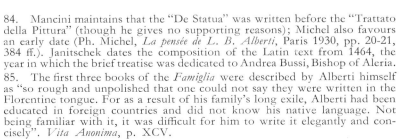

84. Mancini maintains that the "De Statua" was written before the "Trattato della Pittura" (though he gives no supporting reasons); Michel also favours an early date (Ph. Michel, *La pensée de L. B. Alberti*, Paris 1930, pp. 20-21, 384 ff.). Janitschek dates the composition of the Latin text from 1464, the year in which the brief treatise was dedicated to Andrea Bussi, Bishop of Aleria.

85. The first three books of the *Famiglia* were described by Alberti himself as "so rough and unpolished that one could not say they were written in the Florentine tongue. For as a result of his family's long exile, Alberti had been educated in foreign countries and did not know his native language. Not being familiar with it, it was difficult for him to write it elegantly and concisely". *Vita Anonima*, p. XCV.

86. A. Parronchi, *Studi etc.*, op. cit., p. 383.

87. "And I am certainly grateful to all those writers who have clarified the subject before me, without concealing their sources or filling their works with the ideas of others. And since we, too, intend to set down our own, we may write more abundantly and freely with respect to previous authors, in the hope that the new things we say will equal what we quote from them". Ibid., p. 384.

88. Cf. L. Vagnetti, "La Descriptio Urbis Romae", in *Quaderno I dell'Istituto di Elementi di Architettura e Rilievo dei Monumenti, Università degli Studi di Genova*, October 1968, p. 25 ff.

89. See *De Statua*, ed. Janitschek, p. 191: "ambitum circuli istius extremam-

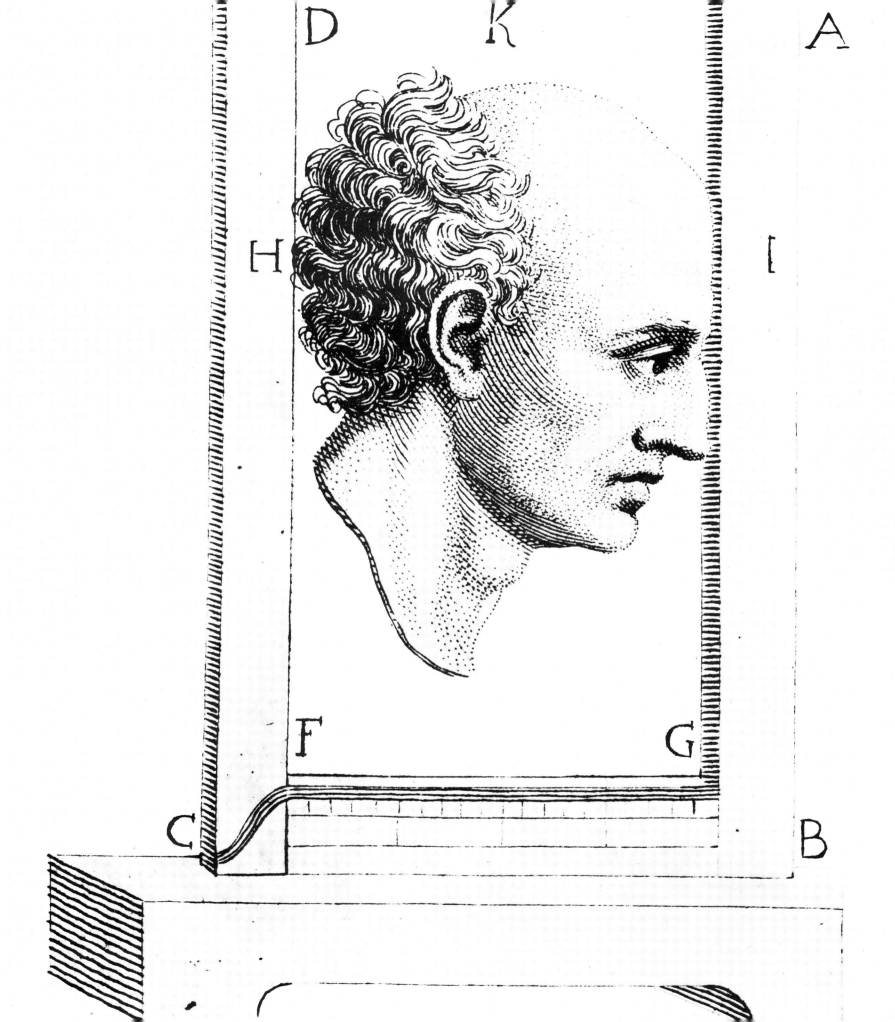

texts, and "horizon" and "radius"[89] are given similar explanations. The circle was divided into equal parts called *gradi*, and these in turn were subdivided into smaller units called *minuti*. In the *Descriptio* there are four (not six) *minuti* to each *grado*, and forty-eight *gradi* in all. Forty-eight *gradi* subdivided into four *minuti* correspond to the "horizon" of thirty-two *gradi* subdivided into six *minuti* in the *De statua*. (The division of the *gradi* into smaller units was caused by the need for greater precision in the measurement of long distances, a problem which does not arise when checking the proportions of the human body or a statue.) Both books conclude with instructions for the use of the instrument, given with practical examples in the *Descriptio* and explained ideally in the *De statua*.[90] The object in each case is to formulate a proportional canon, a kind of aesthetic anthropometry capable of conquering space by means of two simple instruments, the *squadra mobile* and the *definitore*. In this way, a statue, in which the human figure no longer adopts certain obligatory positions or occupies the places usually reserved for it in Gothic buildings, could move realistically in space, in conformity with the corresponding geometrical perspective grid that defined pictorial space.[91]

Though the work has been described as more medieval than Renaissance,[92] the originality of the *De statua* lies in its rationalism. Alberti's devices may indeed resemble the tools of a simple artisan. But it is important to grasp their symbolic significance, and this can only be done by drawing an analogy with the large-scale problems of the city.

The *De statua* failed to have much influence, and little editorial interest was shown in it. This seems strange, considering that it dealt with a problem that was to engage the attention of many future artists, from Leonardo to Dürer, and that its concept of *addendo aut diminuendo* anticipated Leonardo's *crescere* and Michelangelo's *levare*. In the Mannerist period, when sculpture reigned supreme, Cosimo Bartoli's cautious judgement of the treatise was inspired by its theoretical concern with instruments, though he did emphasise the didactic value of the *De statua* as a manual.[93] But in presenting it as a curiosity, he did it a disservice. On the other hand, Michelangelo himself, according to Danti, applied himself to the practical problem of "demonstrating with what instrument or tool one may achieve that perfection of which all artistic proportion is the universal echo and, in particular, that of the human body."[94]

Yet both Condivi and Vasari testify that Michelangelo distrusted all books "that had not tried out what they contained."[95] Danti himself affirms that beauty is not to be found in nature but in

art, and points to the uselessness of Alberti's eclectic method of establishing ideal proportions. But for Alberti, as for the Florentines of the Quattrocento, the highest moment had been reached precisely when they had given "to the fruit of art the value and very instruments of nature."[96]

que circuitionem in partes divido coequales similes partibus quas in astrolabio inscribunt astronomi"; and the *Descriptio* in L. Vagnetti, op. cit., p. 60: "huius horizontis ambitum in partes divido coequales et numero sint octo et quadraginta quas partes gradus appellabimus".

90. "Non unius istius aut illius corporis tantum, sed quoad licuit, eximiam a natura pluribus corporibus, quasi ratis portionibus dono distributam pulchritudinem, adnotare et mandare litteris prosecuti sumus." L. B. Alberti, op. cit., p. 201.

91. "Sic statuo cuiusque artis et disciplinae adsunt natura principia quaedam et prospectiones et executiones quae qui adhibita diligentia adverterit sibique adsumpserit rem ex instituto pulcherrime consequetur." Ibid., p. 173.

92. See A. Parronchi, op. cit., p. 402.

93. Cosimo Bartoli dedicated his translation of Alberti's treatise to Ammannati, describing it as an attempt "to prepare a way for the young, unskilled enthusiasts of this most noble art to follow, encouraging them to carve well according to fixed, stable principles". L. B. Alberti, *Della Pittura e della Scultura*, op. cit., p. 104.

94. V. Danti, "Trattato delle perfette proporzioni", in P. Barocchi, *Trattati d'Arte del '500*, Bari 1962, p. 213.

95. Ibid., p. 214, note 4.

96. A. Parronchi, op. cit., p. 405. On the "De Statua" see also J. Gadol, op. cit., pp. 76-81, 82-84.

Alberti refers to his fondness for mathematical studies more than once;[1] intellectual amusement combined with curiosity and practical application is a constant characteristic of his technical works. This is as true of the geometrical core of his writings on painting as it is of the *Trattato dei pondi* (now lost) and the *Ludi Matematici*.[2] Alberti probably approached the subject of constructional equipment and technique in the same spirit with which he had written the *Trattato della pittura*: the latter was an attempt to theorise Brunelleschi's ideas on perspective; his main object now was to systematize the mechanical principles behind the equipment invented by Brunelleschi for the construction of his prodigious dome, and to explain these devices theoretically in a book that might serve as a practical guide.[3] Brunelleschi's silence on the subject was dictated by prudence. As he told Taccola,[4] many listened only to criticize and then put forward the same ideas they had criticized in illustrated manuals, claiming them as their own. Therefore, "non debetur dona Dei nobis tributa relinquere sed ea sequi ac exercere, quia virtuosi ac ingeniosi a sapientioribus sapientes reputantur."[5] This was certainly not the attitude of a populariser, but that of a Gothic architect jealous of preserving the secrets of his trade.[6]

Francesco di Giorgio's well-known controversy, in the course of which he attempted to formulate the still unfamiliar concept of plagiarism, may have been directed at Alberti. In his sixth tract, which deals with equipment for lifting weights and drawing water, Francesco proclaims: "The ignorant have always taken credit by attributing to themselves the labours of others, and this has never been so true as in our own day. They boast that they know and can do many things, though if the truth were known, all that they know is really the invention of others. This fault is particularly evident in our own times among those who often call themselves architects, though these are nearly all ignorant, incompetent men, who may easily be recognised by their works."[7] The second part of this passage may refer to Francesco's rival for the commission of the fortresses in the area of Urbino; the first may contain a reference to Alberti.[8]

Brunelleschi's legacy was a rich one. Not only is it reflected in the writers who quote him (Biagio da Parma, for example, to whom is attributed a *Trattato dei pesi*), but also in the experiments that followed his own, such as those of Leonardo. Leonardo designed a great number of winches and other devices for lifting weights, drawings of which are scattered throughout his works (though most of them are to be found in the Codex Atlanticus). How many of Leonardo's mechanical ideas were derived from

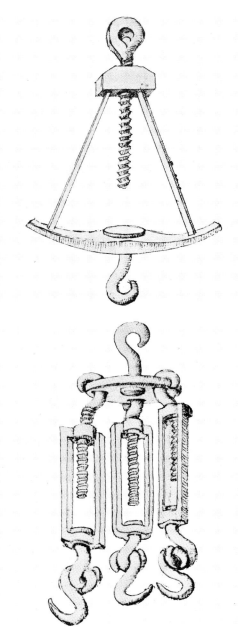

1. *Vita Anonima*, op. cit., p. 95: "... he studied physics and mathematics for twenty-four years. Nor did he snub them for being subjects of a more mnemonic than creative kind". And in the *Profugiorum ab aerumna*: "... and above all, when I began to study them, nothing gave me greater satisfaction, nothing absorbed me so much as mathematical studies and demonstrations, especially when I strove to give them some practical application, as Battista did in this case, for he used mathematics in elaborating his basic rules of painting, and in establishing his incredible propositions regarding the motion of heavy bodies". L. B. Alberti, *Opere Volgari*, Vol. II, p. 182.

2. In referring to the "Trattato dei Pondi", Vasari merges it erroneously with the "Ludi": "... he composed a treatise on traction and the rules for calculating heights". Vasari, op. cit., II, p. 537. Mancini attributes the "Trat-

tato dei pondi, leve e tirari" to Alberti, but Grayson rejects this categorically. Nor is its inclusion in the Chigi codex, together with the "Descriptio Urbis Romae" and the "Cinque Ordini Architettonici", enough to prove Alberti's authorship, since the codex itself is apocryphal. Cf. F. Borsi, I Cinque Ordini Architettonici e Leon Battista Alberti, in *Studi e Documenti di Architettura*, December 1972, 1, p. 57 ff.

3. P. Sanpaolesi "Ipotesi sulle conoscenze matematiche statiche e meccaniche del Brunelleschi", in *Belle Arti*, 1951, II, pp. 25-30: "Filippo's complete silence leaves us no chance of obtaining any precise information on the matter, but one cannot say he was unaware of the theorems involved in these simple machines. It is more difficult to establish whether he discovered a way of deducing the exact theoretical principles of the machinery he invented during

324. *Bonaccorso Ghiberti: drawing of a winch, from the "Zibaldone".* Ms. Br. 228, f.v. 93. Florence, Biblioteca Nazionale.

325. *Mariano di Jacopo, called Taccola: horse-drawn mechanism for lifting weights, from the "De Ingeneis".* Palat. 766, c. 10. Florence, Biblioteca Nazionale.

326. *Bonaccorso Ghiberti: three-speed winch, from the "Zibaldone".* Ms. Br. 228, f.r. 102. Florence, Biblioteca Nazionale.

327. *Bonaccorso Ghiberti: three-speed winch, from the "Zibaldone".* Ms. Br. 228, f.v. 103. Florence, Biblioteca Nazionale.

328. *Mariano di Jacopo, called Taccola: animal-drawn mechanism for lifting weights, from the "De Ingeneis".* Palat. 766, c. 11. Florence, Biblioteca Nazionale.

329. *Giuliano da Sangallo: mills with three-speed transmission, from the "Taccuino Senese", c. 50, ed. Falb., Siena 1902.*

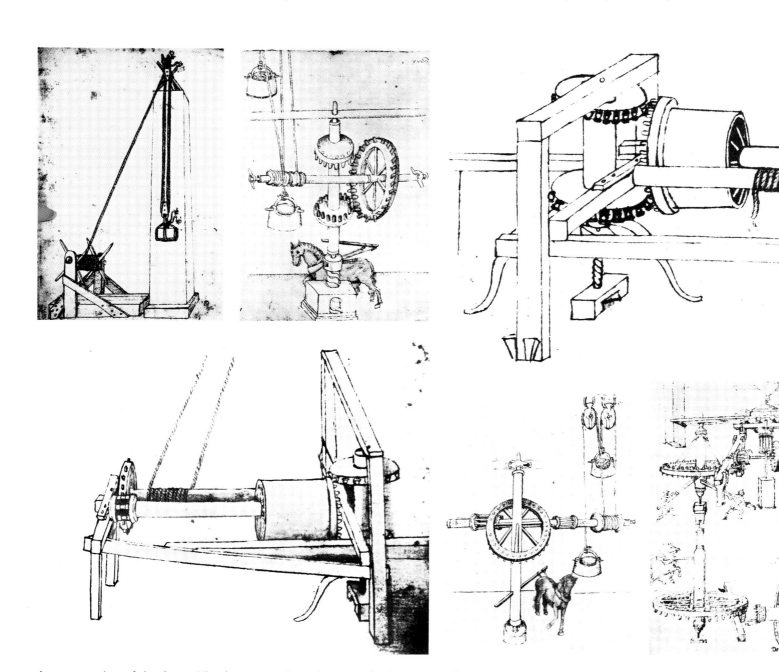

the construction of the dome. The documents show that Brunelleschi built many machines without knowing the principles on which they were based, and which we now call *lavori virtuali* ('potential works'). Such were the three *colle* (pulleys) that lifted the material to the level at which the building was being carried out, up to the very top of the dome itself".

4. "Ex sua benignitate dixit mihi hec (sic) verbis: 'Noli cum multis partecipare inventiones tuas sed cum paucis intelligentibus et amatoribus scientiarum quia nimis ostendere et dicere suas inventiones et facta potes unum derogare sua ingenia". Mariano di Jacopo, called Taccola, *Liber tertius de ingeneis ac edifitiis non usitatis*, Milan 1969, p. 15. Alberti might have met Taccola in Siena when he spent a few months in the following of Eugenius IV (Mancini, *Vita di L. B. Alberti*, p. 255). Cf. F. D. Prager and G. Scaglia, *Mariano Tac-*

cola and his book De Ingeneis, Cambridge (Mass.) 1972, p. 17.

5. Ibid.

6. This also explains how "The principal innovations of Brunelleschian mechanics, the screw actuated reversing clutch and the screw-controlled load positions, are unknown to the architecture books of Alberti, Serlio, Palladio and their successors". F. D. Prager and G. Scaglia, *Brunelleschi. Studies of his Technology and Inventions*, M.I.T. 1970, p. 105.

7. Francesco di Giorgio Martini, op. cit., pp. 492-93.

8. See also the similar statement in the preamble to the treatise: "Not wishing to fall into the vice of ingratitude, or to deck myself out in borrowed plumes ..." This is said in connection with Vitruvius, but there is no

330. *Bonaccorso Ghiberti: crane with rotating platform used to construct the lantern of the dome of S. Maria del Fiore, from the "Zibaldone". Ms. Br. 228, f.r. 105. Florence, Biblioteca Nazionale.*

331. *Bonaccorso Ghiberti: crane with rotating platform, from the "Zibaldone". Ms. Br. 228, f.r. 104. Florence, Biblioteca Nazionale.*

332. *Giuliano da Sangallo: crane with rotating platform, from the "Taccuino Senese", c. 12, ed. Falb, Siena 1902.*

333. *Leonardo: crane with rotating platform, from the "Codex Atlanticus", f.v. b 295. Milan, Biblioteca Ambrosiana.*

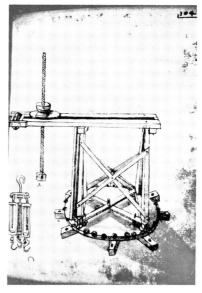
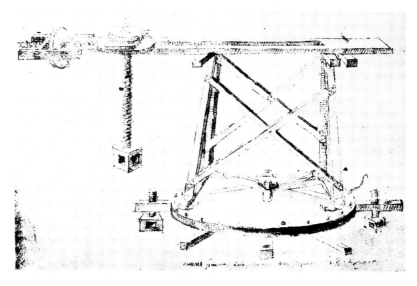
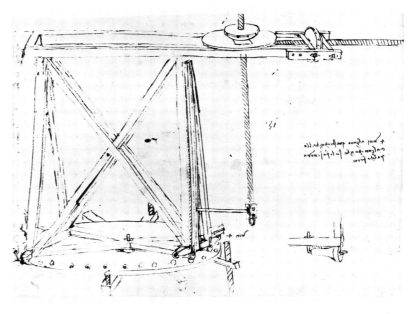

Brunelleschi? It is easier to answer this question by comparing them with those of Sangallo, and particularly with Bonaccorso Ghiberti's.[9] There are noticeable similarities in many of the mechanical devices of all three artists, such as the three-speed winch, the large *colla* (the principal device used in raising Brunelleschi's dome), the crane with rotating platform (used in assembling the lantern), and the adjustable-balancing crane, all of which were derived from the same source. (Francesco di Giorgio was the first to create a myth out of mechanical technology in his bas-relief at Urbino.)

Rinuccini, a near contemporary of Leon Battista, testifies to the latter's interest in the study "machinarum cum bellicarum tum quae magnis trahendis ponderibus valeant."[10] However, no attempt has been made to reconstruct the contents of Alberti's treatise, either on the basis of the meagre sources regarding contemporary scientific and technical literature (collected by Winterberg)[11] or on the evidence provided by Mancini, who tends to distinguish between one treatise written "on weights" and another "on pulleys", that is, between mechanical physics and mechanical technology.[12] Nor is any such attempt to be found in the hurried notes of Gille[13] or in Gadol.[14] Some idea of the content of the lost treatise may be deduced from the *De re aedificatoria*, in which he makes two references to another text. The first occurs in his discussion of motion and the various types of movement;[15] the second — "multa quae ab isto usu pertineant alibi explicabuntur"[16] — refers to operational techniques and immediately precedes Alberti's theory of machines as "animated bodies". This is the key to Alberti's re-interpretation of Brunelleschi's work and contemporary technology, and is wholly consistent with the anthropomorphic organicism that inspires Alberti's entire aesthetics.[17] It is accompanied by an appeal to prudence and caution, and there is a warning as to the consequences success or failure may have on one's credibility and prestige — an exhortation to correct conduct that must have been largely determined by his experience of the quarrels between Brunelleschi and Ghiberti (which Manetti discusses).

The *Pondi, leve e tirari* which Mancini attributes to Leon Battista deals mainly with mills and hydraulic machinery in general; only the final pages are concerned with constructional machinery. There is mention of traction equipment (*tirari*) and winches that are more Brunelleschian than Ghibertian, but there is no reference at all to cranes. Thus the manuscript is more likely to have been written by Martini than by Alberti.

Much more is known about the *Ludi Matematici*, of which the

doubt that the barb is directed at Alberti (Ibid., p. 296).

9. L. Reti, "Tracce dei progetti perduti di F. Brunelleschi nel Codice Atlantico", in *Letture Vinciane* 1960-72, Florence 1974, p. 104.

10. G. Mancini, *Vasari Vite Cinque*, Florence 1917, p. 114.

11. Winterberg, "Leon Battista Albertis technische Schriften", in *Repertorium für Kunstwissenschaft*, 1883, 6, p. 326 ff.

12. G. Mancini, *Vita*, op. cit., pp. 286-89.

13. B. Gille, *Les Ingegneurs de la Renaissance*, Paris 1964, p. 82; p. 11 of the Italian trans., *Leonardo e gli Ingegneri del Rinascimento*, Milan 1972.

14. J. Gadol, op. cit., p. 204.

334. *Bonaccorso Ghiberti: crane with counterbalancing weight, from the "Zibaldone". Ms. Br. 228, f.r. 94. Florence, Biblioteca Nazionale.*

335. *Leonardo: crane with counterbalancing weight, from the "Codex Atlanticus", f.r. 349 a. Milan, Biblioteca Ambrosiana.*

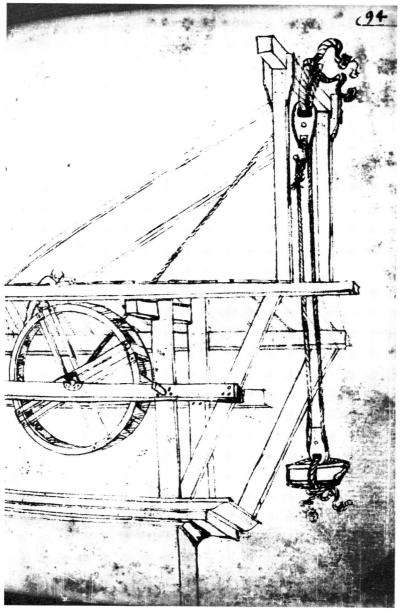

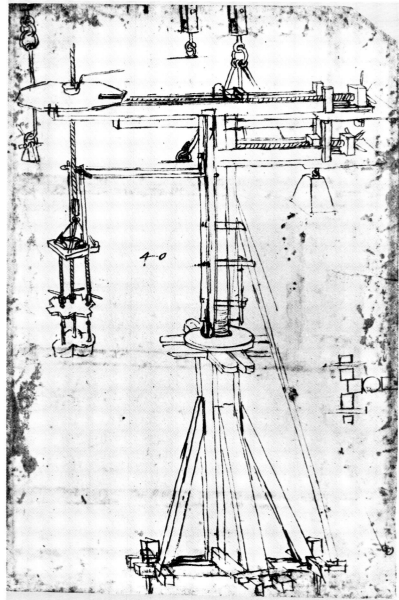

15. "Heavy bodies move in various directions, away from, towards, or around a point, and can be carried, drawn, or pushed". L. B. Alberti, *L'Architettura*, VI, 6, p. 476.

16. Ibid., VI, 8, p. 497.

17. Alberti affirms: "It is enough to point out that all machines may be regarded as inanimate bodies provided with exceptionally strong hands, and that in moving weights, they behave just as we men do. Therefore, when constructing machines, we must reproduce the same measurements and contractions that our members and nerves assume when we pull, push, or carry objects". Ibid., p. 496.

text edited by Grayson is available. Since no autograph copy of the work exists Grayson has based his text on the numerous extant manuscripts and Vagnetti's careful study of the treatise, a study that combines a reliable textual analysis with explanatory drawings and references to the more significant manuscripts.[18] There is just one observation to be made concerning the dedication to Meliaduso d'Este and Alberti's apologies for the "delay" in fulfilling his promise to write the work.[19] The dedication marked the climax in Alberti's relations with the court of Ferrara.[20] Practically all Alberti's artistic interests were engaged in the course of this relationship, so that it serves to complete our picture of the cultural universalism that characterised this period in his career. This universalism should be taken into account in judging the lack of architectural activity on Alberti's part in these years. Meliaduso, the son of Niccolò III and Caterina de' Taddei, had little enthusiasm for the ecclesiastical career planned for him by his father.[21] All we know about him is that he ran away from Ferrara when he was nineteen and that many years later, in 1450, he was granted the income from the Benedictine monastery of S. Bartolo in Ferrara. It is doubtful that he ever went to Pomposa; he was certainly never abbot of Pomposa *in commendam*; and it is very unlikely that he was made abbot under the jurisdiction of an agent of the Estes like de la Sale, who was probably put in charge of the monastery by Meliaduso's father because of the son's weaknesses (which certainly did not include impotence).[22] Alberti may have dedicated the *Ludi* to Meliaduso to compensate for his lack of a religious vocation by providing him with a technical education. This would explain his commission to write a simple, straightforward exposition of all that was necessary for the practical solution of astronomic, hydraulic, and administrative problems which would have completed an abbot's studies most appropriately. The work may even have been written to encourage Meliaduso to face certain practical problems and to help him solve them. Vagnetti's comparison of the treatise with Villard de Honnecourt's notebook is a pertinent one; the latter is another succinct *summa* of medieval knowledge, which was, of course, concentrated in the monasteries.

The *Ludi Matematici* is more an abridged manual of engineering than bedtime reading. But it has a political purpose too, and it is a companion volume to the *Theogenius*. Instead of the perfect prince, its subject is the perfect abbot, who is an agriculturalist, a topographer, and a man who can calculate directions, measurements, weights (especially heavy ones like crops) and great distances. Every one of the twenty exercises set forth by Alberti (even

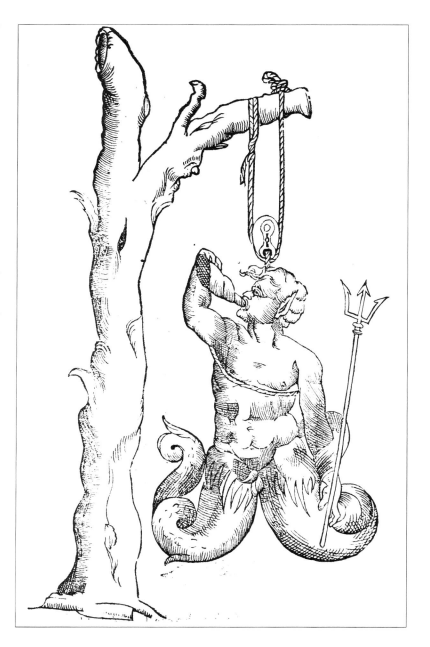

18. C. Grayson (ed.), *Opere Volgari*, Vol. III, p. 352 ff.; L. Vagnetti, "Considerazioni sui Ludi Matematici", in *Studi e Documenti di Architettura*, December 1972, 1, pp. 173-261.

19. See the dedication, *Opere Volgari*, III, p. 133.

20. Alberti had dedicated the *Philodoxeus*, the *De equo animante* and the *Theogenius* to Lionello d'Este, and had expressed his intention of dedicating the *De re aedificatoria* to him as well. The *De Pictura* was dedicated to Giovan Francesco, Prince of Mantua.

21. Much has been written about Meliaduso's mistaken vocation and about the boredom and restlessness that characterised his ecclesiastical career as Abbot of Pomposa, until the Pope's dispensation and his own death freed

him from his vows. Writers have also insisted on the lucid, carefree nature of Alberti's treatise (Bartoli). But if one considers the importance of Pomposa in the area of Ferrara (a kind of northern Montecassino) and its function in the control and organisation of the waters of the Po (always a vital factor in the region), the nomination of a prince of the house of Este as Abbot of Pomposa takes on a political aspect. This would have been consistent with the family's policy of establishing complete control over a State of considerable territorial-technical importance. The Estes had already tried to annex the small independent State of Pomposa in various ways, by instigating internal revolt and forming alliances with other States against it. A radical change took place in the very beginning of the fifteenth century: the series of regular abbots came to an end and Pandolfo Malatesta (of the Pesaro branch of the

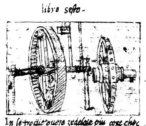

the last one, the "problem of the crown" devised by Archimedes to show how the tyrant Hieron was cheated of gold) is related to a particular field of action, and serves some practical purpose pertinent to the daily management of a large farm, land reclamation, or topography. Even the approximate or erroneous calculations may be understood in the light of an attempt to illustrate certain principles with a practical end in view.

As Vagnetti has pointed out, the fact that the work was largely ignored in its own day is less important than its anticipation of many problems concerning measurement by sight which were to be widely explored later, especially in the following century. Alberti also deserves credit for attempting to assimilate and re-apply medieval scientific knowledge as he had done in the *De statua*. One reason for the delay in the composition of the *Ludi* (apart from practical ones that kept Alberti away from the court of Ferrara) may have been his realisation that it was no longer possible to deal with such problems in this particular way. The same subject is dealt with quite differently in the *De re aedificatoria*, where there is no mention of mathematics. Instead, problems characteristic of the Po valley, such as the plantation of vineyards in damp areas and trees in marshlands, the danger of floods ("as in the areas around the Po"),[23] roads, water-courses, and dykes, are treated on the basis of simple observations of an experimental and traditional nature. Among the few topics the *Ludi* has in common with the tenth book of the *De re aedificatoria* is the problem of measuring the gradient of a canal even where the plain is quite flat. Another is that of channelling water through a city and the consequent need to line up opposite points of direction. The simplicity of the exegesis in the *De re aedificatoria* is an indication, if not proof ("ars paulo secretior haec est"),[24] of how much Alberti studies the subject before ironing out the uncertainties and qualitative lapses that characterise the *Ludi Matematici*.

It is difficult to assign a definite place to the *Ludi Matematici* in Renaissance culture. One may agree with Vagnetti when he describes it as a tardy, half-hearted *divertissement* written to fulfil a promise made to an even more half-hearted prince. Or one may see it as a laboured, uneven work of popularisation written to illustrate practical applications of scientific theory. In both cases the work is consistent with Alberti's desire to "sample" the whole of contemporary culture from the viewpoint of its utility, in the belief that theory and experience, knowledge and practice, could be reconciled. But the reappearance of ideas expressed in the *Ludi* in the writings of Leonardo, in spite of the latter's relative ignorance of Alberti's manuscript, would seem to confirm the second

family) was appointed administrator of the abbey. The agreement between Pandolfo and Niccolò III practically secured the annexation of Pomposa for the Estes. However, events developed gradually. After Pandolfo, Pomposa was administered by Baldassare de la Sale, a faithful follower of Niccolò's, and then by Cardinal Rinaldo, the first commendatory abbot of the house of Este. Cf. A. Ostoja, "Vicende della commenda pomposiana in relazione al piano di assorbimento della Signoria estense", in *Analecta Pomposiana*, Codigoro 1965.

22. I owe the following information about Meliaduso's illegitimate descendants to research carried out in the Modena State Archives by Gianni Baldini: "The illegitimate children of Meliaduso d'Este (3 March 1406-2 January 1452),

340. *Method of measuring the height of a tower. Introduction to the third book of the "De Ingeneis" by Taccola, 1432.*

341. *Method of measuring the height of a tower by means of a mirror. Cod. Lat. VIII 125 (37-17). Venice, Biblioteca Marciana (after Vagnetti).*

342. *Measurement of the height of a tower, from the "Ludi Matematici" (after Grayson).*

343. *Measurement of the height of a tower, from the "Ludi Matematici". Cod. G IV 29. Genoa, Biblioteca Universitaria (after Vagnetti).*

344. *Indirect measurement of the height of a tower (after Vagnetti).*

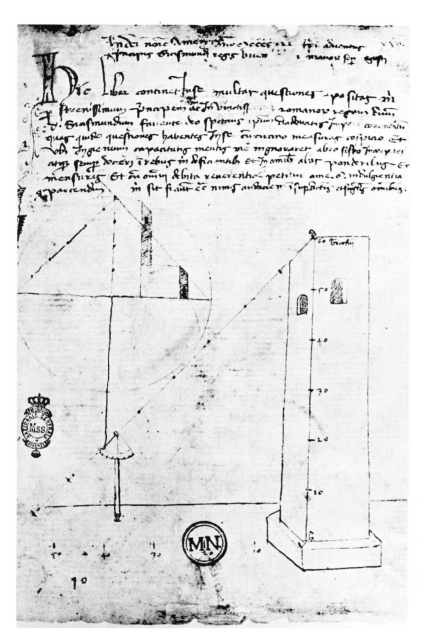

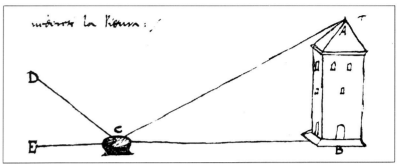

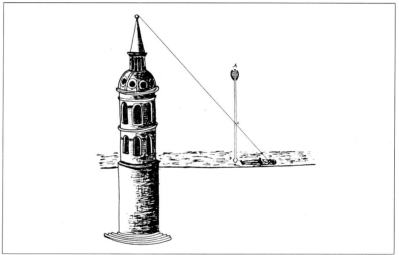

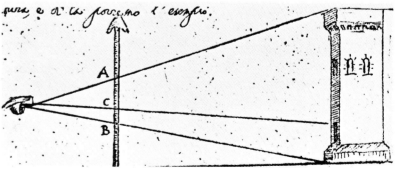

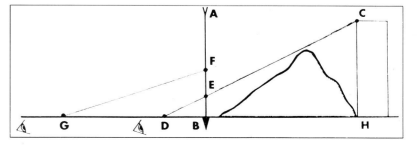

the son of Niccolò III, were: Scipione Maria (died in 1500). Ten letters written between 22 November 1464 and 4 July 1498, to his uncles Borso, Ercole I, Alberto Maria, and his cousin Cardinal Ippolito I are still extant; Polidoro, of whom there are six letters, written to his uncles Borso and Ercole I between 10 November 1467 and 7 September 1472; Suor Laura, three letters to her uncle Borso; Niccolò, whose widow, a certain Lippa, has left a letter to Ercole I dated 17 August 1498; Polissena, the wife of Giovanni Romei. A fifteenth-century summary of the will of Giovanni Romei, her first husband, has survived".

23. L. B. Alberti, *L'Architettura*, X, 9, p. 942.
24. Ibid., p. 921.

345. Indirect measurement of the width of a river (after Grayson).
346. Another method for measuring the width of a river "expeditely" (after Grayson).

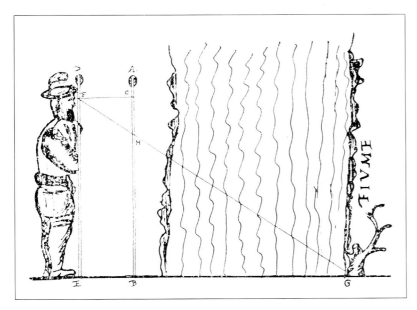

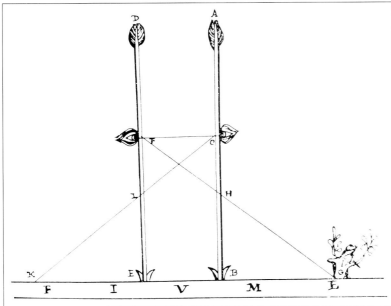

interpretation. Solmi points out that both Alberti and Leonardo were interested in problems of measurement and that their respective explanations of weighing-machines and odometers are similar.[25]

This should caution us against underestimating the work too much with respect to the *Descriptio*, whose method of measurement based on polar co-ordinates was adopted by Leonardo in his plans of Imola, Cesena, and Urbino.[26] Nor should it be neglected in favour of the treatise on painting, a subject which Leonardo explored with quite a different self-assurance.

25. E. Solmi, *Le fonti dei manoscritti di Leonardo da Vinci*, Turin 1908, pp. 39-41. Leonardo makes an explicit, though erroneous reference to Alberti: "Battista Alberti says in a work of his which he sent to the Lord Malatesta of Rimini". He also quotes him: "Battista Alberti says in his work Ex Ludis Mathematicarum". "... and this is in Battista Alberti".

26. M. De Toni, "I Rilievi Cartografici per Cesena e Urbino", in *Letture Vinciane*, op. cit., p. 133 ff.

CHAPTER ELEVEN
The De Re Aedificatoria

Alberti's treatise on architecture, of which some manuscript copies are entitled (in the Vitruvian manner) *De architectura*, is more commonly known by its late medieval title as the *De re aedificatoria*. It is the work of a lifetime and it marks the culmination of an attempt to relate art to politics and morality. The book contains a wealth of autobiographical material, beginning with Alberti's journeys abroad in the company of Cardinal Albergati and continuing in his observations on the monuments of Italy and nature, and in his ransacking of the classics for allusive illustrations of the various subjects he deals with. The autobiographical aspect of the *De re aedificatoria* has already emerged in our discussion of his architectural works.

The circumstances in which the work was written are not entirely clear.[1] There is some doubt, for example, about the evidence of Landino, who "refers inaccurately to Alberti's nine books of architecture"[2] and there is no doubt that the tenth book, which deals with restoration, has the unmistakable air of a later addition. This is apparent from the lofty tone of conclusion that characterises the end of Book Nine, which has all the appearance of a *trait d'union* between the book proper and a later appendix. The impression is confirmed by the amount of space dedicated to the subject of hydraulics: this anticipates Frontinus's additions to Vitruvius and suggests that Alberti wanted to emulate his Latin model on this subject too. Finally, there is the reference to the proposal for the restoration of St. Peter's: the past conditionals *commendassent* and *fecissem* convey the impression that the proposal was overtaken by subsequent events, while "istitueram" clearly refers to a decision that had been shelved. We have already referred to the solid reasons for writing the first nine books together and presenting them to Nicholas upon the completion of his town planning scheme. Indeed, towards the end of the seventh book, which deals with religious architecture, the author considers the climax of Nicholas' building programme at some length. Another puzzling passage occurs at the beginning of the sixth book. This refers to some kind of crisis in the compilation of the treatise.[3] Since we may exclude all suspicion of rhetorical indulgence, this inner crisis must have coincided with a temporary lull in the writing of the treatise. It may not have been actually interrupted, but Alberti may have felt a momentary lack of intellectual energy. With the completion of the fifth book Alberti had dealt not only with the value of the project and constructional technique, but with the entire structure of the city and its typology. These were all subjects he expounded originally, but for which he could rely heavily on personal experience, literary allusion,

and practical situations. Having done this, he now faced the problem of "ornament": that is, he had to define beauty and establish a system of values that would relate religious architecture to public and private architecture. At this point he seems to have felt some dissatisfaction with the subject as treated so far and to have considered revising it. However, he conceals his uncertainty by saying: "I prefer not to choose different principles or to order my material in a different way, but to continue as I have done so far, dealing with one subject after another as it comes into my mind, providing it is relevant to my purpose."[4] Yet he may well have hesitated before tackling the most difficult part of his treatise, which embraced the linguistic problem (the *explicatio*) and the comparison of his own personal findings with Vitruvius — the confrontation of authority with experience. Apart from these two passages (between the fifth and sixth books, and the ninth and tenth) the treatise was checked, polished, and completed in a fairly uniform manner, Alberti's method being to write out a first draft with gaps, especially for names and quotations, which he filled in later.[5]

ALBERTI AND VITRUVIUS

The language difficulties mentioned by Alberti at the beginning of the sixth book had also been pointed out by Vitruvius: "If certain things are explained badly, it is because I have tried to express them not in the style of a great philosopher, learned orator, or fine grammarian, but as an architect with a smattering of these disciplines."[6] Vitruvius's concern, which was even more urgent for Alberti, was to be understood not only by the initiated but by the educated person in general.

There is no questioning Vitruvius's obscurity. On the other hand, there is nothing to confirm Krautheimer's theory[7] that Lionello d'Este suggested Alberti write a commentary on Vitruvius, and that this commentary was later developed into an independent, original work. On the contrary, there is an organic development that links all Alberti's treatises on art. It can be seen, for example, in the evolution of his concept of "natural beauty": in the *Della pittura* it embraces the whole of the visible world; in the *De statua* it consists of the choice and assembly of individual parts; finally, in the *De re aedificatoria*, beauty becomes a question of proportion to be found in the organic nature of an edifice — in certain laws that regulate the harmony of nature.[8] Alberti emphasized the need to be independent of the ancients very early on in his career (in the dedication of the *De Pictura* to Brunelleschi); the same attitude is fundamental to the *De re aedificatoria*. At a time when princes

---

1. Grayson has argued that the whole work was written between 1444 and 1452, in "The Composition of Alberti's Decem Libri De Re Aedificatoria", *Münchener Jahrbuch der Bildenden Kunst*, XI, 1960, pp. 152-61. Mattia Palmieri's reference to the presentation of the books of architecture to Nicholas V in 1452, Flavio Biondo's mention of the attempt to retrieve the ships from Lake Nemi (also referred to in Alberti's treatise) in 1447, and the introduction to the *Ludi Matematici* addressed to Meliaduso d'Este (with its allusion to the "books of architecture" requested by his brother Lionello), which must have been written before Meliaduso's death in 1452, are all factors that help to establish the date of the treatise. To this may be added Facio's testimony of 1456 ("scripsit et de architectura libros duos quos intercoenales inscripsit", where the two works are clearly confused), the reference to a passage of

Theophrastus translated by Teodoro Gaza in 1453, and the note on the building materials needed for Rimini in the letter written to Matteo de' Pasti in 1454. It is uncertain whether the whole work was completed by 1452; there are critics who believe that only some of the books had been written by that year (see P. Portoghesi, *L. B. Alberti, L'Architettura*, op. cit., p. 54). On the other hand, it may be objected that except for the *De Cifris* and the *De Iciarchia*, Alberti always wrote a first rapid version of his work, returning to it later, ironing out its imperfections with patience and at irregular intervals, and sometimes using more than one manuscript whenever time, place, and circumstances allowed him to.

2. C. Grayson, op. cit., p. 155.

and artists were showing an interest in classical antiquity, the explanation and interpretation of Vitruvius had become necessary, but it was a task that could only be undertaken by an original, inquiring mind in the light of contemporary needs. This is what determined Alberti's interest in Vitruvius, though a knowledge of classical culture had prevailed throughout the Middle Ages and was assimilated by men like Boccaccio and Petrarch in the early stages of the new Humanism.[9] Alberti states his position clearly: "In the course of these meditations, I have come across many ideas that have been extraordinarily important, useful, and necessary for mankind, which could not have been ignored in a treatise such as this. And in my opinion, every gentle lover of the arts should feel an obligation to help in restoring this science, for which the most learned of the ancients had the greatest esteem, from its present ruin."[10]

Alberti followed Vitruvius in the formal organisation of his treatise, dividing it into ten volumes and giving it the same title. His interpretation of the orders and columns is particularly indebted to his Roman predecessor, and he either quotes or refers to Vitruvius on no less than fifteen occasions, usually on technical matters. Alberti differs from Vitruvius in his numerous references to classical literature: Livy, Cicero, Pliny, Plato, Herodotus, Thucydides, Servius, Strabo, Diodorus Siculus, Suetonius, Tacitus, Aristotle, Varro, and Demosthenes. He criticises Vitruvius explicitly at times, indirectly at others, enough to invite constant comparison with him. He declares: "It is our concern to include in this work all the most valuable and valid observations written down by the authors of antiquity, together with those rules we have found they applied in the actual construction of their work."[11] Alberti was determined to verify everything for himself: "I have examined all the buildings of antiquity that might be in the least important to see if anything was to be learnt from them. I have been tireless in seeking out, examining, measuring, and drawing everything possible so as to master all that man's labour and intelligence offers in these monuments."[12] There is a polemical note in Alberti's definition of the architect in the preface as a man "who adopts a sound, perfect method and is capable of planning rationally and executing practically by moving weights and joining masses so as to create works which best satisfy man's most important needs. To be capable of this he must have a thorough command of the noblest art."[13]

Later he points out that "the arts that are useful, indeed, absolutely necessary to the architect are painting and mathematics. It does not matter whether he is versed in the others. For we do not

LEONIS BAPTISTE ALBERTI DE RE AEDIFICA
TORIA INCIPIT   LEGE FELICITER

VLTAS ET VARIAS ARTES QVE
ad uitam bene beateq̃ agédam faciant summa industria et diligentia conquisitas nobis maiores nostri tradidere. Quæ omnes et si ferant præ se: quasi certatim huc tendere: Vt plurimum generi hominum prosint: tamen habere innatum atq̃ insitum eas intelligimus quippiam: quo singulæ singulos præceteris diuersosq̃ polliceri fructus uideantur: Nanq̃ artes quidem alias necessitate sectamur: alias probamus utilitate: Aliæ uero q̃ tantum circa res cognitu gratissimas uersentur in pretio sunt: quales autem hæ sint artes non est ut prosequar: inpromptu enim sunt: uerum si repetas ex omni maximarum artium numero nullam penitus inuenies: quæ non spretis reliquis suos quosdam & proprios fines petat et contempletur. Aut si tandem comperias ullam: quæ cum huiusmodi sit: ut ea carere nullo pacto possis: tum et de se utilitatem: uoluptati dignitatiq̃ ɔiunctam præstet: meo iudicio ab earum numero excludendam esse: non duces architecturam: namq̃ ea quidem si quidem rem diligentius pensitaris et publice & priuatim commodissima et uehementer gratissima generi hominum est: digni tateq̃ inter primas non postrema: Sed anteq̃ ultra progrediar: explicandum mihi censeo quemnam haberi uelim architectum: Non enim tignarium adducam fabrū: quem tu summis cæterarᷝ disciplinarum uiris compares: Fabri enim manus architecto pro instrumento ē. Architectum ego hunc fore constituam/qui certa admirabiliq̃ ratione et uia tum mente animoq̃ diffinire: tum et opere absoluere didicerit quecunq̃ ex ponderum motu corporᷝq̃ compactione et coagmentatione dignissimis hominū usibus bellissime cōmodentur: Quæ ut possit cōprehensione et cognitione opus est rerum optimarum et dignissimarᷝ. Itaq̃ huiusmodi erit architectus: redeo ad rem Fuere qui dicerent aquam aut ignem

Architecturæ laus.

Architectus quis.

a i

3. "The reader may judge for himself with what care I have dealt with these matters [in the first five books]. I do not think much more can be expected from works of this kind, and indeed, as God is my witness, this treatise has given me more trouble than I foresaw when I first began it. I have encountered many difficulties in explaining the subject matter, in inventing appropriate terms, and in the presentation of my material; these have tended to discourage me and to incline me to give up the task. On the other hand, the very reasons for which I undertook the work have driven me to continue it". L. B. Alberti, *L'Architettura*, op. cit., VI, 1, p. 440.

4. L. B. Alberti, *De Iciarchia*, 2, in *Opere Volgari*, op. cit., II, p. 219.

5. He had been rebuked for doing this by his friend Leonardo Dati in 1443, when writing the first version of the *Famiglia:* "The second serious mistake

is to quote from other writers without mentioning them, almost as if you hadn't read them, or were inventing what they said and leaving a blank space". (C. Grayson, op. cit., p. 155). A number of blanks in the text (which no amount of comparison between the first edition and the various manuscript copies can fill) show that this work of completion was never fully carried out. In his dedication to Lorenzo the Magnificent, Politian felt obliged to point out that Bernardo, Battista's brother, had gathered together the books on architecture, "descriptos eos ex architipis atque in volumen redactos". This shows he was rather eager to testify to the authenticity of the first edition in comparison with the earlier manuscripts that had been circulating, manuscripts either corrupted by copyists or incomplete from the beginning. Apart from those that might have been lost (in which case there would be some

share the opinion of those who say the architect ought to be a lawyer ... nor do we require him to be a proficient astronomer ... a perfect musician or orator."[14] Vitruvius had written: "There are two terms in architecture, the signified and the significant. The signified is the subject in hand. The significant is what is demonstrated according to the rules of science. Therefore, the architect must be well versed in both. To be so, he must have talent and application, for neither talent without instruction, nor education without talent, will ever produce a perfect artist. Therefore, he must study grammar, have a sound grasp of design, an excellent knowledge of geometry, some idea of optics, and a good knowledge of arithmetic. He must also know history, philosophy, music, medicine, law, and astronomy and the motions of the heavens."[15]

Alberti differs from Vitruvius's abstract encyclopaedism in his emphasis on the architect's need to understand the tools of his profession and to have a specific knowledge of subsidiary, technical matters. In Book Ten he insists: "Painting and mathematics are as indispensable to the architect as the knowledge of metrical feet and syllables is to the poet, and I doubt whether a superficial knowledge of these arts will suffice."[16] In Vitruvius, architecture has a basically representative function and is placed at the service of the State: "I have not hesitated to present you with this treatise immediately, so that not only the republic, recently enriched with provinces, but also the heart of the empire itself may be finely decorated with public buildings."[17] Vitruvius's imperialism contrasts with Alberti's Humanism: architecture "is as necessary to the community as it is to the private citizen. It is particularly pleasing to man as a whole, and certainly one of the most important of all the arts."[18]

Vitruvius's theory of the origin of architecture as a development of the use of fire is based on the naturalistic determinism that was fashionable in the period before the Enlightenment: "Thus, after the discovery of fire, great numbers of men began to gather in groups, assemblies and banquets, all in the same place."[19] Alberti's theory is broader in scope: "Some people have said that fire and water were the original causes that brought men together in communities. But when we consider how useful, indeed, how indispensable a roof and walls are, we are led to believe that the latter were the real reasons why human beings gathered together. Nevertheless, we should be grateful to the architect not only because he provides us with comfort, welcome shelter from the heat of summer and the cold of winter (though this is by no means to be slighted), but above all for his countless

inventions both in the public and private field, which are of the greatest use in satisfying many of man's needs. How many noble families, ruined by the adversities of time, would have disappeared from our city, and from many others throughout the world, had not the home kept their survivors united and preserved them, as it were, in the bosom of their ancestors!"[20] Thus Alberti returns to the theme of the family, replacing a mythological theory of the origins of society with one based on man's concrete historical needs.

Vitruvius wrote at a time when classical architecture was in decline, when the prevailing tendency was to codify Greek influence and consider Greek architectural terms as the only correct ones: "This lack of correspondence between Greek and Latin terminology is very noticeable". He continues: "I have mentioned these things not in order to change the use of terminology and language, but to explain them so that the learned might understand them."[21] Alberti not only adopted a critical approach to antiquity, but rejected Vitruvius's Greek architectural terminology and tried to replace it with Latin terms in order to create an Italic architectural language. He insisted on the historical continuity of an independent Etruscan-Roman-Tuscan-modern tradition: "My readers will have realized that I have preferred clear exposition to rhetorical display. But even this is no small enterprise, as only those who have tried their hand at treatises of this kind can tell. In spite of everything, we believe and hope not to be mistaken in our belief that we have expressed ourselves in a correct, intelligible Latin."[22]

Alberti's brief summary of the history of architecture in the third chapter of Book VI is vitiated by a form of historical teleology, for he writes of the youth of architecture in Asia, its flowering in Greece, and its splendid maturity in Italy. Alberti saw Roman architecture as having the virtue of "innate parsimony", and believed that it was this quality that led the Romans to construct buildings in the shape of animals. He also saw it characterised by a variety of interests, the outcome of which was the discovery of all architecture's secrets: "They established architecture in all its aspects, and there was nothing too hidden or obscure which they did not explore, trace, and reveal in its true light with the help of heaven and of the art itself."[23] This is a very different approach from the eclecticism of Vitruvius: "I have illustrated the different forms of Italian and Greek buildings and given the proportions of their different symmetries."[24] Or: "Harmony is a musical concept, difficult and obscure, especially for those who do not understand Greek. And since we have to discuss it, we

trace of them), there are very few manuscript copies of the treatise, considering the considerable interest it aroused; no more than seven or eight in all, and these were copied in Florence, Rome, Urbino, and Naples, places where interest in Alberti was most pronounced.

6. Vitruvius, *Dell'Architettura*, ed. Galiani 1790, 1, p. 9.

7. R. Krautheimer, "Alberti and Vitruvius", in *Acts of the* 20*th International Congress of the History of Art*, New York, September 1961.

8. On this point see A. Blunt, *Artistic Theory in Italy, 1450-1600*, London 1940.

9. L. A. Ciapponi, "Il De architettura di Vitruvio nel primo Umanesimo", in *Italia Medioevale e Umanistica*, III, 1960, p. 59. F. Pellati, "Vitruvio nel

Medioevo e nel Rinascimento", in *Bollettino del Reale Istituto di Archeologia e Storia dell'Arte*, Rome 1932.

10. L. B. Alberti, op. cit., VI, 1, p. 442.

11. Ibid., I, 1, p. 18.

12. Ibid., VI, 1, p. 442.

13. Ibid., Preface, pp. 6-8.

14. Ibid., IX, 10, p. 860.

15. Vitruvius, op. cit., I, 1, p. 2.

16. L. B. Alberti, op. cit., IX, 10, p. 860.

17. Vitruvius, op. cit., p. 1.

must use Greek terms, many of which have no equivalent in the Latin tongue."[25]

For Alberti, the principle of authority is subordinate to the relationship of the various parts of a building, to "the example of the ancients", the "advice of experts", and constant practice.[26] Thus rules can be formulated, some regarding "the beauty and decoration of the building as a whole, and others its separate parts. The first may be learnt from philosophy; they guide the scope and limits of the art. The second derive from the knowledge we have just described and from experience; when perfected by the principles of philosophy, they regulate the practice of architecture."[27]

ARCHITECT AND PATRON

In distinguishing the architect from carpenter ("fabrum tignarium") and master-mason as one "qui certa admirabilique ratione et via tum mente animoque diffinire tum et opere absolvere didicerit,"[28] Alberti took a big step forward, freeing architectural design from its medieval heritage and placing it at the centre of a cultural activity that was deeply conscious of human needs and of the example of history. This explains his definition of a building as a body which, "like all other bodies, consists of form and matter. The first element in this case is the work of genius; the other the product of good nature. The first requires ratiocination; the other is a question of finding and choosing the material."[29]

Alberti's appeal to rationality is a constant one: "The wise architect must conceive and plan everything in advance, so that he does not find himself regretting, once the work is under construction or completed, that this or that hasn't been done in a different way."[30] And again: "Architecture is a great art, but not one for the majority of men. An architect must have inventiveness, unflagging enthusiasm, a high degree of education, much experience, and above all sound common sense, if he is to master his profession. For the greatest quality an architect can have is the capacity to judge what is most fitting."[31] Discussing Porsenna's labyrinth at Chiusi, Alberti remarks: "Wonderful though they are, I can never bring myself to praise works of this kind, for they have no rational purpose."[32] This rationalism was to characterise the architect's behaviour as well, and it did not permit any facile bursts of enthusiasm: "I would advise you to wait a while until your enthusiasm for your project has boiled over. Afterwards, you may return and consider it more carefully, when your judgement is no longer swayed by fondness for your design but guided by calm reason."[33] And: "When, therefore, you have

examined the whole building carefully on the basis of the various parts of the model, without leaving anything to chance, and after you have finally decided to build in that way and made sure that the money necessary is guaranteed, you must see to all the other things that are indispensable if your work is not to be held up for want of something in the course of construction."[34]

It is essential that the architect's conduct be guided by moral principles. "The architect cannot neglect the following points if he is to approach the preparation, continuation, and execution of his project correctly. He must examine the nature of the task before him, the responsibility he intends to assume, the kind of reputation he wishes to have, the amount of work involved, and the degree of glory, profit, favour, and fame he will acquire among posterity, if he carries out the work as he should. Or, on the contrary, to how much disgrace and indignation he exposes himself, and what a clear, manifest, and enduring testimony of his own folly he leaves behind him, should he carry it out inexpertly, unadvisedly, or rashly."[35]

But the architect's virtues must be matched by the understanding of his patron. Alberti urges diffidence and prudence on the architect's part, both before and after accepting a commission: "I cannot neglect a matter of considerable importance for an architect. You must not offer your services to every man who says he wants to build, like those superficial artists who vie with each other for commissions. Indeed, I wonder whether it is not better to wait until your client has come to you for help more than once. For those who desire your skill must in turn have faith in you."[36] Hence the particular nature of Alberti's treatise, which is aimed above all at the patron. In his own practice as an architect, he was more concerned with establishing the nature of the project and the psychological preparation of the patron than with the work of architecture itself, not to mention its actual construction. Thus Alberti's treatise is not so much a theory of architecture as an analysis of the conditions that determine the aims and purpose of building. This explains his popularisation of culture in the pursuit of political ends: "This work is written not just for members of the profession, but for all who take delight in noble studies. This is why I like to introduce an amusing anecdote from time to time, though you will find that even this is never entirely off the point."[37] All his examples of the social usefulness of architecture are openly propagandistic: the defence of the family in times of adversity; the art of warfare ("most victories are to be attributed more to the skill and valour of the architect than to the leadership and exhortations of the commander");[38]

18. L. B. Alberti, op. cit., Preface, p. 1.
19. Vitruvius, op. cit., II, 1, p. 26.
20. L. B. Alberti, op. cit., Preface, p. 8.
21. Vitruvius, op. cit., VI, 10, p. 147. Cf. also G. Castelfranchi, "Il Neoclassicismo di Vitruvio e il Classicismo dell'Alberti, in Paideia, III, 1948.
22. L. B. Alberti, op. cit., VI, 1, pp. 442-44.
23. Ibid., 3, p. 454.
24. Vitruvius, op. cit., VI, 10, p. 147.
25. Ibid., V, 4, p. 103.
26. L. B. Alberti, op. cit., VI, 3, p. 456.

27. Ibid.
28. Ibid., Preface, p. 7.
29. Ibid., p. 14.
30. Ibid., II, 1, pp. 94-96.
31. Ibid., IX, 10, p. 854.
32. Ibid., VIII, 3, p. 682.
33. Ibid., II, 2, p. 100.
34. Ibid., 3, p. 106.
35. Ibid., IX, 10, pp. 852-54.
36. Ibid., 11, p. 862.

the pride "in the house we inhabit, if it is built with a little more care than usual"; the praise earned for having spent part of one's patrimony for the fame "and splendour of yourself, your family, your descendants, and the whole city"; and the safety of the State ("It must be pointed out that the safety, authority, and decorum of the State largely depend upon the work of the architect").

The patron's essential purpose in building is a historical one: "In fact, whatever serves to keep us and our family in good health, enables us to lead a dignified, pleasant life, and commits our memory to posterity, may be considered an enterprise of the highest order."[39] Alberti accepted the society of his day as he found it; he addressed himself to the social, cultural elite of fifteenth-century northern-central Italy, and avoided passing judgement on it. Nor was he concerned with social forces of a different kind. He withdrew into himself and elaborated systematic plans for his own self-realization. He did not just make ample concessions to the needs of the Renaissance principality; he laid its cultural foundations.[40]

But though he underlined the positive qualities of such a society, Alberti was careful to point out some of the risks it ran. He warned his readers against undertaking "enterprises that cannot be completed,"[41] and emphasised the importance of what was appropriate. Private citizens were urged to be modest, while the public sphere was allowed its splendour. He was quite explicit about the constant threat to society presented by the middle-class *parvenu*, for whom he emphasized that "whoever wants to know what true ornament really is, should realize that it is not something one can simply buy, but that it requires taste and intelligence above all."[42] Again: "In my opinion, it is better for the rich to go without certain decorations in their private houses than to be accused of extravagance in some way by the more discreet and frugal."[43] "I hate excessive luxury, but I love the beauty and good taste of creative works."[44] This was one way of bridling the extravagance of patrons, subjecting them to the restraints of culture, and forcing them to recognise their obligations to society. "I cannot approve of the habit of providing private habitations with battlements and pinnacles. These are more appropriate in fortresses, if at all, especially in those of tyrants, and they are quite alien to the customs of a well-ordered State and a peaceful people, for they imply fear and the abuse of power."[45] The social order, which is reflected in its architectural forms, does not permit such things, and he condemns those private citizens who, "anxious not to be outdone by their rulers in the spending of money,

consumed by an inordinate thirst for glory, and determined to add lustre to the names of their families by every means possible, have squandered indiscriminately, as long as fate allowed them to."[46] Thus beauty becomes a fundamental safeguard against the dangers to society presented by the middle class: "Beauty is of a quality that contributes considerably to the comfort and even to the durability of a building. No one can deny that he feels more at ease living in a decorated house than between bare walls. Nor can human art devise a better way of defending its works against the devastation of man himself, for beauty is such that it calms the destructive fury of the enemy, and a work of art is respected. I would even say that no qualities are more apt to save a bulding from human malice than decorum and gracefulness of form."[47] If one relates this to Alberti's disagreements with Vitruvius, one sees how he substituted the synthetic, the cathartic, even the protective value of beauty for Vitruvius's celebrated triad. Though Alberti's observations were intended for a large élite, they were ultimately directed at the patron par excellence, the Prince. He underlines the prince's political obligations towards architecture and the city, and explains how these are fulfilled according to the way in which a prince governs: "Naturally, the noblest man will be the person in whom power is wholly concentrated. Therefore, one must consider what should be done for such a man. First one must discover what kind of a man he is, whether he rules with justice and righteousness, respecting the wishes of his subjects and guided not so much by self-interest as by a desire to benefit his fellow-citizens, or whether he rules in such a way that the people must obey him *volente nolente*. Nearly all buildings, and cities too, vary according to whether power is exercised by a tyrant (as the latter is called), or by one who acquires and conserves his power as a magistrature granted him by others."[48] The passage evokes the figures of Lionello and Sigismondo, two very different Renaissance princes, whom Alberti could consider as potential patrons without the slightest moral prejudice In the *De Iciarchia*, his concept of a prince is that of a man guided by moderation: "We have pointed out that the prince has the right to control men. We have also said that no one can control many unless he is capable of controlling a few, and that the first task is to control oneself. It is this form of self-control that we have dealt with so far."[49] But the concrete realism of architecture does not allow the architect to favour any one form of political regime: "There are obviously different ways of governing men."[50] The habitation of a king (by which he means a democratic prince) may be situated in the centre of

37. Ibid., II, 11, pp. 156-58.
38. Ibid., Preface, p. 10.
39. Ibid., I, 6, p. 50.
40. Cf. A. Tenenti, *L. B. Alberti*, Milan 1966, pp. 78-79.
41. L. B. Alberti, op. cit., II, 2, p. 102.
42. Ibid., IX, 1, p. 782.
43. Ibid., p. 780.
44. Ibid., 4, p. 802. There are also the words in the *Vita Anonima*, p. 111: "And looking at a luxurious house, he said: 'This pretentious palace will soon collapse, and its owner swept away with it."

45. Ibid., p. 808.
46. Ibid., VII, 17, p. 656.
47. Ibid., VI, 2, p. 446.
48. Ibid., V, 1, p. 332.
49. L. B. Alberti, *Opere Volgari*, op. cit., II; *De Iciarchia*, III, p. 265.
50. Ibid., p. 290.

the town, "whereas that of a tyrant will be built like a fortress, and as such will be neither inside nor outside the town."[51] As Portoghesi has remarked, Alberti had a very clear idea of the estrangement between the feudal castle and the *civitas* it dominated, an idea he must have formed during his travels in Germany. Alberti's realism did not permit him to condemn tyranny openly, but his political thought is dominated by a concept of moral and natural order the logical outcome of which is political moderation.

THE ENVIRONMENT

There is an almost Leopardian feeling for nature in the *De re aedificatoria*: "Seeing the sown fields flower in springtime, and all the trees and plants rich with the promise of fruit, he would be seized by melancholy and rebuke himself thus: 'You too, Battista, must give man the fruit of your studies'."[52] "He used to say he worshipped the beauties of nature, and that quadrupeds, birds, and other resplendent animals should be loved, for all that nature granted in her bounty was beautiful."[53]

His love of natural beauty led him to approve of it in painting; thus he anticipated a middle-class genre of art: "Our soul takes the greatest delight in pictures of charming views, ports, fishing- and hunting-reserves, ponds, country games, and flourishing, luxuriant landscapes."[54] Hence his bourgeois fondness of the villa, his dislike of the town, and his love of gardens: "And it [the villa] should be surrounded on all sides, for reasons of both pleasure and utility, by stretches of flowery meadows, sunny fields, cool shady woods, crystal-clear springs and streams, ponds to bathe in, and many other things."[55] He also expresses a fondness for grottos, an element that was to be so prominent in Mannerist and Rococo landscape architecture: "I was very taken with what I saw in a grotto once, where a spring gushed out from a wall composed of various seashells, including those of oysters. The shells were arranged in such a way as to produce a most pleasant variety of colours, some laid flat and others turned upside-down."[56] The villa, to which more than one passage is dedicated in Book Five, "should have all the advantages and pleasures of good air, sun, and fine views ... and enjoy the view perhaps of some town, fortress, the sea, a vast plain, the tops of some familiar hills or mountains, or beautiful gardens, and should offer plentiful opportunities for fishing and hunting."[57] These passages are full of joie de vivre and deal with a theme that recurs more than once: in the letters written at the time of his flight from Mantua, in the pamphlet entitled *Villa*, and in the relevant passages of the

51. L. B. Alberti, *De Architettura*, V, p. 346.
52. *Vita Anonima*, op. cit., p. 115.
53. L. B. Alberti, ibid.
54. Ibid., IX, 4, p. 804.
55. Ibid., 2, p. 792.
56. Ibid., 4, p. 804.
57. Ibid., V, 17, p. 414.

Famiglia and the *Theogenius*.[58] The *De re aedificatoria* contains images of this kind: "They say that the very sight of the flame and light of the fireside warms the hearts of family-men who sit round it chatting."[59] Alberti's treatise, which is really a discussion of beauty, presupposes an environment in which hygiene, climate, and ecology are objects of constant attention and evaluation. Alberti warns in the first book that though it is possible to eliminate defects in the soil or water, "it is not in man's power to change the heavens. There is no doubt that the air we breathe is what most contributes to the nourishment and preservation of life, and if it is perfectly pure, it will be of the greatest benefit to our health."[60] Thus, the first step in any architectural or town planning scheme is the choice of a suitable site, where the air is pure and free from fog, and where there is no accumulation of noxious vapours. It must have a sufficient amount of sun and water and be well situated with respect to the winds: "Moreover, the place must be neither too damp as a result of too much water, nor afflicted by droughts, but be cheerful and temperate."[61]

Alberti's sites are far from anonymous; they have a number of ideal features, and the architect's first concern, like that of the prince who wishes to found a new settlement, should be to choose the most fitting place for his construction. This idea, which rather anticipates those of the physiocrats, led Alberti towards a modern concept of architecture, according to which the architect takes a whole area into account, not just the town. This provokes a series of observations on hygienics. "Every part of the house must have windows so that the air may circulate and change from time to time, otherwise it will become stale and harmful."[62] Drains too, are important "to prevent the air from becoming infected, and to defend its purity and wholesomeness."[63] Hygienic installations are indispensable: "Care should be taken to set the dunghills in some remote hidden corner so that the farmer's family is not plagued by smells. And yet, in our own houses, almost under our own beds, and in our best rooms where we usually rest, we allow secret privies, which give off most noxious smells."[64] He is worried by the practice of burying people in churches, "for in such cases the purity of the sacrifice may be contaminated by the pestilential stench of putrefaction. Thus cremation is a much better custom."[65] Concerning crowds in public places, "it is advisable above all that the theatres where people gather in August to listen to poets be protected from the sun, for the public needs sweet, cool shade. Otherwise the reflection of the sun inside the building will scorch the spectators, who might easily fall ill as a result of the heating of their humours."[66]

58. Cf. C. Grayson, "Villa: un opuscolo sconosciuto", in *Rinascimento*, IV, 1953, p. 45.
59. L. B. Alberti, op. cit., X, 14, p. 978.
60. Ibid., I, 3, p. 24.
61. Ibid., 4, p. 34.
62. Ibid., 12, p. 80.
63. Ibid., IV, 7, p. 322.
64. Ibid., V, 17, p. 430.
65. Ibid., VIII, 1, p. 670.
66. Ibid., 7, p. 730.

Some of these considerations are motivated by contemporary ideas on medicine, but occasionally one detects a note of snobbery: "Animal organisms emit vapours, and these exhalations have the same characteristics as the body that emits them. In other words, if they come from a foul body they will be foul, but if emitted by a perfumed body they will be sweet. Sometimes we find that certain sweaty secretions or vapours, though not unpleasant in themselves, take on a bad smell because the person's clothes stink."[67]

Alberti provides a clear explanation of the relationship between volume, area, and heating, and he proposes a form of natural air-conditioning based on a system of rooms to be used in summer and winter alternately. Much of Book Ten is taken up with the subject of water, and special attention is given to the characteristics and wholesomeness of spring-water.

According to Alberti, human reason teaches us to find natural antidotes with which to combat the evils of nature. Thus his concept of ecological balance: "The ancients believed that nature had made enemies of certain animals and things to their mutual harm and destruction."[68]

THE TOWN

It was no complacent, sterile hedonism that led Alberti to recognise the importance of environmental factors and the fundamental rules of hygiene. On the contrary, this recognition was motivated by specific objectives that were inseparable from those of human settlement itself. The town depends upon and grows out of the area around it: "It will have healthy, huge, pleasant, fertile, well-defended, and highly productive lands of various kinds, provided with an abundance of crops and water. The surrounding region must have rivers, lakes, and easy access to the sea, so that it may procure what it needs and export its surplus products. Finally, to ensure that its civil and military activities flourish in the best way possible, all the means necessary for the embellishment of the town and the defence of its citizens must be made available, so that it may be made acceptable to friends and fearful to foes. ... The town had best be situated in the centre of its territory, in such a position that it can observe all its boundaries. Thus it can decide what to do and when to take action should the need arise."[69]

Besides the town's general layout and the need for it to be at the centre of its territorial activities, there is the problem of the form it should take with respect to the lie of the land: "The town's boundary and the distribution of its parts will vary, of course,

67. Ibid., X, 1, p. 876.
68. Ibid., 15, p. 982.
69. Ibid., IV, 2, pp. 276-78.

according to the nature of the site it occupies."[70] Alberti rejects all *a priori* notions of an ideal city, as he does all typological codification. Instead, he offers a number of examples that confirm his realism: "The biggest town of all is that with a circular plan; the best defended, that with irregular, winding walls."[71] But "one must also consider what is best suited to the particular nature of the town. We know that the ancients adapted themselves to the characteristics and needs of the places where they built."[72] It is difficult to interpret this as offering "very precise figurative indications denoting the influence of the classical model of a square inscribed within a circle."[73] On the contrary, it seems to illustrate Alberti's characteristic method of considering a number of quite different, if not actually conflicting solutions.

The city is built for man, and it is only realistic to recognise the differences that distinguish one man from another, "to clarify thoroughly the differences that exist between men, ... for which purpose it is well to consider how the wisest of men who established laws and founded States in ancient times divided up the citizens of their communities."[74] Quite apart from the historical examples he takes from Plato and Aristotle, Alberti affirms that the division of the social body into separate parts is inevitable, and that each part has "its own type of building". But the problem is more subtle than this. "In dividing humanity up into separate parts, one immediately discovers a truism: that when one considers the inhabitants of a place en masse, one cannot apply the same method of classification one does when dividing them into separate groups. In the second case, one considers each group according to its particular nature, and one must naturally take account of the fundamental characteristics that distinguish the various groups in order to obtain the necessary data upon which to base our classification."[75] At this point the Albertian theme of virtue and fortune re-appears: "What most distinguishes one man from another is what clearly marks him off from other animals, that is, reason and knowledge of the liberal arts to which we may add the favour of fortune."[76]

Alberti's idea of society is that of an oligarchy headed by a mixed group of virtuous and fortunate men. These are assisted by a class of bureaucrats, to whom they entrust the actual business of government: "On entering into office, they will carry out their duties with flexibility and seriousness at home, with tenacity and patience abroad. They will be judges and generals, and they will dedicate both themselves and others to their country's cause."[77] The governed are defined with the same realism that characterises the definition of the city: "All the other citizens ought to obey

70. Ibid., 3, p. 288.
71. Ibid., p. 294.
72. Ibid.
73. T. Marconi, *La città come forma simbolica*, Rome 1973, p. 57.
74. L. B. Alberti, op. cit., IV, 1, p. 264.
75. Ibid., p. 268.
76. Ibid.
77. Ibid., p. 270.

352. "De re aedificatoria", c. 141r., end of IV. Reggio Emilia, Biblioteca Municipale.

353. "De re aedificatoria", c. 164v., V, 11. Reggio Emilia, Biblioteca Municipale.

libro quarto.

che e lingreso cōtra di le boche morizar
te, e apena [...]li hochij [...] le duersioe di canali
mobile i ciascuna hora cognisciti da li nauigā
ti. Queste sōne le coxe le quale pareuine da
dire di tuequante le pūblice uniuersale.
solo quelo agiugirei, che di partire le pi
aze comādano, i le quale i pace le coxe po
portate si marchadise, e la iuuetude si ex
arcita ouero si abia a exercitare, e i le ba
talie le lignatiō, la pabulatiō, e a questo mo
do da tolerare le asediatiō so da saruare
primedio. L templo e la basilica et l spetiac
lo e cosi magiormēte so piu comuni che pro
prij nō de multi, mà quili sarte di sacerdoti,
ouermēte siene del magistrato. Di questo
adōcha sira da dire al suo loco.

ancora i le coxe i numero di piedi i paro eten
ire a le religione e costumerino di codante lo
ge quidice piedi e [...] profōde noue, Faliat
te drite le spōde de le sose che patischano e
ualmēte al fōdo quanto de sopra distara li lat
ra itrasi, dōda labile sera sate l fōdo, a poca a
poco se andara astrigēdosi la satigatiōne al ba
so sera cauata. E da loci campestri siane de
misse le aque da li siumi oueramēte da lagi
o dal mare derriuate e cōdute siane empit
te. Se questo nō si pottera palli e tōchu do
lati et accuti i e ancora sornite de tribie p le
ripe e p li sōdi semenate se ex asprnuu.

ali e trochi
iolati d ac
ti e tribali.

resentanes

astre mometanie

lle.

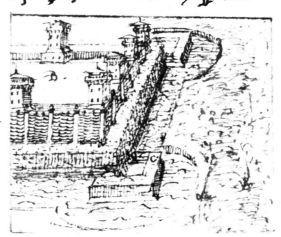

and collaborate with them as the occasion demands."[78] The organisation of a town reflects the structure of the society that occupies it, and it raises a number of practical, functional, and hygienic considerations: "It will add greatly to the beauty of the town if the artisans' workshops are distributed in separate, appropriate areas: the bankers, painters and goldsmiths ought to have their shops near the market place; the apothecaries, tailors, and the crafts generally reputed to be most respectable will be placed a little farther off; finally, the dirty, stinking trades, especially the evil-smelling tanneries, will be hidden away in the outskirts facing northwards, since the wind rarely blows from that direction towards the city, and when it does, it is so strong that it carries the bad smells right over the city instead of into it. Probably some people would prefer to see the residential areas of the top people uncontaminated by any kind of contact with the rabble. Others would prefer each district, without exception, to have all its essential services, and such people would see nothing wrong in the meanest shops interspersed with the houses of the great. But we have said enough. Convenience is one thing, decorum another."[79] The words "others would prefer" are eloquently expressive of a prudent detachment motivated by a rigid sense of class. The happiest and most human of Alberti's ideas — "the city is like a large house, and the house in turn is like a small city"[80] and "the hall, living-room and other such rooms in a house should be like the market-place and large streets of a town"[81] — allow one to believe in the possibility of an orderly co-existence between the different social classes, something that had been realized in the medieval town. Alberti was no doctrinaire theorist applying rigid geometrical patterns to town planning, and he accepted some of the medieval town's essential features, such as the organic layout of its streets. The streets "in the centre of the town should not be straight, but should wind from side to side like the bends in a river. This makes the streets look longer, and consequently the town will seem larger. Moreover, it adds greatly to a city's beauty, practical convenience, and safety. Walking down them, one should gradually discover some new architectural feature with every step one takes. Equally important is the fact that the entrance and façade of each building should look directly onto the street. The very width of the street is an asset in this case [in the small town], whereas elsewhere it would be ugly and unhealthy."[82]

Alberti's concern with perspective resulted in his town's being conceived spatially: "As for the streets of the town, not only will they be finely paved and perfectly clean, but beautifully adorned

78. Ibid.
79. Ibid., VII, 1, p. 536.
80. Ibid., IX, 1, p. 64.
81. Ibid., V, 2, p. 338.
82. Ibid., IV, 5, p. 306.

with two identical rows of arcades or houses of the same height."[83] The new focal point of the urban structure was to be the square: "The city should have large squares. In times of peace they will serve as markets and as places where the young may perform gymnastics. In times of war they can be used for the stockpiling of wood, forage, and other useful materials for resisting sieges."[84] Alberti describes the square in its ideal proportions. Its area is composed of two squares, in such a way "that the colonnade and other constructions all around it correspond to the open space in the middle according to fixed proportions, so that it does not appear too large because of the lowness of the surrounding structures, nor too small because of their excessive height. The height of the roofs should be a third of the width of the square, or at least two-sevenths. I would also advise you to raise the colonnades above ground level by about a fifth of their width, whereas their width should be equal to the height of the columns."[85]

The organic nature of the square must be reinforced by the construction of arches at the points where the streets branch off from it: "the arch is like a door that is always open". "The most suitable position for an arch is where a street runs into a square or market-place."[86] Each square has its precise function: "A square may be used as a market for the exchange of money, or for the sale of herbs, cattle, and even wood. Each of these markets must have its own particular place and decorations, but the most important of all is that where the exchange of money takes place."[87] The theatre, too, "is really a square surrounded by tiers."[88]

This confidence in the square as a place where the different social classes may meet, talk, and co-exist leads Alberti to consider the possibility of reviving other features of the classical city: the theatre, the amphitheatre, the basilica, the court of justice, and the baths. He would certainly not have imitated, but re-interpreted them in the light of contemporary, if not future needs; this is confirmed by the only classical structure Alberti did revive — the basilica.

The most doctrinaire parts of the *De re aedificatoria*, those that are most Vitruvian and archaeological, are the only ones in which Alberti visualises an ideal city or entertains the possibility of a future *renovatio imperii*. This is not conceived as a mere stylistic revival but as a return to antiquity, to the essential, universal human values embodied in the classical city. By its very definition, this was a model of orderly social life, a rational answer to both practical and spiritual needs, and an example to be followed in its treatment of spatial values. This is why the concept of the city animates Alberti's idea both of the house and the fortress, and

83. Ibid., VIII, 6, p. 710.
84. Ibid., IV, 8, p. 330.
85. Ibid., VIII, 6, p. 716.
86. Ibid.
87. Ibid., p. 714.
88. Ibid., p. 710.

356. "De re aedificatoria", c. 282v., V, 16. Reggio Emilia, Biblioteca Municipale.

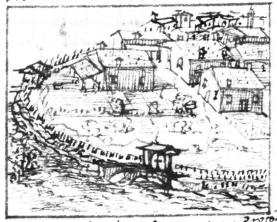

why he sees it as expressing the values of order and tolerance. The people who inhabit Alberti's city credit architecture with an importance greater than that of mere ornament. In the eighth book, Alberti testifies to the intense architectural activity of his day: "And is it not true perhaps to say that the whole of Italy is fired by a kind of rivalry in renewing the old? Great cities, which in our childhood were built entirely of wood, have suddenly been transformed into marble."[89] The *De re aedificatoria*, written when Rome was about to assume the greatest of spiritual responsibilities and to undertake a vast new building programme, reflects similar ambitions, which go beyond mere decorum and involve political considerations. But by the time Alberti wrote the tenth book, the moment had passed, and such ambitions were no longer realizable. So he fell back upon the idea of restoring the city: "We shall now deal with those edifices that can rarely be improved by restoration, beginning with those of a public nature. But the biggest and most important problem of all is the city, or rather, whether the city is situated in a suitable area."[90] This later becomes a question of administrative or bureaucratic efficiency: "The ancients' practice of paying groups of men out of State funds to provide for the care and maintenance of public monuments seems to me to be highly recommendable."[91]

DESIGN AND CONSTRUCTION

In discussing Alberti's idea of the architect and his cultural formation, we have considered his view of design as an intellectual process culturally independent of the end it pursues. What did he actually think of this process? Plotinus had written: "first the Idea comes, co-ordinating and binding the future object into a unity composed of many parts. Then it reduces it to a coherent whole, finally creating a unity by means of correspondences."[92] Alberti says: "The function of design, therefore, is to assign to the edifices and the parts that compose them their proper places and exact proportions, and to order everything suitably and harmoniously so that the whole form of the construction may be found in the design itself."[93]

Plotinus, again, writes: "How can the corporeal accord with what is superior to the body? Well then, tell me how the architect, after harmonising the exterior of a house with its interior, can call it beautiful? The explanation lies in the fact that, apart from the stones, what is exterior is nothing but the interior form, which is certainly divided up in the material mass of the exterior, but is still indivisible though represented in its multiplicity."[94] This is comparable to Alberti: "We can design perfect forms of

89. Ibid., 5, p. 698.
90. Ibid., X, 1, p. 872.
91. Ibid., 16, p. 988.
92. Plotinus, *Enneadi*, Bari 1947, p. 100.
93. L. B. Alberti, op. cit., I, 1, p. 18.
94. Plotinus, op. cit., pp. 100-01.

buildings in our mind, without the help of any materials. One has only to think of the lines and angles drawn according to their exact positions and conjunctions. The design must be an accurate, uniform plan conceived in the mind, carried out by means of lines and angles, and contrived by a person of skill and learning."[95] At this basically geometrical stage of the design the aesthetic criterion of *varietas* re-appears, the same canon that was to animate the painter: "It must not be applied too much or too little, but be subordinated to utility and beauty so that entire parts may correspond to their like."[96] This introduces the concept of symmetry and that of equal values within the symmetrical context itself.

Alberti defines symmetry in this way: "Each of the side lines ought to be equal to the one opposite it, and long lines should never be joined with short ones in any part of the construction. Instead, there should be a just and reasonable proportion between them, which can be established from time to time."[97] This leads to the problem of proportion, which we shall consider in detail later, and to that belief in form which Alberti considered to be the "absolute, exact method" for the attainment of beauty in the face of relativism, subjectivism, flair, and chance: "Some will argue that the beauty of a building is relative, a matter of opinion. They will say that the forms of buildings must vary according to each man's personal taste, and that they cannot be reduced to any rule of art. It is a physical defect of the ignorant to reject what they cannot understand."[98]

Alberti then appeals to history, to "the careful enquiry into the origins of the arts, their underlying principles, and the ways they develop."[99] The idea of an academic Alberti[100] ought really to be rectified in the light of his sense of history. Another of his beliefs was that rules were founded upon experiment. The Greeks "also sought to establish rules by which they could distinguish between well constructed and badly constructed edifices. They carried out all kinds of experiments following the rules of nature. Mixing elements of various proportions, straight lines with curved ones, and light with shade, they strove to discover, as by a conjunction of male and female principles, something new that might help them to achieve their objectives."[101] As Portoghesi has observed, the analogy between the life of forms and organic life, expressed in the reference to male and female principles represents a further development in the concept of organicism which Alberti applied to architecture, and which foreshadows that of *Einfühlung*. The analogy between architecture and animal organism is drawn more than once.[102] For Alberti, the real problem with respect to

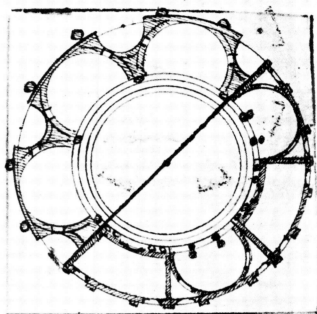

95. L. B. Alberti, op. cit., I, 2, p. 20.
96. Ibid., 8, p. 56.
97. Ibid.
98. Ibid., VI, 2, pp. 448-50.
99. Ibid.
100. Cf. P. Portoghesi, *Architettura*, op. cit., Introduction, p. XXIV.
101. L. B. Alberti, op. cit., VI, 3, p. 452.
102. Ibid., III, 6, pp. 454 and 810.

358. "De re aedificatoria", c. 255r., VII, 4. Reggio Emilia, Biblioteca Municipale.

359. "De re aedificatoria", c. 256v., VII, 4. Reggio Emilia, Biblioteca Municipale.

libro septimo 275·

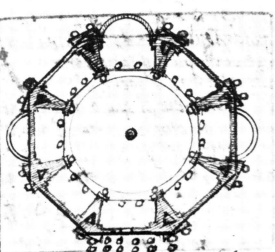

330

vius's obscurities were to have no sequel. Not even Orlandi mentions them in his recent stylish translation of the *De re aedificatoria*, while Bartoli completely ignored them, as later architects were to do. Giuliano da Sangallo's Sienese notebook contains this note among some sketches of elements for the Ionic order: "Words and terms used by Vitruvius: acroteria, sima, timpani, corona, simatio, denticholi, tema, coeforos, fastigio, epistilio". Francesco di Giorgio often made use of the following terms: "abbaco", "zoofero" (for *zooforo*), "trochilo", and "astragolo" (for *astragalo*).[129] Alberti might easily have been led to write an explanatory pamphlet on the subject, similar to the *Elementi della pittura*. But the lack of any such work, together with his use of words of Greek origin taken from Vitruvius, demonstrates the impossibility of attributing the *Cinque ordini architettonici* to Alberti. It also shows once more that the *De re aedificatoria* was written for the man of learning, the patron, and the painter: "This treatise will be so useful that even painters, who are the most refined enquirers into beauty, will judge it to be indispensable."[130] Alberti's aim was to interpret the orders according to a constructive organicism and internal logic, not as a series of academic forms. This can be seen both when he experiments with neologisms and when he analyses the elements: "In placing the capital upon the column, it was found necessary to introduce some point of support to which the architrave might be fastened."[131] Even Alberti's interpretation of architectural style is rooted in history. Discussing the Doric order, he notes that "the Etruscans seem to have used it from the very earliest times,"[132] and he underlines the primacy of its capital, "which we shall call Italic in order to distinguish it from those imported from other countries. It combines Corinthian gaiety with Ionic refinement, and has projecting volutes like the handles of a jar, which makes it pleasing and very popular."[133] Thus Alberti's preoccupation with terminology may be seen as less of an academic exercise than a concern for history. "The Italic capital combines the ornaments of all the others. It contains the same characteristics that we have noted in the Corinthian order as far as its vase, abacus, leaves, and the flower in the abacus are concerned. But instead of shoots there are volutes, and these rise as high as the four corners of the abacus to a height of two modules. The front of the capital, which would be bare otherwise, is decorated in the Ionic style, with its cavetto moulding terminating in volute-shaped handles and the rim of the vase decorated with eggs and berries, like an ovolo."[134]

Though Alberti was obliged to follow the proportions of the orders codified by Vitruvius, he insists upon the logic of his

he had created the premises for qualified artisans or *capomaestri* to carry out such work.

116. Ibid., III, 5, p. 188.
117. Ibid., 14, p. 244.
118. Ibid., p. 246.
119. Ibid., VI, 10, p. 506.
120. Ibid., I, 10, p. 70.
121. Ibid.
122. Ibid., p. 72.
123. Ibid.

124. Ibid., III, 6, p. 194.
125. Ibid., 13, p. 238.
126. Ibid., VI, 13, pp. 517-20.
127. Ibid., p. 524.
128. Ibid., VII, 7, p. 475.
129. Cf. F. Borsi, *I Cinque Ordini Architettonici e L. B. Alberti*, cit.
130. L. B. Alberti, op. cit., VII, 1, p. 528.
131. Ibid., 6, p. 564.
132. Ibid.
133. Ibid., pp. 564-66.

own calculations and on his own personal experience. He emphasizes the fact that his method of tracing entasis is based on personal observation not on books. His explanation of the triglyph emphasizes its structural importance, and he calls Vitruvius's "drops" (*guttae*) nails (*clavicoli*). Thus he transfers a formal analogy of a naturalistic kind into something more concrete and closer to the carpenter's needs[135] (a series of nails, or wedges, used for fastening the end of a beam).

In Alberti's terminology, metopes become *tabulae* and are defined as *vacua inter tigna* (empty spaces between beams). Ovoli are also interpreted constructionally, though with a trace of uncertainty: "Little eggs were so carved, unless I am mistaken, in imitation of the stones that protruded from the pavement which had been covered with an excess of mortar."[136]

In the course of this organic interpretation of the orders Alberti mentions certain examples of late Imperial architecture (thus anticipating certain Mannerist and Baroque interests), and certain naturalistic forms in particular: "Some very beautiful effects were created by architects of great talent. One of these consisted in placing on both sides of the entrance-door to the dining-room huge statues of slaves who held up the lintel. Another was the use of columns, especially in the porticos of gardens: some of these were made to look like tree trunks, with knotted shafts, while others were entwined with boughs, or wreathed and enriched with leaves, rough branches, and little birds."[137] As Portoghesi notes, this anticipates the entrance-door flanked by telamons in Bernini's plan for the Palazzo Montecitorio and Philibert de l'Orme's natural tree-trunk columns. Above all it establishes the anthropomorphic character of the orders as a final solution to the concern for proportion that motivates the concept of *concinnitas*. Thus, Alberti draws these conclusions at the end of the treatise: "At this point we had best clarify the forms and measurements adopted by the ancients in constructing columns, which they distinguished in three orders according to three different ways of conceiving the shaft. Observing the human body, they decided to fashion the columns in its likeness, and on measuring man, they discovered that his width was a sixth of his height, while the distance from his navel to his kidneys was a tenth."[138] "The columns were probably fashioned according to these measurements, so that some were six times as high as their base, and others ten". Alberti then interprets the logic of the orders as a system of mathematical means based on the optimal rule of *mediocritas*: "Thus, with the help of arithmetic, they added the two abovementioned figures and divided the total in half. In this way, they

134. Ibid., 8, pp. 584-86.

135. Galiani failed to understand this in his commentary on Vitruvius, IV, 3, p. 80: "The very word guttae, or drops, as we have seen in the preceding chapter, is clearly intended to convery the meaning of drops of water as figures, not nails, as Alberti would like to believe".

136. L. B. Alberti, op. cit., VII, 11, p. 592.

137. Ibid., IX, 1, p. 786.

138. Ibid., 7, p. 834.

libro decimo

libro decimo

ficanieto si posa uestire isieme.

discovered that the mean number between six and ten was eight. They then took this measurement and established the height of the column as eight times the diameter of its base, calling it Ionic."[139] The same process was followed in establishing the Doric, where the minimum number of six was added to the mean of the Ionic, which made fourteen and a mean of seven. The Corinthian, on the other hand, was produced by adding the mean of the Ionic to the maximum number of ten, which made eighteen and a mean of nine. The natural outcome of organic constructive parameters of this kind was anthropometry and the idea that "naturae sensu animis innatu quo sentiri discimus concinnitates". Once Alberti had established the logic of the orders in this way, he proceeded to deal with the problem of "placing", of establishing the right position for each part, a problem that involved symmetry. This exposition of the optimal measurements of the individual parts is followed by a definition of their optimal proportions in relation to each other. Of course, the simplest ratio of all is 1 : 1, and this is what is determined in symmetry.

PROPORTION

Proportion is to the *De re aedificatoria* what perspective is to the *De pictura*, and the two subjects are fundamentally related. Optics and medieval *perspectiva* had been studied for many centuries, but Alberti (with the experience of Brunelleschi behind him) made a synthesis of all that was known on the subject, his purpose being to establish principles that would help the artist in his knowledge and use of space.

Proportion had been the subject of much speculation in the Middle Ages. St. Augustine held that the pleasure of beauty was a rational one and attributed it to the presence of "quaedam dimensio atque modulatio". St. Thomas's "lucidus ordo" signified that "it was necessary that Divine Providence reach down to the meanest things according to a certain proportion."[140] But it was Nicholas Cusanus who came closest to Alberti, defining transcendence on the basis of "trascensum omnium proportionum", since to know was to measure. Cusanus even affirmed that the concept of proportion contained the possibility of measurement within it and was the principal means of knowledge in general: "Comparativa est omnis inquisitio medio proportionis utens". Proportion was not simply a logical, mathematical concept, but above all an aesthetic one. "Thus, the idea of measurement becomes the mean term which unites the investigator of nature and the artist, that is, the creator of a second nature."[141]

Cusanus held that proportion was a question of number. There could be no proportion without number, and without proportion there could be no form, almost as if proportion were a mirror reflecting an image. Thus number was an element in all things, and the entire universe was the harmony of number: "When, therefore, I consider the unity in number, I see that its composition has no composition, that simplicity and composition, or unity and multiplicity, coincide. Indeed, if I look more carefully, I see that the unity composed of number is like the the octave, fifth, and fourth of the harmonic unities. In fact, harmonic ratio is unity, which cannot be understood without number."[142] This line of thought deserves to be studied more deeply and systematically. Alberti also had the precedent of Brunelleschi before him. But in this particular case, the only relevant evidence regarding Brunelleschi is contained in a phrase of Manetti's: "His [Brunelleschi's] object was to rediscover how the ancients built their fine walls and great buildings, and how they established their musical proportions, so that equally great buildings might be constructed skilfully and economically."[143] This seems to imply a desire to simplify a complex doctrine by breaking it down into practical principles. Vitruvius had said: "Harmony is an obscure, difficult concept, especially for those who do not understand Greek. And since we have to deal with it, we must make use of Greek words, because many of them have no appropriate Latin equivalent."[144] Naturally, Vitruvius was another source, and Alberti made much of the passage in which Vitruvius says: "The design of temples depends upon symmetry, so architects should be well acquainted with its rules. Symmetry is born of proportion, which in Greek is called analogy. It consists of a correspondence in measurement between the third part of the elements in a work and the work as a whole, and upon this correspondence depends its symmetry. Therefore, no building may be said to be well composed unless it has symmetry and proportion, like the members of a well-formed human body."[145] Here the Greek word "symmetry" corresponds to the Latin *commensuratio*, which becomes *compartimento* in Barbaro (from the Latin *pars*). It signified commensuration within a certain field rather than equivalence or equal distance with respect to a given axis. The Greek word analogy led back to Aristotle and to the concept of proportion as a ratio of terms, of which arithmetical proportion was only one example. It also recalls the Aristotelian idea that "things we call beautiful are uneven numbers, the straight line, equality and the powers of certain numbers." The definition of proportion as analogy had been formulated by Plato, and *Timaeus* must have been among the books Alberti had read. Plato had dealt with the intellectual's need for physical exercise, some-

139. Ibid., p. 836.
140. St. Thomas Aquinas, *Summa contra gentiles*, III, 78, pp. 25-35.
141. E. Cassirer, *Individuo e Cosmo nella Filosofia del Rinascimento*, Florence 1935 (1974), p. 87.

142. Nicholas Cusanus, *L'Idiota*, pp. 69-120 (139-41).
143. A. Manetti, op. cit., p. 19.
144. Vitruvius, op. cit., V, 4, p. 103.
145. Ibid., III, 1, p. 49.

thing Alberti did not ignore.

How is the subject of proportion dealt with in the *De re aedificatoria*? The importance of connecting lines according to their mutual ratios is emphasized in the preface, and it is said to be the main factor in beauty.[146] It is one of the most essential elements in the design and construction of architecture, if not *the* ultimate purpose of "design and harmonious order."[147] The definition of architecture as organism is founded upon the need for proportional ratios: "Just as all the individual members harmonise in an animal organism, so all the separate parts of a building should harmonise". This leads to the principle that "the larger a building is, the larger its parts will be."[148] And: "Each part of a building must correspond to all the others so as to contribute to the success and beauty of the whole. The building cannot be beautiful in only one of its parts while the others are neglected; all must harmonise in order to appear as a single, well articulated body, not a jumble of unrelated fragments."[149]

Together with this organic concept goes the need for moderation in the construction of the individual parts: "Let the members be moderately proportioned therefore". Alberti also insists upon variety, the same variety he urged upon the painter of narrative, according to which not all the parts of a work ought to be equal, for some will be larger than others: "In any case, you must be careful to ensure that your building does not become a shapeless lump with disproportionate sides and shoulders."[150] When he comes to the subject of roofs, he emphasizes its importance with a reference to his own experience: "I have had a lot of experience in such matters and must remind you how difficult it is to carry out a work in such a way that its various parts are both practical and beautiful. For rarely does a building deserve praise both because of its practicality and because its parts are harmoniously varied according to a unified vision of its proportions." The word he uses in this case is *concinnitas*, "quantum et partium escultam varietatem qualem proportionum ratio et concinnitas diffinierit."[151] Up to this point, apart from his observations on the appropriate use of uneven numbers in apertures[152] and on the need for different sizes of bricks — something he had seen applied with excellent results in many classical monuments, especially those along the Via Appia[153] — Alberti's theory of proportion seems to be limited to the relationship between the parts of a building seen as an organism and to the definition of unity within variety and of variety within unity. This, of course, is a basically hedonistic, or, at least, wholly aesthetic approach. But there is the famous passage in Book Seven where the term *concinnitas* reappears in the

explanation of the unequivocal nature of the proportional system: "I shall define beauty as a unity of all the parts founded upon a precise law and in such a way that nothing can be added, diminished, or altered but for the worse."[154] Though he limits himself historically to defining the proportions as the fruit of experience, "usum aedificandi,"[155] he is aware of the need to enquire into the nature of proportion and to establish its derivation from symmetry in the Vitruvian manner. Thus symmetry is conceived as a mirror-like equilibrium of the parts. All the ornamental parts of a building must be proportioned in such a way that there is a balance between equal elements in all directions. One must also be careful not to introduce anything that might clash with the quality of the material and its distribution. Everything must be defined according to specific angles and proportioned lines: "Omnia ad certos angulos paribus lineis adaequanda."[156]

Alberti then proceeds to establish a series of norms: the ratios between the voids and solids created by the spaces between columns: "In the closest kind of colonnades, the spaces between the columns should not be less than one and a half times the width of a column. In the widest sort they should not exceed the same by more than three and three-eighths. In those of the intermediate kind, the ratio should be two and a quarter: the closer ones will have a ratio of two; those that are almost wide, a ratio of three."[157] As for the orders: "The following proportions were established so that the columns might enhance the beauty of the building. Doric capitals are best used with columns whose width at the base corresponds to a seventh of the total height of the shaft. This ratio must be a ninth in the case of Ionic capitals and an eighth in that of Corinthian."[158]

Alberti then establishes the proportions of the pediments ("the summit or upper angle of the pediment will not be more than a fourth nor less than a fifth of the width of the front measured along the cornice"),[159] those of the basilica's ground plan,[160] and the rules for arched colonnades, which require square pillars. This last requirement derives from the fact that the lower terminal parts of the arch are never wholly in line with the columns that support them when the latter are cylindrical: "In the close type of colonnade, the height of the space between the two columns should be three and a half times its width. In the wide sort, the height must be one and two-thirds its width. In those that are almost wide, the height will be twice the breadth, in those that are almost close, the width will be a third of the height."[161]

Finally, he establishes the correct proportions for tombs,[162] towers,[163] squares, the arches above streets that run into squares

146. L. B. Alberti, op. cit., Preface, p. 14.
147. Ibid., I, 1, p. 18.
148. Ibid., I, 9, p. 64.
149. Ibid., p. 66.
150. Ibid., p. 68.
151. Ibid., II, 2, pp. 100-01.
152. Ibid., I, 12, p. 84.
153. Ibid., II, 10, p. 148.

154. Ibid., VI, 2, p. 446. For the different versions of Lauro and Bartoli, and their relative interpretations of the concept of *concinnitas*, see L. Vagnetti, op. cit., pp. 146-49.
155. Ibid., 3, p. 451.
156. Ibid., 5, pp. 470-71.
157. Ibid., VII, 5, p. 562.
158. Ibid., 7, p. 566.
159. Ibid., 11, p. 616.
160. Ibid., 14, pp. 636-38.
161. Ibid., 15, p. 642.

(a subject he goes into in great detail),[164] and concludes with those for colonnades[165] and courts of justice.[166]

Having defined the fundamental elements of the proportions relative to town planning, Alberti discusses optimal volumetric ratios: "The ancients seem to have built their walls to a height equal to one and a third the length of the area to be enclosed. Measuring these buildings, we discovered that the height of walls in a rectangular area must vary according to whether the area has an arched or beamed roof. Moreover, large edifices must be dealt with differently than small ones, for the proportions with respect to the distances between the centre of the visible rays and the highest point of visibility are different". Here, Alberti combines perspective with proportion. The "centre of the visible rays" means the position of the eye, and the question of the relationship between height and width arises from the consideration as to whether the whole rectangle can be taken in visibly.[167] In defining the ratios of areas ("according to a traditional, widespread practice of the ancients, the width of the hall was two thirds its length, while the length was equal to its width plus two thirds, or to its width plus two fifths"[168]), Alberti simplified the ratio of 1 to the root of 2 (1 : 1.41421) to a ratio of 1 : 4, in consideration of the fact that the human eye is not as subtle as such a ratio would imply. The substitution of 1 : 4 for 1 to the root of 2 also confirms Alberti's rejection of the use of "irrational numbers" (as Portoghesi has pointed out).

Having dealt with the normative or prescriptive part of his treatise, Alberti enquires more deeply into the nature of beauty: "Beauty is the agreement and harmony of the parts in relation to a whole, to which these parts are connected by specific number, delimitation, and collocation, according to *concinnitas*, that is, to the fundamental, precise law of nature". ("Pulchritudinem esse quendam consensum et conspirationem partium in eo cuis sunt ad certum numerum finitionem collocationemque habitam ita uti concinnitas hoc est absoluta primariaque ratio naturae postularit."[169]) Proportions and their laws are to be found in the order of nature, and "the ancients, reflecting upon the practice of nature as regards both the structure of the organism as a whole and in its single parts, perceived that it was in accordance with nature that the proportions of bodies were not always the same in all cases, for some men are fat, some thin, and others medium. And seeing that buildings were different according to their purposes and functions, as we have shown in the preceding books, they realized it was necessary to build different kinds of structures."[170]

What are these laws derived from nature? First, there is the use of odd and even numbers: "Following nature, they never made such individual parts of a building as columns, corners etc., in uneven numbers, for there is not a single animal to be found that stands or moves on an uneven number of feet. On the other hand, they always made an uneven number of apertures, for this too, corresponds to the rule of nature, as we can see from the fact that though animals have an even number of ears, eyes, and nostrils one on each side of their faces, they have only one large mouth in the centre."[171] There is also a privileged series of numbers, the first being the number three ("all philosophers hold nature to be founded on the number three.") "Five, on the other hand, is considered divine and sacred to the protective deities of the arts, particularly Mercury."[172] (The latter is probably a reference to Mercury Trismegistus, or Hermes. Hermes Trismegistus was translated and popularised by Gemistos Plethon; another translation was begun in 1460 by Ficino on the express wish of Cosimo the Elder.)[173] Of the uneven numbers seven and the fraction of a ninth receive special mention; four, six ("a perfect number because it is the sum of all its divisors"), eight, and ten (whose square is "equal to the sum of the cubes of four consecutive numbers") among the even ones.[174]

Having defined the optimal numbers, Alberti deals with the second aspect of *concinnitas*. This is 'delimitation', or the mutual correspondence between the lines that establish size (length, height, and width.)[175] In this case, the optimal series of ratios is established through analogy with music, though Alberti is quick to inform his reader that "we shall go no further into the matter than is required by the architect's purpose. We shall leave aside questions regarding musical scales, such as the tetrachordal theory, for the only points that concern us are the following."[176] Alberti points out that music, like architecture, is based on proportions or numerical ratios, that movement or beat is regulated in the same way, and that the values of notes are also established by proportional ratios, which in turn correspond to the length of the chords that emit them. "We shall define harmony as a combination of notes pleasing to the ear. The tone of a note may be either deep or high. The longer the chord is, the deeper its note; the shorter it is, the higher." (This may be an allusion to the complicated fourth chapter in Book Five of Vitruvius.)

To establish his optimal ratios, Alberti is obliged to adopt both Greek and Latin terminology. These ratios are the diapente, or fifth, for the series 4, 6, 9 (the number plus one half), which Alberti calls the *sesquialtera* (as he points out, the prefix "sesqui" means "atque potius" or "and besides"); the diatessaron, or fourth

162. Ibid., VIII, 3, pp. 690-92.
163. Ibid., 5, pp. 700-02.
164. Ibid., 6, p. 718.
165. Ibid., 8, p. 756.
166. Ibid., 9, p. 758.
167. Cf. P. Portoghesi, op. cit., p. 797, note 2.
168. L. B. Alberti, op. cit., IX, 3, p. 796.
169. Ibid., 5, pp. 816-17. For the translation of the term *concinnitas*, cf. L. Vagnetti, op. cit., p. 150 ff.
170. Ibid.

171. Ibid., p. 818.
172. Ibid.
173. Cf. F. A. Yates, *Giordano Bruno e la tradizione ermetica*, Bari 1969, pp. 25-27.
174. L. B. Alberti, op. cit., IX, 5, pp. 818-20.
175. Ibid.
176. Ibid., p. 822.

(Alberti's word is *sesquiterzia*) for the series 9, 12, 16 (the number plus one third); the disdiatessaron, or octave, also called the double, for 1 : 2 ratios; and the disdiapason, or quadruple, for 1 : 4 ratios. The tonus, or *sesquiottava*, signifies an 8 : 9 ratio. Alberti applies these ratios simply (with two variants) to the proportions of areas such as squares or uncovered urban centres. With buildings, a third factor has to be taken into account, for volume is conditioned by height too. However, these ratios cannot be adopted indiscriminately; one has to define a field of commensuration — what Vitruvius would have called symmetry — and Alberti distinguishes very simply between areas as *breves*, and *mediae*, *prolixiores*, or small, medium, and large plans. Small areas ("where the measurements are all the same, or where there is a ratio of 2 : 3 or 3 : 4") which correspond to a square and one half or a square and one third, are simple and easily reduced to musical proportions. Medium areas require greater care. The easiest is that which involves a 1 : 2 ratio, or diapason (a double square). When one comes to a 4 : 9 ratio, one must double the *sesquialtera*. For example, once one has traced the smaller side of the square, possibly to the value of four, one then establishes the first *sesquialtera*, which is six. To this is added another area half as long as the first, until the total length becomes nine. Thus, the highest figure in this kind of area will be twice the smallest plus the tonus of the double; and a 4 : 9 ratio will have been obtained through an eight-plus-one operation.[177] One can also double the *sesquiterzia* to obtain a 9 : 16 ratio on the basis of a 9 to 12 scale; both 9 : 12 and a 12 : 16 ratios are equivalent to a one to one and one third ratio.

Large areas too, are produced by a decomposition of ratios. By adding a double to a *sesquialtera* one obtains a triple, that is, proportions based on a 2, 4, 6 series, which are reducible to a 1 : 3 ratio. Or one can add a *sesquiterzia* to a double square and so obtain proportions based on a 3, 6, 8 series, reducible to a 3 : 8 ratio. Then again, by doubling the double square according to a 2, 4, 8 series one can obtain the quadruple ratio of 2 : 8. The harmonic ratios that are called double, triple, and quadruple are made up of simple consonant ratios. This obliges the architect to follow an inner logic, and to choose his contexts carefully. As Alberti points out: "The numbers discussed above are used by architects, not confusedly, in any combination, but in harmonic proportions. Thus, for example, whoever wants to erect walls within an area that is twice as long as it is wide must apply the proportions that are proper to this area, that is, those that produce the double not the triple. He must do the same in an area whose

177. Ibid., 6, pp. 823-26. Cf. also R. Wittkower, *Architectural Principles in the Age of Humanism*, London 1973, pp. 110-16.

I DIECI LIBRI

DE L'ARCHITETTVRA

DI LEON BATTISTA DE GLI ALBERTI FIORENTINO,

Huomo in ogni altra dottrina eccellente, ma in questa singolare; da la cui prefatione breue= mente si comprende

La commodità, l'utilità, la necessità, e la dignità di tale opera, e parimente la cagione, da la quale è stato mosso à scriuerla:

Nouamente da la Latina ne la Volgar-Lingua con molta diligenza tradotti.

Con gratia, & priuilegio de lo Illustris. Senato Vinitiano per anni dieci.

IN VINEGIA,

APPRESSO VINCENZO VAVGRIS.

M D X L V I.

length is three times its width, adopting the equivalent proportions, a 1 : 3 ratio. Nor can he do otherwise in an area whose length is four times its width. Thus, the sizes of areas will be determined in groups of three by means of the numbers mentioned above, according to the measurements best suited to the work."[178] In spite of the normative character and mathematical subtlety of the laws of nature, the artist was still free to choose those solutions that seemed best suited to each particular case.

Following his exhaustive exposition of the numerical ratios, Alberti deals with the *innatae correspondentiae*, or "natural proportions" (Orlandi) that cannot be established numerically, but which are based on the roots and powers of numbers. The cube derived from one is absolute and optimal: "The first cube of all, whose root is one, is consecrated to the deity, for since it is derived from one, it must be one in every way. Moreover, they say that it alone is the basis of all perfect stable forms and can rest upon any base with equal safety". Reference to the world of Pythagoras through Vitruvius is explicit: "once it [the die] is cast, it lies firmly upon the side on which it comes to rest, unless moved. Such is the dice that gamblers use."[179] Alberti discusses the number eight whose cube root is two, and says: "the line drawn from one angle of a square to the angle opposite it is a straight line, and divides the square into two equal parts. Hence the word diagonal, the numerical value of which is unknown, though it is the root of a square measuring eight on all sides."[180]

Alberti then sums up the question of the doubling of the square (the square constructed along the diagonal of another given square). The same subject is dealt with in Plato's *Menon* (where the sophists, like Alberti, call the diagonal the *diametros* and *diameter*) and in Vitruvius: "If there is a square place or area, and it is necessary to provide another square twice its size this can be achieved with any kind of number or multiplication by means of a figure in the following way". And: "Thus Plato demonstrated how the square could be doubled geometrically, as the illustration below shows."[181] The same illustration can be found in medieval writers, from Villard de Honnecourt to Roriczer; Alberti must have found it in some text that remains unknown to us. (We have already seen the close affinities between the *Ludi Matematici* and the Picard architect's notebook, though there is no evidence to show that Alberti was acquainted with the latter.) As we saw of S. Sebastiano, it was a geometrical element Alberti made use of, independently of the fact whether this passage in the ninth book preceded or followed his work in Mantua.

Alberti discusses the cube whose diagonal is the square root of three, and then writes of the hypotenuse of a right triangle whose sides are the square roots of four and twelve, which is equal therefore to the square root of sixteen.

Alberti's discussion of proportion ends with an analysis of the "particular proportions that are established between the two dimensions of a work, regarding which some very useful considerations may be drawn from music, geometry, and arithmetic."[182] These are the proportional means which are obtained arithmetically by adding the major and minor terms and dividing them by two, or geometrically by multiplying the minor term by the major and finding the root of the product. Alberti warns that "in practice it is very difficult to find the numerical value of this [geometrical] mean. However, it can be represented very well by lines, though we shall not go any further into the matter". (This would seem to be an early example of analytic geometry.)

"The third type, the harmonic mean as it is called, is slightly more complicated than the arithmetical, though it can be expressed perfectly with numbers. In this case, the proportion between the minor term and the major must be the same as the distance between the minor term and the mean with respect to that which separates the mean from the major"; in other words, $m - a : a = c - b : c$. Plato had written in the *Timaeus* that the three proportional means determine all the intervals in the musical scale; Alberti may also have been acquainted with Ficino's commentary on the subject. Alberti concludes by affirming that this sophisticated system of means is particularly useful in calculating heights, that is, it has a direct bearing on one of architecture's main problems.[183] The architect has to approach the problem of height in various ways, while the system of means anchors it firmly to the inner logic of the ground plan. Though the sixth chapter of Book Nine is difficult, it is worth analysing, for it shows Alberti going through the same process of reducing a difficult theory to simple practical terms that he followed in the fields of optics and perspective. The difference here is that he succeeds in giving proportion an objective value within the logic of a system that reconciles the natural order of things with the supernatural order of forms. Just as perspective is a symbolic structure capable of providing accurate proportions in the field of vision, so proportion provides the right perspective for focussing the elusive, mystic concept of *concinnitas* from within.

THE INFLUENCE OF THE DE RE AEDIFICATORIA
Even before it was published, when it was still circulating privately in the form of a limited number of manuscript copies — "those

178. Ibid., p. 828.
179. Vitruvius, op. cit., V, Preface, p. 96.
180. L. B. Alberti, op. cit.
181. Vitruvius, op. cit., IX, 1, p. 199.

182. L. B. Alberti, op. cit., p. 830.
183. Ibid., 7, p. 834.

who have a copy are reluctant to part with it" wrote the Ferrarese ambassador in Florence[184] — Alberti's treatise had begun to influence the work of his contemporaries. Filarete was the first to make specific mention of it in his *Sforzinda*: "... Battista Alberti, who, for our times, is a very learned man in different fields, and very skilled in this [architecture], particularly in design, which is the foundation and way of all art. He understands it very well, and is very expert in geometry and other sciences. He has also written an excellent work in Latin."[185]

In mentioning design and geometry, Filarete was alluding to the *Della pittura* and the *Elementi della pittura*, which had a direct influence on some chapters of his own work. The "also" seems to contain a specific reference to the *De re aedificatoria*, and the fact that Alberti wrote in Latin may have induced Filarete to write in the vernacular in order to reach a larger public. His *Sforzinda*, which takes the form of a dialogue written for the education of a prince (was it not the same didactic motive that led Vasari to write his *Ragionamenti* for Francis I?) reflects Alberti's greater concern with the patron than with the architect, even though its explicit experimentalism is directed towards the construction of the city and the definition of its details.

In addition to this general similarity of purpose, many other details relate the *Sforzinda* to Alberti's treatise. From the very *incipit*, the latter is described as the work of a "second Vitruvius". In discussing the measurements of man, Filarete also mentions the *De statua*. But when he deals with the anthropomorphic character of architecture, he really has Vitruvius's *Homo ad quadratum* in mind. He suddenly exclaims, with the characteristic liveliness and lack of pedantry that distinguish his work: "He has to eat like any other man if he wants to live. And like other men, he falls sick and dies, just as he may recover from many illnesses with the help of a good doctor."[186] He believes in the need for models as a necessary stage in the checking of a design before the actual building begins: "Make a wooden model; measure, divide, and establish everything that must be started and completed."[187] Filarete orders his material as Alberti does in the *De re aedificatoria*. He distinguishes between public and private buildings and expresses concern for the healthfulness of the climate and the quality of the building materials, making numerous references to his own experience. He adopts Vitruvius and Alberti's idea of the natural origin of the orders but emphasises its anthropomorphic aspect. He pays homage to both Brunelleschi and Alberti, to the first as the "resuscitator of the ancient style of building", to the second as the designer of the Palazzo Rucellai.

184. G. Mancini, op. cit., p. 352, note 6.
185. Filarete, op. cit., pp. 10-11.
186. Ibid., I, p. 29.
187. Ibid., II, p. 42.

He mentions the $1:2$ and $1:\sqrt{2}$ ratios of the doors of the building and adds a $1:1.5$ ratio of his own.[188] He deviates slightly from the $1:2$ proportions of the square, describing one as 372 feet long and 192 feet wide.[189]

Filarete's treatise is probably the only one that contains an echo of Alberti's architectural terminology. His cymatium (cimagine) has the form of a groove, and the small element attached to it is called a staff, or *ritondino*, which corresponds to Alberti's *gulula*. There are references to monuments and events with which Alberti was personally involved, and he describes both the Ponte Elio and the rescue of a ship from Lake Nemi ("carried out in a strange way").[190] Filarete is much more lively, aggressive, and realistic than Alberti. He has none of Alberti's prudence, subtlety of expression, or philosophical scepticism. He is even more ready to accept society as it is, the impositions of power, and the seething life of nature. All this finds expression in his more courtly, more schematic, Utopian concept of the city. Nevertheless, in all this he was profoundly influenced by Alberti.

Francesco di Giorgio, on the other hand, adopted a critical attitude towards Alberti. He belonged to a line of experimental artists, architects involved in the actual construction of buildings, and antiquarians or technically-minded archaeologists; thus he was very far from Alberti's philosophically orientated, literary-architectural syntheses. There is no explicit mention of Leon Battista in his works, nor is there any evidence that he ever read the *De re aedificatoria*, but there are many factors that suggest he is referring to the work indirectly. In the prefaces to the Sienese and Magliabechi manuscript copies of his work, he expresses his dissatisfaction with those who wrote before him (probably Alberti and Filarete): "For those who have written about the superior art of architecture have either failed to complete their works or have dealt with that aspect of it which interested them most, without mentioning the rest. On the other hand, for the reasons we have already explained, they have adopted terms that have never been used before, and have dealt with many monuments that have been in a state of ruin for centuries."[191] The words "never been used before" may refer to Alberti's terminology, while the buildings "in a state of ruin", of which he writes elsewhere, may allude to the Cathedral of Pienza, and be a hint at the connection between Alberti and Pienza made for the benefit of his contemporaries. Considerations of this kind lead him to insist upon a return to the principal sources "and above all to Vitruvius, who is reputed to be the best. But because of the difficulty of Greek and Latin grammar, it has never been possible to establish his meaning,

even though many learned scholars of these languages have tried to do so, urged on by me and my Lord."[192] This passage refers once more to the difficulties of deciphering Vitruvius, but the allusion to "learned scholars" seems to be a direct hit at Alberti. Francesco emphasises Vitruvius's authoritativeness, and, in doing so, deliberately ignores or slights Alberti's attempt to produce a contemporary version of the Latin theorist. He points out sharply how, among his contemporaries, there are some "who have usurped works of art and claimed to have done what only their real authors were able to carry out." This may be an attempt to formulate the modern concept of plagiarism, and may be directed at Alberti's unacknowledged references to Vitruvius or, more generally, at his unacknowledged debt to Brunelleschi. Francesco's aim, as Maltese has observed, was to bring Vitruvius up to date, to compare his observations with the monuments themselves, and to illustrate the latter with drawings. Alberti was concerned with the cautious formulation of rules; Francesco's treatise is a work of self-discovery: "the various forms and figures of temples, houses, and all the other things dealt with are the fruit of my weak invention."[193] There follows another polemical statement: "Though I am well aware that some modern authors have written about architecture, I think I have dealt with the useful and difficult aspects of this art slightly better than they have". This implies a comparison of his own specific typological solutions with Alberti's generalised models and lack of discussion of style.

Yet in spite of these differences, Francesco was also indebted to Alberti. This is reflected perhaps in the doctrinaire tone with which he prepares to deal with the subject of "parts of houses and palaces". It is even more apparent in his preface, which is full of quotations, though more modern ones than Alberti's (they include Petrarch for example). The division of his material, too, is similar to Alberti's. After saying that "in the first [part] we shall consider common houses and properties; in the second their individual parts,"[194] he proceeds to discuss climate. Then without going into the matter of privileged numbers, he tackles the question of the proportions of rooms and their correct height. Anticipating Palladio, he says they can be established by means of a simple graphical method.[195]

In defining architecture, Francesco hints at a distinction between "construction and design". He places the problem of actual construction before ratiocinative design ("demonstrating things by means of reasoned proportions before they are built"[196]). He then speaks of the architect's cultural development in terms of Vitru-

188. Ibid., pp. 232-33. L. B. Alberti, op. cit., p. 84.
189. Ibid., p. 273.
190. Ibid., p. 588.
191. Francesco di Giorgio Martini, *Trattati di architettura, ingegneria e arte militare*, Milan 1967, II, p. 295.
192. Ibid.
193. Ibid., p. 297.
194. Ibid., p. 327.
195. Ibid., pp. 346-47.
196. Literally, "building and ratiocination". Ibid., p. 36.

vius's universalism. His treatment of the orders is steeped in a vague anthropometry and characterised by numerous references to Vitruvius, though he does express some personal ideas, including a simplification of the proportions of the orders (the Tuscan is given nine parts, while the Ionic column is given nine diameters instead of Vitruvius's eight and a half). But he never elaborates a proportional system, and this confirms both a freer attitude to decoration and a non-structural approach to the orders. On the other hand, he strictly adheres to Vitruvius in his ideas on proportional ratios and optimal numbers, re-affirming the principle of the relationship between architecture and the human body: "with suitable proportions and measurements. It remains for us to adopt the same in the composition of all buildings."[197] As for the various kinds of secular buildings, he makes the same distinction between "particular", "private", "royal", and "noble", but makes no reference to social structure in the way Alberti does, concentrating more closely on the definition of planimetry and measurements.

His treatment of geometry (like that of wheels and mill-wheels) is the same as Alberti's, since they shared the same knowledge of the instruments of their day. But Francesco's handling of the subject has none of the dignity Alberti confers upon it in the *Elementa picturae* and the *Ludi Matematici*. The difference is similar to that between a technical institute and a classics school, between a geometry manual and a noble science, which, for men of letters like Alberti, was a mysterious product of the East and of ancient philosophy, a "formula that could open up new worlds". This is reflected in the almost provocative brevity with which Francesco di Giorgio dismisses the whole question of perspective. Here he offers a little practical device, consisting of a pair of rods with which one may establish the point of vision and measure the diminution of heights as one withdraws from the point of observation; everything can then be resolved with a couple of drawings.

Perhaps the only time Leonardo mentions Alberti explicitly is when he refers to "our present knowledge of how a river flows", adding that "this is in Battista Alberti."[198] "Alberti's method is based upon an experiment where the distance between two points from an island is known. But this experiment can only succeed where the river is similar to that where the experiment was carried out". Leonardo's reference is to a lost work, to that "additional book on ships" which Alberti mentions in the preface and fifth book of the *De re aedificatoria*,[199] where he speaks of methods intended to render his proposals useful in a tone that is almost Leonardesque: "Methods I have thought up for sinking enemy ships."

In one of his architectural drawings, Leonardo uses the very same terms Alberti does — *toro, nestroli, orbicolo, toro inferiore*, and *latastro* — instead of Vitruvius's upper torus, astragals, small square, troclea, and plinth. He adds, in a brief passage entitled the "Staircases of Urbino", "the *latastro* [plinth] must be as wide as the wall against which it is placed."[200] This proves that Leonardo knew the *De re aedificatoria*, and he was probably the only man who realized the nature of the terminological problem Alberti tried to solve. In a famous letter to the administrators of the Cathedral of Milan, Leonardo adopted a comparison Alberti had drawn between architectural restoration and medicine. Alberti had written: "Doctors say that the effectiveness of the treatment depends upon what is known of the disease."[201] Leonardo wrote: "What the sick building or sick cathedral needs is a doctor-architect who understands it fully."[202]

These verbal parallels indicate that Leonardo knew Alberti's works, but one cannot say Alberti was a point of reference for him. On the contrary, he re-assimilated some of the problems dealt with by the Florentine humanist, checked them experimentally, and expounded them in the notes to his manuscripts. Lack of space precludes a systematic study of the problem here, but it may be said that two fundamental aspects of Alberti's thought figure largely in Leonardo's as well: proportion and perspective. They shared the same intellectual approach to painting. "I shall tell you that painting is a question of the mind, and that like music and geometry it takes into account the proportions of even numbers, while arithmetic is concerned with uneven ones. Painting considers all the even numbers and the qualities of the proportions of light, shade, and distance in perspective."[203] Of the proportional bases of music and painting, Leonardo says: "You might say that music is composed of proportions, and that this is what I follow when I paint, as you shall see."[204] Leonardo's *termini delli corpi* corresponds to Alberti's *circoscrizione*, and the concept of the visual pyramid is the object of many of his drawings and written passages. Leonardo re-examined the entire problem in a rather dispersive manner, not without absorbing certain elements proper to medieval optics. Yet he was only endorsing an affirmation of Alberti's when he said that "perspective is the bridle and rudder of painting."[205] All Alberti's preoccupations with the definition of an area are summed up in Leonardo's lapidary statement: "A building must always have a clear outline so that it may reveal its true form."[206] The "clear outline" is

197. Ibid., p. 69.
198. J. P. Richter, *The Literary Works of Leonardo da Vinci*, II, p. 220.
199. L. B. Alberti, op. cit., V, 12, p. 388.

200. J. P. Richter, op. cit., II, p. 55.
201. L. B. Alberti, op. cit., X, 1, p. 868.
202. J. P. Richter op. cit., p. 331.
203. Ibid., p. 78.
204. Ibid.
205. Ibid., p. 127.
206. Ibid., p. 27.

equivalent to his "tracing the edges", which in turn corresponds to Alberti's concept of *circoscrizione* as the basis of design. Thus, the main points of Alberti's thought filtered through into Leonardo's notes, in spite of the latter's completely different *forma mentis* and method of enquiry. (Leonardo, of course, had none of Alberti's fine literary style.)

In the Madrid manuscript discovered in 1967, Leonardo made a "list of the books I have left locked in the trunk". Among the mathematical texts and classical works included in this list is a copy of "Battista Alberti on architecture", "a book on measurement by Battista Alberti" (perhaps the *Ludi Matematici*), and a book "about cutting the ropes of ships" (possibly the *Navis* Leonardo mentions elsewhere.)[207]

Garin catches an echo of Alberti in a passage written in 1494 about the evils of the city: "A goodly-sized stone recently uncovered by the rain lay upon a rise in the ground, on the edge of a delightful little wood, in a stony path among tufts of grass and various flowers of different colours, and it could see a great number of stones lying in the road below it. It was suddenly seized by a desire to roll down and join them, saying to itself, 'What have I in common with these flowers? I would rather be with companions of my own kind',"[208] and so it rolled down and joined the others. But it soon began to feel the weight of carts, the hoofs of horses, the feet of wayfarers, and to be covered with mud and dung. "Such is the case", Leonardo concludes, "with those who want to leave the solitary life of contemplation for the city, where the people are riddled with illnesses of all kinds." There is a similar passage in the *Lapides* (one of Alberti's *Intercoenales*), where the stones jump into the water from a river-bank in order to join their companions and swim with them, but they are overwhelmed by mire, mud, and dung. This too, concludes with a comparison between two kinds of life; the quiet, leisurely life of the river-bank and the giddy, iniquitous world of the river. Garin sums up: "After nearly fifty years, and writing in very different circumstances, Leon Battista Alberti and Leonardo faced the same choice between two concepts of reality, or, in other words, between two kinds of existence: the active or contemplative life, knowledge or action, solitude or society. Both clearly chose the same kind of contemplative life: isolation, peace, and freedom."[209] In the role Landino assigns Alberti in his *Disputationes Camaldulenses*, one can see the logical connection between Alberti's treatment of urban, hygienic problems and his realistic proposal of escape from the city.[210]

Pedretti's comparison of the plans for the castle of Romorantin with the Leonine city raises the question of Alberti's possible influence on the French Renaissance. The plans for Romorantin (Roma minor, according to one etymological interpretation) were drawn up between 1517 and 1519; the *De re aedificatoria* was published in France in 1512 and translated into French for the first time in 1553. This first translation was edited by Jean Martin, who had edited the 1547 translation of Vitruvius. The translator's note refers once more to the obscurity of Vitruvius: "Messer Leon Battista Alberti says at the beginning of his sixth book ... that Vitruvius wrote in a way that seemed like Greek to the Latins and like Latin to the Greeks. In my opinion, he did this deliberately so as not to be understood by his ignorant contemporaries."[211] Fra' Giocondo, Alberti, Serlio, and Filandro are then quoted as authorities for the interpretation of Vitruvius.

By this time, the first phase in the exportation of the Italian Renaissance to France was already over: Leonardo had personified its genius, Cellini had imposed it as a way of life, and Serlio had reduced it to the simple rules of a manual. When the great native tradition of French Mannerism emerged, with Philibert de l'Orme as its leading figure, Alberti's ideas began to exert a fresh influence. Particular attention was paid to his distinction between the "learned architect" and the master-mason, and to his insistence on the need for "wisdom" and "prudence" on the patron's part in controlling his ambitions.

The first book of Philibert de l'Orme's *De l'Architecture*, though enriched by the author's own experience, is Albertian in its concept of the architect as a man who holds a compass entwined with a snake, the symbol of prudence: "For a very great and measured sense of prudence is required of them."[212] De l'Orme also condemns what Alberti had formerly described as graphic "impurities", calling them "deceit" and "abuse": "Therefore, I am of the opinion that we ignore the sound practices of those who built in ancient times, and who did not stop at the depiction of plants, pictures and such things, as Leon Battista says ... he [the patron] must modify the models they [the architects] make out of wood, paper, parchment, or any other material, so that they express his wishes."[213]

Having formulated his moral concept of the architect, de l'Orme appeals to the patron in a manner typical of Alberti: "If it pleases you to read the first chapter of the second book of Leon Battista Alberti's *Dell'architettura*, you will see the excellent advice he gives those who want to build, advice that might well be followed by patrons and architects alike. For after considering all that is necessary for the honour, health, well-being, and hap-

207. C. Maccagni, "Le fonti di Leonardo: l'elenco di libri del codice 1057 della Biblioteca Nacional di Madrid, in *Leonardo da Vinci. Letture Vinciane*, I-XII (1960-1972), Florence 1974, pp. 296, 297, 303-04. Cf. also *Leonardo da Vinci. Scritti Letterari*, ed. by A. Marinoni, Milan 1974, p. 239 ff.

208. E. Garin, *La Città in Leonardo*, op. cit., p. 313.

209. Ibid., p. 314.

210. For the relationship between Alberti and Leonardo, see Zoubov, "Leon Battista Alberti e Leonardo da Vinci", in *Raccolta Vinciana*, XVIII, 1960, pp. 1-14. E. Garin, La Città in Leonardo, in *Letture Vinciane*, XII, Florence 1964, pp. 311-25. Cf. also C. Pedretti, *The Royal Palace at Romorantin*, Cambridge 1972, *passim*.

211. Vitruvius, *Architecture*, Paris 1547, Address to the reader.

212. Ph. de l'Orme, *Architecture*, Rouen 1648, III, c. 50.

213. Ibid., I, c. 22*v*.

piness of the inhabitants, whether they be kings or princes, one must also consider their authority, greatness, and comfort, so that what is built may be worthy of them and such as to ensure their immortal fame and memory. Nor must one forget to see to the lodgings of all those who have dealings with them, according to their particular rank, so that they may be better served and loved, while those who serve and follow them, or attend to their business, will not have to suffer hardship in exchange."[214] De l'Orme differentiates between habitations according to the social class of their occupants (this has affinities with Serlio's detailed division of social classes.)

Another Albertian feature of de l'Orme's work is its concern with sound construction. Where actual building techniques and materials are concerned, he takes his examples from French architecture; his return to the Gothic tradition of the *charpente* (framework construction) and *pierrerie* (stonework) is a wholly personal, though essential feature of his treatise. There are still other aspects of Alberti's work that re-appear in de l'Orme: the preoccupation with climate; the reconciliation of French methods of measurement with Roman; the language question (French being "so poor and sterile that we have no words to explain it [architecture] properly"); the problem of the orders;[215] and the neglect of the ruins of ancient Rome. He is particularly concerned about the marble taken from Roman monuments to make lime; if "they continue like this, Rome will soon be unrecognisable."[216] De l'Orme deals with the *ad quadratum* proportional method, though he approaches it mainly from a practical point of view.[217] However, the idea of architecture that emerges from his treatise is that of the "art of command", which is understandable given the French tradition of the *maîtres maçons*: "The architect must obey his patron and administrative superiors, while the supervisor must obey the architect and do everything he is told to do for the proper construction of the work."[218]

Dürer was acquainted with the drawing and painting of the Italian Renaissance even before his first visit to Italy, during which he may have met Pacioli or Bramante in Bologna.[219] He was aware of Alberti's *costruzione legittima* and supported the *velo*, illustrating it in some very famous, striking drawings. Thus, after nearly a century, he adopted a technical device of Alberti's which had fallen into disuse after being criticised by Leonardo. Moreover, there is a connection between his *Trattato sulle proporzioni umane* and the *De statua*, though he modified Alberti's system of measurement, dividing his *minuta* into three "particles". "His ideas on town planning, expressed in his treatise on fortifications and

214. Ibid., c. 8.
215. Ibid., V, c. 136*v*.
216. Ibid., c. 152*v*.
217. Ibid., VIII, c. 234, 235.
218. Ibid., p. 399.
219. Cf. E. Panofsky, *The Life and Art of Albrecht Dürer*, Princeton 1955.

possibly related to one of the first slum clearance projects in history, — the Fuggerei of Augsburg, demolished in 1519-20 — reveal his knowledge of modern theorists like Leon Battista Alberti and Francesco di Giorgio Martini."[220] Finally, his observations on the lettering of inscriptions are related to the Alberti-Feliciano-Pacioli tradition, though in his treatment of Gothic lettering he substituted small, articulated, square moulds for the Italian *ad quadratum* system.

Dürer rejected Alberti's concept of ideal beauty for the "ugliness of nature", which he considered no impediment to "artistic beauty". When he defines artistic beauty, however, he falls back upon Alberti's concept of *concinnitas*, which becomes *Vergleich-lichkeit*.[221]

The foundations for the new influence of Alberti on the Italian Cinquecento were laid by a number of translations of his treatise. The first was Pieti's. Pieti illustrated his version with some beautiful, technically skilful drawings,[222] but his work was never published and it remained unknown. Only a fragment of it has survived, the manuscript copy at Reggio being completed by Lauro. It is not known whether Pieti left it unfinished, or whether the missing part was simply lost. However, it is significant that an attempt was made to provide it with illustrations like those in the various editions of Vitruvius. In both cases, the illustrations reflect the different styles of the regions where the works were translated rather than an impossible figurative objectivity. That the first translation was done at Reggio is further confirmation of the interest Alberti provoked, and the fame he enjoyed, in that area of the Po valley.

Lauro did his translation not far away, in Modena. It was printed in Venice in 1546 and dedicated to Bonifazio Bevilacqua. The comparison between Vitruvius and Alberti is drawn as early as the dedication, and Alberti's superiority is immediately underlined: "I shall relate here wonderful things regarding his ideas and show that neither Vitruvius nor any other architect has written about the theory and practice of architecture with such clarity and skill as he did."[223] Trusting to his clarity of exposition, Lauro did not illustrate his edition. The most important sixteenth-century translation however, Cosimo Bartoli's, contains Torrentini's beautiful woodcuts. Bartoli's version appeared in 1550, in odd rivalry with the simultaneous publication of the *Lives* of Vasari, who had designed its frontispiece. (A similar episode occurred later when a new issue of Alberti's *Opuscoli morali* came out just after the second edition of the *Lives*.) This explains why Vasari's ideas on architecture were largely ignored at the time, though his

nephew, Giorgio Jr., later did his best to remedy this neglect in an amateurish manner. In his dedication to Cosimo I, Bartoli recalls "the many great and varied edifices he [Alberti] built throughout the State, for its defence, utility, and ornament", and he observes that the Duke, by virtue of "his great experience, natural aptitude, and sharpness of intellect", is "extremely knowledgeable" in architectural matters. He points out that his translation is based on a comparison of various Latin texts and illustrated with "ground plans, sections, and elevations" of the buildings discussed by the author or interpreted by the translator.

The immediate success of this edition in Florentine circles obliged Vasari to include Alberti in his *Lives* as one of the leading figures in Florence's artistic supremacy with the grudging reservations we discussed earlier. Confirmation of this success can be found in a passage by Cellini, which also indicates Alberti's influence in France: "For Leon Battista Alberti, our fellow countryman, has written with great skill and judgement about the architectural orders established by Vitruvius, saying nothing that might diminish their beauty in any way. And wonderful as they are, he has added many beautiful, useful things that Vitruvius left unsaid. Anyone who wishes to follow the architectural profession should read Vitruvius. But let him read Leon Battista's book too, for he will find it very useful and beautiful."[224]

The scope of this work allows only a brief reference to the growth of Alberti's reputation in the sixteenth century, a subject that deserves to be studied at length. Otherwise, one could demonstrate that Ammannati's idea of incorporating his planimetric designs into a treatise on the city was motivated by the need to illustrate Alberti's different architectural categories.[225] The same is true of the more ingenuous, ambitious treatise written by Vasari's nephew, the *Città ideale*. The experimentalism of this period, which reduced architecture to a question of the suitability of various kinds of buildings for different social classes and public functions, was indebted to Alberti. The interest in architectural theory and rules that thrived in the court of Cosimo I, an enlightened prince, of whom Alberti would have approved as a patron, led to a revival of Alberti's thought at the time of the publication of Bartoli's translation, when Alberti's ideas had already been assimilated by Florentine art.

Mannerism too, needed the support of some logical structure and a system of rules. Yet one searches in vain for even a single reference to Alberti in the "divine" Michelangelo's letters, poetry, memoirs, and minor works. Michelangelo was too involved in the culture of his own generation to quote those artists of the

220. Ibid.
221. Ibid.
222. The Municipal Library of Reggio Emilia possesses a manuscript with an eighteenth-century frontispiece: "Leo Battista Albertis Florentinus de Architectura — Manuscript translation by Damiano Pieti of Parma 1538 — For the use of Messer Carlo dal Finale, Captain".
223. "The ten books of architecture by Leon Battista degli Alberti the Florentine", ed. Lauro, Venice 1546, p. 3*v*.

224. B. Cellini, *La Vita*, Milan 1958, p. 715.
225. Cf. B. Ammannati, *La città: appunti per un trattato*, ed. by M. Fossi, Rome 1970.

past who had created the cultural background he rejected. What could Alberti's rigid doctrine of harmony have offered him in his rebellion against classicism?

Outside the world of Florence the situation was quite different. Palladio could refer openly to Alberti as the "second Vitruvius" in the *incipit* to his *Four Books*, and he included Alberti and Vitruvius among the authors of those texts he intended to simplify (in the light of experience) for the benefit of actual builders. His treatise contains numerous references to Alberti, and there are many points of contact between the two (for example, the subject of proportion, and its reduction to a simple question of optimal heights and the sizes of rooms). What stands out in comparison with Alberti's nobility of style is Palladio's skill as a *lapicida* (stonemason). Discussing the same subjects drawn from classical antiquity (the Ponte Elio, for example), Palladio is determined to measure the ruins for himself; Alberti, who had ignored the question of drawings and thereby failed to provide his reader with the possibility of verifying his data, cannot be trusted. For Palladio, who had helped with the illustrations for Barbaro's edition of Vitruvius, drawings were all-important.

The same is true of Serlio, though it is difficult to judge how far he was influenced by Alberti. His work contains no explicit references to, or quotations from Alberti, but the way in which he introduces Bramante into his discussion of classical architecture (that is to say, his habit of discussing classical architects and contemporaries in the same breath) results from an attitude that could only have been formed in the light of Alberti's example. His experimentalism and his analysis of the human condition (which led him to elaborate a detailed classification of the social classes) had their roots in Alberti's realism. Even the eclectic manner in which Serlio combines earlier Venetian and French architectural characteristics with those of Renaissance architecture is the product of the realism personified by Leon Battista.

It is easier to establish Alberti's influence on the artists who continued to enquire into the subject of proportion, from Pacioli to Lomazzo. It is no coincidence that the latter should write: "Since it would take too much time to name all those who have left manuscripts or drawings (some of which have been lost), we shall only mention those whose works have been published, such as Leon Battista Alberti, who wrote about perspective, architecture, and painting, Pomponius Gauricus, Fra' Luca dal Borgo, who has dealt with divine proportion ..."[226] As far as the Platonic, Hermetic Lomazzo is concerned, one may point to his ideas on proportion, the parallel he draws between music

and architecture, and his adoption of Alberti's concept of *concinnitas*.[227] Pacioli, as we have seen, was a guest of Alberti's in Rome when still a young man, and he felt the weight of Alberti's heritage more directly; this is particularly evident in his treatise on the proportions of inscription lettering and in his love of inscriptions. Vasari even attributes some of Pacioli's work to Leon Battista, including a special technique for marble inlay based on the use of a particular kind of drill. "Nonetheless, he used it [porphyry] above the entrance to the main door of S. Maria Novella in Florence, where he carved eighteen very large, well designed Roman letters which can be seen in the front part of the block of porphyry, and which read BERNARDO ORICELLARIO."[228] Pacioli writes (in a very Albertian passage): "What else are fortresses, towers, ravelins, walls, ... battlements, mantelets, and other fortifications in the cities and castles of the territory but geometry and proportion, duly weighed and built by means of a plumb-line?"[229] This seems to echo the cultural conviction that characterises the *De re aedificatoria* where Alberti persuades the prince of the utility of science. Pacioli also mentions Valturius and the Palace of Urbino: "the entire magnificent edifice of your noble, admirable Palace of Urbino."

Cataneo's treatise is something of a curiosity in sixteenth-century architectural literature. Dedicated to Aeneas Sylvius Piccolomini, it mentions that he "built many great temples, shrines, and magnificent buildings in Siena, Pienza, and other places, where they can still be seen today, for which he procured the services of the finest minds."[230] The Sienese writer is indebted to Alberti for his universalistic concept of architecture and his idea of the city: "There is no doubt that the most beautiful aspect of architecture is that which deals with the city, where we find the greatest number of people, and where human knowledge and enterprise flourish most."[231] But Cataneo fails to acknowledge his debt to Alberti and repeats Vitruvius's old formulae regarding the formation of the architect.

Alberti's praiseworthy attempt to eliminate some of the subjects and disciplines the architect was expected to master was misunderstood, because the architectural theorists of the sixteenth century (who by that time had become the purveyors of a second-class culture) were content to foster their pretentious claims for the architect according to the gospel of Vitruvius. Cataneo confirms his Vitruvian orthodoxy and takes sides against those who, as far as the orders were concerned, would dare "establish new orders on their own authority,"[232] though the famous polemical passage in the 1567 edition might have been directed against Serlio rather

226. G. P. Lomazzo, *Scritti sulle Arti*, Florence 1973, pp. 259-60.

227. Cf. the introduction by R. P. Ciardi, op. cit., p. 33.
228. G. Vasari, op. cit., I, p. 110.
229. L. Pacioli, *De divina proportione*, in P. Barocchi, *Scritti d'Arte del Cinquecento*, I, Naples 1971, p. 62.
230. P. Cataneo, *I primi quattro libri dell'architettura*, Venice 1554, Dedication.
231. Ibid.
232. G. Nudi, *Pietro Cataneo, trattatista d'architettura del Cinquecento*, Florence 1968, p. 22.

than Alberti. Apart from his unusual contribution to the subject of fortifications, which tends towards the definition of an urban 'form', Cataneo follows Alberti's typological division of buildings. He even tries to interpret them planimetrically, and this attempt, in spite of its elementary nature, was to be the model for Ammannati's more sophisticated experiments and for the more complete classification carried out by Vasari's nephew.

Alberti's treatise achieved its greatest prominence in the sixteenth century as a result of numerous translations and editions. The revival of interest in Alberti grew in proportion to the spread of classicism and as the need to establish a balance between rule and freedom of expression began to be recognised. But this apparent fame was parallelled by a basic lack of comprehension, the result of the breakdown of a fundamental equilibrium. Men no longer believed that the order of nature could be reproduced in art, and all rules of art were attacked in the name of "genius". The esteem accorded to Alberti and to his anti-Vitruvian views declined in proportion to the consolidation of the Roman Cinquecento and the revival of Vitruvian orthodoxy.

Even when the Baroque age had become saturated in "genius" and Alberti's reputation had reached its nadir (a fact reflected in the complete lack of editorial interest in his works in this period), the classical aspects of his thought still continued to exercise an influence. Bernini, whose theories bear a considerable resemblance to Alberti's (according to Chantelou), made studies and drew sketches which show that he continued to believe in the anthropomorphic relationship between human proportions and architectural forms. This belief reaches its climax in the celebrated "embrace" which prefigures the symbolic structure of the square of St. Peter's.

This is a late but logical realization of the idea of Alberti's that was incorporated into Nicholas's plan of the same square, which was to have consisted of a colonnade surmounted by an architrave. Bernini, of course, conceived the project in a different manner. He detached it from the surrounding urban texture and made it an independent organism. But the concept of perspective that underlies all Bernini's architectural sketches, beginning with those of Ariccia and including those of the Pantheon, S. Andrea al Quirinale, and the colonnade of St. Peter's, is basically related to the spatial vision of the Renaissance codified by Alberti. Chantelou adds: "Bernini said that he had done this only in the case of St. Peter's in Rome, whose front everyone judged to be too low, and that he had managed to remedy this by advising the Pope to build two wings of colonnades so as to make the church

seem higher than it really was. He drew a sketch to illustrate his point, showing that the same effect could be observed in the relationship of the arms of a body to its head. He said the same applied to the relationship between the two galleries and the façade in question, and that architecture was a question of the interplay of proportions derived from the human body. He concluded by saying that this was why painters and sculptors made better architects — because they studied the proportions of the human body."[233]

Though traces of Alberti's thought can be found in the more orthodox, classical Baroque schools, it is difficult to discover any such debt in the Borromini-Guarini current, apart from the importance it attributed to sound construction, geometry or *opus architectonicum*, and functionality. Baldinucci's total silence with regard to Alberti marks the lowest point in the latter's reputation. Once more, it was in the area of the Po valley, and in Padua in particular, that certain ideas implicit in Alberti's treatment of proportion were revived, in Giuseppe Viola Zanini's treatise.[234] Alberti is also mentioned by Roland Fréart de Cambrai in his *Parallèle de l'Architecture Antique et de la Moderne*, in which the author couples the names of architects and compares their ideas in his discussion and illustration of the orders (the architects discussed are Palladio-Scamozzi, Serlio-Vignola, Barbaro-Cataneo, Alberti-Viola, and Bullant-Philibert de l'Orme). John Evelyn, the defender of classicism and the leading figure in the second phase of English neo-Palladianism, included a translation of Bartoli's vernacular version of the *De statua* in his 1664 English edition of Alberti. In the introduction to his work, Evelyn describes Alberti as "a Florentine gentleman of industrious great learning and extraordinary ability in all the polite sciences."[235] No new edition of the *De re aedificatoria* was published either in Italy or France throughout the whole of the eighteenth century (except for that of 1784, which belongs to the neo-Classical, rationalist tradition). The first edition of Leoni's English translation appeared in 1726 (it included the *Pittura* and the *De statua*), and was followed by re-issues in 1739, 1751, and 1755. Alberti came to be known in England through Palladio, at a time when people were moved to enquire into the cultural background of Palladio's architecture. Alberti's prescriptivism, realism, and empiricism were congenial to the English mind. The 1784 edition was undertaken jointly by an architect, Andrea de Dominicis, the son of Raguzzini's disciple Carlo de Dominicis, and a mathematician, Gioacchino Pessutti. Its aim was to keep "the substance of Bartoli's translation and preserve its air of ancient gravity", while purifying it of its

233. Cavaliere di Chantelou, *Bernini in Francia*, Rome 1946, p. 51.
234. G. Viola Zanini, *Dell'Architettura*, Padua 1629.
235. R. Fréart, *A Parallel of Ancient Architecture with the Modern*, London 1664, p. 143.

"Tuscan idioms". (This was rather like removing the rust from a medal while leaving its patina.)

Alberti was not always treated indulgently by the eighteenth-century rationalists. Tiraboschi praised the elegance of his Latin in the *De re aedificatoria*. Milizia, however, attempted a first critical interpretation of the treatise, which he acknowledged as "a distinguished work over-loaded with useless erudition."[236] He tends to play down Alberti's contribution to S. Maria Novella, limiting it to the portal: "The façade is too Gothic and German, which is another reason for believing it to be the work of Giovanni Bettini."[237] He describes the tribune in the Annunziata, with some insight, as a "fantastic, difficult work, with some good qualities and some bad."[238] He points out the "damage" to S. Andrea in Mantua caused by "what are called modern improvements" and writes that "what remains of the original structure is dignified, well designed as a whole, and its every part reflects the soundness of its construction."[239] He describes Alberti's work on S. Francesco in Rimini as a "new wrapping for an old temple" and emphasises its dignity: "one might well believe that Leon Battista increased its height after seeing the magnificent Roman arch and bridge in Rimini."[240] Of the completion of the building, he writes: "It is thought that the plan was to have been a Latin cross, terminating in a semi-circular choir". (This observation is not wholly irrelevant to our own interpretation of the problem.)

Milizia was followed by Memmo, who renewed the accusation that Alberti had burdened the history of architecture with excessive learning. He charged Alberti with failing to put his principles into practice in S. Francesco and in the illustrations to his treatise (which were the work of Bartoli, of course). He praises Alberti's principles generally, though he does not think "they would be sufficient to make an architect."[241] Joining his voice to Lodoli's, he asks: "When and why did they think they had revived the greatness of Italian architecture in the fifteenth and sixteenth centuries? Was it perhaps because some new, more enlightened Vitruvius had appeared on the scene? Did anyone build any faultless structure upon better principles? No."[242] "Then came Leon Battista Alberti, who published his famous book, the *De re aedificatoria*, which Cosimo Bartoli made available to a larger public by translating it from the Latin. He was a great admirer of the Romans, as we have seen, and advanced the reputation of two of his fellow countrymen [Brunelleschi and Filarete], whose example he followed in the construction of his own works. These include the choir and tribune of the Annunziata in Florence, S. Andrea in Mantua, and most

L'ARCHITETTVRA DI LEONBATISTA ALBERTI

Tradotta in lingua Fiorentina da Cosimo Bartoli Gentil'huomo & Accademico Fiorentino.

Con la aggiunta de Disegni.

IN FIRENZE.   M. D. L.

Appresso Lorenzo Torrentino Impressor Ducale.

236. F. Milizia, *Memorie degli Architetti*, Bologna 1827, p. 200.
237. Ibid., p. 201.
238. Ibid.
239. Ibid., p. 202.
240. Ibid.
241. A. Memmo, *Elementi di architettura lodoliana*, Zara 1855, p. 336.
242. Ibid., p. 245.

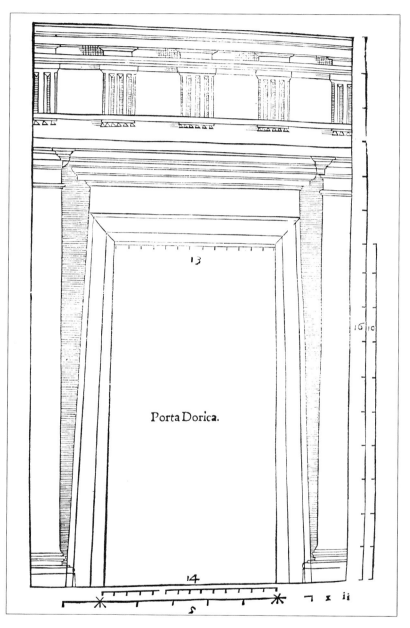

Porta Dorica.

of S. Francesco in Rimini, which is the most beautiful."[243]

Thus Memmo, too, had reservations about Alberti, though he was favourable to him on the whole, especially when he could use him to attack Vitruvius. However, Alberti's entire theory of proportions was contested in the eighteenth century. Milizia wrote: "It would be very convenient indeed if all beauty, that is to say, everything one likes, could be reduced to harmonic proportions. In this case, not only would every architect have to know music, so as to be able to apply it to his buildings, but every artisan desirous of making something pleasant would have to take lessons from the chapel-masters, who would become our universal teachers. Even our pies and bonnets would have to conform to musical proportions."[244]

At the end of the eighteenth century one finds an unusual revaluation of Alberti, Fra Giocondo, and Francesco Colonna (the author of the *Hypnerotomachia di Poliphilo*) in the work of the antisensist Piedmontese nobleman, Galeani Napione di Coccconato. Faced with the contemporary revival of interest in Greek and Egyptian architecture, Galeani fell back on the ideas of Piranesi, arguing in favour of the tradition that led from the Etruscans to the Renaissance and of the work "of most learned men, who were born in the two most favoured regions of Italy, Tuscany and the Venetian State, but who did not develop their ideas in the grand manner until they had drunk of the magnificence of Rome."[245] Leon Battista Alberti is seen as "the father of Michelangelo, and Fra Giocondo as the father of Palladio in architecture."[246]

Two quite different interpretations of Alberti were current in the nineteenth century. According to the first, he was a theorist and codifier, a Florentine Vitruvius laying down the laws of harmony and proportion. This was the Alberti admired by the neo-Classicists such as Quatremère de Quincy, who saw him as the champion of geometrical harmony and musical composition. But the neo-Classical age was more attracted to Palladio, who was looked upon as the true heir of a classicism that was both pure and apparently orthodox. Palladio could be adapted to the new requirements of modern society; above all he was easy to understand, for his treatise was illustrated with explanatory drawings and was extremely varied. Consequently, any fame Alberti enjoyed was the reflection of Palladio's, his real position being that of a kind of background figure within a cultural context founded upon a strong classical bias.

The second Alberti was the one invented by the new Romantic generation, for whom he was an embodiment of the Italian genius,

243. Ibid., p. 246.
244. F. Milizia, *Principi di Architettura Civile*, Bologna 1827, p. 264.
245. F. Galeani Napione, *Monumenti dell'architettura antica*, Pisa 1820, I, p. 245.
246. Ibid., p. 257.

Des cisternes, ensemble de leur vsage & vtilité.

Chapitre huitieme.

E vien maintenant aux cisternes, & dy en premier lieu que ce ne sont que de grās *cisternes.* vaisseaux d'eau, nó gueres differens des ecluses: mais il fault p̄ necessité que leurs fons & costez soient bien serrez & solides, si fermes que l'eau ne les puisse miner. Or en est il de deux especes, l'vne pour boire, & l'autre pour seruir a tous vsages, mais principalement au feu. La premiere donc sera dicte seruante a boire a l'imita- *Cisterna po-* tion des antiques lesquelz souloient appeller la vaisselle d'argent a ce destinée, l'ar- *Argentū e-* gent seruant a viande & la seconde pourtant que c'est son p̄pre de receuoir indiffe *scurium.* remment toutes eaux en sa capacité, nous la dirons gardeuse d'eau. *paquis.*

a symbol of the versatility and universality of the spirit of an oppressed people. This is the concept expressed in the editorial note to the edition of the *De re aedificatoria* published in 1833 with notes by Ticozzi: "To this we must add the great love he bore his country, which did not allow him to follow the example of foreigners, or tolerate those Italians who declared Italy to be poor in works of architecture". Alberti was used to counter the prestige of French architectural theorists, emphasis being placed on the fact that he preceded them chronologically. This was the age in which some of Alberti's architectural forms were assimilated by the eclectic neo-Classical Renaissance, not because of the abstract theories that underlay them, but because they were chaste, simple, elegant, architecturally primitive and pre-Raphaelite. The Romantic interpretation of Alberti was a sentimental one; the Romantics saw something of the simplicity they yearned for in the use of marble and in the men of the Renaissance, whom they saw not so much as philologists and Humanists but as free, adventurous spirits.

The historical interpretation of Alberti and his works in this period includes the accurate studies of D'Agincourt and the reservations of Selvatico and Ricci, but at the same time it places Alberti in his true dimension: an artist at the cross-roads of culture and experience. The reservations spring from a view of Alberti as an "immature" fifteenth-century artist struggling with problems that could not be solved until classicism had reached its zenith in the following century. This was the dominant view before the 1912 German edition of Theuer began a process of re-interpretation that is still going on, but which carries us beyond the scope of an examination of the critical acceptance of the *De re aedificatoria*.

The organicism and nature-worship of Wright, the neat classicism of van der Mies, the regulatory outlines and anthropomorphic, harmonic, modular system of Le Corbusier, and Kahn's revival of the 'antique' are all elements that tempt one to trace Alberti's influence on modern architecture. But it would be difficult to go beyond the bald affirmation and establish the real nature of this influence. One almost agrees with Zevi when he refers to the "perennial untopicality of this disconcerting figure, who is more famous than loved, but whose incisiveness is a constant provocation."[247] There can be no doubt about the untopicality of Alberti's classical code, or about his faith in the capacity of art to reproduce a rational order of things or a natural order of society.

In an age when everything is taken apart and contested, when

247. B. Zevi, "L'operazione linguistica di Leon Battista Alberti", in *L'Architettura*, XVIII, 1972, 140, pp. 142-43.

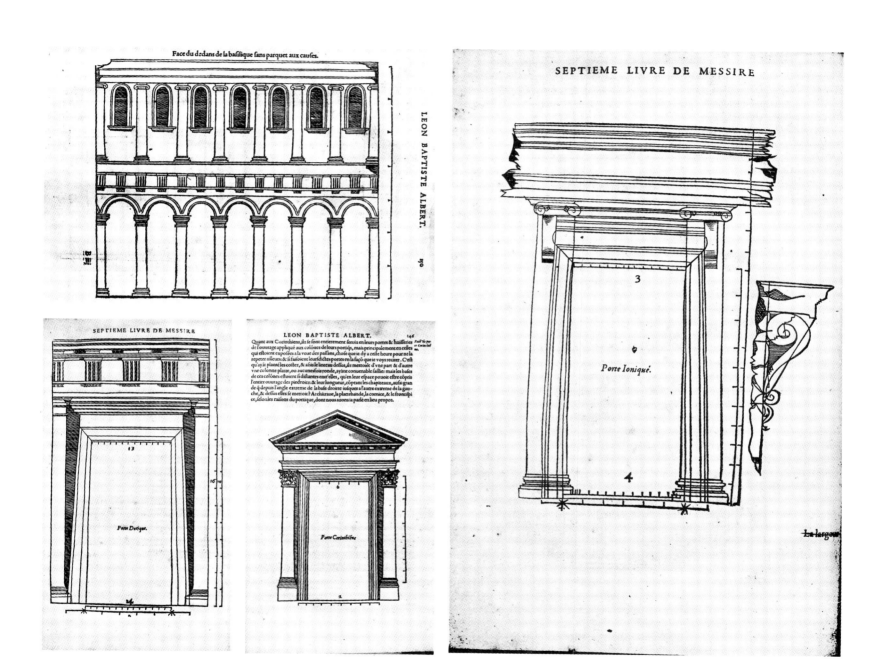

settled values are non-existent, Alberti's belief in correct conduct and social-political conformity — in a word, his conservatism — is not just out-of-date, but culturally anachronistic and, as Milizia would have said, has "an undefinable smell of mould". But if one considers that Alberti did not derive these values from contemporary society, but created them out of a tortured belief in their validity at a time when language, culture, power, the Papacy, and all the historical forces of the Quattrocento were in a state of ferment, then they appear much more real and significant. They are significant, if only because Alberti's attempt to construct a corpus of artistic doctrine capable of embracing both practical and pure theory is just as necessary today as ever, in spite of the enthusiasm with which solutions of a psychological or para-psychological nature are proposed. Particularly relevant for the field of architecture and town planning is Alberti's idea that the builder's craftsmanship needs to be safeguarded, since it is a necessary element in a living culture. Nowadays, of course, such craftsmanship is the slave of technology.

The professional architect today is geared to the needs of commercial consumption and stereotyped standardisation, and is conditioned by a complete lack of values. Bare-faced and disguised corruption is now the accepted rule of professional life, and the architect is forced into any number of compromises in order to satisfy his client, besides having to conform to rules established by public authorities. At such a time, Alberti's concept of architecture as a human science rooted in a Humanistic culture is not only relevant and edifying, it is the only way out for a world fast on its way to being caught between sub-culture and intellectual prostitution.

The "curial attitude" Alberti adopted before Machiavelli is neither academic nor rhetorical. Nor is his thought the expression of a snobbish cultural élite. On the contrary, it is an anchor of salvation in a rising tide of vulgarity, enabling the architect to practise his profession and at the same time fulfil his obligations to culture. Alberti can still help us to lay the foundations of a new architecture designed to satisfy human needs, based on Humanistic values yet shorn of all traces of classicism.

382. *Comparison between Leon Battista Alberti and G. Viola's Corinthian order, from Roland Fréart, "A Parallel ...", London 1664.*

383. *"L'Architettura", frontispiece of the version edited by G. Pessutti the mathematician and A. De Dominicis the architect, Rome 1784.*

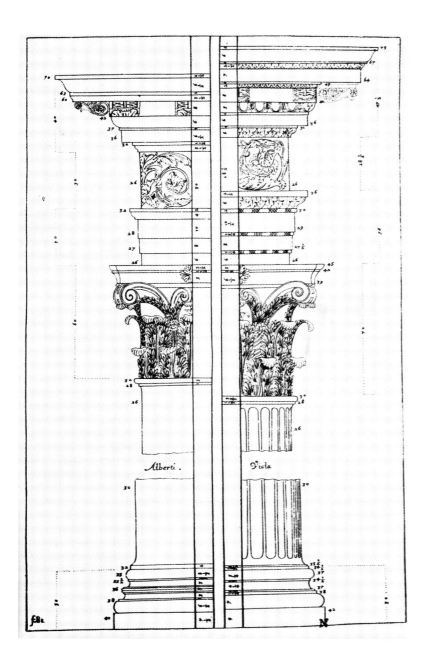

Alberti. *Viola.*

I DIECI LIBRI

DI ARCHITETTURA

D I

LEON BATTISTA ALBERTI

TRADOTTI IN ITALIANO

DA COSIMO BARTOLI

NUOVA EDIZIONE

DILIGENTEMENTE CORRETTA E CONFRONTATA
COLL'ORIGINALE LATINO,

ED ARRICCHITA DI NUOVI RAMI RICAVATI DALLE MISURE MEDESIME
ASSEGNATE DALL'AUTORE.

IN ROMA MDCCLXXXIV.

NELLA STAMPERIA DI GIOVANNI ZEMPEL PRESSO MONTE GIORDANO
CON LICENZA DE' SUPERIORI.

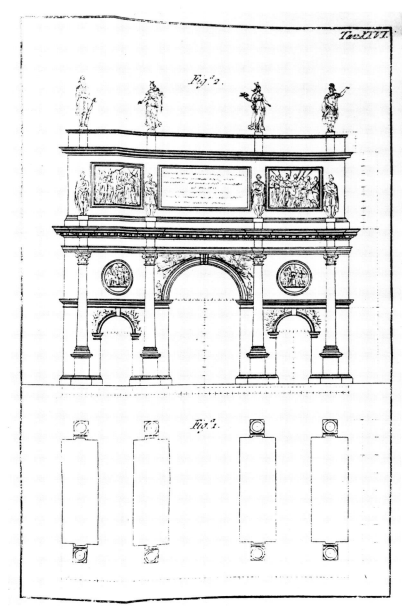

384. "*L'Architettura*", an early indication of neo-Classical taste in the Roman triumphal arch illustrated in plate *XXVI* of the 1784 edition.

385. "*Della Architettura libri dieci*", frontispiece of Stefano Ticozzi's edition, Milan 1833.

386. Portrait of Leon Battista Alberti in an engraving by Lanti, from Ticozzi's edition of the "*Della Architettura libri dieci*", Milan 1833.

DELLA
ARCHITETTURA
LIBRI DIECI
DI
LEON BATTISTA ALBERTI
TRADUZIONE
DI COSIMO BARTOLI
CON NOTE APOLOGETICHE
DI
STEFANO TICOZZI
E TRENTA TAVOLE IN RAME DISEGNATE ED INCISE
DA COSTANTINO GIANNI

MILANO
A SPESE DEGLI EDITORI
MDCCCXXXIII.

AN ANTHOLOGY OF ALBERTI SOURCES FROM THE HUMANIST TO THE NEO-CLASSICAL AGE
by Gabriele Morolli

This anthology follows the most obvious line of development in the history of Alberti criticism, that suggested by the documents themselves: Alberti and the esteem of his contemporaries; the veneration of his classical followers in the sixteenth century; the facile hagiography of the Baroque age; the adverse criticism of the Enlightenment; and Alberti's revaluation by the rationalist critics of the neo-classical period.

As one might imagine, no sensational discoveries have been made. No early stimulating interpretations of Alberti's art have been found; neither have any precocious, irreverent criticisms. Our work has been confined to the modest task of tracing as accurately as possible the changing concept of Alberti in the evaluations, judgements and simple references of artists and men of letters over a period of nearly four hundred years.

The first fact to emerge is that Leon Battista has continued to attract attention throughout this period, and has continued to exercise his fascination in spite of changes of taste and different cultural ideals. Alberti's cultural heritage (unlike that of many of his contemporaries) has survived almost intact, in spite of the most diverse interpretations given to it.

It is indeed astonishing how writers have striven in various ways—sometimes pedantically, at others with keen intelligence—to explain Alberti's multiform activities in every field of human knowledge. It is as though all who have come into contact with him have been fascinated by the systematic, ideological power that informs everything he did, and by his ability to theorize and synthesize the vaguest aspirations of his age and, more generally, the profound structures of every era.

ANONYMOUS, *Life of Leon Battista Alberti.*

The most striking feature of the following excerpts from the anonymous biography of Alberti is the author's evident pleasure in his task. This gives added weight to the theory (supported by many critics) that the work was most probably written by Alberti himself. In this case, there is the interesting possibility that Alberti himself was the first to create the myth of Alberti the "complete man", an idea greatly abused by later generations of scholars and men of letters. The "complete man" is shown as being acutely aware of the ideals of Renaissance Humanism. These range from the human to the tedious, from the spontaneous to the arrogant, from the lively to the bookish. Harmony, empiricism, *aurea mediocritas*, scientific curiosity, the love of literature, the cult of beauty, *mens sana in corpore sano*, the worship of the ancients, the love of glory, deep morality, and philosophical curiosity are some of the ideals the biographer pursues in his ordered universe. They create a picture of man that was destined to take its place among the ideal concepts of human behaviour that have been developed in the course of history.

"From early youth he was instructed in all that was most fitting for a noble, liberal education, so that he certainly could not be considered the least among the most prominent young men of his age ... he practised riding, jousting, and music, and he was passionately fond of literature and the fine arts. There was nothing too mean or too difficult he did not desire to master. His studies and reflections were all praiseworthy. He worked extremely hard at sculpture and painting, not to mention the rest, and neglected nothing in his effort to win the esteem of the best. His talent was of the highest order, and he may be said to have mastered all the arts. He was never idle or lazy, and once he started something he always went through with it. He often said that he found literature free from the cloying quality that is held to be common to all human things. He loved literature so much that sometimes it gave him the same pleasure as the buds of sweetly smelling flowers, and then neither hunger nor sleep could make him leave his books. But so late did he stay up sometimes that his books assumed the aspect of piles of scorpions, so that he could see nothing, let alone his books. Whenever he was reduced to this state, he sought relief in music, painting, and physical exercise. He used to play ball-games and darts, and he ran, wrestled, and danced. Above all, he practised mountaineering, but more to strengthen his body than for relaxation or pleasure. He distinguished himself in military exercises when still a boy, and could jump the height of a man from a standing position; no one could beat him at high-jumping. He could throw a javelin with such power that it would pierce the thickest of iron breast-plates. With his left foot touching the cathedral wall, he could throw an apple right over the roof-tops. Once he threw a little silver coin up against the roof of a high church with such power that his companions heard it strike the vault. He could ride for hours without showing the slightest trace of fatigue, with one end of a rod touching his foot and the other in his hand, without the slightest movement on the part of the rod. He was such a fine horseman

that even the proudest, most mettlesome horses seemed to fear and tremble when he mounted them. He was a self-taught musician and his compositions were highly esteemed by the music-masters. All his life he was given to singing, but he did this when alone or in private, especially at home with his brother and relatives. He loved to play the organ and was reputed one of the best organ-players. Indeed, his advice helped many others to become more proficient in music."

It is perhaps unnecessary to stress that this detailed description of all the most desirable attributes of the typical Humanist is not just a eulogy of Alberti, but a kind of manifesto of early Renaissance ideals. It is quite probable that Leon Battista, with his profound awareness of the new social and cultural tendencies of his age, was not simply concerned with exalting himself in his autobiography, but with immortalizing and codifying an extremely complex ideal of behaviour.

"He considered all those who were famous for their studies as brothers, and willingly shared his knowledge with them. He gave every artist copies of his great, worthy treatises, and when a learned scholar came to town he was quick to make friends with him. He would acquire knowledge from all sorts of people like smiths, architects, painters, and even cobblers. He would try to find out if there were any unusual secrets in their trade, for he was most anxious to know everything. He was always ready to share his knowledge with others who were eager to learn, and he would tell them anything they wanted to know. He often pretended to be ignorant in order to discover the talent and ability of others". No better example could be found of the fervid love of knowledge and the constant desire to bring it into line with the practical things of everyday life that characterised the scientific and artistic research of the finest Humanists.

"He used to summon the friends he was accustomed to discussing literary matters with, and while dictating pamphlets to them, he would make sketches or make wax models of them. He suffered pain and the extremes of heat and cold with great patience. Once, when not yet fifteen years old, he was wounded in the foot and did not so much as flinch when the surgeon stitched the wound. On the contrary, he helped the surgeon, and in spite of a high temperature, dressed the wound himself. Another time, when a fierce attack of lumbago caused him to come out in a cold sweat, he summoned some musicians and forced himself to overcome the pain with a couple of hours of singing. His head was by nature sensitive to the slightest breeze, but little by little he overcame this handicap during the summer months, after which he always rode bareheaded through fog and wind. Through some quirk of nature he was allergic to garlic and especially to honey so that the mere sight of either would make him feel sick. But he overcame this repugnance by forcing himself to look at and touch these things, so that they ceased to have any effect on him in the end. Thus he proved the truth of the saying, 'where there's a will there's a way'". He could not have been more scrupulous, sincere, naively enthusiastic, even touchingly faithful in his application of the great principles of classical antiquity, *ne quid nimis* and

mens sana in corpore sano.

"When he sought relief by walking out-of-doors, he would spend his time watching the artisans at work in their workshops. But as if rebuked by some stern judge, he would often go straight back home saying, 'But we too are workmen in the exercise of our profession'. Seeing the sown fields flower in springtime and all the trees and plants rich with the promise of fruit, he would be seized by melancholy and rebuke himself thus: 'You too, Battista, must give man the fruit of your studies'. And when he saw the fields ripe for harvesting and the trees laden with fruit in autumn, he would become so downcast that some even saw him weep and heard him exclaim: 'There you are, Leon, everything bears witness to and accuses your sloth. What do you do in a year that is of use to mankind? Tell me, what have you done to show you have fulfilled your purpose?' He took extraordinary delight in looking at things in which there was some beauty or ornament. Once he saw a venerable old man full of health and vigour, and he couldn't take his eyes off him. He used to say he worshipped the beauties of nature, and that quadrupeds, birds, and other resplendent animals should be loved, for all that nature granted in her bounty was beautiful. When his own beautiful dog died he wrote a panegyric for it. He looked upon every skilled or beautiful product of man's invention as divine, and so highly did he esteem anything expressed with a certain grace that he could even find something to praise in a poor writer. When ill, the mere sight of jewels, flowers, or some pleasant natural scene would often cure him."

Two things clearly emerge from this excerpt. Firstly, the Renaissance conviction that there was a perfect correspondence and harmony between the microcosm of man and the macrocosm of the universe. Secondly, the detail that is concentrated in the description of episodes and states of mind. It is this that leads one to doubt whether anyone but Leon Battista himself could have written with such abundance of detail, while at the same time retaining the touching Humanistic feeling for the interpenetration of the human and natural worlds. The passage also expresses a broad, optimistic faith in the creative possibilities of the individual, as well as a spontaneous, boundless worship of beauty conceived as a harmony of intelligence and grace — which must have been one of the qualities Alberti cherished most.

(Anonimo, *Vita di Leon Battista Alberti.* In A. Bonucci, *Opere volgari di Leon Battista Alberti,* Florence 1843, I, p. LXXXIX ff.).

GASPARINO BARZIZZA, *Letter to Lorenzo degli Alberti,* 1415.

"Last night our Battista came to me in tears, for he had learnt from our kinsman Leonardo that the plague had killed off your bailiff in four hours and that you risk catching the illness yourself. Your are not acting at all prudently and are driving your children to despair. Think less about your business matters and more of your survival. Flee the danger and put the minds of your family at rest, for they have every reason to be so worried. Avoid the wreck, for the health of your children, wife, and friends depends on the same vessel. Get into a boat at once and come here. Accept my humble, but very warm hospitality. I have many books here to keep your mind off serious matters. Think of your children's peace of mind, not about any possible financial loss".

Barzizza had founded a college in Padua. This provided roughly the same kind of education as a *ginnasio* (first years of a secondary modern school), according to the principles of educationists like Guarino Veronese and Vittorino da Feltre. It propagated the early Humanism that was to have so considerable an influence on Alberti's professional and artistic development. Lionello d'Este, Sigismondo Malatesta, and Lodovico Gonzaga were all products of the same rich cultural background.

It should be remembered that Francesco Barbaro, Antonio Beccadelli (better known as Panormita), and Francesco Filelfo were all school-companions of Leon Battista, and were all to have important roles in the development of Italian Humanism in the Quattrocento.

(Gasparino Barzizza, *Lettera a Lorenzo degli Alberti "uomo insigne ed amico primario"*. In G. Mancini, *Vita di Leon Battista Alberti*, Florence 1911, 2nd. ed., p. 42).

PANORMITA, *Poem from Hermaphroditus*, 1425.
Alberti's old schoolfriend sent him some light verse, a very popular literary pastime in those days. "You are pleasant company, very handsome, witty, wholly dedicated to the liberal arts, born of the true blood of the Albertis, incomparable in the nobility of your manners. You are liked for your rare talents, and I like you for your genuine simplicity. You are a true and honest friend. Tell me how you get on with women …" The serious, sober Leon Battista did not reply to these lines; they may be more biting than they appear. In any case, the invitation they imply was far removed from the *gravitas* that had already been chosen by the young scholar as the ruling principle of his life. The importance of the poem, however, is that it shows Alberti as a promising Humanist who has already found a place in the best new intellectual circles. Panormita acquired a certain prestige by writing to him.

(Antonio Beccadelli, called Panormita, *Ermaphroditus*, ed. Forberg, Coburg 1824, I, Poem 19, p. 64).

CATASTO DEL LION NERO, 1430.
"Messers Battista and Carlo, sons of the late Lorenzo degli Alberti were debtors of the Venetian company known as Benedetto. The debts were for books, school fees, clothing, and other expenses incurred after the decease of their father. And since I had to see to everything and purchase everything out of my own pocket, I have twice withdrawn money from the savings in Bruges. The outcome is that I have lost far more in these dealings than I have gained".

This declaration was made to the taxation authorities by Antonio Alberti, Leon Battista's cousin, the son of Ricciardo, who was a brother of Lorenzo, Leon Battista's father. The declaration reveals an attempt to trick Lorenzo's two sons and deprive them of their inheritance of 4,000 florins each.

It is ironic that Alberti's idealism, which was so nobly (perhaps polemically, even desperately) expressed in his many works on the family and good administration, should have had to encounter such difficulties and selfishness in real life.

(Catasto del Lion Nero. In G. Mancini, *Vita di Leon Battista Alberti*, Florence 1911, 2nd ed., p. 53).

THE FLORENTINE CHANCELLERY, *Letter of recommendation to the Chancellery of Pope Eugenius IV*, 1433.
"There is a highly educated, most promising young man called Battista degli Alberti employed in the papal Curia. We are sure that his excellence is not unknown to you and that you are aware he comes from a very noble, important family". The letter goes on to recommend Leon Battista in his career in the papal Curia, where he was apostolic abbreviator and secretary. It is interesting to note how everyone mentions his "promise". This testifies to his seriousness and talent and is rather touching if one considers how this promise was to reveal itself as the basis of a truly universal genius.

(Florentine Chancellery, *Lettera di Raccomandazione inviata dal Comune di Firenze al Cardinale Francesco Condulmier nipote di Eugenio IV*, 5 December 1433. In G. Mancini, *Vita …*, Florence 1911).

POGGIO BRACCIOLINI, *Letter of Accompaniment to the "Philodoxeos"*, 1436.
"Baptista de Albertis vir singularis ingenii mihique amicissimus, scripsit fabulam quandam, quam philodoxeos appellat, summa elegantia ac venustate … Nam certo scias velim, Baptistam nostrum tam esse erga te affectum benevolentia, quanta esse potest, maxima, cui si respondebis in amoris officio, incitabis alios ad te ornandum litteris, atque excolendum. Hoc nequaquam existimes parum conferre ad gloriam consequendam. Solae enim litterae reddunt hominem apud posteros immortalem." Bologna, 12 October. Here, Leon Battista is included among the other Humanists who brought fame to their patrons. The passage also reflects the close relationship between Alberti and contemporary culture.

(Poggio Bracciolini, *Lettera di accompagnamento al Philodoxeos dedicato da Leon Battista Alberti a Leonello d'Este, datata* 12 ottobre 1436. In A. Bonucci, *Opere volgari di Leon Battista Alberti* Florence 1843, I, p. CXX).

LAPO DA CASTIGLIONCHIO, *Letter dedicating Lucian's "Sacrifices" to Alberti*, before 1438.
This disciple of Filelfo recalls the years in which he and Battista, students of the Bologna "Studium", attended Greek lessons together to perfect their knowledge of the language that had become so fashionable after the studies of the first Humanists. Lapo says he "started Greek to please you because you repeatedly recommended it, and also to take my mind off the troubles oppressing me. There was no greater solace for us, and no one had more influence over me than you. I made progress in those most liberal and complicated studies thanks not only to your friendship and help but to your stimulating example and encouragement".

This already hints at the firm, strong character Alberti is said to have shown from his youth. Lapo then praises his friend further, which is all the more touching if one thinks that he died a few years later, in 1438: "From very childhood you were endowed with so promising a spirit and talent that no one had the slightest doubt you would become the man you are now. Teachers often have difficulty in getting children to stop their childish play. But you despised such games and, leaving them of your own accord, went on with your studies without anyone urging you to do so. This served you in good stead, for you far surpassed your fellow students in knowledge and could already hold your own with the most learned men. I am sure that you possess this vigorous spirit, this talent denied to most men by the direct will of God. Continue in your efforts then, and strive to justify and surpass the hopes everyone has of you".

These are the sincere, moving wishes of a dear school-friend.

(Lapo da Castiglionchio, *Lettera dedicatoria dei "Sacrifizi" di Luciano all'Alberti*. In: G. Mancini, *Vita …*, Florence 1911).

GIROLAMO ALIOTTI, *Letter to Leon Battista Alberti*, 1439.
When the learned Humanist Ambrogio Traversari died, his disciple Fra Girolamo Aliotti asked Carlo Marsuppini to write his biography. Marsuppini declined, so Aliotti asked Alberti, who was also unable to undertake the task. In his letter to Leon Battista, Aliotti addresses him as the "most learned, eloquent, naturally talented and generous [of men], a credit to Florence and Italy, whose wonderful, divine, omnipotent talent is considered by many worthy of praise and admiration".

(Girolamo Aliotti: *Epistola a L. B. Alberti*, in *Epistolario*, I, Letter 32. See G. Mancini, op. cit.).

MICHELE DI NOFERI DEL GIGANTE, *Verses on Friendship*, 1441.
This was one of the poems written for the *Certame Coronario*, the competition Leon Battista organized in Florence to encourage the use of the vernacular:

"Oh high and glorious enterprise.
Oh supreme spirit, Oh noble talent
Overflowing with ardent charity,
The pillar and buttress of this work.
Oh creative mind moving to defend
In divers styles and ways
Our honourable native tongue,
May your sincere purposes be blessed.
    These purposes, willed by your worthy genius,
Which is greater, more lofty, noble, and rare,
Than any other in this age of ours,
And your judgement is more refined
Than gold purified by the flames of fire,
Have brought us here together
For the praise and commendation of the vernacular.
    It is a singularly well-woven vernacular,
Taut and full of true loveliness,
With worthy sonorous verses full
Of sublime art, as poetry itself decrees.
It is both solid and luxuriant

And whoever hears it
Listens in wrapt contentment,
To so sweet a style.
    It was your noble intention,
In carrying out this enterprise,
To bear all the expense yourself,
Rewarding with three prizes
Them who proved the best
(Or so it was hoped),
When anon appeared a gentle spirit,
Burning with love and high virtue.
    Hearing of such a man so ardently
Pursuing the achievement of his high aim,
And since true virtue blossoms
In the understanding mind, he spoke:
'Oh, worthiest of men, I pray thee, cross not the
                                            [threshold
Lest I be by your side.
In the pursuit of your magnanimous purpose,
Let all the expense be mine'.
    'I know not when in all my life
I heard aught worthier or more gracious',
Answered the noble man, whose honoured name
And noble descendancy you must have guessed
(Nor might I pass it o'er in silence,
For it was he who brought about this gentle day),
That is, Messer Battista degli Alberti
To Piero di Cosimo for his high merits.
    And thus Piero spoke: 'Long have
Your virtue and magnificence been known to me,
Though now I see you so fervent and devout,
And may God be witness that I speak the truth.
But I do not wish to break my oath
Made for the glory of our beloved Florence'.
Thus, they joined together in agreement.
Now I shall relate what faithful memory recalls".
Michele then goes on to develop the theme of
friendship, concluding with the wish that the
victor's silver crown be presented to Alberti him-
self, who had thought of the competition:
    "Willingly would I see the brow
Of so excellent a man crowned
With the glorious gift, and hear the echo of his fame
Resound throughout Europe,
So eminent a man of letters is he.
And though I go on like this, please bear with me,
I so yearn to see him leave the cathedral
Accompanied by all the other venerable poets,
Each with a pretty garland on his head,
Their precious little ones of laurel and of myrtle
Enhancing his. And for greater festivity
The air should thunder with the noise,
While he, attended by those worthy, honest men,
Should make his way towards his throne.
Thus his reward would be more sublime
And so I come to the end of my rhyme".
Leon Battista is already thought of as a universal
genius in the poem. No distinction of any kind
is made between the Humanist and the Lord of
Florence, Piero di Cosimo. The poem ends with
the proposal of a real Renaissance "triumph", a
procession of both Humanistic and heraldic emblematic figures. Indeed, the poem celebrates Alberti's
apotheosis, and is a clear indication of the considerable fame he already enjoyed. Its excessive
praise of Alberti may even have resulted in its
exclusion from the competition, for it may have
been feared that the papal court, which was present
together with ambassadors and eminent men from

all over Italy and Europe, would be offended by it.
(Michele di Noferi del Gigante, *Trattato sotto brevità
in 25 stanze, che parla d'amicizia, recitato in Santa
Maria del Fiore di Firenze, addì XXII d'Ottobre
negli anni domini MCCCCXLI.* In A. Bonucci,
Opere Volgari di L. B. Alberti, Florence 1843,
I, pp. CLXVIII ff.).

LEONARDO BRUNI, *Letter to Leon Battista Alberti*,
1442.
Alberti was offended by an ambiguous comment
of Leonardo Bruni's on one of his literary compositions, which had been given to the Aretine
Humanist by a mutual friend, Leonardo Dati.
When Bruni heard of the misunderstanding, he
was quick to avoid any risk of a literary quarrel
with Alberti, showing that he both esteemed Leon
Battista as a man and feared him as a possible
opponent in a scholarly dispute.
"I want to explain my ingenuousness and innocence,
for when you stopped me recently in the church
of Santa Croce and spoke to me about Carlo's
answer, I did not realize you were imputing something to me. I said nothing on that occasion,
for it did not cross my mind that you might be
asking me for an explanation, and I limited myself
to advising you to avoid the ignoble squabbles
of literary men. I then learnt from Jacopo, a
worthy young man whom you had spoken to,
that my answer had led you to think I had written
about envy and stupidity to Leonardo Dati, a
worthy man and a friend of mine, urged to do
so by Carlo. If you have conceived this suspicion,
I beg you to dismiss it. I was neither asked, persuaded, nor agreed with anyone to write. When
I wrote, I did so spontaneously, without malice,
discussing the relative evils of avarice and pro-
digality as one usually does. Really, I am not so
irresponsible as to try to harm anyone merely to
satisfy another's whim or desire, and certainly not
a well wisher or friend, such as I consider you
to be. Therefore, you have no reason to harbour
such thoughts against me. Perhaps Carlo answered
after discovering what had been written, but he
certainly did not talk to me about it. Farewell".
(Leonardo Bruni, *Epistolario*, IX, Letter 10. See
G. Mancini, *Vita ...*, Florence 1911, p. 208).

LEONARDO DATI, *Letter about the "Della Famiglia"*,
1443.
After writing the four books of the *Famiglia*,
Leon Battista entrusted the manuscript to his
Humanist friend Leonardo Dati and another young
scholar, Tommaso Ceffi, so that they could look
over it and make any necessary changes. The tone
of their answer, the thoroughness of their revision,
the frankness with which they point out certain
defects in the work, and the deep respect the
two scholars show for its author all reflect Alberti's seriousness of purpose. They also show
that Alberti's works were known in the best
Humanist circles in Italy.
"We gave you word, and even if we hadn't, we
would still have revised your book as you have
asked us to do in your most recent letters. We
are now examining it carefully and diligently, so
that, to the best of our ability, it will go off to

Sicily revised and corrected. The copyist has made
many mistakes, and we are correcting them all.
If we may speak frankly, you have made two
errors, unless we are mistaken. The style is too
lofty and there is a roughness about it which
accords ill with the the Florentine tongue and
which the general reader may disapprove of; this
is particularly evident in the beginning. However,
we have put up with it because it becomes so
much more graceful and pleasing to the ear later on.
Your second mistake, which we consider more
serious, is that you have quoted the examples
and opinions of other authors without mentioning
their names, almost as if you had not read their
works or were inventing the quotations and leaving
a blank. Now you could have followed the example
of Cicero, who, when he talks about things he
only vaguely remembers, omits names in such a
way that it does not seem negligence or forget-
fulness but unwillingness to repeat things that are
so well-known that they would bore the reader.
We are telling you this so that you may judge
how right you were to entrust the protection of
your good name and dignity to our affection and
diligence. Let us know at once by letter what we
must do with the second half, whether leave things
as they are or alter them in some way. Meanwhile
the other things will be corrected and we will
send you the book after receiving your letters".
(Leonardo Dati, *Epistola sul "Della Famiglia"*. In
G. Mancini, op. cit., p. 231).

FLAVIO BIONDO, *Italia Illustrata*, 1450.
This Humanist was in love with the grandeur of
Rome and wrote two books on the subject: *Roma
Instaurata* and *Roma Triumphans*. In doing this,
he was trying to meet the same need that led
Alberti to write the *Descriptio Urbis Romae* in the
same period. His aim was to clarify the shape
and external aspect of the Rome that was inhabited
by his admired ancients. Biondo and Alberti must
have known and respected each other in spite
of their different methods and outlooks. Leon
Battista presents us with a lucid, balanced, and
scientifically thorough analysis; Biondo provides
us with an enormous amount of material, which
is often confused, not very well selected, and
inspired more by the romantic suggestiveness of
Rome's ruins than by any desire to give a systematic account of them.
Italia illustrata is a kind of guide book to Italy,
in which Biondo talks about the historical, geogra-
phical, literary and artistic characteristics of the
various regions and towns he visited. In discussing
Florence, he praises the city's most famous citizens
and mentions Leon Battista before Donatello but
after Girolamo Manetti. Of Alberti he says: "Baptista Albertus nobili ad multas artes bonas versa-
tili ingenio patriam exornat". There is already a
hint of Alberti's great reputation for universal
knowledge in this remark, and the idea was to
become a constant feature of all later Alberti
criticism.
(Flavio Biondo, *Italia Illustrata*, ed. cons., Brescia
1482, carta 66 verso).

BARTOLOMEO FACIO, *De Viris Illustribus*, 1456.
Facio wrote this work in the last years of his life.

It is a collection of lives of famous men, whom he divides into various groups: poets, soldiers, painters, orators, sculptors etc. Leon Battista is included (significantly enough) among the *oratores* or *letterati*. The reason for this is that at the time the *De viris illustribus* was written, Alberti had not yet produced anything to show his talents as an architect to their best advantage and had a greater reputation as a Humanist among his contemporaries. In fact, his name figures among those of Niccolò Niccoli, Leonardo Giustinian, Vittorino da Feltre and others: "Not only was Leon Battista Alberti an orator, but he seemed born to excel in all the liberal arts. He was an expert mathematician, besides being an orator and philosopher. He had an expert's knowledge and love of painting, and he wrote a book on the principles of this art. He also wrote two books on architecture which he called *Intercenali* [sic]. However, he should be considered more of a philosopher than an orator".

Facio makes a subtle but significant distinction between *orator* and *philosophus*, including Alberti in the nobler category of those who exercised their intelligence out of the pure love of knowledge; the *oratores* utilized knowledge for certain ends, which were always contingent and mechanically *volgari* however noble.

(Bartolomeo Facio, *De Viris Illustribus*, ed. cons., Florence 1745, p. 13).

GIROLAMO ALIOTTI, *Letter to Nicolò Corbizi*, c. 1460. The learned Aretine monk, Girolamo Aliotti, possessed a small treatise on the art of bronze-casting written in the vernacular by an anonymous Florentine. He wrote to Nicolò Corbizi, asking him whether the author might not be Alberti himself: "... whoever he is, he is extremely learned, and it is clear there is nothing he doesn't know. Find out whether he is Messer Battista Alberti by any chance".

This shows that the myth of Alberti's universal knowledge, infallibility, and versatility was already widespread during his lifetime.

(Girolamo Aliotti, *Lettera a Niccolò Corbizi*. In G. Mancini, op. cit., p. 133).

LODOVICO GONZAGA, *Letter to Leon Battista Alberti*, 1461. This is the Marquis's reply to Leon Battista, who had asked him to take his brother Carlo into his service: "... Susceptis litteris vestris quibus nobis Carolum fratrem vestrum commendatis ut sibi apud nos locus pateat breviter respondemus non parum nobis molestum esse votis vestris prout optaremus non posse satisfacere quod libenti animo fecissemus si nobis adesset facultas: verum impresentiarum tantae nobis expensae extraordinariae et familiae nostrae et gentium armigerarum incumbunt, ut non facile quos nunc habemus retinere possimus. Qua re vos rogamus ut nos excusatos suscipiatis. Cum autem res nostras direxerimus quidquid pro vobis et germano vestro facere poterimus libenti animo faciemus ad alia quaeque vobis gratia parati". The refusal is courteous, respectful, and solemn, and it shows the writer trying not to hurt the feelings of a person he

thinks very highly of and upon whom he lavishes expressions of esteem and regard.

(Ludovico Gonzaga, *Lettera del* 12 *febbraio* 1461 *da Mantova*. In W. Braghirolli, *Arch. Stor. Ital.*, Florence 1869, 3rd. Series, IX, Pt. I, p. 20).

FILARETE, *Trattato sull'Architettura*, 1464. Filarete mentions Alberti in the introduction to his treatise and expresses full, unconditional acknowledgement of his superiority. Antonio Averlino wrote for a different public than Alberti. He was a practical man who felt more at home on the actual building-site and he openly confesses his humbler professional status. Nevertheless, he points out that his work has its own precise function and is equally important. Filarete was well aware of the importance of his vernacular writings and practical activity in spreading the 'new architecture' among the "not so learned". For the latter, quantitively speaking, had far more influence than the small Humanist élite for whom Alberti wrote the *De re aedificatoria*.

"Hearing these arguments, I stepped forward, for they were connected with my profession and there was no one else present who knew anything about the subject. And I said: 'It may seem presumptuous of me to want to tell you about such methods and measurements, considering that great men have written some very fine books on the subject, both in ancient and modern times. Vitruvius, who wrote a noble treatise, was one of these. Another is Battista Alberti, who, for our times, is a very learned man in different fields and very skilled in this [architecture], particularly in design, which is the foundation and way of all art. He understands it very well and is very expert in geometry and other sciences. He has also written an excellent work in Latin. For this reason, therefore, and because I have no great experience in expressing myself, I have given more attention to other matters. And this is why my desire to write about the ways and measurements of building will immediately look like temerity and presumption. But I write in the vernacular, and I have found pleasure in designing, carving and building. I have also enquired into other things too, which I shall mention when the time comes. This is why I have taken courage, for I still believe my work will please the not so learned, whereas those who know more and are more skilled in letters will read the above-mentioned authors".

Alberti is quoted many times in the course of the treatise, which demonstrates the undisputed authority the *De re aedificatoria* already enjoyed only a few years after its publication. In talking about the basic principles of design, Filarete urges those who want "to understand them in greater detail" to go "to the mathematicians and to read Battista Alberti's books on painting".

In discussing the basic principles of geometry and draughtsmanship, he refers back to "the ancient mathematicians, and once more to my Battista Alberti, who has dealt briefly with the point, lines, surfaces, and bodies. Therefore, I shall not deal with the subject like the ancients or the above-mentioned Alberti, but shall merely follow what they say".

Thus, Alberti had already been accorded a place

amongst the "ancients", that is, in the world of definite, indisputable truths.

(Antonio Averlino, called Filarete, *Trattato sull'Architettura*, ed. cons., J. Spencer, facsimile, II, Yale 1965).

LODOVICO GONZAGA, *Letter of recommendation for Leon Battista Alberti*, 1465. Paul II had succeeded to the throne of St. Peter and difficult times had begun for all the intellectuals who moved within the circles of the Curia. Alberti's powerful friend interceded on his behalf: "Sanctissime Pater ac beatissime D.ne mi singularissime post pedum oscula beatorum ac mei humilem ac devotam commendationem. Venerabilis ac spectantissimus d. Baptista de Albertis, qui maxima mecum superiori tempore usus est familiaritate sepiusque apud me fuit et mihi eius opera et servitium nunquam defuit ita ut me illi obstrictum profitear cupiens impresentiarum gratiam et favorem a S.te V.ra impetrare me litteris suis plurimum rogavit ut ipsi B.ae V.rae commendatum faciam, existimans preces meas apud eandem pro sua in me clementia et benignitate non parum profuturas. Ipse igitur quod illum propter sua in me obsequia carissimum habeo et sibi pro virili mea satisfacere cupio be. Vestram ea que par est reverentia deprecor ut eundem d. Baptistam mea etiam causa commendatum suscipere dignetur quicquid eius in illum favoris et gratiae mea intercessione collatum fuerit mihi ipsi in singulare munus ascribam ab eadem S.te V.ra cuius pedibus iterum atque iterum commendo".

The Marquis could not have shown greater benevolence or generosity towards Alberti.

(Lodovico Gonzaga, *Commendatizia per il Pontefice Paolo II del* 1 *gennaio* 1465. In W. Branghirolli, op. cit., p. 12).

LODOVICO GONZAGA, *Letter of recommendation for Leon Battista Alberti*, 1465. The letter refers to the same subject as the previous one. This time, however, it is not written to the supreme pontiff but to Lodovico's son in Rome, Cardinal Francesco. The tone is less solemn, but the profound admiration Lodovico obviously nourished for Alberti is just as apparent: "We are sure you are aware of how much Messer Battista has done for us in the past, in providing the plans and supervising the construction of our S. Sebastiano, for which we are obliged to him. Now he has written to us, begging us to be so kind as to recommend him to His Holiness and to you in his present situation. We have been only too happy to help him in every way possible, and so we have written, recommending him to His Holiness. Now it is our concern that you too, out of the respect you bear us, take it upon yourself to recommend him, and that you do everything in your power to help him, doing which, you will give us singular pleasure".

(Lodovico Gonzaga, *Lettera di raccomandazione per il Cardinale Francesco Gonzaga del* 5 *gennaio* 1465. In W. Braghirolli, op. cit., pp. 12-13).

CARLO ALBERTI, *Letter to Lorenzo Vettori*, c. 1470. "Carlo Alberti to His Lordship, Lorenzo Vettori.

Some time ago, you asked me more than once for this book, the "De profugiis aerumnarum", which we had lost (courtesy prevents me from saying how). But you know what my brother Messer Battista is like. He is quite incapable of saying no to anyone who asks him for a favour. One of his servants asked him for the book immediately after he had finished it, almost thirty years ago now, and was given the first original copy. Afterwards he pretended he did not have it, so that we were at a loss how to get it back. Now we have it again. I am glad for your sake and am sending it to you. Messer Battista wrote this work with all the enthusiasm of his youth, provoked by the malice of some of his treacherous rivals ...".

Carlo's simple, sincere words create the image of a warmer, much more human Alberti than that which usually emerges from official documents.
(Carlo Alberti, *Lettera a Lorenzo Vettori cui manda a leggere i tre libri della Tranquillità dell'animo*. In A. Bonucci, *Opere volgari di L. B. Alberti*, Florence 1843, p. 5 ff.).

BERNARDO RUCELLAI, *De Urbe Roma*, 1471 (1496).
On 23 September 1471 Bernardo Rucellai, together with other Florentine 'orators', including Donato Acciaioli, accompanied Lorenzo de' Medici to Rome. The purpose of Lorenzo's visit was to congratulate Sixtus IV on his recent election to the Papacy. The distinguished party seized the opportunity to visit the ruins of the ancient capital of the Empire, Leon Battista Alberti acting as their guide. Bernardo's idea of writing a book on the ruins of Rome clearly dates from 1471, though it was not until about 1496, after he had withdrawn from the frenzy of political life, that Bernardo was able to dedicate himself to his "honestum otium" and actually start writing the work. The Florentine nobleman's description of the city is similar to those in the works of Publio Vittore and Sesto Rufo. It was originally intended as an introduction to a vast historical, political study of Roman civilisation, which was never written. In spite of its brevity, the work won the unanimous approval of all contemporary scholars of antiquity, for it broke through the narrow limits of specialised classical studies. Indeed, it covers various fields of Humanistic enquiry, from Latin and Greek literature to numismatics, archaeological research, the method of drawing explanatory sketches, epigraphy, and antique jewellery. It adopts the most up-to-date contemporary methods of measurement, and reveals a thorough understanding of history.

Alberti, who is the tutelary deity of this vast, complex, archaeological-antiquarian autopsy, must have represented a precedent of exceptional importance for Bernardo, since he was the very embodiment of everything the scholarly Humanists aspired to. In fact, whenever Bernardo Rucellai mentions Alberti he does so with the utmost respect: "Nam lateritia ipsa, [Roma] turribus frequens aliisque id genus munimentis, nullum, praeter magnitudinis, decorem retinet aliis alio more, ut tum res erant, Principibus imperantibus; siquidem Baptista Albertus se in vetustis moenibus pavimentata opera, crustisque perornatos parietes vi-

disse adfirmet, vir sane architecturae peritissimus, ut eius scripta indicant, et qui in prosequendis antiquitatum monumentis huius aevi omnes facile superaverit". (p. 443). This contains an explicit reference to Alberti's descriptions of ancient monuments in the *De re aedificatoria* (VII, 2), and attests to his tireless activity in the exploration of Rome's subsoil. Alberti's profound knowledge of ancient Rome emerges when he is mentioned as having guided the party to the ruins of the Antonine Baths in person: "Ceterum quod substructionum cadavera, duce Baptista Alberto, olim invisimus, eas quoad per vetustatem liquit suis lineamentis describendas curavimus". (p. 444). There is an even more explicit reference to inspections carried out by Bernardo and other Florentines under the guidance of Alberti: "Nam olim Romae, quum ego atque Donatus Acciaiolus et Laurentius Medices, duce Baptista Alberto, prisca monumenta inviseremus, factum est ut in marmoreis elogiis titulisque concertatio oriretur, aliis aliter sentientibus, ut in pervetustis fere inscriptionibus, ambustisque evenit". (p. 445). Particularly touching is the picture he portrays of the party standing among the ruins of Rome discussing the meanings of certain ancient Latin inscriptions.

Rucellai mentions the description of the Tarquinian wall in the *De re aedificatoria* (IV, 4): "Quin etiam perdurasse huiusque aggeris [Tarquinii] vestigia usque ad Baptistae Alberti aetatem ex illius de Architectura Commentariis conligitur, siquidem dicat a Vitruvio praeceptum quod ipse Baptistae passim, in Tarquinii praesertim aggere, observaverat, ut anterides substituerentur". (p. 447).

Another interesting citation is that relative to Alberti's attempt to draw up a scientific planimetry of ancient Rome in the *De Urbis Romae*, which Bernardo was obviously familiar with: "Verum de situ ipso moenium ac mensura Urbis Baptista Albertus scite admodum disseruit, ut qui eam machinis mathematicis summo studio prosequutus, sit; vir, ut diximus, prae ceteris huius aevi antiquitatis amator, architecturaque peritissimus". (p. 455). There is a final quotation from the *De re aedificatoria* (VIII, 6): "De Ponte [Aurelio] iuvat referre quod Baptista Albertus in libro de Architectura scribit, ponti omnium praestantissimo stetisse tectum suffultum columnis quadraginta duabus marmoreis opere trabeato, tectura aenea, ornatu mirifico". (p. 456).
(Bernardo Rucellai, *De Urbe Roma*, c, 1496; ed. by Roberto Valentini and Giuseppe Zucchetti, *Codice topografico della città di Roma*, Rome 1953, IV, p. 440 ff.).

PIETRO DEL TOVAGLIA, *Letter to Lodovico Gonzaga*, 1471.
The plan under discussion is the circular choir of the Annunziata: "Messer Battista continues to say that it will be the most beautiful construction ever built, and that the others can't understand it because they are not used to seeing such things, but that when they see it built, they will say that it is much more beautiful than a cruciform plan". Alberti's words, though reported indirectly by Del Tovaglia, convey all the pride, scorn, and self-assuredness of the Humanist scholar in expressing what he knows to be true. For though his

truths may be misunderstood or even doubted by the common people, they shine with the superior light of philosophical learning.
(Pietro del Tovaglia, *Lettera a Lodovico Gonzaga da Firenze del 27 aprile* 1471. In W. Braghirolli, op. cit., p. 17).

LODOVICO GONZAGA, *Letter to Luca Fancelli*, 1472.
"We have read about what has happened to your wife and the reasons for you going to Mantua in your letter, and we are very sorry. But since our agent tells us that the main reason for your visit is the weakness of the foundations of S. Andrea, for the love of God, take great care and see that the foundations are sound, since one must give much thought and importance to such matters. Thus, measure them three or four times before building them, and take care for the love of God".

Alberti's ghost seems to have watched over the construction, making sure that the proportions of his "harmony" were observed. Evidently the cult of proportion took hold of Lodovico Gonzaga too, who though far from being an intellectual, urged Fancelli to measure the foundations two or three times so that Alberti's precision would be respected.
(Lodovico Gonzaga, *Lettera a Luca Fancelli da Gonzaga del* 22 *luglio* 1472. In W. Braghirolli, op. cit., p. 18).

LUCA FANCELLI, *Letter to Lodovico Gonzaga*, 1472.
"Illustrious Prince and Most Honoured Lord. I am delighted with the design you have sent me, first because it helps me to understand the work, and secondly, because ambassadors and noblemen often pass by, and we have to pay our respects by showing them some fine work. Now I can show them this wonderful design, the like of which does not exist in my opinion, for which I thank Your Lordship". This was a "proportioned" design of S. Andrea which Alberti had made himself. Luca's genuine astonishment at the intellectual thoroughness of the work conveys the admiration that a practical architect like himself must have felt for the clarity and abstraction of a theorist like Leon Battista.
(Luca Fancelli, *Lettera a Lodovico Gonzaga da Mantova del 27 Aprile del* 1472. In W. Braghirolli, op. cit., pp. 21-22).

IANUS VITALIS, *Epitaph on the death of Alberti*, c. 1472.
   "Albertus iacet hic Leo, Leonem
quem Florentia iure nuncupavit
quod princeps fuit eruditorum
Princeps ut Leo solus est ferarum
Latomus denique et ipse hoc Epitaphium dictavit
quisquis barbarus es, rudisque Phoebi
hoc saxum pedibus cave prophanes
quod sane eximium tegit Leonem
peius auge tuum genus Perosum
nam musis sacer est, easque secum
vel hic in cumulo moratur oris
docti blanditiis: vel ipse cum illis
indagat clarios comes recessus
doctis multivagam referre praedam

nam raro unde solet stupenti Apelle
atque Vitruvio sagacitatem.
Sed quid te dubium morer? Leonem
Albertum satis hi loquuntur ungues".
Though the epitaph has no precise date, it must
have been written about the time of Alberti's death.
(Ianus Vitalis, *Epitaffio per Leon Battista Alberti*.
Quoted in Michele Poccianti, *Catalogus scriptorum
florentinorum omnis generis*, Florence 1589, p. 112).

CRISTOFORO LANDINO, *Disputationes Camaldulenses*,
1475.
In the introduction to this philosophical work,
Landino explains that the subject of the dialogue
is a comparison between the active life (defended
by Lorenzo the Magnificent) and the contemplative
life (defended by Leon Battista). Alberti is credited
with markedly neo-Platonic tendencies, and he is
paid a most flattering compliment: "It seemed a
fitting task to write down everything I ever heard
Leon Battista Alberti say, for he was the most
learned man I have ever met and a magnificent
orator ..." (p. 717). He then relates how he climbed
up to the hermitage of Camaldoli with his brother
to escape the summer heat. On reaching their
destination they discovered that Lorenzo was
there too, with his brother Giuliano, Alamanno
Rinuccini, Piero and Donato Acciaioli, Marco Pa-
renti and Antonio Canigiani, all keen scholars of
philosophy. Just as they were all happily greeting
each other and shaking hands, news came that
Leon Battista was about to arrive:
"He was on his way from Rome at the time, and
had left the via Aretina for Figline, where he had
gone to visit Marsilius Ficinus, who is undoubtedly
the greatest Platonist of our time. They had all
agreed to stay at the monastery, and not to return
to Florence until the height of the summer had
passed. Meanwhile, the others [Alberti and Marsi-
lius] had already reached the monastery, and
leaving their horses below, were slowly walking
up the hill towards us, together with Mariotto,
the Father Superior of the Camaldolese, a very
religious, cultured man. When we heard the news,
we were seized by joy and a great desire to see
and talk to them. So we went to meet them. It
was already sunset, and we spent the rest of the
day in conversation with Battista. There had been
no man of such far-ranging knowledge for centuries. I shall not mention his knowledge of letters,
for he had absorbed all that was to be known in
this field with the greatest wisdom".
Though the meeting may be fictitious, its description still has historical value insofar as it expresses
the Humanists' (and above all Alberti's) ideal vision
of life, as well as the image of themselves they
wished to pass on to posterity.
(Cristoforo Landino, *Disputationes Camaldulenses*.
In *La Letteratura italiana, storia e testi*, ed. Milan-
Naples, 13, 1952, p. 715 ff.).

FEDERICO DA MONTEFELTRO, *Letter to Cristoforo
Landino*, c. 1475.
Federico da Montefeltro wrote this letter thanking
Cristoforo Landino for the copy of the *Disputationes
Camaldulenses* he had sent him. Of Alberti, one of
the protagonists in the dialogue, Federico says:
"Nihil fuit familiarius neque amantius amicitia qua

Baptista et ego eramus coniuncti".
This testifies to the friendship and admiration
Alberti and the art-loving prince felt for each other.
It also gives us an insight into the many contacts
that bound Alberti to Urbino, so vital a centre
of Humanist culture and art.
(Federico da Montefeltro, *Lettera a Cristoforo Lan-
dino*. In P. Alatri, *Lettere di Stato e d'Arte di F. da
Montefeltro*, Rome 1949, pp. 102-03).

CRISTOFORO LANDINO, *Apologia for Dante*, 1481.
In a passionate defence of his native city against
"false slanderers", Landino draws up a list of all
the great men who lived and worked in Florence.
Leon Battista Alberti is mentioned among the
"excellent knowledgeable Florentines", between
the Humanist Giannozzo Manetti and the scientist
Guido Bonatto: "But where shall I put Baptista
Alberti? To what category of learned men does
he belong? Among the physicists you will say.
I would certainly agree that he was born to investigate the secrets of nature. Was there any branch
of mathematics that was unknown to him? He
knew geometry, arithmetic, and astrology. He was
a musician, and at the same time knew more about
perspective than any other man had done for
many centuries. His profound knowledge of all
these subjects is clearly manifested in the nine
books of architecture which he expounded with
the greatest, most divine eloquence. He wrote
about painting and sculpture, the second book
being the *De statua*. Not only did he write about
these arts but he also practised them, and we still
have some very fine paintings, statues, engravings
and bronzes of his." (carta 10 recto).
Apart from the space he dedicates to Alberti (he
writes no more than a line or two about the other
men of learning usually, as against the nine dedicated to Alberti), Landino adopts the tone of a
man who knew Leon Battista personally and was
on familiar terms with him.
Landino returns to Alberti when he discusses the
great men who used the vernacular, such as Petrarch
and Boccaccio (carta 14 recto): "Certainly, I doubt
whether anyone did as much as Battista Alberti to
further this language. I beg you to read the many
books he wrote on various subjects and to mark
the industry, elegance, style and dignity with which
he sought to transmit the thoughts of others to
posterity. Battista Alberti did much to improve the
language and bettered all those who excelled before
him in both the spoken and written word".
It is in reference to the language question that
Landino pronounces his important judgement on
Alberti's 'style': "I recall the style of Battista Alberto, which, like a chameleon, always moulded
itself to the subject matter".
(Cristoforo Landino, *Chomento di Christoforo Landino Fiorentino sopra la comedia di Dante Alighieri poeta
fiorentino*. See *Apologia nella quale si difende Dante
et Florentia da falsi calumniatori*, Florence 1481,
carta 10 recto and ff.).

AGNOLO POLIZIANO, *Dedication to the "De re aedificatoria"*, 1485.
This brief masterpiece of Humanist Latin prose
was written as an introduction to the first printed
edition of the *De re aedificatoria* and dedicated to

Lorenzo the Magnificent: "Nullae quippe hunc
hominem latuerunt? Quamlibet remotae litterae,
quamlibet reconditae disciplinae. Dubitare possis
utrum ad oratoriam magis, an ad poeticen factus,
utrum gravior sermo fuerit, an urbanior. Ita
perscrutatus antiquitatis vestigia est, ut omnem
veterum architectandi rationem et deprehenderit,
et in exemplum revocaverit: sicut non solum
machinas et pegmata, automataque permulta, sed
formas quoque aedificiorum admirabiles excogi-
taverit. Optimus praeterea et pictor et statuarius
est habitus; cum tamen interim ita examussim
teneret omnia, ut vix pauci singola: qua re ego
de illo, ut de Carthagine Sallustius, tacere satius
puto, quam pauca dicere".
The quotation illustrates how the myth of Alberti's
universal knowledge had already taken root in
the age of Humanism, even in the most sophisticated cultural circles such as Lorenzo's court.
Politian was also aware of the creative attitude
Alberti adopted in his evaluation of the great
classical tradition: "He fully understands the laws
of architecture as they were established by the
ancients, applying them in useful constructions
of his own ... and created admirable kinds of
wonderful buildings". Thus Politian points out
that Alberti did not merely imitate the ancients
passively but created a valuable repertory of new
architectural structures. Not only was this true;
it was the highest praise a worshipper of classicism
like Politian could bestow on an illustrious colleague. It was as if he were saying: "Not only
have you resurrected the revered ancients; you
have excelled them".
(Agnolo Poliziano, *Lettera di presentazione dell'edizione del De Re Aedificatoria per la prima volta stam-
pata in Firenze nel* 1485. The letter in question is
the seventh in Book X of the standard collection
of *Politian's Epistulae*).

FRANCESCO DI GIORGIO MARTINI, *Architettura civile e militare*, c. 1485.
In the introduction to this treatise (p. 295), Francesco di Giorgio justifies his purpose in writing:
"For those who have written about the superior
art of architecture have either failed to complete
their works or have dealt with that aspect of it
which interested them most, without mentioning
the rest. On the other hand, for the reasons we
have already explained, they have adopted terms
that have never been used before, and have dealt
with many monuments that have been in a state
of ruin for centuries".
This seems to contain a biting reference to Alberti,
whom Francesco di Giorgio (a professional architect and builder) must have considered a man of
letters steeped in Humanist and antiquarian learning
but completely devoid of practical experience. He
adds: "Sometimes one finds a layer of stone or
tufa rock about a foot thick, beneath which the
ground is quite unstable. If you were to build on
it, the foundations would buckle beneath the
weight of the walls and the whole building would
be ruined. This happened at Pienza, a town in
Tuscany, where a fine church collapsed as a result
of this kind of inadvertence ..." (pp. 431-432)
This sharp criticism is undoubtedly aimed at the
man who designed the "noble temple", who was

of course Alberti (though it is uncertain whether he conceived the whole plan of the architectural complex at Pienza). The full sarcasm of the confident, practical architect is conveyed in the juxtaposition of the fine church and the ironic "collapsed".

There are numerous echoes of Alberti's treatise in Francesco di Giorgio's. This shows that, in spite of everything, Alberti was present in Francesco's mind. He repeats Alberti's observation that the steps of a staircase must be set at a particular angle if they are to be climbed easily. He urges the installation of an adjustable fan to draw off the smoke from the chimney-piece (something Alberti had recommended too), and he suggests that the lord of a palace introduce apertures in the walls to listen to what is being said in his absence (another idea proposed in the *De re aedificatoria*).

Francesco di Giorgio ends on an even sharper note of criticism: "For a long time now many noble authors have written about the art of architecture, buildings and machinery, and have written down their ideas without illustrating them. And though these writers think they have fully elucidated their ideas, yet we see that there are very few readers who can understand them without the help of drawings. For the reader has to rely on his own idea of what is being described and sometimes it is as different from the author's as day is from night. Thus the reader is left in some confusion, for there are as many ideas of what the author is trying to describe as there are readers". This is an unkind but justified criticism of Alberti's treatise, which was published without explanatory illustrations.
(Francesco di Giorgio Martini, *Architettura civile e militare*. In Francesco di G. Martini, *Trattati*, ed. by C. Maltese, Milan 1967, p. 290 ff.).

Paolo Cortese, *De hominibus doctis dialogus*, 1490.
"Sed multum duo doctrina praestiterunt: Jannotius Manettus, et Baptista Albertus; quorum alter unus omnium doctissimus putabatur; alter etiam in Architectura disertus fuit; sed in Jannotio admirabile quoddam studium omnium doctrinarum fuit; sed nescio quo pacto sit huius summi viri, quam aliorum paullo ante dictorum nomen obscurius. Ex quo profecto intelligi potest, plus valere ad famam, et celebritatem nominis unius simplicis generis virtutem absolutam, quam multa annexa genera virtutum non perfectarum".

Here the praise of specialisation goes hand in hand with the criticism of universal knowledge, the quality usually cited by Leon Battista's admirers in his defence. This demonstrates that the ideal of a synthesis of all knowledge, a characteristic feature of fifteenth-century Humanism, had begun to lose its appeal and that a whole system of values was on the verge of crisis. It marks the beginning of a tradition that was critical of Humanist dilettantism and which found its most authoritative spokesman in Giorgio Vasari, who attacked some of the basic principles of Alberti's life-work.
(Paolo Cortese, *De hominibus doctis dialogus*. In *Philippi Villani Liber*, ed. by Gustavo Camillo Galletti, Florence 1847, p. 227).

Antonio Manetti, *Vita di Filippo di Ser Brunelleschi*, c. 1490.
Of Brunelleschi and Donatello's archaeological excavations in Rome Manetti writes: "The reason why they [the excavations] were ignored was that no one at the time understood — nor had anyone understood for centuries — how the ancients had constructed their buildings. For though some authors had written down the rules that governed this architecture in the time of the Gentiles (just as Battista degli Alberti did in our own times) little was known about it other than general notions". Here the parallel between Vitruvius and Alberti is not so much exalted as taken for granted.
(Antonio Manetti, *Vita di Filippo di Ser Brunellesco*. In Gaetano Milanesi, *Operette istoriche edite ed inedite di Antonio Manetti*, Florence 1887, p. 96).

Piero della Francesca, *De perspectiva pingendi*, c. 1490.
The many points of contact between the paintings of Piero della Francesca and the writings of Alberti are indirect evidence of the esteem accorded Alberti's even by so thorough an artist-scientist as Piero. Yet there was a profound difference between Alberti's early proto-Renaissance empiricism and the full Humanistic lucidity of Piero's precise, scientific perspective.
"Painting consists of three principal parts, which we shall call design, commensuration, and colouring" (p. 63). These "parts" may be compared to Alberti's *circoscrizione, composizione*, and *ricezione dei lumi*.
The "lines which come from the outer edges of the object and terminate in the eye, so that the eye receives and discerns them" (p. 64) are very similar to the "rays" of Leon Battista's visual pyramid. Piero della Francesca, like Alberti before him, distinguishes between the geometrical point of the philosopher and the real point of the painter: "Therefore, I shall describe the point as the smallest thing visible to the human eye". (p. 65) Leon Battista had written in the De Pictura: "The first thing to know is that a point is a sign which one might say is not divisible into parts. I call a sign anything which exists on a surface so that it is visible to the eye" (p. 37).
In sketching a door for a "temple with eight sides" (p. 120), Piero adopted the typically Albertian 1 : 2 proportional ratio. Again, in the construction of a "base for a round column" (p. 148), the column itself is planned according to the rules formulated by Alberti.
(Piero della Francesca, *De perspectiva pingendi*; ed. cons. by G. Nicco Fasola, Florence 1942).

Luca Pacioli, *Summa arithmeticae*, 1494.
In the "Letter to the Most Illustrious Prince Guido Baldo, Duke of Urbino" which introduces the treatise Luca writes: "Vitruvius too, in his book on the subject, and the Florentine Leon Battista degli Alberti, in his perfectly proportioned works, developed the application of mathematics to architecture. The same is exemplified in our own day by the new wonder of Italy, the noble, admirable palace of Your Lordship, begun and completed by your father of most happy memory. In this

building nature has indeed shown its power and art more than in any other that has yet been seen. No tongue can express the beauty and harmony of its plan better than the building itself, which it does most eloquently, for not only is it immediately pleasing to the eye, but whoever studies all the artifice and ornament that has gone into its construction will be even more astonished". Pacioli's praise of Alberti is no surprise. Nevertheless, it is lavish and one can see how natural it is for him to compare Alberti with Vitruvius. What strikes one most is the perhaps not altogether fortuitous comparison of Alberti's "supreme edifices" (and their harmonious proportions) with the equally wonderful, well-proportioned palace of Urbino. Pacioli seems intent on establishing some kind of intimate connection between Alberti and this Renaissance palace.
(Luca Pacioli, *Summa Arithmeticae*, Venice 1494).

Leonardo da Vinci, *Trattato della Pittura*, c. 1498.
The parallel passages below are significant enough to induce one to believe that Leonardo must have made a thorough, systematic study of Alberti's *Della pittura*. This familarity with the treatise on the part of an artist who described himself rather defiantly as an "unlettered man" represents a deliberate tribute to Alberti, a far more significant tribute than the often general expressions of reverence which so many of Alberti's contemporaries paid him.
"The point is that ultimate unit than which nothing can be smaller". Alberti had written something very similar: "The first thing to know is that a point is a sign which one might say is not divisible into parts" (p. 37). It should be noted that both artists begin their treatises with these respective definitions.
"There are six simple colours, of which the first is white, though some philosophers refuse to accept either white or black as colours, for one is the cause of colour while the other is its absence". (par. 250). Thus Leonardo mentions six not four fundamental colours, adding black and white, which do not appear in Alberti's list. However, he adopts a position that is basically the same as Alberti's, for the latter had said: "The painter, therefore, may be assured that white and black are not true colours but, one might say, moderators of colours, for the painter will find nothing but white to represent the brightest glow of light, and only black for the darkest shadows" (p. 47).
In explaining the treatment of light and shade according to the setting in which the subject is placed, Leonardo says: "If the terrain nearby consists of fields, and a woman stands in a field beneath the sun, you will see the folds of her dress ... take on the colour of the field by means of reflected rays" (par. 774). Alberti had written: "We see this happen when the faces of people walking about in the meadows appear to have a greenish tinge" (p. 47).
As for the position of the point of vision in the perspective construction, Leonardo writes: "The point must be on a level with the eye of a man of average height" (par. 410). This recalls Alberti: "The suitable position for this centric point is no higher from the base line than the height of the

366

man to be represented in the painting ... (p. 55). Both artists attributed a kind of divinity to the art of painting. Leonardo says: "The divinity of the painter's art is such that the mind of the painter is changed into a likeness of God's" (par. 65). Alberti: "The virtues of painting, therefore, are that its masters see their works admired and feel themselves to be almost like the Creator" (p. 61). Their views are also similar as regards the use of the *velo* (net), which has no absolute value in itself and must not be used indiscriminately, but simply as an aid. Leonardo praises "those who are capable of reproducing the fantastic effects of nature, but who use such devices only to avoid unnecessary labour and to include the smallest detail in the faithful imitation of the real" (par. 35). Leon Battista writes: "I will not listen to those who say it is no good for a painter to get into the habit of using these things, because, though they offer him the greatest help in painting, they make the artist unable to do anything by himself without them. If I am not mistaken, we do not ask for infinite labour from the painter, but we do expect a painting that appears markedly in relief and similar to the objects presented. I do not understand how anyone could ever even moderately achieve this without the help of the veil" (p. 69). Leonardo writes: "The painter should delight in portraying scenes of abundance and variety ... so that his novelty and abundance may attract the attention and delight of the observer" (par. 179). Alberti: "The first thing that gives pleasure in a 'historia' is a plentiful variety" (p. 79). Leonardo writes: "The good painter should paint two things above all: man, and the Idea in his own mind. The first is easy, the second difficult, for one must depict a gesture and movement of the body" (par. 176). Alberti: "A 'historia' will move spectators when the men painted in the picture outwardly demonstrate their own feelings as clearly as possible ... Yet these feelings are known from movements of the body" (p. 81). Leonardo writes: "When you paint heads, therefore, you must pretend that the hair of young heads is ruffled by the wind, and they must be depicted with a different grace" (par. 398). Alberti: "Since by nature clothes are heavy and do not make curves at all, as they tend always to fall straight down to the ground, it will be a good idea, when we wish clothing to have movement, to have in the corner of the picture the face of the West or South wind blowing between the clouds and moving all the clothing before it" (p. 87). Leonardo writes: "Let us suppose, my reader, that you take a glance at the whole of this written page. You will immediately come to the conclusion that it is full of different letters. But you will not know what letters they are, nor what they mean. To understand them you must go over them word by word and line by line ... and the same is true of nature with respect to this art [painting]" (par. 47). Alberti: "I would have those who begin to learn the art of painting do what I see practised by teachers of writing. They first teach all the signs of the alphabet separately, and then how to put syllables together, and then whole words" (p. 97). Leonardo writes: "One cannot distinguish the nature of error in small things as one can in big. The reason for this is that if a small object is made in the likeness of a man or other animal, its parts cannot be examined by the artist with due care owing to the drastic reduction in its size" (par. 114). Alberti: "We must beware, however, not to paint on very small panels, as many do. I would have you get used to making large pictures, which are as near as possible in size to the actual object you wish to represent. In small pictures the greatest mistakes are most easily concealed; in a large one even the smallest errors are obvious" (p. 101). Leonardo writes: "Whatever is in the universe by virtue of essence, presence, or imagination, he [the good painter] first conceives it in the mind, and afterwards paints it with his hands" (par. 9). Alberti: "If there are slow artists, they are so because they try slowly and lingeringly to do something which they have not first thought out clearly in their own minds; as they wander, fearful and virtually sightless, in the darkness of their error, like the blind man with his stick they with their brush test and investigate unknown paths and exits. Therefore he should never put his hand to work without the guidance of well-informed judgement" (p. 103). Leonardo writes: "A painter must never reject judgements passed on his painting by others, but should listen to their opinions with eagerness and patience, considering whether the criticism expressed of his work is justified or not. If it is, then he should alter his work ..." (par. 72). Alberti: "When we are about to paint a 'historia', we will always ponder at some length on the order and the means by which the composition might best be done. We will work out the whole 'historia' and each of its parts by making sketch models on paper, and take advice on it with all our friends" (p. 103).

(Leonardo da Vinci, *Trattato della Pittura*, ed. by Gaetano Milanesi, Rome 1890. For the quotations from Alberti, see Leon Battista Alberti, *On Painting and On Sculpture*, ed. by Cecil Grayson, London 1972).

GIROLAMO MASSAINI, *Dedication to the pamphlet "Leonis Bap.ae Alb. Opera"*, 1499.

Massaini was given the task of collecting and publishing Alberti's works by Roberto Pucci. In the introductory letter to his volume he says: "Scriptor profecto adeo foecundus, adeo fertilis, ut luxuriantem hunc quandoque agrum nimio (ut aiunt) ubere glebae, admirari detur. Adde tot et tantarum rerum cognitionem ut hunc non multiscium, sed omniscium merito dicas, ut qui illum non amet, non veneretur; aut insanus omnino, aut prae ceteris aliis individus sit, cum tot huius viri a natura dotibus largitis, tot ornamentis, tanta arte quaesitis, non trahatur. Quid dicam de moribus? Quibus et laudandi et culpandi sumus, cum illi a bonis animi, quae nobis intrinseca, non corporis et fortunae, quae extrinseca sunt, emanent? Quibus adeo sanctis fuit: ut novus hic Socrates se tamquam speculum cunctis semper praebuerit. Refert mihi nonnumquam amicus quidam, qui Baptistae perquum familiaris semper vixit, plura de illo quae dum audio, admirabilitate percitus stupeo magis, quam laudare possim. Quanta fuerit continentia, quanta corporis castimonia, quanta in omnibus rebus vitae integritate! Quibus auditis, et suis lectis scriptis, quae vere hominem temperatum et in omnibus frugi nobis ostendunt, evenerit nonnumquam cum ruri agam (iuxta enim villulam nostram suburbanam ille suum saepius incolebat; si quando hominum satietate ex toto expuere, et se totum meditationi tradere volebat), ut gymnasiolum suum, quod tu gurgustiolum quoddam dicas tanta erat in omnibus summa moderatione et modestia, omni a se (ut alter Diogenes) ambitione pompa et fastu semotis: gymnasiolum inquam et meditullium illud, ubi plura commutatus sit, ego non nisi horrescens, tamquam sacrum ac veris musis quoddam dicatum locum, ingredi potuerim. Sed ad litteras redeo. Qui alter detur tempestate nostra mathematicis disciplinis imbutus, perspectiva et symmetria absolutus, aedificatoria consummatus, omni philosophiae refertus, platonicis sacris initiatus, ut Leo noster fuit? Legatur opus suum De Pictura, opusculumque De Picturae Elementis, et, utrum mathematicus et perspectivus dici possit, apparebit. Inspiciatur illius Statua, et tunc de symmetria loquamur. De Re Aedificatoria non dicam, cum volumen illud iamdiu editum, in decem libros digestum laudibus nostris non egeat. Quam multiplici philosophia redundet morali praesertim, indicant decem Intercenalium libri. Quam dives sit in inventionibus, quam miro in dispositionibus, ordine et distributione uniusquisque rei servatis, quanta arte polleat in praeceptis suis nemo doctus non stupet. Praebet se facilem in rebus vel difficillimis, tanta exprimendorum conceptuum arte valet, latinae linguae numquam oblitus. Licet enim in quibusdam licente nimis agere videatur, id omne ex verborum ignoratione, sed consulto factum ab eo scias: non enim ignorabat quantum in unaquaque re litteraria posset, et cancellos sibi praescriptos recte tenebat, sed memor Ciceronis dicti censebat augentem latinam lingua nova quaedam (licet pauca) nonnulla vero arbitrato suo dicere decere". This emphasises once more the universality of Alberti's knowledge and points to the close ties that bound him to Humanist literary circles. Massaini includes a touching description of a visit to the little country-house near Florence where Leon Battista was said to have retired every so often. For Massaini the visit was a kind of pilgrimage to a dwelling, which, though humble, was still alive, almost sanctified (to use the author's own words) by a sense of the great man's presence.

(Girolamo Massaini, *Dedicatoria a Roberto Pucci dell'opuscolo "Leonis Bap.ae. Alb. Opera"*. In A. Bonucci, *Opere Volgari ...*, Florence 1843, I, pp. CCXXXV ff.).

UGOLINO VERINO, *De illustratione urbis Florentiae*, c. 1500.

"Nec minor Euclide est Albertus; vincit et ipsum Vitruvium: quisquis celsas attollere moles affectat, nostri relegat monumenta Baptistae". No greater praise could have been given Alberti, who, in Verino's words, excelled even his own great master, Vitruvius. One should also notice that Alberti is placed between a doctor and an astrologer, Niccolò del Garbo and Guido Bonatti respectively.

(Ugolino Verino, *De illustratione urbis Florentiae*, first printed ed., Paris 1583; ed. cons., Paris 1790, III, p. 110).

POMPONIO GAURICO, *De sculptura*, 1504.
Gaurico explains the origins of painting as the design of the outlines of the shadows of bodies: "Nam sive casu aliquo sive sollertia coeperint homines, creta truncisque aut lapidibus, ex umbra similitudine imitando, naturam ipsam aemulari ..." (p. 51). Likewise Alberti in the *De statua*: "Nam ex tronco glebave et huiusmodi multis corporibus fortasse aliquando intuebantur lineamenta nonnulla, quibus paululum immutatis persimile quidpiam veris naturae vultus redderetur". Further on: different expressions "Nec Herculem ipsum semper eadem decebunt, vel cum Anthaeo luctantem, vel coelum humeris substinente, vel Deianirae amplexus petentem, vel Hylam quaeritantem" (p. 55). And Alberti: "Namque Hercules quidem vultus in Anthaeum intentis, ut omni ex parte simillimos vivo exprimas, aut quibus sit ille differentiis ab eiusdem vultu Herculis pacato atque in Dejaniram arridentis dissimilis, ut perscribamus nostri non esse artificii aut ingenii profiteor".
This information is scanty and second-hand, but late fifteenth-century Padua was incapable of formulating the subtle rational speculations of a city such as Florence had been years earlier. It is all the more significant, however, for the quotation of an author whose ideas and moral principles one does not share at least testifies to one's consideration for him.
(Pomponio Gaurico, *De Sculptura*. In André Chastel, *Pomponius Gauricus, de Sculptura*, Geneva-Paris 1969. For the quotations from Alberti, see L. B. Alberti, *De Statua*, ed. Janitschek, *L. B. Albertis kleinere kunsttheoretische Schriften*, Vienna 1877, pp. 169 and 179).

FRANCESCO ALBERTINI, *Opusculum de mirabilibus novae et veteris urbis Romae*, 1510.
This pamphlet is less an antiquarian study than a kind of guide to early Cinquecento Rome. Its typically Humanistic description of Roman ruins is accompanied by a discussion of the Papal *Urbs Nova*. By this time Alberti's authority was such that the mere mention of his name was sufficient to guarantee the validity of one's affirmations. Since the book was a work of popularisation, one may presume that Alberti's ideas must have been known to the average cultured man. "Omitto porticum Pantheon a M. Agrippa constructum cum admirabilibus columnis, ut dixi in templo eius, de qua porticu Baptista Leo ait: extant in hunc usque diem ad porticum Agrippae contiguationes aeneis tabulis pedum XL, opus in quo nescias impensam ne magis an artificis ingenium mirere" (p. 486).
In the course of the description of Cardinal Giovanni de' Medici's magnificent library, the *De re aedificatoria* is mentioned as a very valuable work. It figures among the very rare Greek manuscripts translated by Politian and left by Lorenzo to his son, together with the philosophical manuscripts of Marsilius Ficinus: "Extant et opera Baptistae Leonis de Albertis, Florentini, exquisitissimae doctrinae, qui libros X de architectura composuit,

quos Bernardus eius frater, doctissimus vir emendavit, ac Laurentio Medici (ut erat voluntas auctoris mortui) praesentavit cum aliis opuscolis, quae omnia noster Romulus Aretinus efflagitavit, ut imprimerentur, et accepta copia illius Architectura lib. Sigismundo viro doct. et secretario Sanctitatis tuae donavit" (p. 531).
(Francesco Albertini, *Opusculum de mirabilibus novae et veteris urbis Romae*. In Valentini-Zucchetti, *Codice topografico della città di Roma*, Rome 1953, IV).

BENEDETTO VARCHI, *Disputa della maggioranza delle arti*, 1546.
Discussing the excellence of architecture in his first *disputa*, Varchi absolves himself from having to carry out a thorough examination of the subject matter; instead, he refers the reader to Vitruvius, the founder of the art, and to Leon Battista, who is considered almost as his equal: " ... and had not Vitruvius discussed it already at great length in the beautiful, very learned introduction to his books on architecture (though he exaggerates somewhat in our humble opinion) and had not Messer Leon Battista Alberti, a noble Florentine and an extremely learned man in many arts and sciences, dealt with it in the very beautiful, learned introduction to his own books on architecture, we would deal with it in greater detail. But submitting ourselves to their authority ..." (p. 21).
In the second *disputa* Varchi discusses the excellence of painting: "In the same way, Messer Leon Battista Alberti, a most noble, learned man in many arts and sciences, both a very great painter and architect in his time, wrote in his book on painting that painting was a worthier and nobler art than sculpture" (p. 35).
The fact that Alberti's opinions, modified to suit the needs and taste of a new age, were still remembered and quoted with considerable respect, confirms the undisputed fame Leon Battista's thought had acquired.
(Benedetto Varchi, Lecture concerning the importance of the arts and which is the noblest, sculpture or painting, delivered by him publicly in the Florentine Academy on the third Sunday of Lent in the year 1546, and published under the title, Two lectures by Messer Benedetto Varchi, the first of which includes a sonnet by Michelangelo Buonarroti. The second is a discussion as to whether sculpture or painting is the nobler art, and it is accompanied by a letter by the same Michelangelo, together with the opinions of many other famous painters and sculptors regarding the above-mentioned question, Florence 1549. In *Trattati d'Arte del Cinquecento*, ed. by Paola Barocchi, Bari 1962, I).

PHILIBERT DE L'ORME, *Architecture*, 1548.
This pioneer work laid the foundations of the great French tradition of architectural theory. Leon Battista Alberti is mentioned in the introduction to the first chapter dedicated to the "Considerations to be made and precautions taken on the part of those who intend to build, so that they may not be deceived or harmed to their displeasure". Thus his name is invoked in a passage that deals with concrete, practical problems, an aspect of architec-

ture that was to be particularly important for French architectural critics. He is quoted not so much as an authoritative theorist as an expert adviser on practical issues: "If you read the first chapter of the second book on architecture by Leon Baptiste Alberti, you will see the wise advice he gives to those who intend building, both to patrons and architects".
(Philibert de l'Orme, *Architecture*, Rouen 1548, p. 8).

PAOLO PINO, *Dialogo di Pittura*, 1548.
Even in art circles as far removed from the rational, rather abstract culture of Alberti as those of Venice, it was clearly impossible to avoid paying homage to the great fifteenth-century theorist. In spite of his criticism or misunderstanding of much of Alberti's thought, Pino retained a boundless admiration for Leon Battista. Thus when he urges the painter to be versatile and insists that he be an intellectual with numerous interests and activities rather than a mere technician, he is compelled to mention Alberti, whom he describes as "a very learned Florentine, as is proved by his Latin works. In one that deals with perspective, he dared to question Vitruvius's ideas on the subject" (carta 30 verso). This is followed by a typically Venetian expression of anti-rationalist naturalism, the very opposite of Alberti's intellectualism: "And since painting is really poetry, that is to say, invention, causing something to appear that does not exist, it is worthwhile examining some of the canons observed by poets when they write, that of brevity in particular. This is a quality they introduce into their plays and other compositions, and one that the painter should strive to achieve in his pictures. He must not try to include the whole world in his picture, or design with excessive diligence, composing it with light and shade as Giovan Bellino used to do, for then it is wasted labour having to cover it all over with colours. Even less useful is Alberti's *velo* or *quadratura*, a silly, useless invention" (carta 16 verso). This illustrates the triumph of the new Venetian tonal concept of colour, which is consciously opposed to the scientific, intellectual forms of fifteenth-century painting, especially Tuscan.
The anti-rationalism of the circles for which Pino wrote is further confirmed by the reservations with respect to Alberti's studies of geometry and perspective: "It seems to me to be quite intolerable ... but no writer, either ancient or modern, has given a satisfactory explanation of what painting really is. It is true that Pliny wrote many noble things about it, some of which are quoted in the present dialogue. Leon Battista Alberti, the Florentine painter, also wrote a Latin treatise on the subject, but it is more about mathematics than painting, though it promises the contrary" (carta 2 verso).
(Paolo Pino, *Dialogo di Pittura*, Venice 1548. See the reproduction from the original ed. by G. Nicodemi, Milan 1945).

GIORGIO VASARI, *Le vite de' più eccellenti architetti, pittori et scultori italiani*, 1550.
There are no substantial differences between this edition of the *Lives* and that of 1568 as far as the evaluation of Leon Battista's work is concerned;

the same praise and criticism characterise both. Though Vasari respected and exalted a man who was acclaimed by all as an architectural and universal genius — if only because he added to the prestige of Florence — he nourished suspicion, not to mention hostility for all the theory in Alberti's work. This hostility was based on a lack of historical understanding. The cultured, naturally gifted craftsman, the artist who trusted solely in the dexterity of his touch and his exceptional Idea, the new Mannerist painter, sculptor, or architect (including Vasari himself, of course), was bound to be suspicious, even intolerant of the learned Humanist versed in all the liberal arts and sciences; and Alberti was the very personification of such a figure. Different problems, generated by quite different disappointments and fears, afflicted the artistic conscience in the middle of the sixteenth century, and they could hardly be solved (or even alleviated) by the humanistic, rational, harmonious, encyclopaedic, fundamentally optimistic view of life developed by men like Alberti in the creative years of the fifteenth-century Renaissance. The typically Florentine sharpness that creeps into every reference Vasari makes to Leon Battista (even indirectly) and the abrupt, irritable tone of his *Life* (he seems to be saying, "Yes, of course, he was a man of great genius and learning, a great intellectual and thinker, perhaps too great even, for when one has to get down to the actual business of building, things are very different from what they seem on the drawing-board") are all part of an unconscious reaction. For the powerful artist of the Grand Duchy was probably envious of the Humanist who belonged to an already distant past, who had been so much more serene, so much more certain of the existence of a rational order in the universe, so convinced that mathematics and geometry were the keys to reality and that thought alone was the only happiness obtainable on earth. "Artists who are fond of reading invariably derive the greatest benefit from their studies, especially if they are sculptors or painters or architects. Book-learning encourages craftsmen to be inventive in their work; and certainly, whatever their natural gifts, their judgement will be faulty unless it is backed by sound learning and theory ... The truth of these remarks is clearly demonstrated by Leon Battista Alberti. He devoted himself to the study of Latin and the practice of architecture, perspective, and painting, and he left to posterity a number of books which he wrote himself. Now none of our modern craftsmen has known how to write about these subjects, and so even though very many of them have done better work than Alberti, such has been the influence of his writings on the pens and speech of scholarly men that he is commonly believed to be superior to those who were, in fact, superior to him ... It's not surprising, therefore, that the famous Leon Battista Alberti is better known for what he wrote than for the work of his hands. He was born in Florence, into the noble Alberti family (of which I spoke elsewhere). He spent his time finding out about the world and studying the proportions of antiquities; but above all, following his natural genius, he concentrated on writing rather than on applied work".

At the end of his *Life*, however, after many unkind observations and much praise, (closely followed by even subtler criticism), Vasari desists in his disapproval of Alberti. The hagiographical words that conclude the biography refer almost exclusively to the great Humanist's serenity and the harmony of his philosophical way of life: "Finally, having reached a good old age, in tranquillity and contentment he left for a better life, leaving behind him a most honourable name and reputation. In all those who desired fame he left a desire to be like him, for he had truly been what his epitaph says he was: Leon Battista Alberti, the Florentine Vitruvius:
"Albertus iacet hic Leo: Leonem
Quem Florentia iure nuncupavit:
Quod Princeps fuit eruditorum
Princeps ut Leo solus est ferarum".
(Giorgio Vasari, *Le vite de' più eccellenti architetti, pittori et scultori italiani*, Florence 1550, II, p. 85 ff.).

PAOLO GIOVIO, *Imagines clarorum virorum*, 1551.
"Leoni Baptistae, ex Albertorum familia Florentiae clara, Politianus audita eius morte, nobile encomium cecinit; nos autem eius ingenii acumen et styli felicitate in confragosa materia plurimum admiramur. Novum enim opus aedificatoriae facultatis et propter linguae inopiam valde impeditum nec satis eloquentiae capax aggressus est, tanta facundia, ut imperitos obscuro rudique eius saeculo et certa disciplinae luce carentes architectos in semitam rectissimae rationis deduxerit, quum Vitruvii praecepta densissimis obsessa tenebris illustraret ac, inspectis antiquorum aedificiorum reliquiis atque inde accurata dimetiendi ratione initiorum et finium ordinem deprehendisset, ita ut inopem et corruptis artibus incultam aetatem nostram admirabili abditarum rerum copia locupletasse existimetur. Scripsit etiam in pictura de recessibus et umbris lineisque ex optices disciplina, quibus rebus imagines, in eodem sitas plano, tanquam remotas et extantes erudita manus exprimere consuevit. Ex speculo quoque reflexis radiis, suam ipsius effigiem arguto penicillo pereleganter est assecutus quam apud Pallantem Oricellarium in hortis vidimus. Extat etiam apologorum urbanae gravitatis libellus, quo vel Aesopum inventionis amoenitate superasse iudicatur: et "Momus", summae gratiae dialogus, ac ideo cum antiquis operibus multorum sententia comparandus". Giovio's enthusiastic praise, expressed about the same time, serves to balance Vasari's harsh criticism. It shows that no fixed or stereotyped ideal of the artist had yet been formed even a hundred years after Alberti's death, and that his life and works, clearly felt to be still relevant, continued to be the object of heated debate.
(Paolo Giovio, *Imagines clarorum virorum. Elogia virorum litteris illustrium*, elogio XXXIII. In *Pauli Iovii Opera*, ed. by Renzo Meregazzi, Rome 1872, p. 65).

LODOVICO DOLCE, *Dialogo della Pittura*, 1557.
One of the characters in Dolce's dialogue is Aretino, who concludes his discussion of the dignity of painting thus: "This brief discourse of mine describes the very essence of painting. But if you

want to pursue the matter further, you can read Leon Battista Alberti's little book on painting, which, like all his works, has been well translated by Messer Lodovico Domenichi, as well as Vasari's work".
It is significant that people still felt the need to refer others to Alberti's work even in the exacting art circles of mid-sixteenth-century Venice. Though it may have been considered a book for specialists and enthusiasts, it was still one to be remembered. (Lodovico Dolce, *Dialogo della Pittura intitolato l'Aretino*, Venice 1557. In *Trattato d'Arte del Cinquecento*, ed. by Paola Barocchi, Bari 1962, I, p. 187).

BENVENUTO CELLINI, *Discorso intitolato "Della architettura"*, 1565.
"For Leon Battista Alberti, our fellow countryman, has written with great skill and judgement about the architectural orders established by Vitruvius, saying nothing that might diminish their beauty in any way. And wonderful as they are, he has added many beautiful, useful things that Vitruvius left unsaid. Anyone who wishes to follow the architectural profession should read Vitruvius. But let him read Leon Battista's book too, for he will find it very useful and beautiful".
Cellini first mentions Alberti and then recalls the great theorists of the Cinquecento, Daniele Barbaro, Baldassare Peruzzi, and Serlio etc., as if he were attributing to Alberti the paternity of Italian architectural theory. It is interesting to find so bizarre a spirit as Benvenuto, a man so fond of breaking the rules of classical art, feeling the need to pay special tribute to an artist as different from himself as Alberti.
(Benvenuto Cellini, *Discorso intitolato "Della Architettura"*, printed for the first time by Jacopo Martelli. The twelve vernacular manuscripts in the Nanniana Library, Venice 1776, reproduced in *I trattati dell'Oreficeria e della Scultura di Benvenuto Cellini*, ed. by Carlo Milanesi, Florence 1857, p. 224).

COSIMO BARTOLI, *Dedication of the "Della pittura"*, 1568.
The fact that a new edition of Alberti's treatise was published and dedicated to so important a person as Vasari gives some idea of the esteem in which Leon Battista's writings were still held even at the height of the Cinquecento. "Let young artists still run to learn from your designs, your colours, and your precepts. Meanwhile, look kindly upon the publication of this brief work on painting by the most gifted Leon Battista Alberti, which I have translated into our native tongue and dedicated to you. For thus beginners may learn the first elements, as it were, from this little book, and then study the perfections of fine painting later in your own wonderful works".
(Cosimo Bartoli, Dedication of the *Della Pittura* to Giorgio Vasari in the *Opuscoli*, Venice 1568).

COSIMO BARTOLI, *Dedication of the "Della Statua"*, 1568.
Here too, the publication of a new edition of the translated version of Alberti's brief treatise and

its dedication to a famous artist such as Ammannati prove that it continued to be popular. Bartoli's appreciation of Alberti is more flattering than ever, and his words are particularly well-chosen from a historical point of view: "I am well aware, most gifted Messer Bartolomeo, that you, who are equally skilled in both architecture and sculpture, do not need to follow the precepts on sculpture which the most judicious Leon Alberti laid down in his own day. But I have thought that it would cause you no great displeasure if I were to address these precepts to you, as the man best fitted to judge Leon Battista's fine intelligence. At the time Battista wrote, little or nothing was known about sculpture, since the barbarous hordes had destroyed, indeed, eradicated all the fine arts and disciplines, so that he strove to employ his most refined judgement in opening up an easy safe path which the young, inexpert enthusiasts of this most noble art could follow, encouraging them to carve well according to fixed, stable principles".
(Cosimo Bartoli, Dedication of the *Della Statua* to Bartolomeo Ammannati in the *Opuscoli*, Venice 1568).

GIORGIO VASARI, *Le Vite de' più eccellenti pittori, scultori ed architettori*, 1568.
Vasari did not modify his harshness towards Alberti in this revised edition of 1568. On the contrary, since he dedicates more space to him, his criticism is more detailed and insidious. He discusses Alberti's individual works at great length, pointing out his "errors", which he attributes to the fact that Leon Battista "concentrated on writing rather than on applied work".
Of the loggia in front of the palazzo Rucellai he says: "In this loggia he turned the arches over the closely spaced columns in the façade and also over the corbels, in order both to have a series of arches on the outside and to follow the same pattern internally. He had to make projections at the inside corners because he had put a space at each corner between the arches. When he came to vault the interior he was unable to use a semicircular barrel-vault, which would have looked mean and awkward, and so he resolved to throw small arches across from corner to corner. Here he showed a lack of judgement and design, demonstrating very clearly that theoretical knowledge must be accompanied by experience: no one can develop perfect judgement unless his learning is tempered by practical application".
He goes on the discuss the tribune in the Santissima Annunziata. Since this is a circular structure, the concave interior of which is interrupted by the arches of the chapels, the laws of perspective result in the arches appearing as if they lean forward: "Perhaps Alberti would not have done this if his practical experience of architecture had matched his theoretical knowledge. Another man would have avoided the difficulty and have been content to construct a graceful and more beautiful building".
Finally, there is the subtle irony of the phrase with which Vasari claims that Alberti was more fortunate than other architects in finding so faithful and intelligent an interpreter of his designs as

Luca Fancelli. He appears to insinuate that if Alberti did create anything valid and concrete, much if not all of the credit should be attributed to the men who actually carried out his designs: "Alberti was extremely fortunate to have friends who understood him and who were able and willing to serve him, because architects cannot always stand over their work, and it is a great help if they can find someone to execute it faithfully and lovingly. ..."
However, in the conclusion to this biography, as in the first published version, Vasari seems unable to resist the fascination of Leon Battista and presents him as if wrapped in an aura of nobility. In accordance with the highest ideals of the *Cortegiano*, nobility of spirit and nobility of caste merge in the shining splendour of Alberti's profound wisdom and olympic serenity: "Leon Battista was an honourable citizen, a man of culture who was the friend of talented men and very open and courteous with everyone; and he always lived honourably and like the gentleman he was. Finally, having reached a good old age, in tranquillity and contentment he left for a better life, leaving behind him a most honourable name and reputation".
(Giorgio Vasari, *Le Vite de' più eccellenti pittori, scultori ed architettori*, Florence 1568; ed. cons. by Gaetano Milanesi, Florence 1878, II, p. 535 ff.).

DANIELE BARBARO, *La Pratica della Prospettiva*, 1569.
The name of Alberti is noticeably absent from the introduction to this treatise. In discussing the science of perspective and its theoretical foundations in the century that preceded his own, Barbaro writes: "Before our own age painters produced some very fine examples of their art. Not only did they depict landscapes, mountains, woods, and buildings, all very well designed and shaded, but human bodies too, together with other animals, represented by means of lines very subtly drawn in perspective so that they converge on the eye as on a centre. But no one that I know of has explained or recorded in writing how, or according to what principles, these lines were traced. Unless we wish to call rules and precepts certain practices that were loosely set down without any order or thoroughness and roughly explained. These include some by Piero del Borgo Sansepolcro and others [therefore Alberti's as well] ... that might be useful for idiots". The learned Patriarch of Aquileia was severe enough in his judgement of Alberti to leave his name out of the list of those who had studied perspective altogether. But this is explicable enough if one remembers that Barbaro worked in an area and at a time when the strict application of mathematics and geometry to architecture corresponded to a desire to reduce the whole cultural heritage of the Renaissance to the absoluteness of a system.
(Daniele Barbaro, *La Pratica della Prospettiva*, Venice 1569, p. 1).

ANDREA PALLADIO, *I Quattro Libri dell'Architettura*, 1570.
In the introduction Palladio first refers to the barbarians' corruption of classical architecture and

recalls that the renewal of the sound ancient manner was founded on the writings of Vitruvius and Leon Battista (the only modern author Palladio mentions in the same breath as the great Roman theorist): "Whence, seeing how very different was the common manner of building from that which I had seen in these [classical] buildings and read about in Vitruvius, Leon Battista Alberti, and in other excellent writers who came after Vitruvius ...". In conferring such authority upon Alberti, Palladio distinguishes him from many other excellent contemporary writers on architecture and projects him into the mythical past of antiquity, by the side of Vitruvius.
(Andrea Palladio, *I Quattro Libri dell'Architettura*, Venice 1570).

RAFFAELLO BORGHINI, *Il Riposo*, 1584.
In the course of the debate as to whether painting or sculpture was the superior art, Baccio Valori recalls that one of the arguments used by the supporters of painting was that it was the art that had been exalted by Castiglione and Alberti: "They quote as their authorities Count Baldassare di Castiglione's *Cortegiano* and the book on painting by Messer Leon Battista Alberti, a very noble man and extremely learned in many sciences, who was also an excellent painter and architect". The sculptors "... would not recognise Leon Battista Alberti's authority, saying he was a painter not a sculptor, both judge and party in his own cause, and so not to be listened to in this case". It is strange to find Alberti's wealth of theory being bandied about in this manner, like the rope in a tug-of-war. But this kind of debate was very popular with late sixteenth-century theorists.
(Raffaello Borghini, *Il Riposo*, Florence 1584; ed. cons. R. B., *Il Riposo*, Reggio 1826, I, p. 34, and II, p. 44).

ROMANO ALBERTI, *Trattato della nobiltà della pittura*, 1585.
Of perspective the author says: "And many of our painters have taken considerable pains in the study of this science in the past, above all, Paolo Uccello, Masaccio da San Giovanni, Leon Battista Alberti, and first and foremost the never-sufficiently-praised Piero della Francesca". This captures the particular historical and cultural moment in which Alberti lived and worked.
(Romano Alberti, *Trattato della nobiltà della pittura*, Rome 1585. In *Trattati d'Arte del Cinquecento*, ed. by Paola Barocchi, Bari 1962, III, p. 220).

GIOVAN BATTISTA ARMENI, *Dei veri precetti della pittura*, 1587.
At the end of his work Armenini defends theoretical treatises on art and the superiority of intellectual speculation with respect to simple artisan practice, that is, to the actual practice of art. Armenini was only pleading his own cause, for though a learned *conoscitore* of art, he was no artist. It is interesting to see how he consoles himself with Alberti, who, yet again, is presented as the champion of theoretical speculation: "Vitruvius wrote about architecture and machines, and so did

Leon Battista Alberti, ... even though there are no walls, arches, pillars, or roofs that bear their signatures".
(Giovan Battista Armeni, *Dei veri precetti della pittura*, Ravenna 1587; ed. cons. by Stefano Ticozzi, Pisa 1823, p. 262).

MICHELE POCCIANTI, *Catalogus scriptorum florentinorum omnis generis*, 1589.
"Leo Baptista Albertus Laurentii filius amplissimi Cardinalis Alberti de Albertis nepos, Abbatiae Sancti Severini Pisani praesul dignissimus, vir, et rhetoricc liquore, et poetica varietate ac totius philosophae emicantissimo splendore expolitus; Iuris prudentia, Geometria, Astrologia, Musica, pingendi et sculpendi facultate instructissimus, cujus ingenii acumen prope prodigiosum ad omnes scientias, caeterasque artes sic natura convertit, ut potius ad earum secreta divina pervestiganda, singulorumque entium latentes essentias productus crederetur, quam ut mortali corpore interceptus humanam duceret vitam, multa ut doctus, gravis, compositus, eruditus, et excussus conscripsit, in quibus nihil expositum, nihil triviale, sive sententias, sive verba spectes conspicere licet, quin potius in his sui ipsius praestantissimis scriptis sic semper prioribus certant sequentia, et novae fertiliter inter legendum efflorescunt gratiae, ut perpetua quadam acclamatione interspirandi locus non detur". This praise marks the codification of a literay topos that was to last until the early nineteenth century at least, especially amongst the erudite circles of Florentine criticism.
(Michele Poccianti, *Catalogus scriptorum florentinorum omnis generis*, Florence 1589, p. III).

GIOVANNI RUSCONI, *Della Architettura*, 1590.
In the introduction the author says: "the profession [architecture] had its beginnings in and grew up, so to speak, through the construction of buildings and structures of rare device produced by necessity; to its later forms of comfort and delight, which Vitruvius finally gave it, were added various members and components to increase both its comfort and magnificence, as every architect may see for himself in the writings of Leon Battista Alberti, Serlio, Monsignor Barbaro, Palladio, and others". There is no denying the importance Rusconi attributes to the writings of Alberti, which are included among the most authoritative texts of the sixteenth-century classical theorists.
(Giovanni Rusconi, *Della Architettura*, Venice 1590).

GIOVAN PAOLO LOMAZZO, *Idea del Tempio della Pittura*, 1590.
In the fourth chapter of his book Lomazzo traces a short survey of the authors who had written on the rules of art. Brief though it may be, it shows that this Milanese critic-artist, whose artistic formation and interests were so very different from Alberti's, was unable to ignore so universally acclaimed an authority: "Mentioning only those whose works have been published, we have Leon Battista Alberti, who wrote about perspective, architecture, and painting". He then cites Pomponio Gaurico, Luca Pacioli, and Vignola etc.

Nevertheless, one must admit that this brief reference made by a late Mannerist theorist looks more like the pale memory of a tradition now regarded as almost valueless.
(Giovan Paolo Lomazzo, *Idea del Tempio della Pittura*, Milan 1590).

FILIPPO VALORI, *Termini di mezzo rilievo e d'intera dottrina*, 1604.
Leon Battista gets his share of praise in this survey of the great men of Florence. The work takes as its rather unusual point of departure a number of eminent men whose busts decorated the ancient villa of the Albizzi family. The villa later passed into the hands of the Valori family and was furnished with that typically Baroque taste for the hurried, spontaneous accumulation of objects. "Knowledge has its orders and degrees according to whether it be necessary or useful to life or to the information of man, who needs to know about the origins of his country, the simple elements, history, geography, and above all the various kinds of public and private buildings. The latter have been explained by the great master, Leon Battista Alberti, who resurrected architectural theory and who was universally known as the Florentine Vitruvius. Nearly all his books have been translated by Messer Cosimo Bartoli. He also wrote a treatise on economics (of which there is a manuscript copy in the house) and a comedy in ancient Latin, which he did for his amusement".
(Filippo Valori, *Termini di mezzo Rilievo e di Intera dottrina tra gli Archi di Casa Valori. Eccellenza degli scrittori e nobiltà degli studi fiorentini*, Florence 1604).

FEDERICO ZUCCARO, *Origine e progresso dell'Accademia del disegno di Roma*, 1604.
In tackling the definition of painting, Zuccaro quotes Vasari, Lomazzo, Dolce, and finally Leon Battista. Though critical of the latter, he mentions him together with the leading figures of sixteenth-century classicism and Mannerism, evidence that Alberti's thought continued to enjoy great prestige. "In his commentaries on painting, Leon Battista Alberti says that it consists of *circoscrizione, composizione*, and *ricevimento di lume*. This is not to our taste, however, nor is it an adequate definition as far as we understand painting, or would have it explained and defined. Nor do we agree with the rest of his book concerning the teaching and training of young painters. But leaving all this to those who find it interesting, we may say that the *circoscrizione* he talks about is form, which is an aspect of design. *Composizione* is certainly an aspect of painting, but so it is of many other arts. *Ricevimento del lume*, which is mentioned without further explanation, is common to all objects, bodies and matter."
(Federico Zuccaro, *Origine e progresso dell'Accademia del disegno di Roma*, Pavia 1604, pp. 24-25).

FRANCESCO BOCCHI, *Elogiorum quibus viri doctissimi nati Florentiae decorantur*, 1609.
The ninth *Life* in this book is dedicated to Alberti and appears between Pier Vettori's and Amerigo

Vespucci's: "Hic magno praeditus ingenio disciplinis mathematicis institutus permulta virtutis vel primis temporibus aetatis signa dedit. Pingendi studio incensus dedit operam picturae non mediocrem, eoque artificio delectatus, cum litterarum opus non intermitteret, res multas varii generis sua manu pinxit multamque hac industria laudem est adeptus. Nunc igitur doctrinis humanioribus, in quibus eruditissimus evaserat, nunc aliis artibus egregiis edoctus ita suum ingenium ad res varias apposite versavit; et exercuit, ut documenta utraque in re nobilis industriae nobis posteris reliquerit". The author goes on to praise Alberti's treatises on painting and architecture, and his principal architectural works. He concludes: "Inter pictores et architectos nobiles datus est ei locus, ut notum est; sed viri litterati suum omnino sibi vendicant, et pertinere ad se maxime contendunt". Here too, one can see the typically Florentine tendency to establish abstract categories when praising the great fifteenth-century artist and *literato*.
(Francesco Bocchi, *Elogiorum quibus viri doctissimi nati Florentiae decorantur*, Florence 1609, p. 50 ff.).

TEOFILO GALLACCINI, *Degli errori degli Architetti*, 1621.
The Sienese critic describes Alberti as "a noble Florentine architect, the greatest after Vitruvius ...". This is followed by a number of quotations which imply Alberti's indisputable authority. Gallaccini feels that his agreement with Alberti is very much to his own credit.
(Teofilo Gallaccini, *Degli errori degli architetti*, published for the first time in Venice in 1767, and edited by Giovanni Antonio Pecci, p. 5).

RAPHAEL DU FRESNE, *Vita di Leon Battista Alberti*, 1651.
This biography was written by the French critic and man of letters Raphael du Fresne and appeared as the introduction to his edition of the treatises on painting and sculpture. It contains an appreciative evaluation of Leon Battista's works and thought. This shows that not only was there no sign of a decline in Alberti's fame, but that the rational, classical harmony that formed the basis of his thought was fully understood and appreciated in a country closely bound to the canons of classical art: Louis XIV's France. "... it is difficult to say whether he was a better rhetorician or poet, whether he wrote better Latin or Tuscan, whether he was greater in the practical or speculative sciences, whether he was more serious in the discussion of important matters or more urbane and light-hearted in dealing with simple, ordinary things ... He could deal with subjects generally and yet enter into each one in detail. And when he applied himself to a particular subject it seemed as if his noble intellect had never been engaged in anything else, equalling, indeed excelling those considered most expert in that particular branch of knowledge ... [in architecture] he was the first to attempt to revive its early purity and, opposing the barbarism of centuries of Gothic art, he restored its order and proportion, so that he was universally acclaimed as the Florentine Vitruvius; ... [later he wrote the *De re aedificatoria*], in which all the

secrets of the art are revealed with exquisite order and simplicity, whereas previously they had been locked up in the obscure writings of Vitruvius". (Raphael du Fresne, *Vita di Leon Battista Alberti*, 1651. The edition quoted is the Italian one: Raphael du Fresne, *I Tre Libri della Pittura e il Trattato della Statua di Leon Battista Alberti, con la Vita del medesimo*, Bologna 1786, pp. 123-30).

JOHN EVELYN, *Introduction to the "De Statua"*, 1664. The following eulogy served as an introduction to the *De Statua*, which was included as an appendix in the English edition of Fréart's *Parallèle de l'Architecture Antique et de la Moderne:* "There is no man pretending to this Art, or indeed to any other whatsoever, who does not greedily embrace all that bears the name of Leon Baptista Alberti, who was a Florentine Gentleman of illustrious birth, great learning, and extraordinary abilities in all the politer Sciences, as he stands celebrated by Paulus Jovius, and for which he became so dear to that great Maecenas Lorenzo di Medici, who chose him, with Marsilius Ficinus, Christopherus Landinus, and other the most refin'd Wits of that Age, to entertain his Academic retirements and solitude of Camaldoli ... as being indeed one of the very first that polished the now almost utterly lost and extinguished Art of Architecture; in which how successfully he joyned Practice to Speculation, there are abundance of examples, some whereof are wrought by his own hands. He composed three Books De Pictura, full of incomparable researches appertaining to that noble Art. This of Statues ... appeared so apposite and full of profitable instruction to our Workmen, who for want of these or the like Rules, can neither securely work after the life, or their own inventions, to the immense disgrace of that divine Art". It is significant that Alberti's fame crossed the Channel at a time when English art was enjoying a moment of great splendour.
(John Evelyn, Introduction to Leon Battista Alberti's *De Statua*, included in *A Parallel of the Ancient Architecture with the Modern*, London 1664; translation from the French *Parallèle de l'Architecture Antique et de la Moderne*, by Roland Fréart, Paris 1650, p. 143).

GIOVAN PIETRO BELLORI, *Le vite de' pittori, scultori, ed architetti moderni*, 1672.
Bellori first tries to define and clarify the concept of artistic invention. His aim is to explain the imaginative process that produces a work of art — the famous "Idea". Tracing the historical origins of the concept and its indebtedness to the writers of antiquity, he says: "Now comparing the precepts of the wise ancients with the excellent rules established by our modern authors, we may quote Leon Battista Alberti, who teaches that not only is similarity loved in all things, but above all beauty, and that one must choose the finest parts of the most beautiful bodies". He goes on to discuss the ideas of Leonardo da Vinci and Raphael in such a way that Alberti's thought — though exploited in favour of the concept of the "Idea" — is made to appear as a milestone in the development of modern aesthetics.

(Giovan Pietro Bellori, *Le vite de' pittori, scultori ed architetti moderni*, Rome 1672, p. 22).

LE SIEUR DE VARILLAS, *Les anecdotes de Florence*, 1685,
At a certain point in his biography of Lorenzo the Magnificent, De Varillas draws up a long list of the famous people who frequented the court of the Medicis, one of whom was Alberti: "One must acknowledge the tireless genius of Leon Battista Alberti, for no man has ever worked at so difficult and tedious a subject more successfully than he. His family was one of the most illustrious in Florence and connected with the Medicis, this being the first link in his friendship with Lorenzo. He told Lorenzo about his idea of studying ancient architecture and was given all the advice and assistance he needed — which was very great indeed. Lorenzo's letters gave him access to all the countries of Europe and Asia, wherever there were any old ruins that suggested they might once have been great buildings. Alberti visited them at his leisure and noted all their measurements, so that when he returned to Florence he was able to compare his observations with Vitruvius's rules. It was then that he realized that the obscurity of this author was one of the principal causes of the neglect in which architecture had lain for so many centuries. This was why he decided to make Vitruvius more intelligible and to express his own ideas in a more accessible language. He did both in so neat and orderly a manner that after examining his work, the critics proclaimed he had written in such a way that those who read his books could become as skiltul as he was. Later he applied himself to optics, for he saw that the painters of his day were incapable of painting portraits in miniature. He discovered, clarified, and published the laws and principles of this science. He spared himself neither trouble nor expense in encouraging the young to put them into practice. The result was that there was a greater number of fine painters, sculptors, and architects in the Florence of his day than there had been in Greece, when the latter could boast of its being the mother and nurse of the Liberal Arts. I shall not mention them here, for those interested will find them in Vasari, who wrote three volumes in their praise. I shall only repeat that Alberti's imagination was crowded with palaces, decorations, and statues. But he could also relax in the company of the lesser Muses, and whoever takes the trouble to read the fables he wrote in imitation of Aesop will agree (if unbiased) that his are in no way inferior. I do not have so high opinion of the dialogue he published later under the title of *Momus*, for it is much ado about nothing, and its humour is so weak at times that one really has to feel like laughing to appreciate it. Whatever he was, Alberti died (when still very young) in the arms of Lorenzo de Medici and Politian praised him publicly in a discourse that is considered one of the finest of his works".
This passage deserves to be quoted at length, not because of its historical accuracy or because it adds anything to our knowledge of Alberti's life, but for the unusual, fascinating, adventurous,

Baroque image it presents of Alberti. It is interesting to observe how De Varillas transforms the solemn man of letters, the illustrious Florentine Vitruvius who had been celebrated by generations of critics, into a romantic youth travelling to the farthest corners of Europe and Asia, being hailed by the princes of those remote regions as a new Marco Polo, and dying full of the ardour of youth in the arms of his powerful and faithful friend Lorenzo.
This sentimental Baroque interpretation has the vespertine lights of a Claude Lorraine and the mysterious, picaresque scenery of a Salvator Rosa, but it makes a welcome change from the monotonously repetitive, stale eulogising of literary officialdom.
(Le Sieur de Varillas, *Les anecdotes de Florence, ou l'Histoire secrète de la Maison de Medicis*, The Hague 1685, IV, pp. 185-87).

FERDINANDO GALLI BIBIENA, *L'Architettura civile preparata su la geometria, e ridotta alle prospettive*, 1711. In the introduction Bibiena insists that not everything in his book is his own work and that part of the material taken from other authors might seem a little out-of-date. He apologises for this, saying that the material can always be utilised for it is quite orthodox: "certain parts of the cornices, bases, and pedestals are decorated with carvings similar to those used by the ancients, Leon Battista Alberti, the Sienese Pietro Cattaneo, Bramante, Giulio Romano and others. These are no longer fashionable, but since they are intrinsically good, I have thought it better to include them, so that those who want to may make use of them".
This demonstrates the unprejudiced spirit of the author and of the age he lived in. He considers the classical forms of the early Renaissance to be obsolete but accepts them all the same; since they are intrinsically "good", some eccentric may be led to adopt them in seeking originality in the past.
(Ferdinando Galli Bibiena, *L'Architettura civile preparata su la geometria, e ridotta alle prospettive. Considerazioni pratiche*, Parma 1711).

FRANCESCO ALGAROTTI, *Saggio sopra l'Architettura*, 1753).
Algarotti's reference to Leon Battista on page 17 of his treatise is unusual: the *De re aedificatoria* is cited in connection with the theory that classical architecture was derived from primeval wooden constructions and in relation to the durability and use of certain natural materials. Algarotti's rationalism reduces Alberti's treatise to a manual on the art of building, and he is inclined to emphasize those aspects more closely connected with technology.
Alberti's treatise is quoted again on page 27 to confirm the naturalistic origin of the classical elements and orders; the base of the column originated in the iron rings that used to reinforce the point where the tree-trunk was fixed into the ground. This illustrates the typically functionalistic attitude with which a man of the Enlightenment approached the *De re aedificatoria*.
Even Algarotti's explicit praise of Alberti (p. 33)

for having made the cornices of the entablatures of the intermediate storeys of the Palazzo Rucellai less prominent than the upper cornice is motivated by technical reasons and steeped in *esprit positif*. Algarotti seems to reduce the typological revolution implicit in Alberti's classicism to a simple question of respecting the dictates of natural reason. (Francesco Algarotti, *Saggio sopra l'Architettura*, Pisa 1753; ed. cons., Venice 1784).

GIOVAN BATTISTA MAZZUCCHELLI, *Gli Scrittori d'Italia*, 1753.
Mazzucchelli says nothing to alter the traditional view of Alberti as a man of encyclopaedic knowledge. Vasari and all the other more authoritative writers are quoted with an accuracy and scrupulosity typical of the Enlightenment. A scholar of literature, Mazzucchelli was more interested in Leon Battista from a language point of view, and especially in his Latin: "From this point of view, he is all the more exceptional insofar as he wrote about new, very difficult subjects, such as Mathematics and Architecture, with a felicity of style and a wealth of Latin terms and expressions. As Giovio says, no one else could have written about architecture so clearly, or so elegantly at least, because of the poverty of the language at the time. Thus it is said he so clarified the teachings of Vitruvius that it was through his efforts alone that the ancient writer became comprehensible. Indeed, not only was he called the Florentine Vitruvius, but some went so far as to say he excelled Vitruvius himself."
Mazzucchelli then gives an accurate list of all Alberti's written works.
(Giovan Battista Mazzucchelli, *Gli Scrittori d'Italia*, Brescia 1753, I, P. 1, p. 310 ff.).

FRANCESCO MILIZIA, *Le vite de' più celebri architetti d'ogni nazione e d'ogni tempo*, 1768.
The first edition of this work was published anonymously. Undoubtedly revolutionary in its attitude to contemporary Alberti criticism, it begins with the usual laudatory phrases: "Leon Battista was a man of rare, almost universal knowledge ... versed in philosophy, mathematics, poetry, law, rhetoric, and the fine arts. He was well acquainted with painting and sculpture, but was particularly knowledgeable in architecture. He acquired this knowledge through the study and measurement of antique buildings, which he undertook many journeys to see. His treatise, the *De re aedificatoria*, was translated into Italian by Bartoli and consists of ten books on architecture. It is a most valuable work for architects, though over-loaded with useless learning. He is deservedly considered as one of the principal revivers of antique architecture, which he happily re-introduced both in theory and practice". This is a good example of Milizia's lucid, cautious, pungent criticism; perfunctory and partial though it may be at times, it injected new life into the biographical study of Alberti, which had lain beneath a mass of common-places for so long. He refuses to include the façade of S. Maria Novella among Alberti's works ("is too Gothic, or German rather"), but praises the loggias of the houses of the Rucellai family in Via della Scala, the first to have entablatures in the fifteenth

century: "The arches do not rest upon the capitals of the columns. They only appear to do so, for it is the architraves that really rest upon them. It would be ridiculous to stress the importance of this principle, which even young boys know". Of S. Andrea he says that it is "dignified, well designed as a whole, and every part reflects the soundness of its construction. Unfortunately, the projections of the cornices are rather flat, the mouldings slight, and the style very dry in general". Of the Tempio Malatestiano: "The building has a majestic solidity which rivals ancient architecture, while the façade, with its big central arch, has a kind of triumphal quality, well-suited to a temple that commemorates Sigismondo's victories".
These quotations are sufficient to show that Milizia's revaluation of Alberti was not the outcome of any profound research or of any addition to the list of Alberti's works. Nor was it inspired by any revolutionary interpretation of his achievements. The winds of change that blow through the pages of this critic of the Enlightenment are raised by a new approach to Alberti's works, by an interpretation stripped of the traditional reverence for Alberti. Milizia's judgements, though caustic, perfunctory, condescending, and ironic at times, injected new life into the pallid conventional image of a profoundly learned Florentine Vitruvius and transformed him from a symbol of an architectural revival into a living man of flesh and blood working within a particular historical context, fallible therefore, but more real and credible. It is worth noticing the passage Milizia added to the end of his biography of Alberti in the third edition of the *Lives* and which remained an integral part of the work (this edition appeared under the new title of *Memorie degli Architetti Antichi e Moderni*, Parma 1781). In this passage not only is Alberti's "taste" subjected to unfair criticism (being interpreted in the light of Enlightenment classicism) but it is misrepresented. Yet the very fact that an artist who had lived three centuries earlier was judged to be worthy of close critical analysis marks the end of a tradition that tended to mummify Alberti in commemorative indifference, and heralds the beginning of one that considered him a living reality: "Alberti's taste in the decoration of the orders was not the most exquisite, and [his style] has the undefinable smell of the old churches that inspired it. His Doric capital is almost Gothic, and so is his Corinthian, which has only nine diameters. But the strangest fact is that this order has no dripstone".
(Francesco Milizia, *Le vite de' più celebri architetti d'ogni nazione e d'ogni tempo*, Rome, 1768. This first edition was published anonymously).

ANTON FRANCESCO RAU e MODESTO RASTRELLI, *Serie degli Uomini i più illustri nella pittura, scultura e architettura*, 1769.
This hotch-potch of quaint learning and traditional theory quoted without any kind of critical discrimination also contains a few original observations, as in the conclusion for example: "Leon Battista Alberti was undoubtedly a great architect and made many improvements in the art he practised ... But

Raphael du Fresne is mistaken when he writes in his biography that Alberti was the first to attempt to restore architecture to its original purity by opposing the barbarism of centuries of Gothic art and reviving the principles of order and proportion. Many architects had endeavoured to do the same before him, and some had been successful enough. One has only to look at some of the great Brunelleschi's works to see the truth of this; at the beautiful temples of S. Lorenzo and S. Spirito, for example. For though these buildings do not have the elegance and splendour of classical architecture, they have none of that barbarism which deformed the Gothic, or rather, German works.
It is truer to say that our Leon Battista was the first Florentine to write about architecture clearly, methodically, and knowledgeably. This is why many rightly called him the Florentine Vitruvius. One must admit, however, that he is more famous for having elaborated the rules of architecture than for having put them into practice. For, as Vasari says (and we venerate his authority in such matters), his designs have many good points and many bad. This prevents us from including him among the most famous men who have made the city of Florence glorious".
(Antonio Francesco Rau e Modesto Rastrelli, *Serie degli Uomini più illustri nella pittura, scultura e architettura, con i loro elogi e ritratti incisi in rame*, Florence 1769, I, p. 97 ff.).

GIUSEPPE PIACENZA, *Notizie de' professori del disegno*, 1770.
Piacenza begins his work in the usual manner: "The great nobility of his birth, his rare, almost universal knowledge, and his distinction as one of the revivers of architectural theory. ... Nevertheless, the art Leon Battista excelled in most of all and which will render him immortal was architecture; the books he wrote on this subject in Latin provide ample testimony of his skill and genius as an architect. It is rightly claimed that he made the teachings of Vitruvius intelligible, and so our Alberti was deservedly called the Florentine Vitruvius. One cannot admire sufficiently enough the gracefulness of style and abundance of ancient Latin terms and expressions with which he wrote about new and very difficult subjects such as mathematics and architecture".
Piacenza then deals with the life and works of Alberti comprehensively and knowledgeably (he quotes a great number of books about the architect), but the guiding spirit of his biography is still Vasari, of whom we catch an echo in his evaluation of Alberti's personality: "Leon Battista was a calm, honest man, a lover of virtue, generous and courteous to everyone. He always lived honourably like the gentleman he was. He suffered greatly from the attacks of jealous men and had to put up with family troubles. But though ardent and passionate by nature, he knew how to control himself, and despised revenge with sublime philosophy. Though somewhat inclined to solitude and scientific speculation, he could be cheerful with friends and often amused them with shrewd, witty remarks without any loss to his dignity."
Careful research (typical of the eighteenth-century

mentality) and strict adherence to the opinions of the most respectable literary authorities make Piacenza's biography a characteristic example of the moderate, compromising Illuminism that was so prominent a feature of eighteenth-century Italian culture.

(Giuseppe Piacenza, *Notizie de' professori del disegno da Cimabue in qua, opera di Filippo Baldinucci, fiorentino accademico della Crusca, nuovamente data alle stampe con varie dissertazioni, note ed aggiunte*, Turin 1770, II, p. 49).

QUATREMÈRE DE QUINCY, *Encyclopédie Méthodique, Architecture*, 1788.
The first lines of this article, which is written in the strictly economical language of the rationalist encyclopaedists, try to formulate a precise definition of Alberti: "He must be regarded as one of the restorers of architecture, equally versed in its theory and practice. He was the second artist to build according to the principles of Vitruvius and the rules of antiquity, and he contributed greatly to the improvement of architecture. Following the example of Brunelleschi, he strove to make architecture more graceful and decorative than his predecessors". The lucidity of this judgement seems to reflect the intellectual clarity of Alberti's designs. Equally clear, balanced, and rational is the portrait Quatremère draws of Alberti the man. It is very close to the Illuministic ideal of the philosopher who plans his time and existence in order to protect them from the whims of the irrational. "Architecture was not the only fine art Alberti was skilled in. He also practised painting and sculpture. Yet again, he was versed in philosophy, mathematics, poetry, and antiquity.

"One may wonder how he found the time to cultivate so many difficult arts; but exercised in the study of letters at an early age, work became a habit for him. The hours he dedicated to work left him no time for amusement or rest. His spiritual qualities were no less great than his talents.

Alberti was loving and generous; he was never spiteful to his fellow artists, for he never envied their success. He died peacefully in his own country at a very advanced age".

This sounds like an echo of Voltaire's "il faut cultiver notre jardin".

(Quatremère De Quincy, *Encyclopédie Méthodique, Architecture*, Paris 1788, I, p. 22).

CHRONOLOGICAL SUMMARY OF THE LIFE OF ALBERTI

1404
Leon Battista Alberti born in Genoa on 14 February.

1414
His family in Venice, where his father, Lorenzo, was in charge of the Venetian branch of the family's trading company.

1415
The young Leon Battista sent to the boarding-school of Gasparino Barzizza in Padua.

1421
His father died in Padua on 24 March. About the same time Leon Battista was living with relations in Bologna and studying canon law.

1424
He wrote the Latin comedy *Philodoxeus*, which was passed off as the work of Lepidus, a non-existent Roman playwright. So it was believed for ten years, until Leon Battista issued a revised edition purged of all additions, and declared its true authorship.

1426
Alberti entered the service of Cardinal Albergati in Bologna.

1428
He abandoned the study of law because of difficulty in adapting himself to the repetitive, mnemonic methods of study involved (he had only obtained a 'sub-degree' in decrees).
On 22 October the ban that had sent the Albertis into exile was lifted at the request of Pope Martin V.

1429
Leon Battista in Florence. In this year he wrote the *De commodis et incommodis litterarum*, the *Ecatomfilea* (in which a woman talks about the virtues the man she loves ought to possess), and the vernacular dialogue *Deifira* (which discusses how to escape from amorous relationships that have begun badly). He also wrote the strictly classical *Egloghe* in Latin, brief poetic works such as *canzones* and elegies, as well as works in the vernacular like the *Religione*, in which he deals with the hard life of the priest in the tone of an apologia. These were followed by the Latin dialogues, *Intercoenales*, (1429c.) dedicated to Paolo Toscanelli, a famous doctor and mathematician.

1430
In all probability he accompanied Cardinal Albergati on a mission across the Alps, the purpose of which was to settle a dispute between the King of France and the Duke of Burgundy. The diplomatic mission followed first the king and then the duke across France, and returned to Italy two years later via Germany and Basle. The *De re aedificatoria* shows that Alberti was well acquainted with the characteristic buildings and constructional techniques of northern Europe.

1432
About this time he must have settled down in Rome after being appointed an apostolic abbreviator.

1433-34
In this period he wrote the *Della famiglia*. As a result of quarrels with the barons and difficulties

with the Council of Basle, Pope Eugenius IV left Rome for Florence, where he was followed by Leon Battista.

1435
In contact once more with the stimulating atmosphere of Florence, he wrote the *De Pictura* in Latin, a treatise he later translated into the vernacular, dedicating it to Filippo Brunelleschi. It became the basis for all future developments in the study of perspective and proportion, and it was probably accompanied by a series of practical geometrical exercises called the *Elementa Picturae*.

1436
On 18 April Eugenius IV moved from Florence to Bologna, followed by Alberti. The Pope remained in the city with his court for twenty months, during which time Alberti was able to visit Venice. In this period he produced a whole series of brief literary works such as the *De Jure*, a guide to correct legal practice, the *Lettere* in the manner of Petrarch, and the *Apologhi*, a collection of a hundred maxims, a very popular literary genre among contemporary Humanists.

1438
In January Leon Battista was in Ferrara, where a Council was being held in opposition to the one of Basle.

1439
On 10 January the Pope and the Emperor of the Greeks (who had accompanied the representatives of the church of Constantinople to the Council) entered Florence, where the Council of Basle had been transferred and where it ended in the same year with a proclamation reuniting the two Churches. In this period Alberti wrote the *Theogenius*, a dialogue on the State written in the vernacular, which affirmed that virtue and rectitude were the true foundation of society. The work was dedicated to Lionello d'Este.

1441
Leon Battista organized the *Certame Coronario* in Florence. This was a competition which awarded a crown of laurel, as in ancient times, to the author of the best vernacular poem on the theme of "True Friendship", after it had been read before a huge audience in S. Maria del Fiore. Alberti himself, together with various other contemporary writers, took part with a work that was later incorporated in the fourth book of the *Della Famiglia*. The latter, together with many other minor works written during his lifetime, shows the importance Alberti attributed to the vernacular as an instrument in the popularisation of knowledge and instruction, in spite of his great love of classicism.

1442
Leon Battista was invited to Ferrara, a city ruled by his friend Lionello d'Este. During his stay, Lionello may have suggested that he write a treatise on architecture in the vernacular. Alberti gave advice on the erection of the equestrian statue in honour of Lionello's father, Niccolò, and drew up the general plan of the cathedral bell tower. He also wrote the short treatise *De equo animante*, a mine of information about horses; their shapes, colours, breeding, breaking-in, illnesses etc.
In this period Alberti wrote *Mosca*, an improvi-

sation on Lucian's *Eulogy of the Fly*, of which Guarino Veronese had sent him a translation. Prompted by the death of his dog, he also wrote *Canis*, a moralistic eulogy of man's faithful friend. About the same time he wrote the dialogue *Della Tranquillità dell'Animo*, a typical example of Humanist ethics: one must bear with adversities, know oneself, avoid anger and revenge, not be over-talkative, be calm in one's judgements, firm in the midst of inevitable trials, never yield to despair, and keep one's mind constantly occupied with mental exercises when sad and worried.

1443
He wrote a version of the *Della famiglia* in the vernacular, a treatise consisting of four books: the first three on the education of children, conjugal love, and household administration respectively, were written in the Roman period of 1432-34; the fourth, on friendship, was added almost ten years later. It is fundamental for an understanding of Leon Battista's social and ethical thought. In the same year Eugenius IV returned to Rome and Alberti followed him.
In Rome he began *Momus* (ante 1450) an allegorical fable largely indebted to the fantastic adventure stories of Lucian and dealing with the correct conduct of the Prince. It was extremely popular in Humanist circles.

1446
He was commissioned by Cardinal Prospero Colonna to retrieve a Roman ship from the bottom of Lake Nemi. He managed to lift it from the bed of the lake by means of winches and a pontoon, but it broke in half. The experience led him to write *Navis* (1447) (lost), which discussed the shapes of classical ships and the best methods of naval construction.

1447
On 23 February Eugenius IV died. He was succeeded by Pope Nicholas V, or Tommaso da Sarzana, Cardinal Albergati's secretary, a cultured man and a great lover of Humanism. He had known Alberti since the latter had been a student at the University of Bologna and had become a close friend of his during the diplomatic mission to France and Germany.
By 1450 Alberti had completed a number of brief works of various kinds: the *Ludi Matematici* deals with the solution of interesting problems regarding mechanics, physics, optics etc., and was dedicated to Meliaduso d'Este, Lionello's brother and abbot of Pomposa; the *De motibus ponderis* described the behaviour and characteristics of heavy bodies; the *De' pondi e leve di alcuna rota* (considered apocryphal) is a treatise on all kinds of mechanical devices used to convert the force of wind, water, or any other natural phenomenon into motive-power. At about the same time he seems to have taken part in Nicholas V's grandiose project for the reconstruction of Rome, though there is no documentary evidence to prove this. The project included the restoration of the city walls and the "Forty Basilicas", the repair of the city aqueducts, the remodelling of the Vatican quarters, and the construction of a new St. Peter's. There is no doubt that the ideals of the Humanist Pope and Leon Battista coincided quite remarkably in this outstanding building programme.

1446-51

The Palazzo Rucellai in Florence is believed to have been built in this period. Leon Battista provided the plan of its façade and later drew up that of the Loggia in front of the palace. The actual construction was probably carried out by Bernardo Rossellino.

1448-70

The façade of S. Maria Novella was completed on behalf of the Rucellai family.

1450

In this period he seems to have written the *Descriptio Urbis Romae*, in which he deals with the city's ancient monuments. After measuring them accurately, he made a large, very precise map of them. This is reasonably accurate and far superior to any other contemporary map of Rome.

Work was begun on the Tempio Malatestiano in Rimini. This was designed by Leon Battista and executed by Matteo de' Pasti. The work continued for many years, but was interrupted by the death of Sigismondo Malatesta in 1468 and remained unfinished.

1452

According to Mattia Palmieri, Alberti presented Nicholas V with the *De re aedificatoria*, his great treatise on architecture consisting of ten books. Thus the manuscript began to circulate, though it was not until 1485 that the first printed edition of the treatise was published in Florence by Aldus Alamanus, with a dedication to Lorenzo the Magnificent. The first translation into Italian was done by Pietro Lauro and published in Venice in 1546, but the best known one is Cosimo Bartoli's, published in Florence in 1550. The fame of the treatise also spread abroad from the middle of the sixteenth century onwards.

1455

Nicholas V died and was succeeded by Callistus III, a Catalan and uncle of the future Alexander VI.

1458

Aeneas Sylvius Piccolomini was elected to the Papacy as Pius II. He was a friend of Leon Battista's and shared the same Humanistic ideals. In his *Commentaries* he recalls archaeological walks to the aqueducts of Rome in the company of Alberti.

1459

Leon Battista accompanied the Pope to Mantua, where Pius II had summoned a Diet for the organisation of a vast new Crusade. On this occasion the Marquis of Mantua, Ludovico Gonzaga, commissioned Alberti to construct a church dedicated to St. Sebastian. Work was begun on it the same year.

1460

Pius II left Mantua in January, but Leon Battista stayed on to superintend the construction of the new church. In this period he wrote the short Latin treatise *Trivia* on the art of oratory, dedicated to the young Lorenzo de' Medici.

1463

Alberti returned to Mantua, where the church was half built. However, the work gradually slowed down before coming to a complete standstill; it was completed in a hurried fashion towards the end of the century, without any regard for Alberti's original design.

1464

Pius II died at Ancona, preparing for the Crusade. He was succeeded by Paul II, who, unlike his predecessor, had very little sympathy for Humanism. He soon abolished the college of apostolic abbreviators, which included all the most important Humanists in Rome at the time. Consequently, Leon Battista found himself unemployed, though he was sufficiently well-off by this time to be able to maintain his customary standard of living. He remained in Rome and frequented, amongst others, the mathematician Luca Pacioli and the wealthy Florentine Bishop, Leonardo Dati, who had been a friend of his since the time of the *Certame Coronario*.

1466

Alberti wrote the *De componendis cifris*, in which he examined the problem of interpreting the scriptures and established a system of communication by means of an undecipherable code.

1467

He took charge of the work on the Rucellai Chapel in S. Pancrazio in Florence, for which he designed the shrine of the Holy Sepulchre.

1468

He witnessed, but was not involved in, the dissolution of the Roman Academy and the persecution of Humanists like Platina and Pomponio Leto.

He wrote the *De Iciarchia*, in which he discusses government, describing the ideal Prince as a wise, virtuous, just man.

1470

He was entrusted with the construction of the tribune in the church of the Santissima Annunziata in Florence. Michelozzo had already proposed plans for the completion of the apsidal part of the Servite church, while Manetti had drawn up a project for a circular choir. The foundations had been laid in 1460, but nothing further was done until Ludovico Gonzaga, who had made a promise to the Friars, took charge of the project and appointed a new architect. Leon Battista did not live to see the work completed, for it was not finished until 1477.

It had now become a regular custom every autumn for Leon Battista to spend some time with his very close friend, Count Federico da Montefeltro, in Urbino.

1471

In September Alberti sent plans from Rome for the new church of the Gonzagas in Mantua: S. Andrea. Work on the church proceeded rapidly, but Alberti did not live to see even the foundations laid, for he died in Rome in early April of the following year. S. Andrea was continued according to Alberti's original plans thanks to the fidelity of the Florentine architect, Luca Fancelli.

1472

Alberti died, the only mention of his death being a brief note in Mattia Palmieri's chronicle.[1] He was buried in Rome, in a church that was demolished a few decades later.

1. Mattia Palmieri, who died in 1483, continued the history of the world that Matteo Palmieri had written from the earliest times up to 1443 under the title of *De temporibus suis*.

BIBLIOGRAPHY

The most up-to-date Alberti bibliography is that published by Renato Bonelli and his assistants in the Library Bulletin of the Faculty of Architecture of the University of Rome, Nos. 2-3, April 1973. Its general section covers Alberti's literary works and their editions, and it is reproduced below in full. The section dealing with Alberti's architectural works has been adapted to the needs of the present volume.
The bibliographical material regarding the treatises on art is included in the second part, which is more specifically concerned with the subject.

THE LITERARY WORKS OF LEON BATTISTA ALBERTI
(In chronological order)

1424
Philodoxeus, a Latin play, with a *Commentarium Philodoxo fabulae* written in 1434.

1429-30
De commodis et incommodis litterarum, a dissertation on literary studies in Latin.

c. 1429
Amator, a discourse on the nature of love, in Latin. Translated into the vernacular by Carlo Alberti, Leon Battista's brother, with the title of *Ephoebia*.
Intercoenales, a collection in ten books of dialogues, apologias and short stories in Latin. Books I, II and IV (the *Defunctus*) have survived together with the *Uxoria* and *Anuli*.

c. 1429-30
Deiphira, a dialogue in the vernacular.
Ecatonfilea, a dialogue in the vernacular.
Poesie ("Agiletta" and "Mirzia", elegies; sonnets; a madrigal; a love story; sestinas; "Corinto" and "Tyrsis", eclogues), in the vernacular.

1433
Vita Sancti Potiti, in Latin.

1433-34
Della famiglia, a treatise in the form of a dialogue, in the vernacular (Books I, II and III; Book IV was written in 1440 or 1441 and entitled *De amicitia*).

1434
De statua, a brief treatise on sculpture in Latin.

1435
De pictura, a treatise in Latin, with a note entitled "De punctis et lineis apud pictores" written a few years later.
Elementa picturae, a technical-didactic treatise in Latin.

1436
Della pittura, a vernacular version of the above.

c. 1436
Elementi di pittura, a vernacular version of the above.

1437 ss.
Lettere sull'amore (to P. Codagnello, *Lettera consolatoria* and *Avvertimenti matrimoniali*, a translation into the vernacular of the "Uxoria", see above) in the vernacular.

1437
Sofrona, a dialogue on love in the vernacular.
De iure, a Latin pamphlet.
Pontifex, about ecclesiastical life, in Latin.
Apologi, a hundred short stories in Latin.

c. 1439
Villa, a pamphlet on agronomy in the vernacular.

1440 c.
Teogenio, a treatise on fortune in the vernacular.

1441
De amicitia (Book IV of the "Della famiglia" in the vernacular. It was presented at the Certame Coronario held in Florence on 22 October 1441).

1441-42
Della tranquillità dell'animo, a dialogue in the vernacular.
Mosca, a Latin pamphlet.
Canis, a Latin pamphlet in praise of dogs.
Passer, a Latin poem (lost).

1442
De equo animante, a Latin treatise on the training of horses.

ante 1450
Momus, a political, moral, and satirical treatise in Latin.

c. 1450
Grammatica della lingua toscana.
De Lunularum quadratura, on the calculation of circular segments and sections, in the vernacular.
Descriptio urbis Romae, an exposition of the method used for establishing the topography of Rome, in Latin.

c. 1450-51
Ludi rerum matematicarum, the solutions of twenty geometrical and mechanical problems, in the vernacular.

1452
De re aedificatoria, a Latin treatise on architecture in ten books (probably written in 1443-45 and 1447-52).

c. 1452
Literary works (some written at an earlier date) which Alberti included in an appendix to the "De re aedificatoria", but which were not published and are now lost: *Navis aeraria* (1447), *Historia numeri et linearum*, *Quid conferat architectus in negotio*.

1453
De porcaria coniuratione, a Latin epistle.

c. 1460
Trivia senatoria, a Latin pamphlet on the art of public speaking.

1460-62
Cena familiaris, a dialogue on the family in the vernacular.

1460 ss.
Istorietta amorosa fra Leonora de' Bardi e Ippolito Bondelmonti.

1462
Sentenze pitagoriche, aphorisms in the vernacular on virtuous behaviour.

c. 1462-65
Epistulae septem Epimenidis nomine Diogeni inscriptae, imaginary replies to Diogenes.

Epistola Leonem ad Cratem philosophum, a letter to Krates.

c. 1466
De componendis cifris, a Latin pamphlet on the use of the alphabet in secret codes.

1468
De Iciarchia, a dialogue on the head of the family.

The following cannot be dated:
Commentaria rerum matematicarum (lost).
De literis et ceteris principiis grammaticae (lost).

The following are considered apocryphal:
I cinque ordini architettonici, by a sixteenth-century author of Serlio's circle.
Della prospettiva.
Trattato dei Pondi, Leve e Tirari.
Trattato del governo della famiglia (in two different versions).
The *Tre concioni*, written by Stefano Porcari.
Amiria and *Ephoebia*, by his brother, Carlo Alberti (see *Amator*).
Intorno al tor donna, a translation and adaptation of the "Dissuasio Valerii ad Ruffinum philosophum ne uxorem ducat" by the medieval Welsh writer, Walter Map.
Some poems (see G. Ponte, in *Rass. Lett. It.*, 1958, 2, and C. Grayson, ibid., 1959, LXIII, 1).
A vernacular version of the *De statua*, probably the work of Cosimo Bartoli.
A vernacular version of the first three books of the *De re aedificatoria* by an anonymous translator.
A version in ottava rima of the *Istorietta amorosa di Ippolito e Leonora*.

EDITIONS OF THE LITERARY WORKS OF LEON BATTISTA ALBERTI
A list of the most important and recent editions. Those recommended for consultation and for their textual commentaries are marked (.).

Leon Battista Alberti Opera, Florence 1499, ed. by G. Massaini. It includes the *De commodis et incommodis litterarum, De iure, Trivia, Canis, Apologi*.
Opuscoli morali di Leon Battista Alberti, Venice 1568, ed. by C. Bartoli.

Opere volgari di Leon Battista Alberti, annotate e illustrate da A. Bonucci, 5 Vols., Florence 1843-49. They include: I. Philodoxeus fabula (Latin text), Della tranquillità dell'animo, La cena di famiglia, Avvertimenti matrimoniali, Intorno al tor donna, Sofrona. II. Della famiglia, Sentenze pitagoriche. III. De iciarchia, Teogenio, Ecatonfilea, Ippolito e Leonora, Ippolito e Dianora, Deifira. IV. Della pittura, Della prospettiva, Della statua, Dell'arte edificatoria (preface and three books), I cinque ordini architettonici, Lettera per il San Francesco di Rimini, Ludi matematici. V. Trattato del governo della famiglia (in two versions), Epistola a Paolo Codagnello, Epistola consolatoria, Amiria, Ephoebia, Lettere amatorie, Concioni, Poesie.

Opera inedita et pauca separatim impressa di Leon Battista Alberti, H. Mancini curante, Florentiae 1890. Latin works ed. by G. Mancini. They include:

Amator, Frottola, Madrigale, Psalmi, Descriptio urbis Romae, Elementa picturae (in the vernacular and in Latin) De punctis et lineis apud pictores, Pontifex, Intercoenales (Books I, II, IV and the Anuli), De amicitia, De equo animante, De porcaria coniuratione, Epistulae septem Diogeni inscriptae, Epistola ad Cratem, Epistulae, Frottola (pt. III), De Lunularum quadratura, Nota de casu ad pontem Aelium, De cifra proemium, De B. Alberti quadam testamentaria voluntate.

I libri della famiglia, ed. by G. Mancini, Florence 1908. *I primi tre libri della famiglia*, with notes by F. C. Pellegrini, Florence 1911; revised with an introduction by R. Spongano, Florence 1946 (.) *I libri della famiglia, Cena familiaris, Villa*, ed. by C. Grayson, in L. B. Alberti, *Opere volgari*, I., Bari 1960 (.) *I libri della famiglia*, ed. by R. Romano and A. Tenenti, Turin 1969 (.) (follows the text established by Grayson).

Venticinque inediti e sconosciuti di Leon Battista Alberti (Intercoenales) ed. by E. Garin, in "Belfagor", 1964, XIX, pp. 377-96 (.). *Intercenali inedite*, ed. by E. Garin, in "Rinascimento" 1964, IV, pp. 125-258 (.) *Una intercenale inedita di L. B. Alberti: "Uxoria"*, by C. Grayson, in "Italia medievale e umanistica", 1960, III, pp. 291-307.

L. B. Albertis Kleinere Kunsttheoretische Schriften, ed. by H. Janitschek, Vienna 1877 (see Bibl.) It contains the *De statua* (Latin text), the *Della pittura* (vernacular version), and *I cinque ordini architettonici* (in the vernacular), with translations in German. *Della pittura*, critical edition ed. by L. Mallè, Florence 1950 (.) See also *L. B. Alberti, Opere volgari*, ed. by C. Grayson, Bari 1973, III (.).

Elementa picturae, Latin and vernacular text with a critical essay and explanatory illustrations by A. Gambuti in "Università di Firenze, Facoltà di Architettura, Istituto di Composizione architettonica I-II. Studi e documenti di Architettura, 1 December 1972: Omaggio ad Alberti" (.) See also *L. B. Alberti, Opere volgari*, ed. by C. Grayson, Bari 1973 III (.).

De re aedificatoria, Florence 1485 (First edition). *Libri de re aedificatoria decem*, Paris 1512. Idem, Strasbourg 1541. *I dieci libri de l'Architettura*, Venice 1546 (first translation into Italian, by P. Lauro). *L'Architettura ... tradotta in lingua fiorentina da Cosimo Bartoli*, Florence 1550, *The architecture ... Of painting and of statuary*, London 1726 (first translation into English, by G. Leoni). *Della architettura, della pittura e della statua*, Bologna 1782 (translations by C. Bartoli). *L'architettura (De re aedificatoria)*, Milan 1966, ed. by G. Orlandi and P. Portoghesi (Latin text and translation) (.).

Descriptio urbis Romae, Latin text and translation by G. Orlandi, critical essay and graphic reconstruction by L. Vagnetti, in "Quaderni dell'Istituto di Elementi di Architettura e Rilievo dei Monumenti di Genova", 1 October 1968, (.).

Ludi matematici, text with critical essay and graphic reconstructions by L. Vagnetti in "Università di Firenze, Facoltà di Architettura, Istituto di Composizione architettonica I-II. Studi e documenti di architettura 1, December 1972: Omaggio ad Alberti" (.) See also *L. B. Alberti, Opere volgari*, ed. by C. Grayson, Bari 1973, III (.)

De componendis cifris, in A. Meister, "Die Geheimschrift im Dienste der päpstlichen Kurie", Paderborn 1906, pp. 125-141.

Momus o Del Principe, critical text, translation, introduction and notes by G. Martini, Bologna 1942 (.)

Opuscoli inediti: Musca, Vita S. Potiti, ed. by C. Grayson, Florence 1954 (.)

Opere volgari, ed. by C. Grayson (.) I, Bari 1960. It includes: *I libri della famiglia, Cena familiaris, Villa*. II, Bari 1966. It includes: *Rime, Theogenius, Profugiorum ab Aerumna Libri III, De iciarchia, Epistula consolatoria, Sentenze pitagoriche, Uxoria, Naufragius*, the vernacular version of the *Dissuasio Valerii* by Walter Map. III, Bari 1973. It includes: *De pictura, Elementi di pittura, Ludi rerum matematicarum, Grammatica della lingua toscana, Ecatonfilea, Deifira, De amore — a P. Codagnello, Sofrona, Istorietta amorosa, Lettere*.

BOOKS AND ARTICLES OF GENERAL INTEREST

1859

Voigt G., *Die Wiederbelebung des klassischen Altertums oder das I Jahrh. des Humanismus*, Berlin, Bk. III, 3, (translated into Italian with the title "Il risorgimento dell'antichità classica", Florence 1888, I, Bk. III, 3, pp. 368-74).

1860

Burckhardt J., *Die Kultur der Renaissance in Italien*, Basle, I, pp. 162-66.

1867

Burckhardt J., *Die Kunst der Renaissance in Italien: Renaissance Architektur*, Stuttgart (Vol. I of the "Geschichte der neuren Baukunst" by L. B. Wilhelm and C. Gurlitt, the continuation of the "Geschichte der Baukunst" by F. Kugler written in 1856-59).

1867

Springer A., *Bilder aus der neuren Kunstgeschichte*, Bonn, pp. 68-103.

1868

Popelin C., *Leon Battista Alberti*, in "Gazette des Beaux-Arts", XXV, pp. 403-21.

1878

Redtenbacher R., *Leon Battista Alberti*, in "Dome, Kunst und Künstler", II, pp. 3-21.

1882

Mancini G., *Vita di Leon Battista Alberti*, Florence, (second revised and extended ed., Florence 1911).

1886

Von Pastor L., *Geschichte der Päpste* (Ital. trans., Rome 1900, I, Bk. III, 5).

1888

Geymüller H. and Stegmann C., *Die Architektur der Renaissance in Toscana*, Munich 1885-1909.

1889

Müntz E., *Histoire de l'art pendant la Renaissance*, Paris 1889-91, III.

1904

Per Leon Battista Alberti, a collection of articles published in commemoration of the 5th centenary of his birth, Bologna 1904.

Ricci C., *Leon Battista Alberti. Discorso*, Bologna.

1906

Londi E., *Leon Battista Alberti architetto*, Florence.

1907

Suida W., article on Alberti in U. Thieme and F. Becker, *Allgemeines Lexikon der bildenden Künstler*, Leipzig, 1907-50, I, pp. 196-211.

1909

Lugli V., *I trattatisti della famiglia nel Quattrocento*, Bologna.

1913

Aubel E., *Leon Battista Alberti e i libri della Famiglia*, Città di Castello.

1917

Ricci C., *Leon Battista Alberti architetto*, Turin. Venturi L., *La critica d'arte in Italia durante i secoli XIV e XV*, in "L'Arte", XX, p. 315 ff.

1919

Guzzo A., *Leon Battista Alberti*, Naples (rep. in "Idealisti ed Empiristi", Florence 1935).

1920

Gentile G., *Il pensiero italiano del Rinascimento*, Florence 3rd (ed.).

1923

Venturi A., *Storia dell'arte italiana. L'architettura del Quattrocento*, Milan, VIII, Pt. I, 3, pp. 152-99. Venturi A., *Architetti dal XV al XVIII secolo: Leon Battista Alberti* (Biblioteca d'Arte illustrata, ser. 2, issue 17), Rome.

1924

Schlosser Magnino J., *Die Kunstliteratur*, Vienna (trans. into Italian with the title "La letteratura artistica", Florence 1935, pp. 114, 121-29).

1927

Semprini G., *Leon Battista Alberti*, Milan.

1928

Saitta G., *Leon Battista Alberti*, in "L'Educazione dell'Umanesimo italiano", Venice.

1929

Schlosser J., *Ein Künstlerproblem der Renaissance: Leon Battista Alberti*, in "Sitzungsberichte der Wiener Akademie Phil. Hist. Kl.", Vienna (trans. into Italian with the title "Il non artista: L. B. Alberti", in "Xenia", Bari 1938).

1939

Gengaro M. L., *Leon Battista Alberti teorico ed architetto del Rinascimento*, Milan.

1940

Wittkower R., *Alberti's approach to antiquity in architecture*, in "Journal of the Warburg and Courtauld Institutes", 1940-41, IV, 1-2, pp. 1-18.

1942

Garin E., *Filosofi italiani del Quattrocento*, Florence.

Saitta G., *Il pensiero Italiano nell'Umanesimo e nel Rinascimento*, in "L'Umanesimo", Bologna 1943, pp. 393-424.

1943

Kristeller O. P., *The place of classical humanism in Renaissance thought*, in "Journal of the history of ideas", IV, pp. 59-63.

1949

Garin E., *L'educazione umanistica in Italia*, Bari.

Wittkower R., *Architectural principles in the age of humanism*, London (trans. into Italian with the title "Principi architettonici nell'età dell'Umanesimo", Turin 1964.

1951

Borissalievitch M., *Les théories de l'architecture*, Paris, pp. 74-82.

1952

Garin E., *L'Umanesimo italiano*, Bari pp. 9, 60, 87 ff.

1954

Acton H., *Alberti, uomo universale*, in "Il Quattrocento" (Libera Cattedra di Storia della Civiltà Fiorentina), Florence, p. 225 ff.

Garin E., *Medioevo e Rinascimento*, Bari, p. 93 ff.

1957

Grayson C., *The Humanism of Alberti*, in "Italian Studies", XII, pp. 37-56.

1958

Zevi B., article on Alberti in "Enciclopedia Universale dell'Arte", Venice-Rome, I.

Zubov. V., *Leon Battista Alberti et les auteurs du moyen-age*, in "Medieval and Renaissance Studies", IV, pp. 245-66.

1959

Chastel A., *Art et Humanisme à Florence au temps de Laurent le Magnifique*, Paris (trans. into Italian with the title "Arte e Umanismo a Firenze al tempo di Lorenzo il Magnifico", Turin, 1964.

Vasoli C., *L'estetica dell'Umanesimo e del Rinascimento*, in "Momenti e problemi di storia dell'estetica", Milan, I, p. 400 ff.

1960

Argan G. C., article on Alberti in "Dizionario Biografico degli Italiani", I, pp. 709-713.

Grayson C., article on Alberti in "Dizionario Biografico degli Italiani", I, pp. 702-709.

1961

Aurigemma M., *Leon Battista Alberti*, in "I Minori", I, Milan.

Garin E., *La cultura filosofica del Rinascimento italiano*, Florence.

1962

Muscetta C., *Leon Battista Alberti*, in L. Russo, "I Classici italiani", Florence I, (4th ed. p. 1139 ff.).

Parronchi A., *Leon Battista Alberti as a painter*, in "The Burlington Magazine", LIV, 712, pp. 280-88 (rep. in "Studi sulla Dolce Prospettiva").

Santinello G., *Leon Battista Alberti. Una visione estetica del mondo e della vita*, Florence.

1964

Gille B., *Les ingénieurs de la renaissance*, Paris (translated into Italian with the title "Leonardo e gli ingegneri del Rinascimento", Milan 1972).

Pereira Brandâo A., *Retrato un arquitecto renascentista, Leon Battista Alberti*, Lisbon.

1966

Tenenti A., *Leon Battista Alberti*, Rome-Milan.

1967

Quintavalle A. C., *Prospettiva e ideologia. Alberti e la cultura del secolo XV*, Parma.

1968

Rodenwaldt E., *Leon Battista Alberti ein Hygieniker der Renaissance*, Heidelberg.

1969

Romano R. Tenenti A., Introduction to *Leon Battista Alberti, I libri della Famiglia*, Turin.

Gadol J., *Leon Battista Alberti*, Chicago-London.

1971

Chirici C., *Il problema del restauro dal Rinascimento all'età contemporanea*, Milan, p. 25 ff., p. 35 ff.

Romano R., *Tra due crisi: L'Italia del Rinascimento*, Turin, pp. 137-65.

Tateo F., *Alberti, Leonardo e la crisi dell'Umanesimo*, Bari.

1972

Garin E., *Il pensiero di Leon Battista Alberti e la cultura del Quattrocento*, in "Belfagor", XXVII, 5.

Zevi B., *L'operazione linguistica di Leon Battista Alberti*, in "L'Architettura. Cronache e Storia", XVIII, 1972, 140, pp. 142-143.

THE THEMES OF ALBERTI'S LIFE

1843

Vita Anonima di Leon Battista, in A. Bonucci, *Opere volgari . . .*, Florence, I, p. LXXXIX ff.

1869

Passerini L., *Gli Alberti di Firenze. Genealogia, storia, documenti*, Florence 1869-70, II, p. 131 ff.

1881

Cortesi V., *Osservazioni sul libro "Il Governo della Famiglia" di A. Pandolfini*, Piacenza.

1882

Mancini G., *Vita di Leon Battista Alberti*, Florence (2nd ed., 1911).

Neri A., *La nascita di Leon Battista Alberti*, in "Giornale Linguistico", IX, pp. 165-69.

Scipioni G. S., *Leon Battista Alberti e Agnolo Pandolfini. Lettere al Dott. R. Renier*, Ancona.

1883

Scipioni G. S., *Di una vita inedita di Leon Battista Alberti*, in "Giornale St. della Lett. It.", II, pp. 156-62.

1890

Mancini G., *Opera inedita et pauca separatim impressa di Leon Battista Alberti*, Florence, p. I ff.

1891

Scipioni G. S., *L'anno della nascita di Leon Battista Alberti*, in "Giornale St. della Lett. It.", XVIII, pp. 313-19.

1892

Mancini G., *Un nuovo documento sul Certame Coronario di Firenze nel 1441*, in "Archivio Storico Italiano", 5th ser. IX.

1897

Mancini G., *Nuovi documenti e notizie di Leon Battista Alberti*, in "Archivio Storico Italiano", 4th ser. XIX.

1907

Cessi R., *Gli Alberti di Firenze in Padova*, in "Archivio Storico Italiano", ser. 5, XL.

1908

Dolci G., *Intorno alla fede di Leon Battista Alberti*, in "V. Cian e i suoi scolari dell'Università di Pisa", Pisa, 1900-08.

1910

Cessi R., *Il soggiorno di Lorenzo e Leon Battista Alberti a Padova*, in "Archivio Storico Italiano", ser. 5, XLIII.

Dolci G., *La fede religiosa di Leon Battista Alberti*, Camerino.

1912

Rajna P., *Le origini del Certame Coronario*, in "Scritti vari in onore di R. Renier", Turin, pp. 1027-56.

1913

Mancini G., *La pedagogia nel Trattato della Famiglia di Leon Battista Alberti*.

1915

Mancini G., *Il testamento di Leon Battista Alberti*, in "Archivio Storico Italiano", 1914, LXXII, p. 20 ff.

1922

Venturini L., *Ragione e Dio nell'estetica di Leon Battista Alberti*, in "L'Esame", p. 325 ff.

1923

Semprini G., *Le idee pedagogiche di Leon Battista Alberti*, in "Rivista pedagogica".

1925

Ricci C., *Il Tempio Malatestiano*, Milan-Rome, 5, p. 73 ff.

1930

Michel P. H., *Un idéal humain au XV siècle: la pensée de Leon Battista Alberti*, Paris.

1938

Lang R., *Leon Battista Alberti, die Sancta Masseritia*, Saint Gall.

1942

Martini G., *Momus*, Bologna.

1948

Ceschi C., *La Madre di Leon Battista Alberti*, in "Bollettino d'Arte", XXXIII, pp. 191-92.

1950

Sapori A., *Gli Alberti del Giudice di Firenze*, in "Studi in onore di G. Luzzato", Milan, I, pp. 161-92.

Schalk F., *Leon Battista Alberti und das Buch "Della Famiglia"*, in "Romanische Forschung", LXXII.

1952

Altamura A., *Il Certame Coronario*, Naples.

1953

Grayson C., *Studi su Leon Battista Alberti. Villa: un opuscolo sconosciuto*, in "Rinascimento", Florence, IV, p. 45 ff.

Sasso G., *Qualche osservazione sul problema della virtù e della fortuna nell'Alberti*, in "Il Mulino", II, pp. 600-618.

1957

Tateo F., *Dottrina ed esperienze nei Libri di Famiglia di Leon Battista Alberti*, in "Tradizione e realtà nell'Umanesimo Italiano", Bari, pp. 279-318.

Watkins R., *The Authorship of the Vita Anonima of Leon Battista Alberti*, in "Studies in the Renaissance", IV, pp. 101-12.

1958

Biondillo F., *Il concetto dell'uomo in Leon Battista Alberti*, in "Nuova rivista pedagogica", VIII, 5-6, pp. 22-27.

1960

"Opere volgari" di Leon Battista Alberti, Vol. I, I Libri della Famiglia, Cena familiaris, Villa, ed. by C. Grayson, Bari.

Watkins R., *Leon Battista Alberti's emblem, the winged eye, and his name Leo*, in "Mitteilungen des Kunsthistorischen Institutes in Florenz", 9, pp. 256-58.

1961

Bertin G. M., *La pedagogia umanistica nei secoli XV e XVI*, Milan.

Randall J. H. Jr., *The School of Padua and the Emergence of Modern Science*, Padua.

1962

Draghi G., *Incertezza e coraggio in Leon Battista Alberti*, in "Letterature moderne", XII, 2-3, pp. 239-47.

1963

Martines L., *The Social World of the Florentine Humanists* 1390-1460, Princeton.

1964

Bialostocki J., *The power of beauty: an utopian idea of Leon Battista Alberti*, in "Festschrift für L. H. Heydenreich", Munich.

Martelli M., *Una delle "Intercenali" di Leon Battista Alberti fonte sconosciuta del "Furioso"*, in "Bibliofilia", LXVI, 2, pp. 163-70.

1965

Segre C., *Nel mondo della luna ovvero Leon Battista Alberti e Lodovico Ariosto*, in "Studi in onore di A. Schiaffini", Rome, pp. 1024-53.

1972

Grayson C., *Four love-letters attributed to Alberti*, in "Essays on Italian Language and Literature presented to Kathleen Speight", Manchester 1971, pp. 30-44.

Zevi B., *L'operazione linguistica di Leon Battista Alberti*, in "L'Architettura", XVIII, pp. 142-143.

ALBERTI'S DEBUT AT FERRARA

1890

Mancini G., *Opera inedita et pauca separatim impressa di Leon Battista Alberti*, Florence, text of the "De equo animante", p. 238 ff.

1914

Venturi A., *Un'opera sconosciuta di Leon Battista Alberti*, in "L'Arte", XVII, p. 153 ff.

1922

Venturi A., *Le opere primitive di Leon Battista Alberti*, in "Lo Spettatore", I, 1.

1954

Grayson C., *La prima edizione del "Philodoxeus"*, in "Rinascimento", V, pp. 24-93.

THE ROME OF NICHOLAS V

1880

Dehio G., *Die Bauprojekte Nikolaus V und Leon Battista Alberti*, in "Repertorium für Kunstwissenschaft", III, pp. 241-75.

1885

Marcotti G., *Il Giubileo dell'anno 1450 secondo una "Relazione" di Giovanni Rucellai*, Florence.

1889

Müntz E., *Histoire de l'art pendant la Renaissance*, Paris, 3 Vols., pp. 101-124.

1890

Mancini G., *Opera inedita et pauca separatim impressa*, Florence, text of the "De Porcaria Coniuratione", p. 275 ff.

1908

Geymüller H., *Leon Battista Alberti peut-il être l'architecte du palais de Venise à Rome?*, in "Revue de l'art ancien et moderne", XXIV.

1914

Dehio G., *Die Bauprojekte Nikolaus V und Leon Battista Alberti*, in "Kunsthistorische Aufsätze", p. 163.

1935

Krautheimer R., *Santo Stefano Rotondo a Roma e la chiesa del Santo Sepolcro a Gerusalemme*, in "Rivista di Archeologia Cristiana", XII.

1939

Gengaro M. L., *L'architettura romana nell'interpretazione teorica di Leon Battista Alberti*, in "Boll. dell'Ist. di Archeologia e Storia dell'Arte", IX, pp. 37-42.

1942

Krautheimer R., *Iconography of Medieval Architecture*, in "Journal of the Warburg and Courtauld Institutes", London.

1953

Valentini-Zucchetti, *Codice topografico della città di Roma*, Rome; text of the "De Urbe Roma" by Bernardo Rucellai, p. 437 ff.

1954

Magnuson T., *The project of Nicolas V for rebuilding the Borgo Leonino in Rome*, in "The Art Bulletin", XXXVI, pp. 89-115.

1956

Frutaz A. P., *Il Torrione di Nicolò V in Vaticano*, in "Città del Vaticano".

1959

Rossi S., *Santo Stefano Rotondo a Roma*, in "L'Architettura. Cronache e Storia", IV, pp. 774-79.

1962

Frutaz A. P., *Le piante di Roma*, Rome, I, p. 127, 2, plate 151.

1974

Cassinelli L., Delfini G., and Fonti A., *Le mura di Roma*, Rome.

IN FLORENCE FOR THE RUCELLAI

1899

Guasti G., *La Cappella Rucellai in San Pancrazio*, Florence.

1917

Ricci C., *Leon Battista Alberti Architetto*, Turin, p. 22 ff.

1919

Venturi A., *Intarsi marmorei di Leon Battista Alberti*, in "L'Arte", XXII, pp. 34-36.

1920

Diaccini R., *La Basilica di Santa Maria Novella*, Florence.

1934

Neri D., *Il Santo Sepolcro nella Cappella Rucellai*, Florence.

1938

Braunfels W., *Santa Maria Novella, Florenz, Kirche und Kloster des heiligen Domenicus*, Florence.

1955

Orlandi S., *Necrologia di Santa Maria Novella*, Florence, p. 305 ff.

1959

Mardersteig G., *Leon Battista Alberti e la rinascita del carattere lapidario romano nel Quattrocento*, in "Italia Medioevale e Umanistica", II, p. 285 ff.

1961

Heydenreich L. H., *Die Cappella Rucellai von San Pancrazio in Florenz*, in "De artibus opuscula XL: Essays in Honor of E. Panofsky", ed. by M. Meiss, New York, pp. 219-29.

1963

Dezzi Bardeschi M., *Nuove ricerche sul Santo Sepolcro nella Cappella Rucellai a Firenze*, in "Marmo", 2.

1967

Dezzi Bardeschi M., *Il complesso monumentale di San Pancrazio a Firenze ed il suo restauro: nuovi documenti*, in "Quaderni dell'Istituto di Storia dell'Architettura", Rome, 73-79.

1970

La facciata di Santa Maria Novella a Firenze, Facoltà di Architettura, Università degli Studi di Firenze. Diagram carried out by the Istituto di Restauro dei Monumenti and a critical essay by M. Dezzi Bardeschi, Pisa.

1972

Sanpaolesi P., *Sulla cronologia dell'architettura romanica fiorentina*, in "Studi di Storia dell'Arte in onore di Valerio Mariani", Naples, p. 57 ff.

THE TEMPIO MALATESTIANO IN RIMINI

1893

Seitz F., *San Francesco in Rimini*, Berlin.

1894

Bernich E., *Leon Battista Alberti e le chiese pugliesi*, in "Rassegna Pugliese", XI.

1904

Kuzmany K. M., *Malatesta Tempel in Rimini*, in "Neues Wiener Tageblatt", May.

1907

Waldner H. A., *Leon Battista Alberti und die Kirche "S. Francesco" in Rimini*, in "Deutsche Bauhütte", XI.

1908

Grigioni C., *I costruttori del Tempio Malatestiano*, in "Rassegna Bibilografica", XI.

1913

Grigioni C., *L'abside antica e la torre campanaria del Tempio Malatestiano*, in "Rassegna Bibliografica".

1915

Orsini L., *Il Tempio Malatestiano*, Milan.

1923

Supino I. B., *Leon Battista Alberti e il Tempio Malatestiano*, in "Memorie dell'Accademia delle Scienze", Bologna, ser. 2, 1923-25, VIII-IX, p. 171 ff.

1925

Ricci C., *Il Tempio Malatestiano*, Milan.

1927

Tosi A., *Alcune note sul Tempio Malatestiano*, in "La Romagna", II-III.

1928

Del Piano G., *L'enigma filosofico del Tempio Malatestiano*, Bologna.

1930

Pica A., *La chiesa di San Francesco in Rimini*, in "Italia Sacra. Le Chiese d'Italia Illustrate", Turin.

1937

Brigante Colonna G., *Il Tempio Malatestiano di Rimini*, in "Illustrazione Toscana", October.

1938

Milan G. B., *Agostino di Duccio architetto e il Tempio Malatestiano in Rimini*, Rome.

1948

Degenhart B., *Zur Wiederherstellung des Tempio Malatestiano in Rimini*, in "Zeitschrift für Kunstgeschichte", 2.

1950

Lavagnino E., *Restauro del Tempio Malatestiano*, in "Bollettino d'Arte", ser. 4, XXV, April-June.

Pecci G., *Guida al Tempio Malatestiano*, Rimini.

1951

Campana A., *Per la storia delle cappelle trecentesche della chiesa malatestiana di San Francesco*, in "Studi Romagnoli", II, p. 17 ff.

Garattoni D., *Il Tempio Malatestiano, leggende e realtà*, Bologna.

Pächt O., *Giovanni da Fano's Illustrations for Basinio's Epos Hesperis*, in "Studi Romagnoli", II, p. 91 ff.

Ravaioli C., *Agostino di Duccio a Rimini*, in "Studi Romagnoli", II, p. 113 ff.

Ravaioli G., *Il Malatestiano: studi, realizzazioni e proposte*, in "Studi Romagnoli", I, Faenza, pp. 121-36.

Ruiz Beliscauro C., *Estetica del Tempio Malatestiano*, Bologna.

Salmi M., *Il Tempio Malatestiano di Rimini*, in "Atti dell'Accademia Nazionale di San Luca", 1, pp. 56-73; rep. in "Studi Romagnoli", Faenza 1952, II, pp. 151-67.

1952

Mitchell C., *The Imagery of the Tempio Malatestiano*, in "Studi Malatestiani", Faenza.

1956

Brandi C., *Il Tempio Malatestiano*, Turin.

1957

Grayson C., *Alberti and the Tempio Malatestiano: an autograph letter from Leon Battista Alberti to Matteo de' Pasti*, New York.

1958

Soergel G., *Die Harmonien in L. B. Albertis Tempio Malatestiano*, in "Untersuchungen über den theoretischen Architekturentwurf von 1450-1500 in Italien", Cologne, pp. 8-22.

1965

Ragghianti C. L., *Tempio Malatestiano*, in "Critica d'Arte", XII, 71, p. 23 ff., and 74, p. 27 ff.

Portoghesi P., *Il Tempio Malatestiano*, Florence.

1969

Pasini P. G., *Vicende e frammenti del Tempio Malatestiano*, in "Rimini. Storia, Arte e Cultura", Rimini, p. 201 ff.

1970

Pasini P. G., *Il tempio Malatestiano*, in "Catalogo della Mostra su Sigismondo Pandolfo Malatesta e il suo tempo", Rimini, p. 125 ff.

ALBERTI AT URBINO

1839

Gaye G., *Carteggio inedito d'artisti dei secoli XIV-XV-XVI*, Florence, I, pp. 179-180.

1863

Guasti C., *Inventario della Libreria Urbinate compilate nel secolo XV da Federigo Veterano*, in "Giornale Storico degli Archivi Toscani", VII, p. 46 ff. and p. 130 ff.

1945

Salmi M., *Piero della Francesca e il Palazzo Ducale di Urbino*, Florence, p. 38 ff.

1949

Alatri P., *Lettere di Stato e d'Arte di Federico da Montefeltro*, Rome, pp. 102-103.

1951

Clark K., *Piero della Francesca*, London, pp. 31-35.

1968

Dezzi Bardeschi M., *Gli architetti dalmati ed il ricorso all'antico nel Rinascimento italiano*, p. I, in "Bollettino degli Ingegneri", 11.

THE WORKS AT MANTUA

1612

Donesmondi I., *Dell'Istoria Ecclesiastica di Mantova*, Mantua, p. 381 ff.

1797

Tonelli F., *Ricerche Storiche di Mantova*, Mantua, p. 369 ff.

1869

Braghirolli W., *Leon Battista Alberti a Mantova*, in "Archivio Storico Italiano".

1872

Appello ai Cittadini, Provinciali e Cultori di Belle Arti, della Commissione promotrice dei restauri ai dipinti classici dell'insigne Basilica di Sant'Andrea in Mantova, e del ricordo monumentale al celebre suo architetto Leon Battista nel IV centenario della rispettiva fondazione e morte, Mantua.

1876

Braghirolli W., *Luca Fancelli*, in "Archivio Storico Lombardo", III, Milan, p. 611 ff.

1882

Intra G. B., *La Basilica di Sant'Andrea in Mantova*, Milan.

1883

Intra G. B., *Mantova: La Basilica di San Sebastiano*, in "Arte e Storia", II.

1892

P. Orioli, *Arte ed iscrizioni nella basilica di Leon Battista Alberti fiorentino a Sant'Andrea in Mantova*, Mantua.

1899

Ritscher E., *Die Kirche Sant'Andrea in Mantua*, Berlin.

1900

Grugnola G., *La chiesa di Sant'Andrea in Mantova*, Turin.

1901

Bellodi R., *La basilica di Sant'Andrea in Mantova*, in "Emporium", XIV, pp. 343-358.

1902

Intra G. B., *La basilica di Sant'Andrea in Mantova*, in "Arte e Storia", XXI.

1904

Fabriczy C., *Die Baugeschichte von San Sebastiano in Mantua*, in "Repertorium für Kunstwissenschaft", XXVII.

1924

Schiavi A., *Il Famedio di San Sebastiano*, in "Bollettino del Collegio degli Ingegneri e Architetti di Mantova", Mantua, March.

1932

Schiavi A., *Il restauro della chiesa di San Sebastiano di Leon Battista Alberti in Mantova*, Mantua.

1947

Bellonci M., *Segreti dei Gonzaga*, Milan.

1952

Pelati P., *La basilica di Sant'Andrea*, Mantua.

1955

Amadei F., *Cronaca universale della città di Mantova*, Mantua, II, p. 49 ff.

1956

Rodolico F., *Ricerca ed acquisto di "pietre antiche" alla Corte dei Gonzaga*, in "Archivio Storico Italiano", Florence, 114, p. 749 ff.

1960

Hubala E., *Sant'Andrea in Mantua: Beobachtungen zur ersten Bauphase*, in "Kunstchronik", XIII.

1961

Hubala E., *Leon Battista Albertis Langhaus von Sant'Andrea in Mantua*, in "Festschrift Kurt Behrendt", Berlin.

Krautheimer R., *Alberti's Templum Etruscum*, in "Münchner Jahrbuch der Bildenden Kunst", XII, 3, pp. 65-72.

Marani E., *Luca Fancelli*, in "Mantova. Le Arti", Mantua II, 3, p. 63 ff.

Marani E., *Esordio del Rinascimento*, in "Mantova. Le Arti", Mantua, II, p. 45 ff.

Marani E., *Leon Battista Alberti*, in "Mantova. Le Arti", Mantua II, p. 117 ff.

Muraro M., *Mantegna e Alberti*, in "Arti del VI° Convegno Internazionale di Studi sul Rinascimento", Florence, p. 103 ff.

1965

Fasolo V., *Osservazioni sul Sant'Andrea di Mantova*, in "Atti del VI° Convegno Internazionale di Studi sul Rinascimento", Florence, pp. 207-217.

Perina C., *La Basilica di Sant'Andrea in Mantova*, Mantua (the appendix contains a very full bibliography on the subject).

Sanpaolesi P., *Il tracciamento modulare armonico del Sant'Andrea di Mantova*, in "Atti del VI° Convegno Internazionale di Studi sul Rinascimento", Florence, pp. 95-101.

1967

Coniglio G., *I Gonzaga*, Varese, p. 52 ff.

1969

Carpeggiani P., *Luca Fancelli architetto civile nel contado mantovano: ipotesi e proposte*, in "Civiltà Mantovana", IV.

1971

Carpeggiani P., *Luca Fancelli architetto civile nel contado Gonzaghesco*, in "Arte Lombarda", Milan, XVI.

1972

Brown C. M., *Luca Fancelli in Mantua*, in "Mitteilungen des Kunsthistorischen Institutes in Florenz", XVI, 2.

Celebrazioni dell'Alberti e della Basilica di Sant'Andrea, in "Civiltà Mantovana", VI, pp. 217-69.

TWO OTHER FLORENTINE WORKS

The Tribune of the Annunziata:

1879

Braghirolli W., *Die Baugeschichte der Tribuna der SS. Annunziata in Florenz*, in "Repertorium für Kunstwissenschaft", II.

1930

Heydenreich L. H., *Die Tribuna der SS. Annunziata in Florenz*, in "Mitteilungen des Kunsthistorischen Institutes in Florenz", III.

1973

Roselli P., *Rilievo della tribuna e Coro della SS. Annunziata*, Pisa.

The apse in San Martino a Gangalandi:

1890

Mancini G., *Opera inedita et pauca separatim impressa*, Florence, text of the "Epistolae", p. 272 ff.

1895

Carrocci G., *Il Comune di Lastra a Signa*, Florence, p. 10 ff.

1914

Mancini G., *Il Testamento di Leon Battista Alberti*, in "Archivio Storico Italiano", LXXII.

1972

Moretti L. and Pica A., *Celebrazioni di Leon Battista Alberti* 1404-1472, Exhibition of Documents Rome, p. 22 ff.

THE TREATISES ON PAINTING AND SCULPTURE

CODICES OF THE "DELLA PITTURA"

Manuscripts in the vernacular:

Florence, Biblioteca Nazionale, Cod. II. IV, 38, dated "finis laus deo die XVIII iulii MCCCC36".

Paris, Bibliothèque Nationale, Cod. Ital. 1692 (16th century).

Verona, Biblioteca Capitolare, Cod. CCLXXIII (16th century).

Manuscripts in Latin:

Florence, Biblioteca Nazionale, Cod. II. VIII. 58, 1r-26r (15th century).

Florence, Biblioteca Laurenziana, Cod. Ashb. 1155, 1r-89r, "MDXLI, iulii".

Florence, Biblioteca Riccardiana, Cod. 767, 65r-103v (15-16th centuries).

Florence, Biblioteca Marucelliana, Cod. B. VI. 38. (An eighteenth-century copy of the Riccardiana codex).

Genoa, Biblioteca Universitaria, Cod. B. II. 50, 1r-37r (16th century).

Leghorn, Biblioteca Labronica, Cod. Arm. CXII (misc. 16th century).

Lucca, Biblioteca Governativa, Cod. 1448, 8v-54r. "Finis laus deo 1518. 13 februarii".

Milan, Biblioteca Ambrosiana, Cod. O. 80. Sup., 1r-52r (15th century).

North Carolina, University of North Carolina Library, Cod. 90, 1r-32v (16th century).

Oxford, Bodleian Library, Cod. Canon. Misc. 121, 1r-45r (15th century).

Ravenna, Biblioteca Classense, Cod. 146, 1r-65r (misc. 15th century).

Rome, Biblioteca Vaticana, Cod. Vat. lat. 3151, 21v-66r (misc. 15th century).

Rome, Biblioteca Vaticana, Cod. Vat. Lat. 4569, 119r-162v (16th century).

Rome, Biblioteca Vaticana, Cod. Ottobon. Lat. 1424, 1r-25v (15th century).

Rome, Biblioteca Vaticana, Cod. Ottobon. Lat. 2274, 1r-42 (16th century).

Rome, Biblioteca Vaticana, Cod. Reg. Lat. 1549, 1r-33v (15th century).

Trent, Biblioteca Comunale, Cod. 3224, 105r-161v (misc. 15th century).

Waltham (Mass.), U.S.A., Brandeis University Library, Cod. not numbered, 3r-20v (15th century).

EDITIONS OF THE "DELLA PITTURA"

1540

De Pictura praestantissima et numquam satis laudata arte libri tres absolutissimi Leonis Baptistae de Albertis viri in omni scientiarum genere et praecipue mathematicarum disciplinarum doctissimi, Basle, Th. Venatorius.

1547

La Pittura di Leon Battista Alberti tradotta per M. Lodovico Domenichi, Venice.

1568

Opuscoli Morali di Leon Battista Alberti gentil'huomo fiorentino ... tràdotti, e in parte corretti da M. Cosimo Bartoli, Florence.

1649

De Pictura praestantissima et numquam satis ..., in the volume *M. Vitruvii Pollionis, De Architectura Libri decem*, followed by the *Lexicon Vitruvianum* and the *Excerpta ex dialogo De Sculptura Pomponii Gaurici*, Amsterdam, L. Elzevirum.

1784

Translation into Spanish by *De Silva*, Madrid.

1804

Della Pittura e della Statua con vita di Leon Battista Alberti scritta da Girolamo Tiraboschi, Milan.

1847

Della Pittura di Leon Battista Alberti libri III, in *Opere Volgari di L. B. Alberti ... annotate e illustrate dal Dott. Anicio Bonucci*, Florence, IV, pp. 11-86.

1868

De la Statue et de la Peinture, Traités de Leon-Baptista Alberti noble florentin, traduits du latin en français par Claudius Popelin, Paris.

1877

L. B. Albertis Kleinere Kunsttheoretische Schriften mit einer Einleitung und Excursen versehen von Dr. H. Janitschek, Vienna.

1913

L. B. Alberti, *Il Trattato della Pittura e i Cinque Ordini architettonici*, with a preface by Giovanni Papini, Lanciano (almost a reproduction of Janitschek's edition).

1950

L. B. Alberti, *Della Pittura*, a critical edition by L. Mallé, Florence (a collation of the Florentine manuscript generally used since the time of Janitschek with the printed Basle edition of 1540).

1972

L. B. Alberti, *On Painting and On Sculpture*, edited with translations, introduction, and notes by C. Grayson, London.

1973

Critical edition by C. Grayson of L. B. Alberti, *Opere Volgari*, Bari, III, p. 7 ff.

BIBLIOGRAPHICAL NOTE ON THE TREATISE ON PAINTING

1864

G. Mancini, *Leon Battista Alberti, Gli Elementi di Pittura per la prima volta pubblicati*, Cortona.

1877

H. Janitschek, *L. B. Albertis Kleinere kunsttheoretische Schriften* in "Ilg-Eitelberger Quellenschriften", XI, Vienna (introduction to the German translation of the "De Pictura", the "De Statua", and the "Cinque Ordini Architettonici").

1881-82

H. Ludwig, *Leonardo da Vinci Malerbuch*, in "Ilg-Eitelberger Quellenschriften", XV-XVIII, Vienna.

1890

G. Mancini, *Opera inedita et pauca separatim impressa di Leon Battista Alberti*, Florence.

1891

H. Steigmüller, *Kannte L. B. Alberti den Distanzpunkt?*, in "Repertorium für Kunstwissenschaft", XIV, p. 301 ff.

1892

V. Brun, *Leonardo da Vinci und Leon Battista Alberti*, in "Repertorium für Kunstwissenschaft", XV, p. 267 ff.

1900

P. Toesca, *Precetti d'arte italiani. Saggio sull'estetica della pittura del XIV e XV secolo*, Leghorn.

1901

S. Davari, *Ancora della Chiesa di S. Sebastiano in Mantova e di Luca Fancelli*, in "Rassegna d'Arte", Milan, 6.

1906

P. Duhem, *Etudes sur Leonardo da Vinci*, 3 Vols., Paris, 1906-12.

1908

E. Solmi, *Le fonti dei manoscritti di Leonardo da Vinci*, in "Giornale storico della letteratura italiana", 10-11.

1912

K. Birch-Hirschfeld, *Die Lehre von der Malerei im Cinquecento*, Rome.

C. J. Kern, *Die Anfänge der zentralperspektivischen Konstruktion in der italienischen Malerei des XIV Jahrh.*, in "Mitteilungen des kunsthistorischen Institutes in Florenz", II, pp. 39-65.

1914

J. Mesnil, *Masaccio et la théorie de la perspective*, in "Revue de l'Art ancien et moderne", p. 145 ff.

1915

E. Panofsky, *Das perspektivische Verfahren L. B. Albertis*, in "Kunstchronik", ser. 26, L, 42, p. 505 ff.

1920

H. Wieleitner, *Zur Erfindung der verschiedenen Distanz-Konstruktionen in der malerischen Perspektive*, in "Repertorium für Kunstwissenschaft", LXII, p. 249 ff.

1924-25

E. Panofsky, *Die Perspektive als "symbolische Form"*, in "Vorträge der Bibliothek Warburg", pp. 258-330.

J. Mesnil, *Die Kunstlehre der Frührenaissance im Werke Masaccios*, in "Vorträge der Bibliothek Warburg", p. 122 ff.

1930

L. Olschki, *Der geometrische Geist in Literatur und Kunst*, in "Deutsche Vierteljahresschrift für Literatur und Geistesgeschichte", VIII, pp. 615-38.

1934

P. H. Michel, *L'Esthétique arithmétique du Quattrocento*, in "Mélange Hauvette", Paris.

1935

K. Siebenhüner, *Über den Kolorismus der Frührenaissance, vornehmlich dargestellt in dem "Trattato della Pittura" des Leon Battista Alberti* (doctoral thesis), Leipzig.

1936

G. Wolff, *Zu L. B. Albertis Perspektivlehre*, in "Zeitschrift für Kunstgeschichte", V, pp. 47-54.

G. Wolff, *Leon Battista Alberti als Mathematiker*, in "Scientia", LX, pp. 353-59.

1938

W. M. Ivins Jr., *On the Rationalisation of Sight. With an Examination of three Renaissance Texts on Perspective*, in "Metropolitan Museum of Art Papers", New York, 8.

1940

M. S. Bunim, *Space in Medieval Painting and the Forerunners of Perspective*, New York.

R. W. Lee, *Ut pictura poesis: the Humanistic Theory of Painting*, in "The Art Bulletin", XXX, pp. 197-269.

1942

G. Nicco Fasola, *Pier della Francesca "De prospectiva pingendi"*, Florence (Introduction and critical commentary).

G. Nicco Fasola, *Lo svolgimento del pensiero prospettico nei trattati da Euclide a Piero della Francesca*, in "Le Arti", 1942-43, V, 2, pp. 59-71.

1946

K. Clark, *Leon Battista Alberti on Painting*, London.

G. C. Argan, *The Architecture of Brunelleschi and the Origins of Perspective Theory in the Fifteenth Century*, in "Journal of the Warburg and Courtauld Institutes", IX, pp. 96-121.

1947-48

A. Corsano, *Motivi della civiltà umanistica e rinascimentale. I. Il trattato "Della Pittura" di Leon Battista Alberti*, in "Atti dell'Accademia Pontaniana" (rep. in "Studi sul Rinascimento", Bari 1949).

1949

J. White, *Developments in Renaissance Perspective*, in "Journal of the Warburg and Courtauld Institutes", XII, pp. 58-79.

1950

L. Mallé, *Leon Battista Alberti "Della Pittura"*, Florence.

1953

C. Grayson, *Studi su Leon Battista Alberti, II. Appunti sul testo della Pittura*, in "Rinascimento", IV, pp. 54-62.

R. Wittkower, *Brunelleschi and "Proportions in Perspective"*, in "Journal of the Warburg and Courtauld Institutes", XVI, pp. 275-91.

1955

R. Watkins, *Note on the Parisian Mss. of L. B. Alberti's vernacular "Della Pittura"*, in "Rinascimento", VI, 2, pp. 396-72.

1956

J. R. Spencer, *Leon Battista Alberti on Painting*, London (translation of the "Della Pittura" with introduction and notes).

1957

D. Gioseffi, *Perspectiva artificialis*, Trieste, p. 85 ff.

J. R. Spencer, *Ut Rethorica Pictura. A Study in Quattrocento Theory of Painting*, in "Journal of the Warburg and Courtauld Institutes", XX, pp. 26-44.

E. Battisti, *La visualizzazione della scena classica nella commedia umanistica*, in "Commentarii", 8, pp. 248-56.

E. H. Gombrich, *A Classical Topos in the Introduction to Alberti's "Della Pittura"*, in "Journal of the Warburg and Courtauld Institutes", XX, p. 173 ff.

A. Parronchi, *Le fonti di Paolo Uccello*, in "Paragone", 95, p. 3 ff.

J. White, *The Birth and Rebirth of Pictorial Space*, London (Ital. trans. *Nascita e rinascita dello spazio pittorico*, Milan, pp. 152-59).

1958

K. Badt, *Drei plastische Arbeiten von Leon Battista Alberti*, in "Mitteilungen des Kunsthistorischen Institutes in Florenz", VIII, pp. 78-87.

K. Birkmeyer, *Leon Battista Alberti and Jan van Eyck on the Origin of Painting*, in "Italian Quarterly", 2, pp. 35-54.

1960

V. Zoubov, *Leon Battista Alberti et Léonard de Vinci*, in "Raccolta Vinciana", XVIII, pp. 1-14.

1961

P. H. Michel, *Le Traité de la Peinture de Léon-Baptiste Alberti version latine et vulgaire*, in "Revue des Etudes Italiennes", pp. 80-91.

R. Klein, *Pomponius Gauricus on Perspective*, in "Art Bulletin", XLIII, pp. 211-30.

1962

T. K. Kitao, *Prejudice in Perspective: a Study of Vignola's Perspective Treatise*, in "Art Bulletin", XLIII, pp. 173-95.

A. Parronchi, *Il "punctum dolens" della "costruzione legittima"*, in "Paragone", 195, pp. 58-72 (rep. in "Studi su la dolce prospettiva", Milan 1964).

A. Parronchi, *Leon Battista Alberti as a Painter*, in "The Burlington Magazine", LIV, 712, pp. 280-88 (rep. in "Studi su la dolce prospettiva", Milan 1964).

1963

J. Gadol, *Leon Battista Alberti. The Renaissance of Geometric Space in Art and Science* (doctoral thesis), Columbia University, New York.

M. Baxandall, *A Dialogue on Art from the Court of Leonello d'Este*, in "Journal of the Warburg and Courtauld Institutes", 26, pp. 304-26.

1964

C. Grayson, *L. B. Alberti's "Costruzione Legittima"*, in "Italian Studies", XIX, pp. 14-27.

A. Parronchi, *La "costruzione legittima" è uguale alla "costruzione con punti di distanza"*, in "Rinascimento", ser. 2, IV, pp. 35-40.

1966

S. Y. Edgerton Jr., *Alberti's Perspective: a New Discovery and New Evaluation*, in "The Art Bulletin", XLVIII, pp. 367-78.

1967

A. Parronchi, *Sul significato degli "Elementi di Pittura" di Leon Battista Alberti*, in "Cronache di archeologia e di storia dell'arte", University of Catania, 6, pp. 107-15.

1968

C. Grayson, *The Text of Alberti's "De Pictura"*, in "Italian Studies", XXIII, pp. 71-92.

A. Parronchi, *Due note*, in "Rinascimento", ser. 2, VIII, pp. 351-63.

1971

M. Picchio Simonelli, *On Alberti's Treatises on Art and their Chronological Relationship*, in "Italian Studies Annual", Toronto, 1.

1972

A. Gambuti, *Nuove ricerche sugli Elementa Picturae*, in "Studi e Documenti di Architettura", Institute of Architectural Composition in the Faculty of Architecture, University of Florence, 1, December.

CODICES OF THE "DE STATUA"

Florence, Biblioteca Nazionale, Cod. Magl. IV. 39.

Florence, Biblioteca Nazionale, Cod. Magl. XVII. 6, 176-186 (misc. 17th century).

Florence, Biblioteca Riccardiana, Cod. 767 (16th century).

Florence, Biblioteca Riccardiana, Cod. 927 (16th century).

Rome, Biblioteca Vaticana, Cod. Ottobon. 1424 (15th century).

EDITIONS OF THE "DE STATUA"

1547

Walter Rivius, *Vornehmster Notwendigster angehend mathematische und mechanische Künste eigentlicher Bericht*, Nürnberg (translation which fails to mention that the author of the treatise was Alberti).

1568

Opuscoli morali di Leon Battista Alberti gentil'huomo fiorentino ... Tradotti, e in parte corretti da M. Cosimo Bartoli, Venice.

1664

J. Evelyn, *Leon Baptista Alberti, Of Statues* (an English translation included as an appendix to Roland Fréart de Chaunbray's *A Parallel of the Ancient Architecture with the Modern*, London 1664, Paris 1651).

1804

Della Pittura e della Statua, con vita di Leon Battista Alberti scritta da Girolamo Tiraboschi, Milan.

1868

De la Statue et de la Peinture. Traités de Leon Baptista Alberti noble florentin, traduits du latin en Français par Claudius Popelin, Paris.

1877

L. B. Albertis Kleinere Kunsttheoretische Schriften mit einer Einleitung und Excursen versehen von Dr. H. Janitschek, Vienna.

1972

L. B. Alberti, On Painting and on Sculpture, edited with translations, introduction and notes by C. Grayson, London, pp. 117 ff.

Bibliographical Note on the *De Statua*

1924

E. Panofsky, *Idea*, Leipzig-Berlin (Ital. trans. *Idea, contributo alla storia dell'estetica*, Florence 1952, p. 108).

1959

A. Parronchi, *Sul "De Statua" albertiano*, in "Paragone", X, pp. 3-29.

1960

E. Panofsky, *Renaissance and Renascences*, Uppsala (Ital. trans. *Rinascimento e Rinascenze nell'arte occidentale*, Milan 1971, p. 43).

1962

G. Flaccavento, *Per una moderna traduzione del "De Statua" di Leon Battista Alberti*, in "Cronache di Archeologia e Storia dell'Arte", II, pp. 50-59.

1964

A. Parronchi, *Studi su la dolce prospettiva*, Milan, p. 381 ff.

1965

G. Flaccavento, *Sulla data del "De Statua" di Leon Battista Alberti*, in "Commentarii", XVI, 3-4, pp. 216-21.

1971

M. Picchio Simonelli, *On Alberti's Treatises on Art and their Chronological Relationship*, in "Italian Studies Annual", Toronto.

THE TECHNICAL WRITINGS

CODICES OF SCIENTIFIC TREATISES

De Punctis et Lineis apud Pictores

Turin, Biblioteca Universitaria, Cod. 1184, cc. 60 ff.

Lucca, Biblioteca Governativa, Cod. 1448, cc. 52 ff.

First Edition: G. Mancini, *L.B. Alberti Opera inedita et pauca separatim impressa*, Florence 1890.

De Lunularum quadratura

Florence, Biblioteca Magliabechiana, Cod. 243, cl. VI, cc. 77 ff.

Florence, Biblioteca Riccardiana, Cod. 2110 and Cod. 2942.

First Edition: G. Mancini, *L. B. Alberti Opera inedita et pauca separatim impressa*, Florence 1890.

Descriptio Urbis Romae

Milan, Biblioteca Ambrosiana, Cod. O. 80. sup., 73-78 (16th century).

Rome, Biblioteca Vaticana, Cod. Chig. M. VII. 149, 3r-8v (16th century).

Rome, Biblioteca Vaticana, Cod. Barb. Lat. 6525, 21r-24v (17th century).

Venice, Biblioteca Marciana, Cod. Ital. Zeniano. XI. 67. (7351), 122-127 (15th century).

Critical edition by G. Orlandi, *La Descriptio Urbis Romae ...*, in "Quaderno N. 1 dell'Istituto di Elementi di Architettura e Rilievo dei Monumenti di Genova", October 1968, pp. 60-88.

De' pondi e leve di alcuna rota (apocryphal)

Florence, Biblioteca Laurenziana, Cod. Ashb. 361, 33-47 (15th century).

Milan, Biblioteca Ambrosiana, Cod. 191, 26-84 (in the transcription of Georg von Hoffkirchen, Venice 1576).

Rome, Biblioteca Vaticana, Cod. Chig. M. VII. 149 (16th century).

Turin, Biblioteca del Duca di Genova, Cod. 148 (15th century).

First Edition: G. Mancini, *Vasari vite cinque*, Florence 1900.

Ludi matematici

Florence, Biblioteca Nazionale, Cod. Magl. VI. 243, 64r-74r (16th century).

Florence, Biblioteca Laurenziana, Cod. Ashb. 356, 26r-31v (misc. 16th century).

Florence, Biblioteca Riccardiana, Cod. 2110, 25r-45v (16th century).

Florence, Biblioteca Riccardiana, Cod. 2942, 46r-67r (15-16th centuries).

Florence, Biblioteca Riccardiana, Cod. Moreni 3, 54r-73r.

Genoa, Biblioteca Universitaria, Cod. G. IV, 29, 33r-55r (15-16th centuries).

Ravenna, Biblioteca Classense, Cod. 208, 1-28 (16th century).

Rome, Biblioteca Nazionale, Fondo Vittorio Emanuele, Cod. 574, 1r-36r (16th century).

Rouen, Bibliothèque Municipale, Cod. Leber. 1158 (3056), 1r-36r (15th century).

Venice, Biblioteca Marciana, Cod. Ital. XI. 67 (7351), 130r-141r (misc. 15-16th centuries).

Cambridge (U.S.A.), Harvard College Library, Cod. Typ. 422/2 (15th century).

Editions: *Opuscoli Morali di Leon Battista Alberti gentil'huomo fiorentino ... Tradotti, e in parte corretti da M. Cosimo Bartoli*, Venice 1958, pp. 225-55.

Opere volgari di L. B. Alberti annotate ed illustrate dal Dott. Anicio Bonucci, Florence 1847, IV, pp. 405-40.

Opere Volgari, ed. by C. Grayson, Bari 1973, III.

Elementi di Pittura

Vernacular version: Cambridge (U.S.A.), Harvard College Library, Cod. Typ. 422/1 (15th century).

Verona, Biblioteca Capitolare, Cod. CCLXXIII, 138r-143v (misc. 16th century).

First Edition: G. Mancini, *L. B. Alberti Opera inedita ed pauca separatim impressa*, Florence 1890.

Latin version: Bologna, Biblioteca Comunale dell'archiginnasio, Cod. A. 266, 122-126 (misc. 16th century).

Cues, Biblioteca dell'Ospedale, Cod. 112, 67-73 (misc. 15-16th centuries).

Florence, Biblioteca Nazionale, Cod. Magl. XVII, 6, 169r-175v (misc. 17th century).

Florence, Biblioteca Riccardiana, Cod. 927, 1r-10v (16th century).

Lucca, Biblioteca Governativa, Cod. 1448 (16th century).

Milan, Biblioteca Ambrosiana, Cod. O. 80, sup., 53r-60r (15th century).

North Carolina, University Library, Cod. 90, 33 ff (16th century).

Oxford, Bodleian Library, Cod. Canon, Misc. 172, 221r-225r (15th century).

Paris, Bibliothèque Nationale, Cod. Lat. 10252.

Rome, Biblioteca Vaticana, Cod. Ottobon. Lat. 1424, 26r-30v (15th century).

Turin, Biblioteca Nazionale, Cod. 1184 (destroyed).

Verona, Biblioteca Capitolare, Cod. CCLXXIII, pp. 300-41 (misc. 16th century).

First Edition: G. Mancini, *Gli Elementi di Pittura per la prima volta pubblicati con un discorso sulla parte avuta dall'Alberti nel rimettere in onore la lingua italiana*, Cortona 1864.

BIBLIOGRAPHICAL NOTE ON THE TECHNICAL AND SCIENTIFIC WRITINGS

1838

G. Libri, *Histoire des sciences mathématiques en Italie*, 4 Vols., Paris 1838-41.

1877

H. Janitschek, *L. B. Albertis Kleinere Kunsttheoretische Schriften mit einer Einleitung und Excursen versehen von Dr. H. Janitschek*, Vienna.

1879

G. B. De Rossi, *Piante iconografiche e propettiche di Roma anteriori al secolo XVI*, Rome, pp. 110 ff., 130 ff.

1883

C. Winterberg, *L. B. Albertis technische Schriften*, in "Repertorium für Kunstwissenschaft", VI, pp. 326-56.

1885

D. Gnoli, *Di alcune piante topografiche di Roma ignote e poco note*, in "Boll. Comm. Archeol. Comunale di Roma", 13, pp. 63-82.

1891

R. Caverni, *Storia del metodo sperimentale in Italia* 5 Vols., Florence 1891-98.

1892

V. Braun, *Leonardo da Vinci and Leon Battista Alberti*, in "Repertorium für Kunstwissenschaft", XV, pp. 267 ff.

1894

G. Uzielli, *La vita e i tempi di Paolo dal Pozzo Toscanelli*, in "Raccolta di Documenti e Studi, R. Commissione Colombiana", P. 5, I, Rome.

1906

P. Duhem, *Etudes sur Leonardo da Vinci*, 3 Vols., Paris 1906-12.

1908

E. Solmi, *Le fonti dei manoscritti di Leonardo da Vinci*, in "Giornale Storico della Letteratura Italiana", 10-11.

1910

J. Waterhouse, *Camera Oscura*, article in the "Encyclopaedia Britannica", XI ed., 1910-11.

1912

J. H. Haswel, *Secret Writing: the Ciphers of the Ancients, and some of those in Modern Use*, in "Century Magazine", 1912-13, 85, pp. 82-92.

1914

A. Favaro, *Un ingegnere italiano del secolo XV*,

Padua.

1926

V. Malfatti, *Le navi romane del lago di Nemi*, in "Rivista Marittima", pp. 693-700.

1934

P. H. Michel, *L'esthétique arithmétique du Quattrocento*, in "Mélange Hauvette", Paris.

1936

G. Wolff, *Leon Battista Alberti als Mathematiker*, in "Scientia", LX, pp. 353-59.

1939

W. B. Parsons, *Engineers and Engineering in the Renaissance*, Baltimore.

1940

J. Ch. Mendelsohn, *Bibliographical Note on the "De Cifris" of L. B. Alberti*, in "Isis", XXXII, pp. 48-51.

1942

A. Uccelli, *I Libri di Meccanica di Leonardo da Vinci*, Milan.

1945

E. Uccelli, *Storia della tecnica dal Medioevo ai nostri giorni*, Milan.

1947

L. Sacco, *Un primato italiano: la crittografia nei secoli XV e XVI*, in "Boll. Ist. di Cultura Arma del Genio", Rome, XXIII.

1950

G. Uccelli, *Le Navi di Nemi*, Rome.

1953

R. Valentini and G. Zucchetti, *Codice topografico della città di Roma*, Rome, IV, p. 209 ff.

1955

C. Sarton, *The Appreciation of Ancient and Medieval Science during the Renaissance (1450-1600)*, Philadelphia.

1957

C. Singer, E. J. Holmyard, A. Rupert Hall, I. Trevor, A. Williams, *A History of Technology*, Oxford (It. trans. *Storia della Tecnologia*, Turin 1963, pp. 257-456).

1960

V. Zoubov, *Leon Battista Alberti e Leonardo da Vinci*, in "Raccolta Vinciana", XVIII, pp. 1-14.

O. Lehmann-Brockhaus, *Albertis "Descriptio Urbis Romae"*, in "Kunstchronik", XIII, 12, pp. 345-48.

1961

J. H. Randall Jr., *The School of Padua and the Emergence of Modern Science*, Padua.

1962

F. Frutaz, *Le piante di Roma*, Rome, I, p. 127; II, plate 151.

1963

J. Gadol, *Leon Battista Alberti. The Renaissance of Geometric Space in Art and Science* (doctoral thesis), Columbia University, New York.

1968

L. Vagnetti, *La Descriptio Urbis Romae, contributo alla storia del rilevamento architettonico*, in "Quaderni dell'Istituto di Elementi di Architettura e Rilievo dei Monumenti di Genova", I, October.

1972

F. Borsi, *I Cinque Ordini Architettonici e L. B. Alberti*, in "Studi e Documenti di Architettura", Istituto di Composizione Architettonica della Facoltà di Architettura di Firenze, 1, December, p. 57 ff.

A. Gambuti, *Nuove Ricerche sugli Elementa Picturae*, in "Studi e Documenti di Architettura", Istituto di Composizione Architettonica della Facoltà di Architettura di Firenze, 1, December, p. 131 ff.

L. Vagnetti, *Lo Studio di Roma negli scritti albertiani*, paper read at the International Congress on L. B. Alberti held at the Accademia Nazionale dei Lincei, Rome.

L. Vagnetti, *Considerazioni sui Ludi Matematici*, in "Studi e Documenti di Architettura", Istituto di Composizione Architettonica della Facoltà di Architettura di Firenze, 1, December, p. 173 ff.

DE RE AEDIFICATORIA

CODICES

Eton College Library, Cod. Mss. 128 (15th century).

Chicago, University of Chicago Library, Goodspeed Fund, 1 (15th century).

Florence, Biblioteca Laurenziana, Cod. Plut. 89, sup., 113 (15th century).

Florence, Biblioteca Riccardiana, Cod. 2520 (sixteenth-century trans. of the first three books).

Modena, Biblioteca Estense, Cod. a. O. 3. 8. Lat. 419 (15th century).

Olomouc (Moravia), Chapter Library, Cod. CO. 330 (15th century).

Reggio Emilia, Biblioteca Municipale, Cod. Mss. Vari, G. 3. (trans. by Damiano Pieti, 1538).

Rome, Biblioteca Vaticana, Cod. Urb. Lat. 264. (Explicit 1483).

Rome, Biblioteca Vaticana, Cod. Ottob. Lat. 1424, 39-64 (misc. 15th century).

Venice, Biblioteca Marciana, Cod. Lat. VIII. 125 (3717), (15th century).

EDITIONS

1485

Leonis Baptistae Alberti de re aedificatoria incipit ... Florentiae accuratissime impressum opera Magistri Nicolai Laurentii Alamani. Anno salutis millesimo octuagesimo quinto quarto calendis januarias.

1512

Libri De re aedificatoria decem ..., Paris, Berthold Rembolt.

1541

De re aedificatoria Libri decem ..., per Eberhardum Tappium Lunensem, Strasbourg, Giacomo Cammerlander.

1546

I Dieci Libri De L'architettura di Leon Battista degli Alberti fiorentino novamente da la Latina ne la Volgar Lingua con molta diligenza tradotti da Pietro Lauro, Venice, printed by Vincenzo Valgrisi.

1550

L'architettura (De Re Aedificatoria) di Leon Battista Alberti tradotta in lingua fiorentina da Cosimo Bartoli ... con l'aggiunta de disegni, Florence, printed by Lorenzo Torrentino.

1553

L'Architecture et art de bien bastir ... divisée en dix livres, traduicts de Latin en Francois, par deffunct Jan Martin, Parisien, Paris, printed by Robert Massellin for Jacques Kerver.

1565

L'architettura tradotta in lingua fiorentina da Cosimo Bartoli ..., Venice, Francesco Franceschi (rep. of the 1550 edition).

1582

Los diez libros de architectura ..., Traduzidos de latin en romance, Madrid, Alonso Gomez.

Late sixteenth-century.

Translation into Portuguese by Andre de Resende for King John III, unpublished manuscript.

1640

Rep. of the Spanish translation of 1582, Madrid (uncertain).

1726

The Architecture ... in Ten Books. Of Painting in Three Books. And of Statuary in One Book. Translated into Italian by Cosimo Bartoli. And now first into English ... by James Leoni, Venetian architect, London, Thomas Edlin.

1739

Rep. of the English edition of 1726, London.

1755

Rep. of the English edition of 1726, London.

1782

Della Architettura, della Pittura e della Statua ... Traduzione di Cosimo Bartoli, Bologna, Studio dell'Istituto delle Scienze.

1784

I dieci libri di Architettura di Leon Battista Alberti tradotti in italiano da Cosimo Bartoli. Nuova edizione diligentemente corretta e confrontata coll'originale latino, ed arricchita di nuovi rami ricavati dalle misure medesime assegnate dall'autore, Rome, in the printing-house of Giovanni Zempel.

1797

Los diez libros de Architectura. Secunda edition en castellano, corregida por D.R.B., Madrid, Joseph Franganillo.

1804

Rep. of the Roman edition of 1784, Milan.

I dieci libri d'Architettura, ossia dell'Arte di edificare ... scritti in compendio ed illustrati con note ... da B. Orsini, Perugia, Carlo Baduel.

1833

Della architettura libri dieci. Traduzione di Cosimo Bartoli con note apologetiche di Stefano Ticozzi, e trenta tavole in rame disegnate ed incise da Costantino Gianni, Milan, in "Raccolta dei Classici Italiani".

1847

Della architettura libri dieci. Traduzione di Cosimo Bartoli con note apologetiche di Stefano Ticozzi, e trenta tavole in rame disegnate ed incise da Costantino Gianni, Milan, in "Raccolta dei Classici Italiani".

1847

Dell'arte edificatoria, in *Opere volgari di Leon Battista Alberti a cura del Dott. Anicio Bonucci*, Florence, Galileiana, IV, pp. 187-371 (contains only the translation of Books I-III).

1912

Zehn Bücher über die Baukunst. In Deutsche übertragen, eingeleitet und mit Ammerkungen und Zeichnungen versehen von Max Theuer, Vienna, H. Heller (first German edition).

1935

Russian edition, trans. by V. P. Zoubov, Moscow, 1935-37.

1955

Ten Books on Architecture by Leon Battista Alberti, New York.

Ten Books on Architecture. Translation by James Leoni, ed. by J. Rykwert, London, Alec Tiranti.

1956

Deset Knih o Stavitelstvi, Prague (first Czechoslovak edition).

1960

Ksiag dziescoc o Sztuce Budowania, Warsaw, Paustwowe Wydawnictwo Naukowe (first Polish edition).

1966

L'Architettura (De Re Aedificatoria). Latin text and translation ed. by Giovanni Orlandi, with introduction and notes by Paolo Portoghesi, Milan, Il Polifilo.

BIBLIOGRAPHICAL NOTE ON THE "DE RE AEDIFICATORIA"

1877

H. Janitschek, *L. B. Albertis kleinere kunsttheoretische Schriften*, in "Ilg-Eitelberger Quellenschriften", XI, Vienna (Introduction).

1883

P. Hoffmann, *Studien zu L. B. Albertis zehn Bücher, De Re Aedificatoria*, Frankenberg.

1911

J. W. Berrer, *L. B. Albertis Bauten und ihr Einfluss auf die Architektur* (doctoral thesis), Heidelberg-Cassel.

1916

W. Fleming, *Die Begründung der modernen Aesthetik und Kunstwissen durch Leon Battista Alberti*, Berlin-Leipzig.

1929

L. Olschki, *Der geometrische Geist in Literatur und Kunst*, in "Deutsche Vierteljahresschrift für Literatur und Geistesgeschichte", VIII, pp. 615-38.

1934

P. H. Michel, *L'esthétique arithmétique du Quattrocento*, in "Mélange Hauvette", Paris.

1939

M. L. Gengaro, *L'architettura romana nell'interpretazione teorica di L. B. Alberti*, in "Bollettino dell'Istituto di Archeologia e Storia dell'Arte", IX, pp. 37-42.

F. Pellati, *Vitruvio e il Brunelleschi*, in "Rinascita", pp. 343-65.

1943

W. A. Eden, *Studies in Urban Theory: the "De Re Aedificatoria" of L. B. Alberti*, in "Town Planning Review", 19, pp. 10-28.

1946

G. C. Argan, *The Architecture of Brunelleschi and the Origins of Perspective Theory in the Fifteenth Century*, in "Journal of the Warburg and Courtauld Institutes", IX pp. 96-121.

1947

G. Castelfranchi, *Il neoclassicismo di Vitruvio e il classicismo dell'Alberti*, in "Paideia", III, pp. 140-44.

1948

R. Krautheimer, *The Tragic and Comic Scene of the Renaissance*, in "Gazette des Beaux Arts", ser. 6, XXXIII, pp. 327-46.

1949

J. White, *Developments in Renaissance Perspective*, in "Journal of the Warburg and Courtauld Institutes", XII, pp. 58-79.

1953

V. Golzio, *Il V Centenario del "De Re Aedificatoria" di L. B. Alberti*, in "Studi Romani", I, 6, pp. 638-47.

1955

Raphael Du Fresne, *The Life of Leon Battista Alberti*, in "Ten Books on Architecture", ed. by J. Rykwert, London (rep. of the seventeenth-century English translation).

1956

Y. Khouri-Haddad, *The Climatic Approach to Architecture in the Literature of Vitruvius, Alberti and Palladio*, in "Term Paper", Columbia University, 6.

1957

E. R. De Zurko, *Alberti's Theory of Form and Function*, in "Art Bulletin", XXXIX, 2, pp. 142-45.

C. Schädlich, *L. B. Albertis Schönheitsdefinition und ihre Bedeutung für die Architekturtheorie*, in "Wissenschaftliche Zeitschrift Hochschule Weimar", 1957-58, V, 4, pp. 217-84.

1958

G. De Angelis d'Ossat, *Enunciati euclidei e "divina proporzione" nell'Architettura del primo Rinascimento*, in "Atti del V° Convegno Internazionale di Studi sul Rinascimento", Florence, pp. 253-64.

1960

L. A. Ciapponi, *Il "De Architectura" di Vitruvio nel primo Umanesimo*, in "Italia Medioevale e Umanistica", III, pp. 39-99.

C. Grayson, *The Composition of L. B. Alberti's Decem Libri De Re Aedificatoria*, in "Münchener Jahrbuch der bildenden Kunst", III, 11, pp. 152-61.

R. Wittkower, *The Changing Concept of Proportions*, in "Daedalus", pp. 199-215.

V. Zoubov, *Quelques aspects de la théorie des proportions esthétiques de Leon Battista Alberti*, in "Bibliothèque d'Humanisme et Renaissance", p. 54 ff.

1961

A. Bruschi, *Osservazioni sulla teoria architettonica rinascimentale nella formulazione albertiana*, in "Quaderni dell'Istituto di Storia dell'Architettura", Rome, 31-48, pp. 115-30.

R. Krautheimer, *Alberti and Vitruvius*, in "Acts of the 20th International Congress of the History of Arts", New York, II, pp. 42-52.

R. Krautheimer, *Alberti's Templum Etruscum*, in "Münchener Jahrbuch der bildenden Kunst", XII, 3, pp. 327-46.

1963

S. Lang, *"De Lineamentis, L. B. Alberti's Use of a Technical Term*, in "Journal of the Warburg and Courtauld Institutes", XXVIII, pp. 331-35.

P. Tigler, *Die Architekturtheorie des Filarete*, Berlin.

1966

P. Portoghesi, *Leon Battista Alberti, "L'Architettura" (De Re Aedificatoria)*, Milan (introduction and notes. Latin text and translation by G. Orlandi).

1967

Z. Wazbinski, *La maison idéale selon Alberti*, in "Acta Historiae Artium", XIII, pp. 13-16.

1971

M. Picchio Simonelli, *On Alberti's Treatises on Art and their Chronological Relationship*, in "Italian Studies Annual", Toronto, I.

1972

F. Borsi, *I Cinque Ordini Architettonici e L. B. Alberti*, in "Studi e Documenti di Architettura", Istituto di Composizione Architettonica della Facoltà di Architettura di Firenze, 1, December, p. 57 ff.

ADDENDA

The following books and articles appeared in the course of the present volume's publication (up to March 1975):

E. Battisti, *Il Metodo progettuale secondo il "De Re Aedificatoria" di Leon Battista Alberti*, in "Il Santo Andrea di Mantova e Leon Battista Alberti" (Acts of the Congress organised by the city of Mantua with the collaboration of the Accademia Virgiliana in honour of the fifth centenary of the Basilica of S. Andrea and the death of Alberti, Mantua 1972).

M. Dezzi Bardeschi, *Sole in Leone. Leon Battista Alberti: astrologia, cosmologia e tradizione ermetica nella facciata di Santa Maria Novella*, in "Psicon", October-December 1974.

C. Ricci, *Il Tempio Malatestiano*. Anastatic rep. with an appendix by Pier Giorgio Pasini, Rimini, 1974. See also the review by Agnoldomenico Pica in "Domus", 539, 1974.

C. Eisler, *Portrait of L. B. Alberti*, in "Burlington Magazine", September 1974.

L. B. Alberti, *De Pictura*, ed. by Cecil Grayson, rep., Bari 1975.

INDEX

LIST OF ILLUSTRATIONS

PHOTOGRAPHIC SOURCES

Alinari, Florence: 203, 303, 306, 310.

Sergio Anelli, Electa: 8, 10, 11, 13, 45, 46, 47, 48, 52, 53, 54, 65, 66, 67, 68, 72, 74, 147, 149, 150, 151, 152, 153, 154, 156, 157, 158, 159, 160, 161, 164, 167, 168, 169, 170, 171, 172, 173, 175, 176, 177, 178, 179, 180, 181, 182, 183, 184, 185, 186, 187, 188, 189, 190, 191, 192, 193, 194, 195, 196, 197, 198, 199, 200, 201, 223, 224, 225, 228, 229, 230, 231, 232, 234, 235, 248, 251, 252, 255, 268, 274, 275, 276, 282, 284, 288.

Bazzecchi, Florence: 83, 84, 85, 86, 87, 88, 89, 90, 91, 92, 93, 94, 95, 96, 97, 98, 99, 100, 101, 102, 103, 104, 105, 106, 107, 108, 109, 110, 111, 112, 113, 114, 115, 116, 117, 118, 119, 120, 121, 122, 123, 124, 125, 126, 127, 128, 129.

Electa Archives: 2, 3, 4, 5, 6, 7, 14, 16, 59, 63, 64, 69, 130, 131, 132, 133, 148, 155, 165, 172, 174, 204, 205, 206, 207, 208, 209, 213, 237, 238, 239, 262, 287, 301, 304, 305, 307, 308, 309, 311, 312, 313.

John G. Johnson Collection, Philadelphia: 302.

The Metropolitan Museum of Art, New York: 202.

Paolo Monti, Milan: 44, 49, 50, 60, 62, 71, 73, 75, 163, 221, 222, 226, 227, 249, 250, 253, 254, 256, 257, 258, 260, 261, 263, 264, 265, 266, 267, 269, 270, 271, 272, 273, 278, 283.

Oscar Savio, Rome: 30, 32, 33, 34, 35, 259.

The drawings have been executed by Studio Di Grazia of Rome, except for those of S. Maria Novella and Annunziata which have been taken from books published by the Istituto di Restauro of Florence, edited by Nistri Lischi, Pisa.
We wish to extend our sincere thanks to the Istituto di Restauro della Facoltà di Architettura of Florence and especially to Prof. Piero Sanpaolesi for having allowed us to use the architectural drawings of Palazzo Rucellai and S. Martino a Gangalandi. We have received invaluable assistance from our friend Prof. Marco Dezzi Bardeschi who kindly supplied the photographs (Bazzecchi, Florence) and the architectural drawings of S. Pancrazio. Finally we are indebted to the Academy of S. Luca and particularly to Agnoldomenico Pica for the iconography on Alberti.